Educational Psychology

Recent Title in Essentials of Psychology and Health

Transgender Health and Medicine: History, Practice, Research, and the Future
Dana Jennett Bevan, PhD

Educational Psychology

HISTORY, PRACTICE, RESEARCH, AND THE FUTURE

Jennifer L. Martin and Sarah E. Torok-Gerard

Essentials of Psychology and Health

PRAEGER®

An Imprint of ABC-CLIO, LLC
Santa Barbara, California • Denver, Colorado

Library of Congress Cataloging-in-Publication Data
Names: Martin, Jennifer L. | Torok-Gerard, Sarah E.
Title: Educational Psychology : History, Practice, Research, and the Future /
    Jennifer L. Martin and Sarah E. Torok-Gerard.
Description: Santa Barbara, California : Praeger [2019] | Series: Essentials
    of Psychology and Health | Includes bibliographical references and index.
Identifiers: LCCN 2019019353 (print) | LCCN 2019022275 (ebook) |
    ISBN 9781440864490 (alk. paper) | ISBN 9781440864506 (ebook)
Subjects: LCSH: Educational psychology—History. | Educational psychology—
    Research. | Learning, Psychology of. | Educational equalization.
Classification: LCC LB1051 .E3623 2019 (print) | LCC LB1051 (ebook) |
    DDC 370.15—dc23
LC record available at https://lccn.loc.gov/2019019353
LC ebook record available at https://lccn.loc.gov/2019022275

ISBN: 978-1-4408-6449-0 (print)
          978-1-4408-6450-6 (ebook)

23 22 21 20 19   1 2 3 4 5

This book is also available as an eBook.

Praeger
An Imprint of ABC-CLIO, LLC

ABC-CLIO, LLC
147 Castilian Drive
Santa Barbara, California 93117
www.abc-clio.com

This book is printed on acid-free paper ∞

Manufactured in the United States of America

Contents

Series Foreword

Dozens of subfields exist in the academic disciplines of psychology and health, which help train many different types of specialists in the helping professions, from an array of counselors, social workers, and psychologists to public health scientists, medical researchers, and physicians. Yet, short of finding and completing a course concentrated on the subfield, or shadowing a particular professional at length, students and interested lay readers may have no substantial information on any particular subfield or specialty. Books in this series serve that need.

The *Essentials of Psychology and Health* series includes books that provide an introduction to, and deeper understanding of, academic subfields and resulting specialties in professions intended to understand disorders and improve physical and mental health, whether on individual or societal levels. These books are designed to be inclusive, research and case study strong, compact, and easy to use to locate particular information.

The text in these volumes includes the history of the subfield or profession, perspectives from various schools of thought, theoretical basis, demographics, roles, relationship to other fields, case studies, classic and emerging research, current events, and a look to the future of the subfield or profession. Core obstacles and, where appropriate, controversies are also addressed. Features include a glossary of terms, references, index, and a resource list for further information.

Acknowledgments

I have many people to thank for their support of my work. I thank my institution, the University of Illinois at Springfield, and specifically the Department of Teacher Education for their encouragement. I thank my students, past and present, for challenging me to do a better job every single day. A very special thank you goes to my former research assistants, to whom I refer to as my "forever students," Brianna Boehlke and Courtney Cepec. I thank my friends and my family for understanding my need to do social justice work, despite the repercussions that undoubtedly affect them.

I thank my coauthor, Dr. Sarah Torok-Gerard, for providing me with guidance, critique, and support.

I also thank I wish to thank Debbie Carvalko at Praeger for suggesting this project to us, and for believing in it from its inception.

—Jennifer L. Martin

First, I would like to thank all of my mentors at the University at Albany, State University of New York, in the Division of Educational Psychology and Methodology. These professionals introduced me to the field of educational psychology and provided me with rigorous training during my graduate program.

I would like to thank my students and colleagues at the University of Mount Union, specifically in the Department of Psychology, Neuroscience, and Human Development, for their insights, flexibility, and words of encouragement during this project. I would also like to thank my family for their unconditional support and willingness to put up with the demands that a job in academia often presents.

Finally, I would like to thank the folks at Praeger and my colleague, Dr. Jennifer Martin, for approaching me with this opportunity and providing me with time, invaluable guidance, and a tremendous amount of patience during the writing process.

—Sarah E. Torok-Gerard

OUR THANKS TO THE FOLLOWING CONTRIBUTORS, WHO ASSISTED WITH THE BOXED SPOTLIGHTS

Brianna Boehlke; Caitie Boucher; Courtney Cepec; Taylor Cook; Halle O. Devoe; Evan Hopkins; Grace A. Moll; Dr. Kristine Turko.

PORTIONS OF THIS BOOK HAVE BEEN REPRINTED OR ADAPTED FROM THE FOLLOWING SOURCES, WITH PERMISSION

Beese, J. A., & Martin, J. (2018). "Socioeconomic status and student opportunity: A case of disrespect or teenage rebellion?" *Journal of Cases in Educational Leadership* 21(1).

Martin, J. L., & Beese, J. A. (2016). *Teaching for educational equity: Case studies for professional development and principal preparation, Volume 1.* Lanham, MD: Rowman and Littlefield. Roman and Littlefield, all rights reserved.

Martin, J. L. (2017). "Bullying, gender-based." In K. Nadal (Ed.), *The SAGE encyclopedia of psychology and gender.* Thousand Oaks, CA: SAGE.

Martin, J., & Smith, J. (2017). "Subjective discipline and the social control of black girls in pipeline schools." *Journal of Urban Learning, Teaching, and Research, 13.*

Martin, J. L. (2019). "Factors contributing to microaggressions, racial battle fatigue, stereotype threat, and imposter phenomenon for nonhegemonic students: implications for urban education." In G. C. Torino et al. (Eds.), *Microaggression theory: Influence and implications.* Hoboken, NJ: John Wiley & Sons.

Martin, J. L., Sharp-Grier, M., & Smith, J. B. (2016). "Alternate realities: Racially disparate discipline in classrooms and schools and its effects on black and brown students." *Leadership and Research in Education: The Journal of the Ohio Council of Professors of Educational Administration (OCPEA), 3*(1).

Martin, J. L., Martin, T., & Capel, M. (2014, October). "Apple Pie and Ebonics: Language Diversity and Preparation for a Multicultural World." *OCPEA* 1 (October 2014).

Torok, S. E. (2008, July). *Cognitive and metalinguistic precursors to emergent literacy: Revisiting the roles of metalinguistic awareness in reading instruction and remediation.* Saarbrücken, Germany: VDM Verlag Dr. Müller Aktiengesellschaft.

Timeline

1869

Sir Francis Galton publishes *Hereditary Genius,* arguing that intellectual abilities are biological in nature.

1879

Wilhelm Wundt opens the first formal psychology laboratory at the University of Leipzig in Germany.

1883

G. Stanley Hall publishes *The Contents of Children's Minds on Entering School,* which was based on a large study of kindergarten-aged children and intended to inform elementary school teachers.

Hall also establishes the first laboratory of psychology in America at Johns Hopkins University.

The Child Study Movement officially begins.

1888
G. Stanley Hall founds the Child Study Association of America.

1889
Jane Addams and Ellen Starr establish the Hull House in Chicago, which promoted philanthropic, social, and educational experiences for members of the community and would ultimately provide a community-education model seen in modern programs like the YMCA and Head Start.

1890
William James gives a series of lectures entitled *Talks to Teachers about Psychology* to students around the United States.

1892
The American Psychological Association is established at a meeting hosted by G. Stanley Hall at the University of Pennsylvania.

1893
The National Education Association establishes a Department of Child Study.

1899
William James lectures *Talks to Teachers about Psychology* are published as a book.

John Dewey addresses the American Psychological Association and explicitly emphasized psychology's connections to the field of education.

1903
E. L. Thorndike publishes research on learning and teacher training in formal educational contexts.

1905
Educational psychology is formalized as a specific subdiscipline in psychology.

The first formalized standardized intelligence test, the Binet-Simon Intelligence Scale, is published by Alfred Binet and Theódore Simon.

1907
Maria Montessori opens the first Casa dei Bambini (a.k.a. Children's House), providing the basis for her educational methods.

1910
The *Journal of Educational Psychology* is first published.

1913
John Watson publishes *Psychology as a Behaviorist Views It*, marking the beginnings of behavioral psychology.

1916

The Measurement of Intelligence is published by Lewis Terman, describing how he updated Alfred Binet's and Theódore Simon's intelligence test to create the Stanford-Binet Intelligence Scale.

1917

With the advocacy of Cora Bussey Hillis, the University of Iowa Child Welfare Research Station is established.

1921

Jean Piaget begins publishing research on children's reasoning.

1941

Jean Piaget and Bärbel Inhelder publish *The Child's Construction of Quantities* discussing the use of problem solving while performing conservation tasks in children.

1942

Jean Piaget publishes *Psychology of Intelligence* discussing his theory of cognitive development in children.

1946

The American Psychological Association formally recognizes educational psychology as a formal subdiscipline and establishes Division 15: Educational Psychology.

1954

Mamie Phipps Clark and Kenneth Clark testify to the Supreme Court using their research on the Doll Study regarding the effects of racial segregation on African American children's self-concept and educational experiences. Their research is used as part of the testimony in the landmark case *Brown v. Board of Education, Topeka*, which results in the desegregation of public schools in the United States.

1956

Jerome Bruner publishes the book *A Study of Thinking*, which formally initiated the study of cognitive psychology.

Benjamin Bloom edits and publishes the *Taxonomy of Educational Objectives: The Classification of Educational Goals, Handbook I: Cognitive Domain*.

1960

Jerome Bruner publishes *The Process of Education*, which influenced the field of education and served as a powerful spur to the curriculum-reform movement of the period.

1963

Alfred Bandura introduces the idea of observational learning on the development of personality.

1964

David Krathwohl, Benjamin Bloom, and Bertram Masia publish the *Taxonomy of Educational Objectives: The Classification of Educational Goals, Handbook II: Affective Domain.*

1965

With the help of Jerome Bruner, Head Start programs are established in the United States to improve preschool development and school readiness for at-risk youth.

1968

Jane Elliott conducts the first iteration of the Brown-Eyed vs. Blue-Eyed classroom exercise.

Benjamin Bloom introduces the educational philosophy of mastery learning.

1969

Carl Rogers publishes *Freedom to Learn* introducing the educational philosophies behind learner-centered teaching and experiential learning.

1972

Title IX of the Education Amendments of 1972 are passed into law to prohibit discrimination on the basis of sex in any federally funded education program or activity.

1975

The All Handicapped Children Act (Public Law 94-142) is enacted by Congress.

1983

Howard Gardner introduces his theory of multiple intelligences, changing views on the nature of intelligence and how it is defined.

1989

Kimberlé Crenshaw publishes *Demarginalizing the Intersection of Race and Sex: A Black Feminist Critique of Antidiscrimination Doctrine, Feminist Theory and Antiracist Politics*, introducing readers to the concept of intersectionality in racial and gender oppression.

1990

The American Psychological Association Presidential Taskforce is created to create the Learner-Centered Psychological Principles to provide a framework for educational reform and school redesign efforts; these were revised in 1997.

1995
Claude Steele and Joshua Aronson perform the first experiments demonstrating that stereotype threat can undermine intellectual performance in racial and gender minorities.

1997
Public Law 94-142 is amended to become the Individuals with Disabilities Education Act (IDEA).

2000
The American Academy of Pediatrics issues *Policy Statement on Corporal Punishment in Schools* and calls for banning all forms of corporal punishment in educational settings; the AAP cites its ineffectiveness as a classroom management strategy as well as several adverse effects on the students' psychological and educational well-being; the policy statement is reaffirmed in 2018.

2002
The Partnership for 21st Century Learning creates the 21st Century Learning Framework to provide a framework for 21st-century student success in the new global economy.

2004
Congress amends IDEA by calling for early intervention, greater accountability, and improved educational outcomes including requiring states to track school districts for labeling disproportionate numbers of students of color as "learning disabled" for reasons other than disability.

2010
Linda Darling-Hammond publishes *The Flat World and Education: How America's Commitment to Equity Will Determine Our Future* discussing the implications of educational equity, poverty, and teacher preparation in the 21st century.

2015
Joseph Flynn Jr. publishes *White Fatigue: Naming the Challenge in Moving from an Individual to a Systemic Understanding of Racism,* introducing the concept of white fatigue and how it impacts white students' understanding of race, racism, racial representation, and self-identification in and outside the context of education.

2017
The American Academy of Pediatrics publishes *Policy Statement on the Detention of Immigrant Children* and discusses the known implications of such a practice on the short- and long-term impacts on the physical, psychological, intellectual, and educational well-being of the detained children.

PART 1

Overview

1

The Historical Origins of Educational Psychology: An Overview

---

Teaching is not a lost art, but the regard for it is a lost tradition.
—Jacques Barzun

Reading, writing, and arithmetic. When we think of formal scholastic education, we may readily associate these distinct subsets of content learning with school. But anyone who operates in the trenches of a contemporary classroom knows that formal scholastic education involves so much more. Practitioners in these settings (a.k.a., teachers) are expected to wear many hats and provide a wide array of services to their students on any given day during the designated academic year. Teachers are expected to successfully deliver a set curriculum, one that results in proficient, if not above average, outcomes when assessing their students, using state-mandated standardized tests. They must deliver these curricula to a room full of learners who possess diverse sets of social and academic abilities, home lives, cultural values, SES backgrounds, racial/ethnic backgrounds, motivation levels, attention spans, and learning differences. If that weren't challenging enough in and of itself, they are also expected to implement skills that may extend beyond their formal training, acting as mentors, social workers, mediators, advocates, and disciplinarians.

Teachers' roles are increasingly multifaceted. But how did educators go from filling the more singular role of transmitting content knowledge to being responsible for teaching such a wide range of academic and life skills to their students? This evolution is in part because of research and contributions made by educational psychologists. Broadly stated, *educational psychology* is the scientific study of theories and principles related to human learning. These theories and principles involve a plethora of concepts related to the learner, including but not limited to:

- cognitive and intellectual development,
- learning exceptionalities (e.g., mental retardation, giftedness, learning disabilities),
- individual and group differences,
- motivation and affect,
- socio-emotional development,
- moral development,
- self-concept and identity development (e.g., academic, racial/ethnic, gender, etc.),
- curricular and instructional strategies,
- educational assessment,
- impacts of the immediate home environment,
- impacts of the educational environment, and
- impacts of the overall cultural environment.

The field of educational psychology hasn't always had such a wide range of focus. Like teachers, educational psychologists have been impacted by social, cultural, and temporal changes. It is important to take a look back on how the field has progressed over time. This chapter will explore the evolution of educational psychology and its synergetic relationship with the educational setting. We will discuss:

1. the formal beginnings of educational psychology as a distinct field of study,
2. the major paradigmatic shift in the field from a narrow focus on educational training to the gradual integration of socialized education and the child study movement,
3. the prominent theorists and educational advocates who contributed to the field as it evolved over time, and
4. the current state of the field.

CONSIDERING CONTEMPORARY ISSUES IN EDUCATION

With the recent rash of school shootings, a new debate about teachers' roles and responsibilities has emerged: whether they should be armed while in the classroom. In a recent Pew Research Center survey, 57 percent of 743 of teens, aged 13–17, said they were either "very worried" or "somewhat worried" that a shooting could happen at their school. In the same survey, 63 percent of the 1,058 parents surveyed said they were also "very worried" or "somewhat worried" that a school shooting would occur at their child's school (Graf, 2018). In a separate, but related Pew Research Center survey, 2,541 adults were asked whether they thought teachers and school officials should be allowed to carry guns in schools. A total of 47 percent of the 2,541 participants agreed that teachers and school officials should be allowed to carry weapons. There were partisan differences in how participants responded to the question, though. Only 24 percent of participants identifying as Democrat agreed that arming teachers was acceptable, but 78 percent of participants identifying as Republican agreed with this strategy (Graf, 2018). Only time will tell how policy makers address this issue, but their decisions will likely inevitably leave teachers with a continued responsibility of protecting their students. Some teachers embrace the many responsibilities that are expected of them and do so with an unwavering conviction and love of their profession. Others succumb to challenges like unlivable wages, limited resources, time-intensive schedules that take them away from their own families, low morale, student disciplinary issues, and a general lack of support from their campus administrators, among other things (Rafferty, 2002). In their myriad roles, teachers also have the incredible responsibility and opportunity to positively influence their students' lives. Many do, and many enter the profession with a full awareness of this prospect.

PARADIGMATIC SHIFTS IN EDUCATIONAL PSYCHOLOGY

Learning is not attained by chance, it must be sought for with ardor and attended to with diligence.

—Abigail Adams

Education and educational psychology are interdisciplinary fields of study. Both are impacted by cultural and historical influences. When we talk about a paradigmatic shift, we are referring to a changing paradigm. According to Kuhn (1962), a *paradigm* is the entire collection of beliefs, values, and techniques shared by a group of scientists and research practitioners. Paradigms, including those in educational psychology, are influenced by the current zeitgeist. A *zeitgeist*, which is sometimes referred to as the "spirit of the times," emphasizes the influences of developments in other sciences, political climate, technological advancements, and economic conditions on the development of psychology (Hergenhahn, 2014). Scientists can become emotionally attached to their paradigms, which can make it difficult for them to consider other viewpoints or ways of thinking. Large-scale historical events can prompt a shift in a paradigm. Once observations can no longer be explained by a current paradigm because of the emergence of new cultural phenomena, science progresses, and scientists are forced to change their belief systems. These shifts can sometimes involve contentious, long-standing debates. Several have existed in the study of educational psychology.

Paradigmatic shifts occur with specific psychological constructs as well as entire fields of study. When educational psychology was formalized as a specific subdiscipline of psychology in 1905, it was a very different than the one that exists in the modern era. According to Church (1971), as educational psychology emerged and gained momentum in the world of formal scientific study, its focus was myopically fixed on instructional techniques, assessment, and training in specific academic disciplines. Prominent members in the field rejected the paradigm of socialized education that was being promoted by other educational and social reformers like Jane Addams (1860–1935), John Dewey (1859–1952), and their ilk. Essentially, child development and the educational context were divorced during this era of educational psychology. For all intents and purposes, pedagogy was restricted to the transmission of specific knowledge in subject areas like reading, writing, and arithmetic.

Church (1971) reviewed the research in educational psychology starting in 1905 and ending in 1920. He noted that in 1910, the *Journal of Educational Psychology* made its debut as a published work. According to his findings, the beginnings of educational psychology as a formal science were marked by the publication of a paper written by behaviorist E. L. Thorndike (1874–1949) in 1903 and the creation of the first formal standardized intelligence scale, published by Alfred Binet and Theódore Simon in 1905. What was left out of the early research were discussions of the work done by prominent psychologists who viewed learning and educational development more progressively and holistically. Theorists like James Mark Baldwin (1861–1934), George Herbert Mead (1863–1931), Charles Horton Cooley (1864–1929), and G. Stanley Hall (1844–1924) were either completely ignored or mentioned in unfavorable ways. John Dewey was mentioned, but only in reviews of his books.

Instead, Church (1971) noted:

The profession's journal—doubling the number of pages it devoted to charts, graphs, and tables each year—published almost exclusively articles dealing

JANE ADDAMS

Jane Addams (September 8, 1860–May 21, 1935) was an activist, social worker, and writer in the 20th century and was heavily influenced by the ideas of John Dewey. She was born in Cedarville, Illinois, and passed away in Chicago, Illinois. She was considered underprivileged during her time period because she was not married and lived in an impoverished area of Chicago (Ostman, 2006). Her main focus was on social justice work in the attempt to unify the social classes. Addams was known as the mother of social work, for she advocated for welfare, education reform, peace activism, women's rights, and workers' rights (Ostman, 2006). She spent most of her life as an activist for the underprivileged, and in attempt to better unite the social classes, cofounded Hull House in 1889.

Hull House was a safe place for those of any social class to come and discuss their experiences in hope to resolve any inequitable issues within society; it was a representation of a community who shares its ideas and values (Klosterman & Stratton, 2006). Addams's overall goal for Hull House was to reduce the social distance of the social classes and to increase needed resources necessary to forgo the objective (Klosterman & Stratton, 2006). Hull House discussions focused on the environment in which the poor were required to work and live in, teaching its residents to advocate for necessary resources in order to reach a central belief of equality for all residing within the community—the advocates within the house simply wanted a sanitary working and living environment (Klosterman & Stratton, 2006).

Jane Addams also advocated for women's suffrage and worked against World War I. She was considered a feminist, advocating for women to be placed in political office in order to lead a more humane and peaceful society among the nations (Klosterman & Stratton, 2006). Addams believed that placing women in office would help reach world peace more efficiently due to their feminine sense of nurture and cooperation (Klosterman & Stratton, 2006). She was a known American leader, especially in the international women's peace movement and within her social justice work, which lead to her winning of the Nobel Peace Prize in 1931.

Addams spent time advocating for adolescents within her Chicago neighborhood as well, for she detailed the lives of the underprivileged and underrepresented youth in order to bring attention to the lack of funding for public recreation. She concluded in this movement that members of society often neglected the founding of self-government, focusing more on materialistic items than the youth that will soon lead the future; two members of the younger generation she represented were a 19-year-old awaiting the death penalty for killing a police officer, and an overworked factory girl (Chernock, 2001). Addams believed the voices of and opportunities for the youth were being disregarded; therefore she took it upon herself to rebel against wealth and power to let the young voices rise above and be heard.

After her death in 1935, her legacy lived on throughout the world and has since been implemented into the classroom. Addams believed education was a "tool to teach civic action" (Alonso, 2016, p. 262). Educators across the globe use her theories and practices to better inform their students about the inequalities the world faces. Addams was a firm believer in conversations involving class, race, ethnic, and gender; she believed that "talking and collaborating lead to group consensus, conflict resolution, civic responsibility, and true reform" (Alonso, 2016, p. 261). Many teachers today use her ideas in service-learning projects to involve their students in social justice work while also providing the students with valuable lessons they can use in and outside the classroom; one can say she influenced the well-known pedagogical strategy of service learning. Overall, Jane Addams was not only an American leader and social justice advocate, but also an influencer in the field of education without ever truly knowing her impact.

—*Courtney Cepec*

with the transfer of training, with the nature-nurture controversy, with the concepts of intelligence, achievement, and aptitude, with the best means of teaching this or that subject and how to determine which method was best, with problems of introducing experimental psychology in the normal schools, and with ways of identifying and responding to individual differences. (p. 392)

Church (1971) also pointed out that educational psychology's seemingly intentional disconnect of the research on human development and the educational context was counterintuitive. He cited Dewey's ideas as a hallmark of the educational reform movement. Dewey, recognized as both an educator and a psychologist, had built a reputation as a reformer using research collected at his Laboratory School. He thought learning was an active process and that formal schooling, depending on how it was structured, could be a somewhat restrictive environment that hindered adaptation to the real world. He believed that schooling should reflect and be applied to life experiences. To him, this meant intentionally integrating the social aspects of life into the classroom. For instance, he suggested bringing math lessons to life by teaching children how to measure foods while cooking.

His philosophy asserted that educational reform should ultimately impact the greater society in beneficial ways and that learning should not (and does not) occur in a vacuum. At his address to the American Psychological Association in 1899, he explicitly emphasized psychology's connections to the field of education. He stressed that education should focus more on the teaching and learning of "habits" that focused on intellectual inquiry (e.g., critical thinking), healthy emotional and interpersonal development, and how to turn those habits into observable behaviors. He suggested that simply focusing on how to deliver and assess specific content to students limited the impact of their educational experience. He also thought that schools were the perfect place to study the evolution of these skills in learners and the interaction of learning and social development (Church, 1971).

If the progressive, reformist philosophy of Dewey sounds familiar, it is because it is still touted as being a more effective approach in current educational practice, despite the fact that much of the contemporary educational policy imposed on educators and students by politicians has emphasized a "drill and kill" type of approach to instruction and standardized assessment of learning outcomes. With the creation of the APA's learner-centered psychological principles and the 21st-century learning goals, educational psychologists formally recognize the more complex and applied view of socialized education.

Despite Dewey's research and notoriety, the *Journal of Educational Psychology* published work from psychologists like E. L. Thorndike, who focused primarily on instructional technique (Church, 1971). Thorndike, a socially awkward and shy man, conducted his graduate studies first at Harvard University, and then Columbia University after being the recipient of a rejected marriage proposal in Massachusetts. As student of James McKeen Cattell (1860–1944), a prominent researcher in the study of intelligence at Columbia, Thorndike continued his work with animals like chickens, cats, and dogs. He constructed mazes and what he called *puzzle boxes*. These were elaborately redesigned fruit crates intended to test the ability of cats and dogs to press a lever or pull a loop to escape and find a reward (e.g., food). What he found was that the animals escaped the boxes as a result of trial-and-error learning, not reasoning, observation, or insight (Hunt, 2007). Thorndike defined *trial-and-error learning* as the process of exhibiting chance behavior that was sporadically successful, gradually becoming more precise. Over time and successive trials, Thorndike found that animals were able to find their way out of the puzzle boxes faster and easier, especially during learning trials where food was presented as a reward (Fancher & Rutherford, 2016).

These early studies involving puzzle boxes helped Thorndike formulate two laws that would influence his views of how animals and humans learn: the law of effect and the law of exercise. His *law of effect* asserted that if an animal or person received a pleasant or rewarding outcome after performing a behavior, then that animal or person would be more likely to perform the behavior again, in anticipation of the pleasant outcome. He proposed that the type of outcome that occurred as a result of a behavior determined how it became "stamped" into memory. Pleasant outcomes reinforced the connection between the behavior and the result, in the form of a stimulus-response relationship. Conversely, if an animal or person performs a behavior and the outcome is unpleasant, then they are less likely to perform the behavior again, diminishing the connection between the stimulus and response. If this sounds familiar, it is because the law of effect was the precursor to the idea of positive reinforcement, a primary component of operant conditioning. His *law of exercise* asserted that the more an animal or person is compelled to complete an action to receive a pleasant outcome, the stronger the connection between the behavior and the outcome becomes. This law validated a longstanding philosophical notion of associationism, (a.k.a. associative learning). Together, these two laws would formulate his theory of "connectionism," which would eventually evolve into modern-day behaviorism (Hunt, 2007).

Thorndike's work quickly became known in the field of psychology after he was invited to speak at the New York Academy of Sciences in 1898. From there, his research on learning was published in *Science* and *Psychological Review*. In December 1898, he was invited to present his puzzle box studies at the meeting of the American Psychological Association, where he would solidify his status as a major player in the science of psychology (Hunt, 2007).

Thorndike's early work and ambitions gave rise to a prolific research career. Over the course of his professional life, most of which was spent at Columbia Teachers College, he researched and authored 50 books and 450 articles. His interests were varied, including topics related to educational psychology, learning theory, psycho-educational assessments, and social psychology, among others (Hunt, 2007). In 1899, he collaborated with a friend and colleague, Robert Sessions Woodworth (1869–1962), studying *transfer of training*. This involved the ability of a person to apply a behavior, knowledge, and skills acquired in one learning context to a different learning context. They gave their subjects tasks like estimating weights and then examined how that skill would transfer to other contexts. Some of the contexts were very similar to the activity of estimating weights, while others were very different. What they found was that transfer of training was fairly limited. They published the results of their work in *Psychological Review* in 1901. Ultimately, this research validated Thorndike's original findings with puzzle boxes and his theory of connectionism. The research also refuted C. K. Lyans's "Doctrine of Formal Discipline" in education, which asserted that if the mind can be trained to learn by studying some subjects first (e.g., logic, mathematics, linguistics, philosophy), then it will be easier to learn others (Lyans, 1914). Thorndike and Woodworth suggested that educators should use more task-oriented educational practices that promoted rote learning of specific skills (Fancher & Rutherford, 2017).

Thorndike's work was featured in the very first volume of the *Journal of Educational Psychology*. In the article, he asserted the importance of establishing criteria that would allow for consistently assessing the success or failure of a particular teaching technique. He saw psychology's role as identifying what education could and could not accomplish in shaping the student. Influenced by the likes of Sir Francis Galton, cousin of Charles Darwin and promoter of eugenics and social Darwinism, Thorndike believed that a child's intelligence was bestowed upon him by his genetic endowment. As a result, the classroom environment was limited in (1) the degree to which the child could learn and (2) the effectiveness of the teaching methods used to instruct that child (Church, 1971).

In the grander scheme of psychology, there were different paradigms that impacted the views of researchers like Dewey and Thorndike. Even though they both were considered functionalists, they had differing views about the applied nature of psychology and were influenced by different theorists of their time. Both Thorndike and Dewey were interested in how learning about one's immediate environment could lead to adapting, surviving, and even thriving in that environment. Thorndike took a more restrictive, experimental approach to the study of educational psychology, echoing the philosophy of predecessors like Wilhelm Wundt and Edward Titchener. Dewey, in contrast, aligned his views more closely to those of William James and G. Stanley Hall.

FORERUNNERS OF PSYCHOLOGY AND THE CHILD STUDY MOVEMENT

Education has now become the chief problem of the world, its one holy cause. The nations that see this will survive, and those that fail to do so will slowly perish. . . . There must be re-education of the will and of the heart as well as of the intellect; and the ideals of service must supplant those of selfishness and greed.

—*G. Stanley Hall*

Wilhelm Wundt (1832–1920) is considered by many to be the founding father of psychology. His formal background was in physiology, which may have influenced his strict orientation to laboratory experimentation. He opened the first psychology laboratory (or "Konvikt") in 1879 at the University of Leipzig in Germany. His influence on the field was far-reaching at the time, with scholars from across the world coming to sit in on his immensely popular lectures. His research focus was on sensation and perception, and he published several books and research articles. In addition to authoring formative texts in the field, he trained close to 200 graduate students. This work is what facilitated the spread of his ideas. He believed that, in order for psychology to be considered a legitimate science, the research needed to take place in a controlled laboratory setting and be done using methodical experimentation. He suggested that different psychological phenomena be studied in different ways. *Voluntarism* is considered the first school of thought in psychology. It refers to Wundt's study of reaction times, perception, and attention, things he associated with a person's will and voluntary effort. They could be observed and measured. For those phenomena that could not be carefully observed and measured in a laboratory, like religious beliefs, mythology, customs, and language, he proposed a field of study that he called *Volkerpsychologie*. He believed that historical and comparative analysis was more appropriate in studying these higher-level mental functions (Fancher & Rutherford, 2017).

Wundt's work would eventually spark a paradigm in psychology coined structuralism by his student Edward Titchener (1867–1927). *Structuralism* defined Titchener's approach to psychology, which emphasized the discovery of the basic structure of mental phenomena as collections of sensations and feelings, before considering their functions. While publicly a devout student of Wundt's, Titchener started to question some of his mentor's research methods and ideas. Eventually Titchener's work would give rise to another competing paradigm known as functionalism. *Functionalism* denoted the broad approach adopted by many American psychologists who focused attention on the utility and purpose of behavior. It was much more applied compared to the theoretical and rigidly experimental principles of voluntarism and structuralism (Fancher & Rutherford, 2017).

While Wundt's and Titchener's work facilitated the study of physiological psychology, which intersected with fields of study like sensation and perception as well as primitive neuroscience, other researchers of the time like William James and G. Stanley Hall wanted to know how to use psychology in a more pragmatic way. They felt that in order for psychology to gain legitimacy and truly reflect the human condition, it needed to escape the confines the laboratory and be used to study everyday life. Thus, they sought to create a "new psychology" that could be introduced and applied to the lives of everyday people.

William James (1842–1910) is considered by many to be the father of American psychology. Like Wundt, his influence was far-reaching and shifted the way people viewed the relatively new science. James was the older brother of famous author Henry James Jr. and three other siblings. They grew up in an affluent family with a father who was prone to anxiety and drawn to the spiritual teachings of Swedenborgian philosophy. His father also was also obsessive about providing all of the James children with an excellent education, which resulted in travelling to various countries around the world. These childhood experiences would affect James throughout his life and career. While studying at Harvard, James studied many subjects including chemistry, physiology, medicine, and biology (Fancher & Rutherford, 2017).

After contracting smallpox on an expedition to the Amazon, James returned to Harvard with an eye condition and issues with lower back pain. As a result, he travelled to Germany in 1867 to rehabilitate his back injury using the mineral springs. While there, he first encountered the emerging field of physiological psychology and the work of Wundt. James returned to the United States to resume and complete his medical studies. He did not feel fulfilled in his career path and remained intrigued by what he read of physiological psychology. Eventually, an opportunity came about when he was invited to teach part of a new course on the subject at Harvard. Thus, began James's illustrious career as a professor of psychology (Fancher & Rutherford, 2017).

Like Wundt, James became an immensely popular professor, but his appeal was a more personal one than Wundt's. Wundt's lecture style was rigid, authoritarian, and more of a solitary endeavor. It gave him an opportunity to showcase his expertise and espouse his ideas regarding the directions that psychology should take in order to establish itself as a science. In contrast, James was known to students by being charismatic, engaging, and approachable. He gained a reputation for treating students as his equal. He even solicited feedback from them about his courses, a practice that was not mandated by the university or implemented by the majority of his colleagues. He also made a point to discuss the topics and theory he presented with his students and provided examples that were relatable to everyday life, making psychology more accessible and applied (Fancher & Rutherford, 2017).

James also authored a few important works in 1890. The first was entitled *The Principles of Psychology*, covering a variety of topics including aspects of physiological psychology like sensation and perception, and comparative psychology. But it was his writings on stream of consciousness, emotion, habit, will, and pragmatism that laid the groundwork for a more applied version of psychology. *Pragmatism*, a termed coined by one of James's friends and fellow scholars, Charles Sanders Pierce (1838–1941), is the view that scientific ideas and knowledge are constantly evolving based on the temporal, social, and cultural context. In short, the philosophy asserted that the ways we think and behave adapt to our changing environments (Fancher & Rutherford, 2017). While pragmatism was never directly applied to the field of education, it is apparent how it could be applied to student learning.

In 1890 James also gave a lecture series for teachers titled "Talks to Teachers about Psychology." These lectures were given in summer schools for teachers around the country and then published in 1899 both as a book and in the *Atlantic Monthly* magazine. Aligned with the principles of pragmatism, James's pedagogical ideas were quite modern. He supported and promoted the use of discussion, projects and activities, laboratory experiments, writing, drawing, and concrete materials in teaching (James, 1983).

James taught many students that would go on to be influential in the field, including G. Stanley Hall (1844–1924). G. Stanley Hall is considered to be the father of the concept of the distinct period of development known as adolescence and is also considered a forerunner of the Child Study Movement. These two contributions took psychological study in a much different direction from Wundt's and Titchener's ideas. Hall, like many early psychologists, started out studying theology and had a brief stint at Union Theological Seminary in 1867. He soon was introduced to the increasingly popular theory of evolution asserted by Charles Darwin. Hall preferred this theory to his seminary studies and eventually left theology to pursue the study of philosophy and physiology in Germany. After he ran out of funds, Hall returned to the United States to complete his postbaccalaureate degree. He briefly taught philosophy and religion at Antioch College, where he was introduced to Wundt's newly published book *The Principles of Physiological Psychology.* Intrigued by what he read, he made a plan to study under Wundt and left his position at Antioch. Before he could get to Wundt's lab in Leipzig, Germany, he landed at Harvard where he was offered a teaching position in English. While there, he met William James who was, at that point, a new professor. James encouraged Hall to conduct research and write a paper that involved muscular and perceptual functioning. This ultimately served as Hall's dissertation, granting him the first PhD in the United States that involved experimental psychology (Fancher & Rutherford, 2017).

After earning his doctorate, James headed to Wundt's research institute in Leipzig as planned. Wundt was still establishing his experimental laboratory, and Hall served as his first official American student. Hall was only there briefly and participated in some of Wundt's studies. Hall established a favorable relationship with Wundt and was able to procure recommendations from him as an established psychologist upon returning to the United States. Hall eventually wound up back at Harvard, delivering a special lecture series on the subject of education. This brief opportunity would ultimately lead Hall to pursue a focus on developmental psychology and pedagogy. It would also lead him to a job opportunity at the newly established Johns Hopkins University. There, he would become the first professor of psychology and pedagogy in 1884, a mere eight years after the university was established. He also was granted the first psychology laboratory in the United States and started the *American Journal of Psychology.*

A short four years after establishing himself at Johns Hopkins, Hall was appointed as the first president of Clark University in 1888. Hall would stay at Clark for the duration of his career and, for a time, continued to teach psychology and pedagogy, mentoring more than half of the new American PhD graduates in psychology during the 1890s. Among his students was the progressive education reformer John Dewey. In 1888 Hall also founded the Child Study Association of America followed by a second journal, *Pedagogical Seminary*, in 1891. This is still published today under the name *Journal of Genetic Psychology*.

One of his greatest legacies to the field of psychology was established in 1892, when he hosted a national professional society at Clark. He invited several colleagues who were interested in the new science of psychology to meet and discuss current research. Later that same year, those scholars met again at the University of Pennsylvania, and the result was the founding of the American Psychological Association. Hall was promptly elected the APA's first president (Fancher & Rutherford, 2017). The APA started with 31 members, but grew to 308 members by 1916. As of 2019, the APA's membership has grown to 118,000 researchers, educators, clinicians, consultants, and students (American Psychological Association, 2019).

HALL AND THE CHILD STUDY MOVEMENT

While Hall had a similar reach and notoriety to Wundt, his research interests resembled the Jamesian philosophy of pragmatism. Hall maintained his interests in psychology, pedagogy, and evolutionary theory. At the start of the 1880s, he conducted large-scale survey research with kindergarten-aged children. The questions focused on myriad topics including the children's fears, interests, dreams, knowledge and musings of their bodies, games, toys, stories, zoology, astrology, theology, and their experiences with friendships and bullying. In 1883, he published *The Contents of Children's Minds on Entering School*, with the intent of informing classroom teachers on their students. His systematic research on young children would shape educational practice in the late 19th and early 20th centuries and usher in the formal and systematic study of children (Fancher & Rutherford, 2017).

Hall also conducted survey research with older children. In 1904 he published *Adolescence: Its Psychology and Its Relation to Physiology, Anthropology, Sociology, Sex, Crime, Religion, and Education*. The 626-page work introduced Americans to the term *adolescence*. Hall's research described this time during the developmental trajectory as an emotionally laden tumultuous phase. The book also served to solidify his interests in developmental psychology and provided further evidence that childhood was a period of time that involved constant emotional, physical, social, and intellectual change and growth (Fancher & Rutherford, 2017).

With Hall's work and the work of other researchers and educational reformers like John Dewey, Jane Addams, Arnold Gesell, and Cora Bussey Hillis, the Child Study Movement was born. This movement would eventually reshape the field of educational psychology beginning in the 1920s. The primary intent of the movement was to establish empirically researched pedagogy, by using experimental psychology as a means of studying aspects of children's development including their sensory-perceptual development, physical development, and ideas about religion; the role of play in their development; and the development of their memories and attention spans. The idea behind this research was for formal education to become more systematic and structured in a way that suited a wider range of learners. By incorporating formal research of children's development, a link was created between the university and K–12 setting. This link would facilitate a revision to, and broader acceptance of, the field of educational psychology (Davidson & Benjamin, 1987).

In 1893, the National Education Association established a Department of Child Study. Child Study clubs were formed in locations across the United States. Teachers, parents, and researchers collected data into the early 1900s. The Child Study Movement that was sparked by Hall and his colleagues was in full swing by the end of the 1880s, reaching its peak in the 1920s and early 1930s. Elementary and secondary educators were encouraged to collect data about their students' learning experiences as well as their own teaching practices. This data would eventually contribute the reimagined focus of educational psychology (Huntsinger, n.d.).

While Hall had some interesting views on race and gender that were heavily influenced by evolutionary theory and the social milieu of the time, he was a progressive thinker and educator. Hall worked with female students at Clark, not a common practice during his time, and also oversaw the dissertation of the first African American psychology PhD candidate in the United States, Francis Cecil Sumner (1895–1954). Sumner earned his doctorate in 1920 and eventually landed at Howard University, where he became the head of the psychology department. He had a variety of research interests but held a special focus on the psychology of religion. While at Howard, he mentored and supervised Mamie Phipps Clark (1917–1983) and Kenneth B. Clark (1914–2005). The Clarks would become best known for their "Doll Studies" on racial identity in black and white children, the results of which were used in a brief submitted to the U.S. Supreme Court during the historic 1954 court case *Brown v. Board of Education of Topeka*. This marked the first time that social science research was used in Supreme Court deliberations—deliberations that would ultimately lead to the desegregation of public schools (Fancher & Rutherford, 2016).

Hall also taught Arnold Gesell (1880–1961). Gesell contributed to the field of developmental psychology by conducting large-scale research on infants at his "psycho-clinic" housed in Yale's New Haven Dispensary. He intensely studied the motor skills, social behavior, and personalities of middle-class, Caucasian infants. His research led to the creation of developmental "norms." Like Hall, he believed that humans develop in a typical fashion based on the interaction between their genetic tendencies and immediate environment. He also believed that, as a member of the human species, all infants demonstrated similar qualities and abilities as certain ages. Hall and Gesell helped to create what we now refer to as *developmental milestones* in infancy, childhood, and adolescence (Huntsinger, n.d.).

Cora Bussey Hillis (1858–1924) was a child welfare activist who became an agitator for and influencer in the Child Study Movement. She was born in Bloomfield, Iowa, but spent most of her early life in New Orleans, where her family relocated after the Civil War. She was educated in an all-girls private school there. In 1880, after returning to Iowa, she married attorney Isaac Hillis and settled in Des Moines. She helped to cofound the Des Moines Women's Club in 1886. Soon after, she joined the New Iowa Child Study Society and embarked on other philanthropic endeavors that benefitted families in the area. Hillis was also the first president of the Iowa Congress of Mothers, which would evolve into the Congress of Parent-Teachers Associations. She lobbied for a juvenile court system in her state that would separate juveniles from adults during detainment and in prison. In 1901 and 1908, she advocated for the creation of a research center at the University of Iowa that focused on the study of children and child rearing. Hillis's advocacy work led to the establishment of the University of Iowa Child Welfare Research Station in 1917. This facility along with the Merrill-Palmer Institute in Detroit became the models for other child study centers that appeared during the 1920s and 1930s. The establishment of these institutes sparked the creation of a number of publications including formal journals like *Child Development* and popular magazines like *Parents' Magazine*. The goal of these publications and institutes was to share information about children with parents, teachers, and college faculty (Swaim, 2009; Huntsinger, n.d.).

With the development of the child study institutes came government funding to support initiatives in developmental psychology and parent education. The Laura Spellman Rockefeller Memorial allocated millions of dollars to the study of development in foster children. Additionally, funds were awarded to establish major child research centers at the University of California, Berkeley; Columbia University; and the University of Minnesota under the direction of Lawrence Frank. Financial support was also provided to existing research centers at Yale and the University of Iowa. Smaller research institutes were launched at the University of Michigan and in Washington, DC, and funds were provided for individual research projects. The Society for Research in Child Development was founded in 1930 as a result of the growing interest and importance attributed to the study of child development (Huntsinger, n.d.).

JANE ADDAMS AND PROGRESSIVE EDUCATION

The ultimate aim of education is to modify the character and conduct of the individual, and to harmonize and adjust his activities.

—*Jane Addams*

Jane Addams (1860–1935) was another pioneer of the Child Study Movement and progressive education. *Progressive education* flies in the face of the traditional educational training model. It emphasizes the role of a student's experience over rote learning of facts and figures. It shifts the focus from simply training and testing students to teaching students how to use critical thinking skills, creativity, and social-emotional skills. Active engagement, experiential learning, and exploring the goals of learning are hallmarks of this approach.

Addams was influenced by theorists like John Dewey and William James. Born the eighth of nine children in Cedarville, Illinois, she is known as the "Mother of Social Work," a forerunner of agitators for women's suffrage, and an internationalist. Her pioneering work resulted in her being the second woman to receive the Nobel Peace Prize, in 1931. In 1881, she graduated as the valedictorian of her class at Rockford Female Seminary. Headed toward a career in medicine, her education was interrupted by ailing health and hospital visits. Ultimately, after extensive travel in Europe that included a visit to a settlement house in London's East End with her friend and eventual romantic companion Ellen G. Starr, she set out to create a similar setting for the underprivileged in Chicago. With Starr's help, Addams founded Hull House in 1889 (Haberman, 1972).

The mission of Hull House centered on becoming a hub of civic, philanthropic, and educational endeavors that would ultimately lead to the improvement of more industrialized and urban areas of Chicago. During its second year of operation, it hosted more than 2,000 people each week. Addams and Starr were very adept at calling upon the well-to-do women of Chicago to donate their funds and their time to Hull House. The facility would eventually grow to be a 13-building complex that included an art gallery, second public kitchen and coffee house, gymnasium, pool, boarding club for young women, drama group, and employment bureau, among other things. Hull House would also become a place where social services and cultural events were housed for local residents, many of whom were immigrants. It also operated a night school where people could acquire continuing education credits and new social workers could complete extra training. Addams was friends with John Dewey, who eventually became a board member of the Hull House (Haberman, 1972).

Addams maintained a specific educational philosophy at the Hull House. She cultivated an art education program that challenged the standard, industrialized education that emphasized technical training for future employment. The art program allowed individuals to think outside of the box and engage in independent, creative thinking that allowed for cooperative interaction and self-discovery. A relentless advocate for the underserved and immigrant populations, she also saw art as a way to disrupt the cultural and political status quo and unlock the diverse perspectives of the community through multiculturalism (Davis, 1973).

Addams believed that lifelong engagement with learning was imperative to a functional and vibrant democracy. Her educational and philanthropic programming at Hull House served a variety of people in a variety of ways and would solidify her role in the progressive education movement. With the opening of Hull House, her reputation grew, and she was called upon to participate in larger civic roles. Among these included being named to the Chicago Board of Education in 1905, where she was eventually made chairman of the School Management Committee. She also played a major role in the founding of the Chicago School of Civics and Philanthropy in 1908; in 1909 she became the first female president of the National Conference of Charities and Corrections. Not a stranger to dirty work, Addams also conducted investigations on midwifery, narcotics consumption, milk supplies, and sanitary conditions. In 1910, she was the first woman to be awarded an honorary degree by Yale University. In 1920, she cofounded the ACLU. She was involved in creating legislation that reduced child labor, sponsored a kindergarten at Hull House, and worked with John Dewey and fellow educational pioneer and suffragette Ella Flagg Young (1845–1918) to create teaching techniques that emphasized the needs and abilities of the students, making their educational experience more relevant to them. She emphasized the role of play and argued that the industrialized nature of urban settings was destroying the experience of youth. Addams also endeavored to educate adults who did not have previous access to education (Davis, 1973).

Ultimately, Addams's educational philosophy embodied a feminist perspective, social responsibility, and moral awareness. She recognized the role of education in improving her community as well as the larger democracy that it functioned in. She felt that education should allow for creative, diverse thought and be accessible to everyone, including the poor, immigrants, women, and children. To her an educated society was a peaceful, creative society. The legacy of Hull House can be seen in modern-day educational programs like Head Start, the YMCA/YWCA, free school lunch programs, the Boys and Girls Clubs of America, and more.

Florence Goodenough identified several contributions of the Child Study Movement in 1930. These included the development of mental testing and intelligence, the study of behavioral and emotional development, the study of growth and physical maturation, and the betterment of research method like naturalistic observation (Cairns, 1998). These developments, coupled with the progressive education movement, eventually helped to transition the primary focus of educational psychology from the rote transmission of knowledge in the very specific and limited context of the classroom to a much broader focus that considered the larger social and cultural contexts of the learner. As a result, the discipline has become much more dynamic and multifaceted and better serves students, educators, and policy makers.

EDUCATIONAL PSYCHOLOGY IN THE MODERN ERA

We must merge our traditional sense of schooling with the real world. What we do in school must not insult the child's past but must build upon his past and encourage future learning.

—Sigmund Boloz

Division 15 of the APA

The American Psychological Association formally recognized educational psychology as a distinct subdiscipline of psychology in 1946. During this year, Division 15 was established and a set of formal bylaws were created. These bylaws were most recently revised in May 2016, stating:

> The purposes of this organization shall be to expand psychological knowledge and theory relevant to education, to extend the application of psychological knowledge and services to all aspects of education, to develop professional opportunities in educational psychology, to further the development of psychological theory through the study of educational processes, and to promote cooperation and joint action with others having similar or related purposes. (American Psychological Association, 2016)

APA Learner-Centered Principles

In 1990, in light of many misguided and arguably ineffective policies emphasizing standardized assessment, which inevitably led to a return to the standardization of educational curricula, the APA Presidential Taskforce was formed to create the learner-centered psychological principles. This task force recognized a need for a paradigmatic shift in how we design and deliver educational content. The principles addressed the multiple roles that teachers serve in their students' learning experiences and highlighted the complexities of the learning environment, including the myriad characteristics that the learners themselves bring to the classroom.

They also emphasize diversity and the active and reflective nature of learning. The purpose was twofold:

1. To provide a framework for educational reform and school redesign efforts, and

2. To promote a dialogue between educators, researchers, and policy makers that would encourage a society that valued lifelong learning, among other things.

The principles, being learner centered, focused on internal characteristics that the learners could control. This approach differed from focusing solely on the delivery of instructional methods and the conditioned habits of the learner. They were also intended to be inclusive, holistic, and applicable to the real world.

Below is an abridged list of the learner-centered psychological principles, which were revised in 1997. It is taken from "Learner-Centered Psychological Principles: A Framework for School Reform and Redesign" and was produced by the Learner-Centered Principles Work Group of the APA's Board of Educational Affairs (BEA) (1997). The principles are grouped into four broad categories:

I. Cognitive and Metacognitive Factors

    1. *Nature of the learning process.* The learning of complex subject matter is most effective when it is an intentional process of constructing meaning from information and experience.

    2. *Goals of the learning process.* The successful learner, over time and with support and instructional guidance, can create meaningful, coherent representations of knowledge.

    3. *Construction of knowledge.* The successful learner can link new information with existing knowledge in meaningful ways.

    4. *Strategic thinking.* The successful learner can create and use a repertoire of thinking and reasoning strategies to achieve complex learning goals.

    5. *Thinking about thinking.* Higher order strategies for selecting and monitoring mental operations facilitate creative and critical thinking.

    6. *Context of learning.* Learning is influenced by environmental factors, including culture, technology, and instructional practices.

II. Motivational and Affective

    7. *Motivational and emotional influences on learning.* What and how much is learned is influenced by the motivation. Motivation to

learn, in turn, is influenced by the individual's emotional states, beliefs, interests and goals, and habits of thinking.

8. *Intrinsic motivation to learn.* The learner's creativity, higher order thinking, and natural curiosity all contribute to motivation to learn. Intrinsic motivation is stimulated by tasks of optimal novelty and difficulty, relevant to personal interests, and providing for personal choice and control.

9. *Effects of motivation on effort.* Acquisition of complex knowledge and skills requires extended learner effort and guided practice. Without learners' motivation to learn, the willingness to exert this effort is unlikely without coercion.

III. Developmental and Social

10. *Developmental influences on learning.* As individuals develop, there are different opportunities and constraints for learning. Learning is most effective when differential development within and across physical, intellectual, emotional, and social domains is taken into account.

11. *Social influences on learning.* Learning is influenced by social interactions, interpersonal relations, and communication with others.

IV. Individual Difference Factors Influencing Learners and Learning

12. *Individual differences in learning.* Learners have different strategies, approaches, and capabilities for learning that are a function of prior experience and heredity.

13. *Learning and diversity.* Learning is most effective when differences in learners' linguistic, cultural, and social backgrounds are taken into account.

14. *Standards and assessment.* Setting appropriately high and challenging standards and assessing the learner as well as learning progress—including diagnostic, process, and outcome assessment—are integral parts of the learning process.

For a closer look of the principles and their descriptions, visit: http://www.apa.org/ed/governance/bea/learner-centered.pdf.

THE 21ST-CENTURY FRAMEWORK

I am not a teacher, but an awakener.

—Robert Frost

Educators and parents agree that the formal transmission of specific content knowledge should no longer be considered the primary focus of education. In a study conducted by the Pew Research Center and the Markel Foundation in 2016, 60 percent of adults surveyed said that the public K–12 system had "a lot" of responsibility in preparing students with the skills needed for the U.S. workforce (Bialik, 2017). K–12 educators are addressing this and other emerging needs in their students. According to the Partnership for 21st Century Learning's (P21) Framework, content learning is still a relevant and valuable focus for student outcomes, but it has evolved beyond the basics of reading, writing, arithmetic, and history. It includes teaching mastery in skills like global awareness and literacy in the domains of finance, civics, health, and the environment. Additional P21 outcomes focus on

- learning and innovation skills (e.g., critical thinking, creativity, communication and collaboration);
- information, media, and technology skills; and
- life and career skills (e.g., flexibility and adaptability, initiative and self-direction, social and cross-cultural skills).

In essence, contemporary educators are expected to prepare students both in the realm of the classroom and the world beyond (Partnership for 21st Century Learning, 2019).

REFERENCES

Alonso, H. (2016). Jane Addams in the classroom. *Peace & Change, 41*(2), 261–263.

American Psychological Association. (2019). APA history. Retrieved from https://www.apa.org/about/apa/archives/apa-history

American Psychological Association. (2016). Division 15 by-laws. Retrieved from https://apadiv15.org/wp-content/uploads/2016/08/D15-Bylaws-2016.pdf

Bialik, K. (2017, August 25). Most Americans say K–12 schools have a lot of responsibility in workforce preparation. Pew Research Center. Retrieved from https://www.pewresearch.org/fact-tank/2017/08/25/most-americans-say-k-12-schools-have-a-lot-of-responsibility-in-workforce-preparation/

Cairns, R. B. (1998). The making of developmental psychology. In R. M. Lerner and W. Damon (Eds.), *Handbook of child psychology: Theoretical models of human development* (pp. 25–105). New York, NY: Wiley.

Church, R. (1971). Educational psychology and social reform in the progressive era. *History of Education Quarterly, 11*(4), 390–405. doi:10.2307/367038

Davidson, E. S., & Benjamin, L. T. (1987). A history of the child study movement in America. In J. A. Glover & R. R. Ronning (Eds.), *Historical foundations of educational psychology* (pp. 41–60). Boston, MA: Springer.

Davis, A. F. (1973). *American heroine: The life and legend of Jane Addams*. New York, NY: Oxford Press.

Fancher, R. E., & Rutherford, A. (2017). *Pioneers in psychology: A history* (5th ed.). New York, NY: W. W. Norton.

Graf, N. (2018, April 18). A majority of U.S. teens fear a shooting could happen at their school, and most parents share their concern. Pew Research Center. Retrieved from https://www.pewresearch.org/fact-tank/2018/04/18/a-majority-of-u-s-teens-fear-a-shooting-could-happen-at-their-school-and-most-parents-share-their-concern/

Haberman, F. W. (Ed.). (1972). Jane Addams: Biographical. In *Nobel lectures, peace 1926–1950*. Amsterdam: Elsevier. Retrieved from https://www.nobelprize.org/prizes/peace/1931/addams/biographical/

Hergenhahn, B. R. (2014). *An introduction to the history of psychology* (7th ed.). Belmont, CA: Wadsworth.

Hunt, M. (2007). *The story of psychology* (2nd ed.). New York, NY: Anchor Books.

Huntsinger, C. S. (n.d.). *Early childhood education: Child study movement*. Retrieved from http://schoolbag.info/pedagogy/early/50.html

James, W. (1983). *Talks to teachers on psychology and to students on some of life's ideals*. Cambridge, MA: Harvard University Press. (Original work published 1899)

Klosterman, E. M., & Stratton, D. C. (2006). Speaking truth to power. *Affilia, 21*(2), 158–168.

Kuhn, T. (1962). *The structure of scientific revolutions*. Chicago, IL: University of Chicago Press.

Learner-Centered Principles Work Group of the American Psychological Association's Board of Educational Affairs (BEA). (1997). Learner-centered psychological principles: A framework for school reform and redesign. American Psychological Association. Retrieved from http://www.apa.org/ed/governance/bea/learner-centered.pdf

Lyans, C. K. (1914). The doctrine of formal discipline. *Pedagological Seminary, 21*, 343–393. Retrieved from http://www.archive.org/stream/doctrineofformal00lyanrich/doctrineofformal00lyanrich_djvu.txt

Ostman, H. (2006). Maternal rhetoric in Jane Addams's twenty years at Hull-House. *Philological Quarterly, 85*(3/4), 343–370.

Partnership for 21st Century Learning. (2019). *P21 network: Frameworks & resources*. Retrieved from http://www.battelleforkids.org/networks/p21/frameworks-resources

Rafferty, M. (2002, December 4). *The effects of teacher morale on teacher turnover rates*. Retrieved from http://webb.nmu.edu/Webb/ArchivedHTML/UPCED/mentoring/docs/TeacherMorale.pdf

Swaim, G. (2009). Hillis, Cora Bussey. *The biographical dictionary of Iowa*. Retrieved from http://uipress.lib.uiowa.edu/bdi/DetailsPage.aspx?id=173.

2

Perspectives: How Students Think— Neuroscience and Theories of Cognition

---

Learning is in the eye of the mind.

—French proverb

DEFINING LEARNING

Learning involves many components including changes in the brain, changes in behavior, memories of previous experiences, adaptations to new environments, and problem-solving skills. In this chapter we will examine neurological, cognitive, and behavioral perspectives on learning and their implications for the classroom environment. As we discussed in Chapter 1, educational psychology has evolved to consider many facets of learning and does not believe it to occur in the vacuum of school. Students bring a whole host of characteristics to the learning environment with them, including their intellectual ability and curiosity, their individual home and life experiences, their temperaments, their school readiness, their level of motivation, their emotional and physical well-being, their sense of competence (or self-efficacy), and the various aspects of their identities. Once in the classroom, these components mesh together to impact how individual students interact with each other and their teachers. The next two chapters will focus on a variety of theories that have been used to explain how we think, how we form memories and create knowledge, how we speak, and how we behave.

MARIA MONTESSORI

Maria Montessori is known for her creation of the Montessori School and Method. She was also an Italian physician, educator, and innovator. She began her career in the medical field, graduating from the University of Rome's medical program in 1896, after being rejected once before admittance. She focused on psychiatry, later developing an interest in education and attending classes about pedagogy and educational theory. Her interest in education led her to focus on children with developmental and intellectual disabilities. In 1907 she opened her first school, Casa dei Bambini (Children's House) in Rome.

Her focus was on how children learn naturally from birth to childhood. Casa dei Bambini was opened in an impoverished, inner-city district and quickly became an environment where children were teaching and learning from themselves. Montessori's overall goal was to create a learning center where students could engage in a child-centered approach, focusing on physical, social, emotional, and cognitive learning abilities. By doing this, Montessori believed she could bring more peace to the world, as explained by Priya Darshini Baligadoo (2014). Montessori argued that traditional schooling often discouraged students, later causing them to be ambivalent people: "Little opportunity is giving to students to discover their personality, to be creative, and become autonomous persons" (Baligadoo, 2014, p. 429). By teaching students through sensory-motor activities, they are able to feel, taste, hear, see, and smell their educational resources; this also helps them relate their education to their everyday lives.

Overall, there are multiple benefits for students of a Montessori School. Students are able to learn on their own through their sensory-motor skills, while relating the senses they experience at school to senses at home and throughout their everyday lives. Not only is Montessori education engaging for students, but it is also reliable. Montessori's method has been tested for over 100 years and has been proven successful around the world. Today, there are more than 22,000 Montessori schools around the world. Montessori's overall goal was to create a learning center where students could engage in a child-centered approach, focusing on physical, social, emotional, and cognitive learning abilities, in which she did just that, for her method has furthered even after her death 67 years ago.

—*Courtney Cepec*

HOW OUR BRAINS DEVELOP

Biology gives you a brain. Life turns it into a mind.

—Jeffrey Eugenides

It is important to recognize the connection between cognitive neuroscience and education. With that said, we must be careful not to overstate their connections or incorrectly apply research findings to the classroom setting. Purdy and Morrison (2009) cite research on how cognitive neuroscience is being inaccurately implemented in K–12 curricula. The "zero to three movement," learning styles, left- and right-brain thinking, and "brain gym" exercises are among these neuro-educational fads.

What we can apply from cognitive neuroscience are the established lessons about how the brain works with respect to human development and cognitive functioning. The following sections describe what we know to be true.

Neurons

The brain and body are composed of billions of *neurons* that serve as our information superhighway. These cells transmit information within the brain and throughout the body. The connections between neurons, called *synapses*, are assumed to be the primary means by which people think, learn, and form memories.

The anatomy of a neuron includes two major components: the cell body and the nerve processes. The *cell body*, sometimes referred to as the *soma*, contains the nucleus of the neuron. The cell body is responsible for (1) creating proteins to develop other parts of the neuron and (2) determining whether the neuron should transmit an electrical signal within the neuron. The nerve processes are composed of the axon and the dendrites. *Axons* are responsible for carrying electrical signals, called *action potentials*, away from the cell body. Some are coated with a protective layer of cells known as *glial cells*. These glial cells help form the *myelin sheath* around the axon, which facilitates the speed the electrical impulse travels through the axon. Some neurons are not myelinated, which results in slower transmission of the electrical impulse. The axon is responsible for sending messages out to various areas. Once the electrical impulse travels through the axon to the *axon terminals*, a release of chemicals called *neurotransmitters* is sent out across the synapse. Those neurotransmitters are sent across the synapse to the next neuron. *Dendrites* are the branchlike structures on the receiving end of the synapse that carry incoming signals from synapses to the next neuron's cell body.

Neurons are classified as either motor, sensory, or interneurons. *Motor neurons* carry information from the central nervous system to organs, glands, and muscles. *Sensory neurons* send information to the central nervous system from internal organs or from external stimuli. *Interneurons* relay signals between motor and sensory neurons.

Neural Connectivity

Neural connections (synapses) undergo a lot of construction over a person's lifetime. We go through periods of *synaptogenesis*, or growth of synaptic connections, as well as through periods of *synaptic pruning*, or removal of synaptic connections. These processes are the result of nature (e.g., growth spurts) but also heavily dependent on environmental experiences. Neurological growth spurts correspond with development in motor and cognitive skills.

Brain plasticity refers to the ability of the brain to reorganize itself due to experience. Because many of its synapses are not yet established, the brain is more plastic during the first few years of life than at any later time. Early flexibility in neuronal development allows children to adapt to their environments better.

Myelination is the process of wrapping myelin sheath around neural circuitry, and results in more efficient firing of neural impulses. It is rapid during first two years of life and continues through adolescence. During childhood and adolescence, the brain also becomes increasingly *lateralized*, which means that certain skills become more localized in their functioning and are subsequently attributed to either the right or left hemisphere of the brain. Lateralization is linked to many skills, including language learning, handedness, spatial perception, facial recognition, higher-order thinking, and artistic ability (Galin & Ornstein, 1972; Sperry, 1977; Ruoff, Doerr, Fuller, Martin, & Ozols-Ruoff, 1981). There are frequent growth spurts early in the infant's life, but the periods of both growth and stability become longer as the child grows older. Many growth spurts are localized or restricted to one or a few parts of the brain.

By the age of 10, we have more synapses than we will have at any point in our lives (Bruer, 1997). These synapses operate on a *use it or lose it principle*. Those that are engaged on a regular basis will remain functional, while those that are not used regularly will be pruned away. This pruning is important because it allows for more efficiency of the synaptic connections that remain and makes room for future synaptic connections as we acquire different skills over our lifetime. There are also two major brain growth spurts in the teenage years. The first occurs between ages 13 and 15 and takes place in parts of the brain that control spatial perception and motor functions. The second brain growth spurt begins around age 17 and continues into early adulthood and focuses on the frontal lobes of the cerebral cortex.

Language learning provides a good example of how synapses are pruned over time. When we are born, we are biologically prepared to make vocalizations that occur in any language. We are also biologically prepared to tune into the melody of our native language. In fact, we can start doing this prenatally from within the womb, by listening to the muffled sound of our moms' voices (Webb, Heller, Benson, & Lahav, 2015). Within the first few months to a year, we begin to more closely mimic the sounds of our native language. We do this first through cooing, then by babbling, and eventually by speaking in one-word, then two-word sentences. As we hone our speaking skills, we refine the neural circuitry needed to speak in our native language. By the end of the first decade of life, if we haven't acquired a second language, we tend to lose our readiness to do so. In other words, those synaptic connections that were present at birth for all languages start to get pruned away. This is one reason why it is more difficult and seems less natural to acquire a second language once we enter high school, or later on.

Brain Growth

In addition to changes in the synaptic connections within our neural circuitry, our neural structures also undergo "growth spurts," which involves the proliferation (growth) and refinement (pruning) of synapses.

These spurts occur starting in infancy and continue into emergent adulthood. They occur in different parts of the brain at different points in life. While all of the structures of the brain are in place when we are born, the brain further develops from back to front, and this growth occurs into our early twenties.

At birth, the *midbrain* and the *medulla* are the most fully developed parts of the brain. These two structures control functions like our heartbeat and breathing as well as attention, sleeping, waking, elimination, and movement of the head and neck. The least developed part of the brain at birth is the *cerebral cortex*, the largest, most complex brain structure involved in perception, body movement, thinking, and language (Casey, Giedd, & Thomas, 2000). The cerebral cortex is the last brain structure to stop growing and is sensitive to environmental influences for much longer than other parts of the brain.

The brain develops in spurts followed by periods of stability. During infancy, intervals of growth and stability are very short, occurring at one-month intervals for approximately the first 5 months. After this, the periods of growth and stability become longer and occur around 8 months, 12 months, and 20 months. When a child reaches age two, the periods of growth and stability slow down until about age four, when she typically undergoes another spurt. Growth spurts tend to correlate with very local-ized parts of the brain during development. Some of these spurts occur as children are reaching cognitive milestones. According to Boyd and Bee (2012) some examples of when these spurts occur include:

a) A growth spurt at 20 months of age that corresponds with an infant's first demonstration of goal-directed behavior.

b) A growth spurt at age four that corresponds with the acquisition of fluency in both speech comprehension and speech production.

c) Between six and eight years, a growth spurt that corresponds with refinements in fine motor skills and hand-eye coordination.

d) Between 10 and 12 years, a growth spurt that occurs in the frontal lobes of the cerebral cortex and leads to better logic, planning, and memory formation.

Cognitive Development

Myelination theory asserts that the more a child practices a particular skill set, the more myelin will wrap around his neural circuitry involved in executing that skill set. This is a process that happens naturally and facili-tates neurological development from infancy into adulthood (Paus et al., 1999; Casey, Giedd, & Thomas, 2000).

Experience-dependent changes can lead to individual differences in the rate of development for certain neural circuitry. For instance, a child who is bilingual might have more refined language centers at an earlier age compared to a child who only speaks one language, or a child who has played a sport that requires hand-eye coordination from an early age may have more refined neural circuitry in the parietal lobe for spatial skills. Generally speaking, humans' neurological development proceeds in a rela-tively stepwise, predictable manner.

If someone is trying to learn to play the piano, she would engage a cer-tain segment of her neural circuitry to do so. The more she engaged in learning to play the piano, the more this neural circuitry would be acti-vated. Over time, this neural circuitry becomes more coated with myelin sheath. The myelin can wrap up to 40 times. As the neural circuitry becomes more coated, the experience of executing the particular skill set becomes more efficient and automated. In other words, the longer one practices playing the piano, the easier it becomes. With myelination, the progress is slow, and typically requires error-filled practice. It requires that a learner practice intently at the edge of her ability (Coyle, 2009). This the-ory is very applicable to educational settings.

HOW WE THINK

Whenever I think of something but can't think of what it was I was thinking of, I can't stop thinking until I think I'm thinking of it again. I think I think too much.

—Criss Jami

Cognition is a mental process that helps us acquire knowledge and understand the world we live in through our thinking. It involves a variety of abilities like sustaining attention, forming memories, using judgement to make decisions, problem solving, comprehending and producing language, and using existing knowledge to create new knowledge. While cognition involves what some cultures would consider intelligence, these two things are not the same. *Intelligence* is the general capacity to use all of the mental processes associated with cognition. It is a slightly more controversial concept because there has been a pretty long history of debate about which cognitive skills should be emphasized when measuring intelligence. Some researchers view intelligence as how "book smart" someone is, while others think that people's abilities to adapt to the world around them and use their "common sense" is just as important. We will discuss this debate and theories a bit later in the chapter. First, let's discuss some well-known theories of cognitive development.

PIAGET AND INHELDER'S CONSTRUCTIVIST THEORY OF COGNITION

We call a child's mind small simply by habit; perhaps it is larger than ours is, for it can take in almost anything without effort.

—Christopher Morley

Constructivist theories assume that we actively construct our own knowledge through experience. Swiss psychologists and constructivist theorists Jean Piaget (1896–1980) and Bärbel Inhelder (1913–1997) created the well-known stage theory of cognition. The theory became immensely popular by the 1940s and 1950s and made a lasting impression of the field of developmental psychology. Inhelder, a student, long-time colleague, and academic successor to Jean Piaget, is often overlooked when discussing this theory. Inhelder was an established and prolific researcher in her own right who contributed much to the stage theory that is commonly associated with Piaget. In addition to doing seminal work on conservation tasks, during the 1950s she proposed the formal operations stage of development, asserting that children transitioning into adolescence developed the ability to use experimentation and inductive thinking (Nguyen, 2016; Daly & Canetto, 2018).

Piaget got his start in biology and zoology. It was those interests, and the influence of Darwin's ideas about evolution, that shaped his theory of human development. An intellectually curious child, Piaget began intensely studying mollusks at the Museum of Natural History in Neuchatel, Switzerland, at the age of 10. He wrote his first formal scientific paper on the albino sparrow in high school. By the age of 15, his published writings on mollusks gained him a reputation among European zoologists. He attended the University of Neuchatel, studying zoology and philosophy. He earned his doctorate in 1918, and in the same year, he attended the University of Zurich, where he pursued a budding interest in psychoanalysis. While there, he spent a semester studying under Carl Jung and Paul Eugen Bleuler. After his time in Zurich, he attended the Sorbonne for a period of two years, studying abnormal psychology.

While in Paris, he began working with Theodore Simon at the Alfred Binet Laboratory. He devised reading tests that he administered to school children. He also evaluated the results on standardized tests of reasoning that Simon and Binet had developed. These tests were intended to measure a child's ability to correctly respond to age-appropriate academic tasks. It was this work that eventually led him to question how psychologists and educators defined intelligence and how children think. The tests that were used to measure intelligence suggested that a child's age had a connection to the types of errors they would make in solving certain academic problems. These tests also implied something about the connection between their instruction and how they learned the information.

Piaget was not satisfied with how these standardized tests measured a child's ability to learn. He thought the tests were too limited. After revising how the test was administered, he began asking children *why* they solved a problem or answered a question in a particular way. After reading responses from a variety of children, Piaget concluded that children's ability to reason was not wrong; rather, it was dependent on a child's level of life experience. He determined that children have an innate curiosity and are active in their own learning. Their life experiences, or lack thereof, determine how they approach a problem when solving it. When children lack experience in a given situation, they adapt by using their imagination and creativity in responding. This outlook was very different from the views of some of Piaget's contemporaries. For some, intelligence was thought to be primarily inherited and fixed.

Piaget started publishing his research on children's reasoning in 1921. At that point he had also returned to Switzerland to assume the role of director of the Institut Jean-Jacques Rousseau in Geneva. This is where he met Bärbel Inhelder (Nguyen, 2016). By 1925, Piaget was teaching at the University of Neuchatel and in 1929, he transitioned to the University of Geneva where he spent the rest of his career teaching and researching child psychology. He developed several theories about how children develop, but the one that gained the most notoriety was his stage theory of cognition. Inhelder had been training to become a school teacher at the Rorschach Teacher's College. She was driven enough to want to attend university, so she took private lessons in subjects like Latin, science, the arts, and other disciplines. A French course brought her to the University of Geneva in 1932, where she subsequently became involved in the Institute of Educational Services, a.k.a. the Institut Jean-Jacques Rousseau. By that point, Piaget was the codirector, also researching and teaching courses in developmental psychology. She studied under Piaget, then eventually became his research assistant. Her work led to a bachelor's degree and the first published paper on children's development of conservation through observation, reasoning, and experience. This paper eventually turned into the basis for her dissertation, which focused on the understanding of conservation in children who were developmentally delayed. This work also led to coauthoring a book with Piaget on the topic. She completed her dissertation in 1943, two years after publishing her book with Piaget. She then formally joined Piaget at the University of Geneva where she was made a professor in 1948 (Nguyen, 2016).

Stage theories are theories that break down development into distinct periods of development. Each stage is assumed to be somewhat culturally universal, chronologically fixed, and qualitatively different from the other stages. The classical constructivist stage theory of cognitive development (Piaget, 1952, 1954, & 1962) asserts the following major principles:

- Human development has its basis in biological maturation. (In other words, as the brain develops, it allows for more advanced cognitive reasoning.)
- Children and teens actively seek out (or construct) information from their environment.
- Children and adolescents develop in predictable stages.
- These stages are culturally universal.
- Each stage marks new developmental milestones.
- Humans can't regress in these stages.
- Development in one domain (e.g., cognition) impacts development in other domains (e.g., language, emotional/social development, moral development, etc.).

Piaget identified four causes of cognitive development. Two of these were internal in nature. The first involved *equilibration*, or an innate tendency to achieve cognitive balance. More on that in a bit. The second internal cause involved *brain maturation*. The older children get, the more neural connections they make, and the more refined parts of their brains become (e.g., the prefrontal cortex). Piaget noted that biological development facilitates development in all other domains (e.g., thinking, speaking, socializing, behaving, etc.).

The other two causes of cognitive development were external. The first external cause Piaget notes was *social transmission*. This involves information that children get from other people. For instance, when children learn to speak, they are biologically prepared to do so, but they must learn their native language from listening and interacting with those around them. Finally, children's *experiences* facilitate cognitive development. This includes their own opportunities to act on the world and to observe the results. Again, Piaget considered children to be active participants in their own learning. According to him, this active role started in infancy and was based in the immediate experiences of the infant.

Piaget's theory is associated with a number of concepts. *Genetic epistemology* is the idea that as humans we have a framework and timeline for developing how we think and what we think about. This framework is based on the four causes we just discussed, but more specifically it involves *mental schemas*. Mental schemas are basic units of knowledge about objects, events, and actions. According to Piaget, schemas are built on a small group of sensory and motor skills that we utilize during the very first stage of our cognitive development, the sensorimotor stage.

Piaget also suggested that we use several processes to build our framework. First is *organization*, which in Piaget's view refers to an inborn mental process that helps us to derive generalizable schema from specific experiences. For example, a child's pet poodle gives them knowledge about the schema of "dog." Organization requires the use of two subprocesses: accommodation and assimilation. *Accommodation* requires a child to change a schema as a result of new information she is taking in. *Assimilation* involves absorbing some new event or piece of information to make it part of an existing schema. Assimilation requires us to be selective and to pay attention to cognitive schemas that already exist in our knowledge base.

In order to better explain these concepts, one can use the analogy of a filing system. Pretend a child's brain is like the desktop on a computer. She has all of her existing knowledge stored on this desktop, and it is organized in a way that makes sense to her and relates to her own past experiences. This experiential and conceptual knowledge is organized in separate folders, and she has labeled them in her own special way. Suddenly, her mental desktop has a new incoming piece of information. She has to evaluate that new piece of information and see if she can file it in any of her existing mental desktop folders. If she can link the new knowledge to something she already knows, then she can file it in a folder. In this instance, she would be assimilating that new piece of information to her existing knowledge base. If she could not find a logical place for the new piece of knowledge in her existing knowledge base, she would have to create a new space for it on her mental desktop. In this instance, she would have to accommodate that new piece of knowledge.

According to Piaget, the goal of engaging in organization, accommodation, and assimilation is to achieve equilibration, that state of cognitive balance that we discussed earlier. When children are younger, they oftentimes find themselves in a state of *cognitive disequilibrium*, or imbalance. Another way to think of it is to say that the younger a child is, what they do not know tends to outweigh what they do know. Their natural curiosities allow them to adapt to the world they live in and drives these processes, leading to the acquisition of new knowledge. For Piaget, equilibration guided infants and children through the four stages of cognitive development.

The Sensorimotor Stage

The *sensorimotor stage* (birth to 18 months) is characterized by thought that is based in action. Because infants have limited mobility and can't speak yet, they use sensory and motor skills to interact with the environment. Over the course of this stage, the actions based on these sensory and motor skills become more intentional as infants gain more control over their bodies. Reflexive behaviors like sucking and grasping become more goal directed. For instance, an infant might accidentally start blowing bubbles with their saliva to make "raspberries." The more he does it, the more he realizes he has control over doing it, so he eventually does it on purpose. This is an example of what Piaget referred to as a *primary circular reaction*. These allow for the formation of new schemas because they provide the infant with new experiences. There are a few other substages that occur during sensorimotor stage, which are discussed in the following sections.

Substages of Piaget's Sensorimotor Stage

Reflexes: This substage occurs from birth to one month. Inborn reflexes and sensory experiences are the primary means through which infants explore their environment during this stage. Infants are not yet able to imitate others and cannot integrate information from separate sensory experiences. Examples of reflexes include rooting, sucking, blinking, looking, and grasping. Examples of sensory experiences include seeing, tasting, and hearing.

Primary Circular Reactions: This substage occurs from one to four months. During this substage, infants develop new schemas through their immediate experiences. They build on (or accommodate) their reflexive behaviors, which become more controlled, and they start to integrate their sensory experiences. Infants do not yet connect their physical actions and the reactions that may occur in the environment. An example of reflexive behaviors becoming more intentional would be when the grasping reflex turns into the ability to reach and grab an object in an infant's environment. An example of coordinating schemas of different senses would be when an infant looks toward a sound she hears in her environment.

Secondary Circular Reactions: This substage occurs from four to eight months of age. Infants start to pay attention to the world around them and will perform actions to create a response. Repetition of actions occur at this stage. Imitation may also occur at this stage, but only for schemas that infants already have. Infants may also start to understand the *object concept*, or knowledge that objects are permanent entities that exist independently in space and time even when the infant cannot perceive or act on them. Actions are still not fully intentional at this point, but infants are increasingly aware that they are separate entities in the world. An example of intentional actions would be when an infant strikes a mobile and sees it move. She repeats that action because she realizes she made the mobile move.

Coordination of secondary schemas: This substage occurs from 8 to 12 months of age. During this stage, actions become more intentional and demonstrate *means-end behavior*, which is behavior that is intended to have a specific purpose and lead to a specific result. Infants act with purpose and can coordinate two or more schemas. Imitation of novel behaviors occurs along with *cross-modal transfer*, which is transfer of information from one sense to another. An example of means-end behavior that involves cross-modal transfer would be when an infant shakes his toy repeatedly, because he knows when he does this, the toy will make a noise.

During coordination of secondary schemas, *object permanence*, or the infant's realization that things continue to exist even though they are not in her immediate field of vision, begins but is not mastered. Infants in this substage also commit the "A not B error," also known as a perseverative error (Piaget, 1954). This is an error that involves the mental perception of objects and occurs in infants younger than one year. Around eight months, infants are capable of realizing that objects, when hidden from view, still exist and have not disappeared. This realization illustrates an infant's ability to mentally represent objects in her mind.

Tertiary circular reactions: This substage occurs from 12 to 18 months. This stage is also referred to as the *trial and error* learning stage, which involves experimentation that results in infants trying out new ways of playing with or manipulating objects. This type of "play" is very active and intentional. They no longer commit the A not B error and are able to imitate a wider range of behaviors. An example of trial and error learning would be when an infant throws his bowl of cereal off his high chair repeatedly because he knows doing so will lead to his caregiver picking it up.

Beginning of representational thought: This substage occurs from 18 to 24 months. During this stage, infants develop the use of symbols to represent objects or events. There is an understanding that the object and the symbol are separate. Deferred imitation also begins to occur. Examples of representational thought include language, playing (especially imaginary play), drawing, and storytelling. An example of deferred imitation would be when a toddler starts to sing the "Alphabet Song" because her parent has been teaching her how to sing it over the last two weeks.

It is important to note that object permanence facilitates social attachments. Infants have a strong preference for their primary caregivers from birth. They can recognize their scents and the sounds of their voices. Their ability to orient toward the sound of their caregivers' voices also provides them with information about the appearance of their faces. Once infants realize their caregivers continue to exist even when they cannot see them, they experience separation anxiety and will send signals (crying) to try to regain close proximity to them.

According to Piaget, imitation and deferred imitation also develop during the sensorimotor stage. *Imitation* occurs when infants can perform something they see or hear someone else do. At two months of age, infants can imitate behavior they already possess that is modeled by someone else. For example, if an infant hears another infant cry, they may begin crying too. At 8 to 12 months of age, infants can imitate other people's facial expressions. At one year of age, imitation of any action that wasn't already in an infant's repertoire begins. *Deferred imitation* occurs when an infant imitates a behavior that she has watched at a previous time, and Piaget suggested it begins around 18 months.

Challenges to the Sensorimotor Stage

While Piaget suggested that object concept and object permanence did not occur until a few months into the sensorimotor stage, habituation and dishabituation studies suggest memory abilities are present at birth (Baillargeon & DeVos, 1991). Rovee-Collier (1999) also demonstrated that three-month-old babies can remember a specific learning experience through reinforcement. In regards to imitation, infants are able to imitate simple facial gestures at birth, much earlier than Piaget predicted (Meltzoff & Moore, 1977, 1983, 1989). Piaget also was disputed with respect to when he thought deferred imitation appeared. Piaget said this did not occur until 18 months of age, but more contemporary research found that infants as young as nine months could demonstrate some deferred imitation (Klein & Meltzoff, 1999; Meltzoff, 1988).

The Preoperational Stage

As the sensorimotor stage comes to an end, emerging toddlers begin to demonstrate the use of symbolic representation of objects and events. This is demonstrated in their budding use of language, as they begin to use verbal labels (e.g., "mama," "doggie") to identify the objects and people in their environment. This skill facilitates the transition into the *preoperational stage* (18 months to 6 years). During this stage, young children become more adept at using symbolic thinking to communicate. Piaget referred to this symbolic thinking as the *semiotic function*. They continue to develop their language skills and use symbolic representation through drawing, storytelling, make-believe play, and their imaginations. During make-believe play, they may use *animism*, which involves assigning real-life qualities to inanimate objects. For instance, a child may pretend that her stuffed teddy bear can talk to her.

According to Piaget, a child's thinking during this stage is also egocentric. *Preoperational egocentrism* occurs when a child displays the inability to distinguish personal perceptions, thoughts, and feelings from those of others. In other words, a preoperational child is unable to think about another person's perspective. She may use egocentric speech when explaining something. When this occurs, the preoperational child might leave out important details because she assumes her audience has the same amount of knowledge about the topic as she does.

Piaget tested egocentrism using the *three-mountain task*. The task involved a child and experimenter seated at table with a model of three mountains. Each mountain was a different size and had different details. For example, one mountain could have been covered with trees and mountain goats, while another could be covered with snow and have a cabin on it. A doll was also seated at the table in a different location from the child. The child was allowed to look at all sides of the mountain before he was asked to return to his seat. Once he was seated, the experimenter asked him what he saw in front of him when looking at the mountains. The child typically would give an accurate and detailed description of what he saw. Then, he was asked what the doll saw. Piaget found that a preoperational child would typically provide a description that was similar to his own view of the mountain. Piaget concluded that the child's perspective was limited due to a naïve idea that the doll had the same perspective of the mountains as he did.

Another characteristic of the preoperational stage asserted by Piaget and Inhelder (1974) was that children lack mental reversibility to solve conservation tasks. *Mental reversibility* involves the knowledge that reversing a transformation brings about the conditions that existed before the transformation. *Conservation* is the ability to understand that the quantity or amount of substance remains the same even when there are external changes in its shape or arrangement. Piaget and Inhelder had a series of tasks that measured conservation of liquid, mass, area, length, and volume. According to them, children did not develop this skill until around the age of five or later. They suggested that children at this stage experienced *centration*, or a tendency to think of the world in terms of a single aspect of a problem at a time. Most of the time that single aspect was the end result of the problem, or a focus on end states. They further asserted that as a child progresses into the concrete operational stage, he begins to experience *decentration*, or the ability to think about a variety of aspects of a problem.

Challenges to the Preoperational Stage

Views of early childhood and preoperational thinking have suggested that Piaget's and Inhelder's conservation studies are generally supported. Children as young as two to three years old have some ability to understand that another person sees things differently than they do; thus they demonstrate less egocentric thinking. Flavell (1966, 1974) developed a theory of perspective taking, which he concludes can be broken down into two levels:

- Level One—the child knows that another person experiences something differently.
- Level Two—the child develops a whole series of complex rules for figuring out what the other person sees or experiences.

Ultimately, movement away from egocentrism helps development of understanding differences in appearance and reality. Another aspect of perspective taking is theory of mind. *Theory of mind* involves an awareness of what others are thinking and the realization that it may differ from what you are thinking. In other words, theory of mind is related to perspective taking. A child's theory of mind correlates with her conservation abilities, her degree of egocentrism, and her understanding of appearances. Pretend play and shared pretense help develop theory of mind in children.

The *false belief principle* (Gopnik & Astington, 1988; Gopnik, 1990; Wellman, 1990; Astington & Gopnik, 1991; Taylor, 1996) is the understanding that another person might have a false belief and the ability to determine what information might cause the false belief. The *false belief task* is a task that measures theory of mind and is based on the false belief principle. It requires a child to infer that another person possesses the level of knowledge about a task that they do. During the task, an experimenter shows a child a box of crayons, but reveals that the box of crayons actually contains candles. A young child that is still developing theory of mind may assume that her friend also knows that the box of crayons contains candles even if the friend was not there to see what the experimenter had revealed. An older child will figure out that if her friend was not present when the experimenter revealed that candles were in the box of crayons, her friend will assume that there are crayons in the box.

Theory of mind develops into middle childhood. At 18 months, a child understands that people are goal directed, which means that their behaviors typically have some purpose. By age three, a child understands some link between feelings and behaviors. By age four, a child's beliefs influence their behaviors. By age six a child understands that knowledge can be derived from inference. This can also be linked to a child's ability to express his own emotions and read the emotions of other people. By age seven children understand the reciprocal nature of thought, which is needed to develop friendships.

Certain things can influence theory of mind. Children can possess a sibling advantage. Interactions with siblings, especially older siblings, may enhance theory of mind development. Language skills can also enhance or detract from the speed of theory of mind development. The more robust a child's language skills, the more expressive and better he will be able to articulate what he is thinking and what others are thinking. Cross-cultural research suggests theory of mind development may be universal.

During the *concrete operations stage* (6 to 12 years) children get better at thinking logically. They are less limited by the constraints of the preoperational child and can perform conservation tasks with better accuracy. With that said, they have a better chance at solving these when they are being asked to think about them in concrete, tangible terms. At this stage, a few things have occurred that allow for this. The first is that concrete operational children have acquired mental reversibility, meaning they understand that actions and mental operations can be reversed. Second, at this stage children focus more on the process of transformation during the conservation tasks rather than the end result.

Some other things also occur during this stage. There is a decline in egocentric thinking. As children move through this stage, they get better at inference and perspective taking, which makes them aware that other people have different experiences and knowledge. Children have acquired numerical concepts (or as Piaget referred to it, *numeration*) like addition and subtraction and other mathematical operations, which facilitate seriation. *Seriation* involves sorting objects or situations according to any characteristic, such as size, color, shape, or type. *Classification*, or the ability to structure objects hierarchically, develops for more complex categories. This impacts *class inclusion*, which is the understanding that an object is part of a subset included within a hierarchical set (e.g., both robins and blue jays belong to a larger category of animal, birds). Play becomes more cooperative and based in reality.

During this stage different types of logic develop. Seriation facilitates *transitive inference*, which is a type of inferential reasoning that involves the ability to compare two objects via a transitional object. A common example is the statement: A > B and B > C and C > D and D > E. Knowing this, a child can conclude without being told that B > D. The use of inductive and deductive logic also occurs more frequently. *Inductive logic* involves reasoning from the particular to the general, from experience to broad rules. *Deductive logic* involves reasoning from the general to the particular, from a rule to an expected instance or from a theory to a hypothesis. Finally, *horizontal decalage*, or the ability to apply new kinds of thinking to new kinds of problems, begins to occur more frequently.

Finally, according to Inhelder and Piaget (1958), during the *formal operations stage* (13 years and older) teenagers develop the ability to manipulate hypothetical concepts and think logically using abstract concepts. They engage in systematic and complete approaches to problem solving, are better at using strategies, and implement more organization to problem solve. Teenagers at this stage also are better at formulating and testing hypotheses, as well as separating and controlling variables. They can implement both hypo-deductive reasoning and proportional reasoning. *Hypothetical reasoning* involves deriving logical outcomes after considering hypotheses or hypothetical premises. *Proportional reasoning* involves understanding proportions (e.g., fractions, decimals, ratios, etc.) well enough to apply them to mathematical concepts.

Egocentric thinking reemerges at this stage. *Formal operational egocentrism* occurs when teenagers are unable to separate their own abstract logic from the perspectives of others. This also often involves disregarding any sort of practical implications to their thinking. According to more contemporary research, egocentric thinking can also lead to things like naïve idealism, imaginary audience, personal fable, and the invulnerability fallacy. *Naïve idealism* (Elkind, 1984, 2001; Opper, Ginsburg, & Brandt, 1987) involves thinking about solutions and beliefs that are very optimistic and positive but not realistic or well thought out. This type of thinking is typical of adolescents. Individuals who think this way believe that something will work out exactly as desired without actually thinking the plan through. According to Elkind (1967) an *imaginary audience* occurs when teenagers believe that everyone is focused on them or some small flaw of theirs. Elkind also suggested *personal fables* occur when teenagers think that they are unique and no one else understands them. The *invulnerability fallacy* (Lapsley & Duggan, 2001; Lapsley, 2003) occurs when teens' false sense of security leads them to believe that they cannot get hurt, even when engaging in high-risk behaviors.

Additional Criticisms of Piaget's Stage Theory of Cognitive Development

Some of Piaget's ideas have been revisited and revised. His initial ideas about when children and teens learn were too rigid. What contemporary research has found is that some cognitive attainments occur at earlier ages than Piaget suggested. Other contemporary research disagrees with Piaget and Inhelder's assumption that everyone achieved formal operations (Keating, 1979). Piaget also initially deemphasized the role of culture in learning; however, other theorists have emphasized the role of culture in what, how, and when we learn (Dasen, 1994; Vygotsky, 1978). Piaget also did not initially pay much attention to individual differences, but we now know that experience and culture can play a role in what skills are refined and how quickly they are refined (Segall, Dasen, Berry, & Poortinga, 1990; Vygotsky, 1978).

Some additional assertions by Piaget have been refuted or reformulated by more contemporary theories. These include:

- Cognitive development does not seem to show stage-like qualities (Brainerd, 1993; Flavell, 1982).
- Some preverbal children with autism spectrum disorders can understand the intentions of others, and thus possess some degree of theory of mind (Aldridge, Stone, Sweeney, & Bower, 2001).
- Children do not understand concepts like transitivity and class inclusion the way that Piaget initially proposed (Kail & Bisanz, 1982).
- Study and practice lead to expertise, not formal operational thinking. This involves three stages: acclimation, competence, and expertise. Thus, the more experience children and teens have with something, the more logically and abstractly they can think about it (Byrnes, 1988).

LEV VYGOTSKY'S SOCIOCULTURAL THEORY

Learning is more than the acquisition of the ability to think; it is the acquisition of many specialised abilities for thinking about a variety of things.

—Lev Vygotsky

Lev Semyonovich Vygotsky (1896–1934) was born in Orsa, Russia (present-day Belarus), into a wealthy Jewish family. He grew up during the political strife that followed the Bolshevik Revolution, and the experiences of his culture would impact his future theory. His father was a banker and his mother took care of him and his six siblings, even though she had been formally trained as teacher. Vygotsky was a strong student in his youth and entered the University of Moscow in 1913. At first, he pursued medicine, then switched to legal studies and philosophy. Ultimately, he did not attain a formal degree, but in 1917 he returned to his hometown and began a career as an educator at the Teacher's College of Gomel. In 1924, he attended a national neuropsychology conference known as the Psychoneurological Congress in Leningrad. There he gave a presentation on methods of reflexological and psychological inquiry. His presentation made an impact, as it earned him an invitation to become a research fellow at the Psychological Institute of Moscow (Fancher & Rutherford, 2017; Vygotsky, 1978).

While at the Psychological Institute of Moscow, he conducted research on the psychology of art, and the psychology of education and remediation, focusing on children with learning disabilities. He eventually founded the Institute of Defectology and directed the department for the education of physically "defective" and mentally retarded children in Narcompros. During this time, he also taught at the Krupskaya Academy of Communist Education, the Second Moscow State University, and the Hertzen Pedagogical Institute in Leningrad. In 1925, while in his late twenties, he experienced his first bout of tuberculosis after returning to Russia from a trip to England. This resulted in extended hospital stays, leaving him unable to officially return to work until 1926. Despite his extended illness, he managed to continue to produce publications during this time. He also became an influential leader of a group of Soviet psychologists that became known as the Vygotsky Circle. He maintained a lingering interest in medicine by resuming his medical training at the institute in Moscow and then at Kharkov, where he taught a course in the Ukrainian Psychoneurological Academy (Fancher & Rutherford, 2017; Vygotsky, 1978).

From 1926–1930, Vygotsky created an active research program with several students. Their focus included the study of advanced memory function, selective attention, decision making, and language development. These things were studied using three different perspectives; among them was the cultural-historical approach. He was also very influenced by the *Gestalt Psychology* movement. This approach to psychology viewed sensory, perceptual, and cognitive functions in a holistic manner and asserted that the whole of these experiences was greater than the sum of their parts (Vygotsky, 1978).

Vygotsky never fully recovered from his first bout of tuberculosis, and it returned at the age of 37. This resulted in an untimely and premature death in 1934. Prior to his passing, he was offered a position to head the department of psychology in the All-Union Institute of Experimental Medicine.

His life and career were relatively short, but history would provide him with deserving recognition. Despite skepticism from colleagues about some of his theories while alive, his work became highly influential to the field of educational psychology decades after his death, when they were introduced to Western culture. American psychologist Jerome Bruner played a large role in getting Vygotsky's work translated because he realized how it would impact the field of education in the 1950s and 1960s (Fancher & Rutherford, 2017; Vygotsky, 1978).

The Role of the Social Context in Our Thinking

Vygotsky's theory, which was heavily influenced by the socialist/communist ideology of his culture, asserted that knowledge was acquired through social interactions with individuals who knew more and had experienced more in life and in the cultural context. These individuals were referred to as the *more knowledgeable other* (MKO). The MKO could guide the learning through what Vygotsky referred to as the *zone of proximal development* (ZPD), which had two levels of development: actual development and potential development. According to Vygotsky, the learner's actual development involved the accumulated knowledge and potential for developing other cognitive abilities. The learner's potential development represented functions that had not materialized yet, but were developing with environmental experiences. Thus, the ZPD was the difference between what the learner could do with assistance (from MKOs) and what the learner could do alone (Vygotsky, 1978).

Instructional scaffolding is the process by which one structures the ZPD so that a child can solve problems on their own. Through this process, cognitive skills required for success in each culture are socially transmitted from generation to generation. Scaffolding is commonly associated with Vygotsky's theory because it is one way to guide a learner through their ZPD, but the term was actually coined by Jerome Bruner, the American cognitive and educational psychologist.

According to Bruner and colleagues:

> This scaffolding consists essentially of the adult "controlling" those elements of the task that are initially beyond the learner's capacity, thus permitting him to concentrate upon and complete only those elements that are within his range of competence. The task thus proceeds to a successful conclusion. We assume, however, that the process can potentially achieve much more for the learner than an assisted completion of the task. It may result, eventually, in development of task competence by the learner at a pace that would far outstrip his unassisted efforts. (cited in Wood, Bruner, & Ross, 1976, p. 90)

An example of instructional scaffolding would be teaching a science class about the scientific method. First, the teacher would go over what the scientific method was and describe each step involved in it. Then the teacher might ask her students to tell her what the steps are, and why they are important. Once basic knowledge of the process was achieved, she could provide her students with a structured lab opportunity to demonstrate the steps of the scientific process. Once they applied the scientific process to an experiment that the teacher created, the students could develop their own original experiment using the steps of the scientific method.

Guided participation (Rogoff et al., 1993; Rogoff, 1990, 2003) is another derived concept from Vygotsky's sociocultural theory. It is the tendency for adults to provide scaffolding to children so they can engage in mature activities (e.g., learning to mow the lawn or bake a cake). Rogoff and colleagues assert that parents, teachers, coaches, and other adults who interact with younger and/or more novice individuals naturally engage in the process of guided participation as a means for social transmission of everyday knowledge. Thus, guided participation might be a more organic and less structured experience than instructional scaffolding. Guided participation should be collaborative between the expert and the learner in these exchanges and is intended to eventually lead the novice/learner to become more independent at a particular task.

Vygotsky's Views on Language and Cognition

For Vygotsky, the role of language was imperative to the social transmission of knowledge pertaining to everyday tasks and about the larger cultural context of the learner. He asserted that language was the medium for thinking, and without it, cognition was limited. He proposed stages that represent a step towards the learner's internalization of the ways of thinking used by adults in society. The first stage was the primitive stage that involved animal-like knowledge. The second stage was the naive stage or psychology stage, which involved the learner using language without an understanding of its symbolic character. The third stage was the egocentric speech stage, where the learner uses language to solve problems. The fourth stage was the ingrowth stage, where the learner internalized egocentric speech, leading them to more logical thinking (Vygotsky, 1986).

Vygotsky emphasized role of language in cognition and self-regulation. He asserted that younger learners will use *private speech*, audible speech used to guide them through solving a problem or engaging in an activity. A young child talking aloud to herself while solving a subtraction problem in math class would be an example of private speech. By her talking her way through the problem, she is actively thinking about it and self-regulating her behavior to guide herself to a solution. She might be repeating what her teacher told her earlier in class, thus demonstrating that she has internalized the transmission of that knowledge. *Inner speech* is intended to serve the same purpose for older/adult learners and is internalized. For example, a high school student may be reciting the equation needed to solve his calculus problem in his head, during an exam (Vygotsky, 1986).

COMPARING CONSTRUCTIVIST AND SOCIOCULTURAL THEORIES OF COGNITIVE DEVELOPMENT

Through others, we become ourselves.

—*Lev Vygotsky*

Inhelder, Piaget, and Vygotsky made substantial and lasting impacts on the fields of developmental and educational psychology. Even though Vygotsky preceded Piaget in death by several years, many in these fields compare their theories when discussing cognitive development. To summarize the chapter, here is a list of major points where the two theories differ the most.

Cognition and Education

Constructivist theory asserts cognition is a distinct aspect of development, separate from formal or informal education. Sociocultural theory asserts that education influences the development and growth of cognition.

The Rate of Cognitive Development in Children

Constructivist theory, at least in the early stages of Piaget's theory, asserts cognitive achievements are universal for all children regardless of background. Sociocultural theory asserts that the social and cultural contexts in which children grow up in will vary, and thus cognitive growth will vary for individuals.

The Active Role of Children in Their Own Cognitive Development

Constructivist theory asserts children actively organize cognitive schemas and knowledge to adapt more effectively to the demands of the environment. Sociocultural theory also emphasizes the active role of the child in their own cognitive development but suggests his role is a collaborative one with the more knowledgeable other.

The Role of the Sociocultural Context in Cognitive Development

Constructivist theory emphasizes common, universal features of thought displayed by all children. Piaget did acknowledge that children will move through the stages at varying rates. Sociocultural theory asserts that children will show individual differences in development depending on the values of their culture and what is transmitted to children by older, more competent adults. There are no universal stages.

The Role of the More Knowledgeable Other in Cognitive Development

Constructivist theory asserts children make journey of childhood alone. Other people may influence the direction a child may take, but the child is seen as a solitary adventurer. Sociocultural theory asserts that children rarely make progress on the developmental path without the help of an expert partner.

The Role of Language in Cognitive Development

Constructivist theory asserts thought is required for and precedes language. Sociocultural theory asserts internalized language is the medium for thought.

REFERENCES

Aldridge, M. A., Stone, K. R., Sweeney, M. H., & Bower, T. G. R. (2001). Preverbal children with autism understand the intentions of others. *Developmental Science, 3*(3), 294–301.

Astington, J. W., & Gopnik, A. (1991). Theoretical explanations of children's understanding of the mind. *British Journal of Developmental Psychology, 9,* 7–31.

Baillargeon, R., & DeVos, J. (1991). Object permanence in young infants: Further evidence. *Child Development, 62,* 1227–1246.

Baligadoo, P. D. (2014). Peace profile: Maria Montessori—peace through education. *Peace Review, 26*(3), 427–433.

Boyd, D., & Bee, H. (2012). Physical development. In *The developing child* (13th ed., pp. 81–114). New York, NY: Pearson.

Brainerd, C. J. (1993). Cognitive development is abrupt (but not stage-like). *Monographs of the Society for Research in Child Development, 58,* 170–190. doi:10.1111/j.1540–5834.1993.tb00460.x

Bruer, J. T. (1997). Education and the brain: A bridge too far. *Educational Researcher, 26*(8), 4–16.

Byrnes, J. P. (1988). Formal operations: A systematic reformulation. *Developmental Review, 8,* 66–87.

Casey, B. J., Giedd, J. N., & Thomas, K. M. (2000). Structural and functional brain development and its relation to cognitive development. *Biological Psychology, 54*(1–3), 241–257.

Coyle, D. (2009). *The talent code: Greatness isn't born. It's grown. Here's how.* New York, NY: Bantam Dell.

Daly, J. C., & Canetto, S. S. (2018). Bärbel Inhelder (1913–1997). Retrieved from http://www.apadivisions.org/division-35/about/heritage/barbel-inhelder-biography.aspx

Dasen, P. (1994). Culture and cognitive development from a Piagetian perspective. In W. J. Lonner & R. S. Malpass (Eds.), *Psychology and culture*. Boston, MA: Allyn and Bacon.

Elkind, D. (1967). Egocentrism in adolescence. *Child Development, 38,* 1025–1034. doi:10.1111/j.1467–8624.1967.tb04378.x

Elkind, D. (1984). Teenage thinking: Implications for health care. *Pediatric Nursing, 10*(6), 383–385.

Elkind, D. (2001). *The hurried child*. Cambridge, MA: Da Capo Press.

Fancher, R. E., & Rutherford, A. (2017). *Pioneers of psychology* (5th ed.). New York, NY: Norton.

Flavell, J. H. (1966). Role-taking and communication skills in children. *Young Children, 21,* 164–177.

Flavell, J. H. (1974). The development of inferences about others. In T. Mischel (Ed.), *Understanding other persons*. Oxford, England: Blackwell.

Flavell, J. H. (1982). On cognitive development. *Child Development, 53*(1), 1–10.

Galin, D., & Ornstein, R. (1972). Lateral specialization of cognitive mode: An EEG study. *Psychophysiology, 9*(4), 412–418. https://doi.org/10.1111/j.1469–8986.1972.tb01788.x

Gopnik, A. (1990). Developing the idea of intentionality: Children's theories of mind. *Canadian Journal of Philosophy, 20,* 89–114.

Gopnik, A., & Astington, J. (1988). Children's understanding of representational change and its relation to the understanding of false belief and the appearance-reality distinction. *Child Development, 59,* 26–37.

Inhelder, B., & Piaget, J. (1958). *The growth of logical thinking from childhood to adolescence: An essay on the construction of formal operational structures.* New York, NY: Routledge.

Kail, R., & Bisanz, J. (1982). Information processing and cognitive development. *Advances in Child Development and Behavior, 17,* 45–81.

Keating, D. (1979). Adolescent thinking. In J. Adelson (Ed.), *Handbook of adolescent psychology* (pp. 211–246). New York, NY: Wiley.

Klein, P. J., & Meltzoff, A. N. (1999). Long-term memory, forgetting, and deferred imitation in 12-month-old infants. *Developmental Science, 2*(1), 102–113.

Lapsley, D. K. (2003). The two faces of adolescent invulnerability. In D. Romer (Ed.), *Reducing adolescent risk: Toward an integrated approach* (pp. 25–32). Thousand Oaks, CA: SAGE.

Lapsley, D. K., & Duggan, P. M. (2001). *The Adolescent Invulnerability Scale: Factor structure and construct validity*. Paper presented at the biennial meeting of the Society for Research in Child Development, Minneapolis.

Meltzoff, A. N. (1988). Infant imitation and memory: Nine-month-olds in immediate and deferred tests. *Child Development, 59*(1), 217–225.

Meltzoff, A. N., & Moore, M. K. (1977). Imitation of facial and manual gestures by human neonates. *Science, 198*(4312), 75–78.

Meltzoff, A. N., & Moore, M. K. (1983). Newborn infants imitate adult facial gestures. *Child Development, 54*(3), 702–709.

Meltzoff, A. N., & Moore, M. K. (1989). Imitation in newborn infants: Exploring the range of gestures imitated and the underlying mechanisms. *Developmental Psychology, 25*(6), 954–962.

Nguyen, T. (2016). Profile of Bärbel Inhelder. Retrieved from http://www.feminist voices.com/baerbel-inhelder/

Opper, S., Ginsburg, H. P., & Brandt, S. O. (1987). *Piaget's theory of intellectual development* (3rd ed.). Englewood, NJ: Prentice-Hall.

Paus, T., Zijdenbos, A., Worsley, K., Collins, D. L., Blumenthal, J., Giedd, J. N . . . Evans, A. C. (1999). Structural maturation of neural pathways in children and adolescents: In vivo study. *Science, 283*(5409), 1908–1911.

Piaget J. (1952). *The origins of intelligence in children*. New York, NY: International Universities Press.

Piaget, J. (1954). *The construction of reality in the child*. New York, NY: Basic Books.

Piaget, J. (1962). *Play, dreams and imitation in childhood*. New York, NY: Norton.

Piaget, J., & Inhelder, B. (1974). *The child's construction of quantities*. London, England: Routledge & Kegan Paul.

Purdy, N., & Morrison, H. (2009). Cognitive neuroscience and education: Unravelling the confusion. *Oxford Review of Education, 35*(1), 99–109.

Rogoff, B. (1990). *Apprenticeship in thinking. Cognitive development in social context*. New York, NY: Oxford University Press.

Rogoff, B. (2003). *The cultural nature of human development*. New York, NY: Oxford University Press.

Rogoff, B., Mistry, J., Göncü, A., Mosier, C., Chavajay, P., & Brice Heath, S. (1993). Guided participation in cultural activity by toddlers and caregivers. *Monographs of the Society for Research in Child Development, 58*(8), 1–79.

Rovee-Collier, C. (1999). The development of infant memory. *Current Directions in Psychological Science, 8*(3), 80–85.

Ruoff, P., Doerr, H., Fuller, P., Martin, D., & Ozols-Ruoff, L. (1981). Motor and cognitive interactions during lateralized cerebral functions in children: An EEG study 1. *Cortex, 17*(1), 5–18.

Segall, M. H., Dasen, P. R., Berry, J. W., & Poortinga, Y. H. (1990). *Human behaviour in global perspective: An introduction to crosscultural psychology* (2nd ed.). New York, NY: Cambridge University Press.

Sperry, R. W. (1977). Forebrain commissurotomy and conscious awareness. *Journal of Medicine and Philosophy*, 2(2), 101–126.

Taylor, M. (1996). A theory of mind perspective on social cognitive development. In E. C. Carterette, M. P. Friedman, R. Gelman, and T. Au (Eds.), *Handbook of perception and cognition: Vol. 13. Perceptual and cognitive development* (pp. 283–329). New York, NY: Academic Press.

Webb, A. R., Heller, H. T., Benson, C. B., & Lahav, A. (2015). Mother's voice and heartbeat sounds elicit auditory plasticity in the human brain before full gestation. *PNAS Early Edition*, 1–6. https://doi.org/10.1073/pnas.1414924112

Wellman, H. M. (1990). *The child's theory of mind*. Cambridge, MA: MIT Press.

Wood, D., Bruner, J. S., & Ross, G. (1976). The role of tutoring in problem solving. *Journal of Child Psychology & Psychiatry*, 17, 89–100.

Vygotsky L. S. (1986). *Thought and language* (A. Kozulin, Ed.). Cambridge, MA: MIT Press.

Vygotsky, L. S. (1978). *Mind and society. The development of higher psychological processes* (M. Cole, V. John-Steiner, S. Scribner, and E. Souberman, Eds.). Cambridge, MA: Harvard University Press.

3

Theories: Intelligence, Memory, Language, and Reading Acquisition

The measure of intelligence is the ability to change.

—Albert Einstein

Intelligence is a complex construct that has historically been defined and measured in a number of different ways. Three broad definitions represent the varied ways in which psychological theorists have conceptualized this construct: (1) individual differences in how people process information or think, (2) the magnitude, pattern, origins, or stability of individual differences in mental functioning, and (3) acting or thinking in ways that are goal directed and adaptive.

Because intelligence has been redefined over time, there have also been many controversies regarding how it is conceptualized and measured. Some theorists view intelligence as a general, singular factor (e.g., cognitive reasoning) while others view it as a set of specific factors (e.g., analytic reasoning vs. mathematical reasoning vs. linguistic abilities, etc.). Some theorists view intelligence as an inherited quality that is predetermined and fixed, while others view it as being culturally dictated. Viewing intelligence as being culturally dictated suggests that intelligence should involve some level of adaptability to an environment. Thus, if a subset of skills is more highly valued in one culture (e.g., spatial abilities in Aboriginal tribes versus "book smarts" in Western Europe), then those who possess higher levels of those skills will be perceived to be more intelligent because they have been able to adapt and excel at them. Some theorists view intelligence as being quantifiable and measurable using standardized tests and intelligence quotients, while other theorists view intelligence as more qualitative and immeasurable. Finally, some theorists view intelligence as a static ability that is unchangeable, while other theorists view it as being more fluid and context dependent.

GALTON, EUGENICS, AND THE NATURE OF INTELLIGENCE

The law of competition may be sometimes hard for the individual, [but] it is best for the race, because it insures the survival of the fittest in every department.

—Andrew Carnegie

The first attempts to develop intelligence tests occurred in late 19th-century England and early 20th-century France. At that time, theorists like British statistician and eugenicist Sir Francis Galton (1822–1911) were strongly influenced by the principles of *evolutionary theory*. A cousin of British naturalist, geologist, and biologist Charles Darwin (1809–1882), Galton adopted the more restrictive view of evolution asserted by theorists like French biologist Jean-Baptiste Lamarck (1744–1829). Unlike Darwin, Lamarck thought that the objective of evolution was ultimately the perfection of a species. He believed that animals and humans would eventually evolve to meet the needs of their environments over a period of time (Fancher & Rutherford, 2017; Hergenhahn, 2014).

In contrast to Lamarck, Darwin believed in *survival of the fittest*, a phrase originally coined by English philosopher, biologist, and sociologist Herbert Spencer (1820–1903). Survival of the fittest asserts those animals and humans with physical features that were most evolved to match the constraints of their current environment would survive and reproduce, but those who did not possess such features would eventually die off. To Darwin, the goal of evolution was not perfection; it was simply to adapt to an environment through the process of *natural selection*, an idea cocreated by Darwin and British naturalist, anthropologist, and biologist Alfred Wallace (1823–1913). If Darwin would have considered intelligence as a psychological quality, he may have conceptualized it as being more vulnerable to environmental factors and as an indicator of how an individual or group has been able to successfully adapt to an environment over time.

Galton applied the concept of Lamarckian evolution to psychological characteristics like personality and intelligence. He believed that through selective breeding—or as he referred to it, *eugenics*—the human race could evolve to be a highly intelligent species. Galton and his associates created intelligence tests to promote the idea of eugenics. He asserted that intelligence could be determined by measuring various aspects of the human brain and nervous system, thus he developed tests of sensory abilities and reaction times. He administered these tests in his Anthropometric Laboratory and debuted them at the World Fair in London in 1885. Over his career, Galton tested more than 9,000 subjects. Galton also invented the basic mathematics behind correlational statistics (the Pearson r correlation coefficient) to assess how intelligence was passed down from one family member to the next. This work was done in collaboration with his colleague, British mathematician and biometrician Karl Pearson (1857–1936) (Fancher & Rutherford, 2017; Hergenhahn, 2014).

While Galton's tests were ultimately found to be ineffective predictors of intelligence, he did have a huge impact on how certain influential members of Western European and U.S. societies viewed intelligence. Galton published his first book, *Hereditary Genius*, in 1869. In it he hypothesized, "A man's natural abilities are derived from inheritance, under exactly the same limitations as are the form and physical features of the whole organic world" (p. 1, Preface). This view of intelligence and how he attempted to measure it had social and political implications. More often than not, people (primarily Caucasians) from wealthier backgrounds would perform better on Galton's intelligence tests and would be deemed "fit" to reproduce. Conversely, people of a lower economic class (who were also typically people of color, from inner cities or impoverished rural areas, convicted of criminal offenses, wards of the state, and/or first- or second-generation immigrants to the United States) would underperform on tests of intelligence. In most of these cases, these individuals did not have the same access to educational opportunities, demonstrated obvious cultural differences to the American ideal, and lacked a familiarity with the etiquette of high society. Galton and other prominent and wealthy members of Western European and U.S. societies just assumed these individuals were inherently less intelligent, and, being such, should be prohibited from reproducing for the overall benefit of society. Thus, the practice of *eugenic sterilization*, or forced reproductive sterilization, rose in popularity for those deemed intellectually "unfit."

The American Eugenics Society (AES) started in 1925, four years after the Second International Conference on Eugenics was held in New York City. The founders of the AES were Harry Crampton, Harry H. Laughlin, Madison Grant, and Henry Fairfield Osborn. Other high-profile individuals who were either associated with the group or members included John D. Rockefeller; Andrew Carnegie; J. P. Morgan Jr.; Mary Duke Biddle, the tobacco fortune heiress whose family founded Duke University; Leon F. Whitney, the son of Eli Whitney, inventor of the cotton gin; Dr. John Kellogg (of Kellogg's Cornflakes fame); Alexander Graham Bell; Miss E. B. Scripps, of the Scripps-Howard newspaper chain and from United Press; Dorothy H. Brush of Planned Parenthood; and Margaret Sanger, the founder of Planned Parenthood. The membership peaked at about 1,250 people in 1930. AES became highly effective at disseminating practical and scientific information on genetic health and promoting eugenical research. There was initial support of and even admiration for the ideals of the Nazi movement among members of the American Eugenics Society. With the progression of WWII and the Holocaust, public pro-eugenics sentiments started to wane. The eugenical sterilization laws stayed in effect in some states into the late 1970s and early 1980s, disproportionately impacting women of color and Native American women (Black, 2003; Cohen, 2017; Greenwald, 2009).

The landmark case *Buck v. Bell* set the precedent for the practice. Originating in Virginia, the case was taken to the U.S. Supreme Court two years after the American Eugenics Society was established in 1925. On May 2, 1927, an 8 to 1 majority ruled in favor of forcible eugenic sterilization of the "unfit." Eventually 38 states would enact such laws. The eugenics movement also asserted that racial integrity must remain intact for the benefit of society. As a result, interracial marriage was also frowned upon and a rise in antimiscegenation laws like Virginia's Racial Integrity Act of 1924 occurred. These laws made it illegal for members of different races marry (Black, 2003; Cohen, 2017). (For more information on *Buck v. Bell*, see Lombardo, 2009 or National Public Radio, 2019.) While the eugenics movement eventually fell out of favor as a result of the Holocaust, Galton made other lasting impacts on the field of psychology. He became known as the father of modern-day *behavior genetics*, a group of theories that examine how the inherited qualities of a person interact with his environment to create certain psychological and behavioral characteristics. These theorists emphasize the role nature plays in a person's development and suggest that a person's natural tendencies and attributes drive or influence the environment he puts himself in and how it responds to him. Galton also would influence the future field of psychometrics and standardized testing movement.

Binet and Simon: Intelligence and the Environment

The intelligence is proved not by ease of learning, but by understanding what we learn.

—Joseph Whitney

While Galton used intelligence testing to promote eugenics and racial integrity, French psychologists Alfred Binet (1857–1911) and Théodore

Simon (1872–1961) used their intelligence test to help identify children who needed additional educational assistance in French public schools. Upon request of the French government, which had introduced a law mandating universal education, Binet and Simon developed the first accepted standardized test of intelligence: the Binet-Simon Intelligence Scale (1905). The test was intended to help diagnose children who were academically and intellectual "subnormal" so they could be filtered into special education programs rather than be deemed sick or too ignorant for school. Unlike Galton and members of the eugenics movement, the original intent of this intelligence test was to tailor educational experiences for children of all backgrounds, not alienate or shut them out. Binet and Simon were also the first to use the concept of mental age. *Chronological age* is how old a person is from the time of his birth. *Mental age* represents the age that a person should function intellectually, compared to average intellectual performance for that actual age. In most standardized intelligence tests, age is typically associated with a child's level of performance. To Binet and Simon, *remedial age* occurred when a child's mental age was less than their chronological age. Binet felt that intelligence was not entirely inherited and that a person's intellectual ability could be influenced by other factors, like motivation and access to appropriate learning resources. This is another philosophical departure from Galton and the eugenicists (Fancher & Rutherford, 2017; Hergenhahn, 2014).

Lewis Terman and the Stanford-Binet Intelligence Scales

Binet and Simon's test became the standard template for modern-day intelligence tests. Their own test was revised in 1916 by American psychologist and Stanford professor Lewis Terman. Binet and Simon's test would henceforth be known as the Stanford-Binet Intelligence Scale. Terman heavily revised and elaborated on many of Binet and Simon's original subtests after they translated and revised the scale for use in the United States. They originally developed six sets of tests, one set for children of each of six consecutive ages. This test was most recently revised in 2003 in its fifth edition and is still in use.

THE WESCHLER INTELLIGENCE SCALES

We function on a dozen different levels of intelligence.

—*Bergen Evans*

There are other common standardized tests of intelligence. American clinical psychologist David Weschler (1896–1981) created a series of intelligence scales. In 1939, he published the Weschler-Bellevue Intelligence Scale after working at the Bellevue Psychiatric Hospital in New York City. The scale was used with an adult population in a clinical context. Wechsler defined intelligence as an individual's ability to adapt and constructively solve problems in the environment. Wechsler viewed intelligence in terms of performance rather than intellectual capacity. Thus, the Wechsler scales are not intended to measure a person's quantity of intelligence, but instead measures their intellectual performance. Additionally, contrary to his predecessors, he rejected the idea of a mental age and believed that normal intelligence was the mean test score for all members of an age group. He converted the raw scores on the test to a standard scale, with the mean score represented by 100. The Weschler-Bellevue Intelligence Scale (WBIS) became widely used as an intelligence scale for adults. In 1942, Weschler produced a revision of the test (Saxon, 1981).

In 1949, Weschler published another version of his intelligence scale geared toward children aged 6 to 16 known as the Weschler Intelligence Scale for Children (WISC). The WISC-IV is the test most often used in schools to diagnose children's learning problems and consists of 15 different tests. Five of the tests comprise the *verbal comprehension index* and rely strongly on verbal skills. The remaining 10 tests measure nonverbal types of thinking (known as the *performance scale*), and are divided among the perceptual reasoning index, processing speed index, and working memory index. Each group of tests generates a separate IQ score, and the WISC-IV also provides a comprehensive *full-scale IQ* score that takes all four types of tests into account. The WISC-IV is helpful in determining a child's intellectual strengths and weaknesses (Saxon, 1981).

In 1955, he created another adult intelligence scale, the Weschler Adult Intelligence Scale (WAIS) which is geared for people aged 16 and over. The WAIS, which Weschler initially revised in 1981, was similar in format and content to the Weschler-Bellevue Scale, but for this scale Weschler standardized his scores using a more diverse, nonclinical adult sample, with 10 percent being nonwhite; this reflected the U.S. population at the time. The most recent version of the WAIS, in its fourth edition, was published in 2008 (Saxon, 1981). It remains the most widely used assessment for adult intelligence. The WAIS-V is set to be released sometime in 2019.

In 1967 Wechsler created another test that was adapted from the WISC, known as the Weschler Preschool and Primary Scale of Intelligence (WPPSI; Saxon, 1981). This scale was intended for children aged 4 to 6 1/2 years of age. It has been revised three times, with the most recent revision (WPPSI-IV) occurring in 2012. The test contains 15 subscales, including Block Design, Matrix Reasoning, Picture Concepts, Vocabulary, Comprehension, and Object Assembly, among others.

QUANTIFYING AND VALIDATING INTELLIGENCE SCORES

Standardization in testing requires that (1) all test takers answer the same questions or complete the same set of tasks, (2) these questions or tasks are administered to the test taker in the same way, and (3) the questions or tasks are scored in a "standard" manner. These requirements make it possible to compare relative performances of individual students or groups of students and yield normative data. *Norms* are test scores that accurately represent a group. These scores are typically used as a standard against which subsequently collected data is compared. Normative data provides insight into the distribution or prevalence of the characteristic being assessed in the larger population.

Standardization is required for high-stakes achievement and aptitude tests. For instance, in order to become a licensed school psychologist and be able to use the Weschler Scales for diagnostic and clinical purposes, one must undergo extensive and meticulous training on how to administer every subtest. To ensure accuracy and the same testing experience for all test takers, the delivery of the instructions and the time limits for each subscale must be exact. The scoring for each subscale and raw full-scale score must be also exact in order to convert the test taker's score to a standard score. Another example of standardization occurs with statewide scholastic achievement tests that are administered in the same way regardless of where the students go to school within the district or state.

The approximate distribution of scores on modern IQ tests like the Weschler scales is standardized so that the average score is 100 and 96 percent of the scores fall between 1 and 2 standard deviations of the average score (with a range of scores from 70 to 130). Scores that fall between 90 and 109 are considered average, 85–89 are low average intelligence, 70–84 indicate borderline mental functioning, 50–69 indicate mild mental retardation, 35–49 indicate moderate mental retardation, 26–34 indicates severe mental retardation, and 25 indicates profound retardation. Scores between 110 to 119 indicate above-average intelligence, 120–129 indicate very high intelligence, 130–144 indicate superior intelligence, and scores at 145 or above indicate giftedness.

Reliability refers to the stability of a test score. By definition, a reliable test yields scores that are stable over time. Generally, IQ scores become more stable after the age of three. Biological maturation (resulting from better health and access to nutrition) and environmental variables have influenced how children's IQ scores have changed over the past 70 years, particularly in western cultures (Williams, 1998). *Validity* indicates whether a test is measuring what it is intended to measure. IQ scores are predictive of children's grades in school both at the time they are taken and in the future. Children with high IQs fare better overall socially and academically, while children with low IQ (specifically, verbal IQ) are more likely to be delinquent in adolescence, to be illiterate later in life, and to exhibit criminal behavior in adulthood (National Research Council & Institute of Medicine, 2001).

MULTIFACETED THEORIES OF INTELLIGENCE

If the Aborigine drafted an I.Q. test, all of Western civilization would presumably flunk it.

—Stanley Garn

Cornell professor of human development Robert Sternberg (1949–) created the *triarchic theory of intelligence*, which asserts that there are actually three aspects, or types, of intelligence. The first is *analytical intelligence* and includes abilities such as planning, organizing, and remembering facts and applying them to new situations. The second is *creative intelligence*, which measures how well a person can see new connections between things, is insightful about experiences, and is able to "think outside the box" about various kinds of problems. The third aspect is *practical intelligence*, sometimes called "street smarts." People with a high degree of practical intelligence are good at applying information or finding some practical solution to real-life problems (Sternberg, 1985).

Harvard professor and developmental psychologist Howard Gardner (1943–) created a *theory of multiple intelligences*, arguing that there are eight distinct types of intelligence. In his book, *Frames of Mind* (2011), Gardner suggested that all humans possess each type of the eight intelligences but the interaction between their genetic and environmental experiences determine which intelligences manifest at any given point. Gardner's intelligence types are linguistic, logical/mathematical, musical, spatial, bodily kinesthetic, interpersonal (understanding other people), intrapersonal (understanding oneself), and naturalistic (recognizing patterns in nature). The underlying philosophy of Gardner's theory has been adopted by many educators. Because his theory conceptualizes intelligence as multidimensional, it allows for a broad consideration of a variety of differences, both individual and group differences. It also validates instructional approaches that serve a wider variety of learning styles. It should be noted that empirical support for this theory is limited.

INFORMATION PROCESSING THEORY

Memory . . . is the diary that we all carry about with us.

—Oscar Wilde

Information processing (IP) theories are a set of theories that focus on the way people process information using internal mechanisms like cognition, attention, and memory. These theories, which emerged during the 1960s, assert that due to maturational changes in the brain, cognitive processes become more sophisticated and efficient as children get older. IP theories also liken the human brain to a computer that involves three memory stores that take in information from the external environment, make sense of it, and then retain it. This is known as the *three-stage memory model.* There are several processes involved in transferring the information from one memory store to the next, and if these become disrupted in some way, a person may not be able to store and retain the information for the long term.

The first type of memory is *sensory memory,* in which information from the external environment is processed via the body's sensory registers (eyes, ears, mouth, nose, and skin). The capacity or size of sensory memory is theoretically unlimited and does not require conscious attention, unless the sensory information needs to be processed further to get it into the next memory store. Humans need to pay attention to the sensory information long enough to perceive and interpret it, otherwise the information is forgotten. Given the amount of sensory information the human body is exposed to at any given moment, the duration of sensory memory is fleeting, lasting one to four seconds depending on the type of sensory information being processed. There are two types of sensory memory that have been more extensively studied: iconic sensory memory and echoic sensory memory. *Iconic sensory memory* is memory of visual stimuli in its exact original form. Its capacity is very large, but its duration lasts less than a second. *Echoic sensory memory* is memory for auditory stimuli. It also has a larger capacity and a shorter duration, but it is said to last a bit longer than iconic memory, fading after three to four seconds.

If sensory information is attended to long enough to be perceived and interpreted, then it can be moved to the second memory store, short-term memory (a.k.a. working memory). *Short-term memory* is where information that is consciously recognized and interpreted from sensory memory enters the mind. It requires intentional, conscious cognitive processing, and it is where humans actively rehearse information in order to process it for the next memory store, long-term memory. Because short-term memory requires more time and energy to process, it has a smaller capacity than sensory memory but a longer duration (30 seconds). The capacity for short-term memory is 7 +/- 2 meaningful units of information (e.g., the length of a phone number). This range of 5 to 9 units (sometimes referred to as "chunks") of information is known as *Miller's magic number,* after the pioneer of cognitive psychology George Miller (1920–2012) conducted studies testing the short-term memory using memory span tasks (Miller, 1956). *Memory span tasks* are tests for the capacity of short-term memory by giving a series of items one at a time in a given order. These items can be words, letters, or numbers. The WISC intelligence scales, discussed earlier, include a digit span task. Short-term memory also involves the process of *encoding*, which involves modifying information in a way that makes sense in order to help store it in long-term memory and retrieve it at a later time. *Storage* is the acquisition of new knowledge and involves the process of putting what is learned into memory initially. *Retrieval* is the process of remembering previously stored information.

Because people actively attend to and manipulate information in short-term memory for long-term storage, and because it also is where stored memories are retrieved for real-time use (e.g., taking an exam, driving to the store, or making a cake), short-term memory is also referred to as *working memory*. In the analogy of the human mind being like a computer, working memory is the Internet because it is pretty constantly "online," getting people through the tasks of their day.

According to information processing theories, the final memory store is long-term memory. *Long-term memory* is considered to have a limitless capacity and duration, at least theoretically. There are a two main types of long-term memories: explicit memories and implicit memories. *Explicit memories* (a.k.a. declarative memories) involve memories for facts, figures, and personal experiences. These require conscious recall. One subtype of explicit memory is *semantic memory*, which involves factual knowledge that is universal for everyone (e.g., facts and figures from a book). The other subtype of explicit memory is *episodic memory*, which involves memories for personal experiences. *Implicit memories* (a.k.a., nondeclarative memories) involve long-term memories that influence behavior but do not require conscious recall.

One type of implicit memory is *procedural memory*, which involves memory for some sort of physical process (e.g., playing the piano, kicking a ball, driving a car). The more a person engages in a task, the more accurate and efficient they can become at performing the task. When someone experiences this, it is a process known as *automaticity* because the behavior becomes somewhat automatic to perform. The other type of implicit memory is *conditioning memory*, which involves some sort of automatic response to an external stimulus that is learned from previous experience or associations (e.g., flinching when one sees a needle, getting nauseated when one smells a food that has made one ill previously).

Some long-term memory storage processes are better than others at facilitating learning. *Rote learning* is learning primarily through repetition and practice, with little or no attempt to make sense of what is being learned (e.g., playing scales on the piano). It does not require as much effortful processing as other learning strategies. *Rehearsal* is a cognitive strategy that involves repeating information over and over repeatedly as a means of keeping it in memory and learning it (e.g., memorizing a piano sonata). When this is done to hold information in short-term memory, it is referred to as *maintenance rehearsal*. Rehearsal is a strategy that occurs more frequently when children progress through elementary school (Kail, 1990).

Meaningful learning involves making connections between new information and prior knowledge (e.g., elaboration, organization, visual imagery). *Organization* is a cognitive strategy that involves pieces of information into meaningful categories. This is a strategy that improves during the elementary and secondary school years (DeLoache & Todd, 1988). *Elaboration* is a cognitive strategy that involves connecting one's existing knowledge to incoming knowledge to expand what one knows. This strategy is used in a more intentional way starting in adolescence (Flavell, Miller, & Miller, 1993). In general, meaningful learning provides more effective approaches to learning and retaining declarative content.

How children think about their learning can also impact how and what they retain. *Metacognition* involves children's beliefs about their own cognitive processing and the strategies they use to regulate their thinking. In other words, metacognition is thinking about thinking. Educators can use a variety of strategies to assist children in regulating their learning and thinking in the classroom and help students retain and transfer their knowledge.

LANGUAGE ACQUISITION

Language comes first. It's not that language grows out of consciousness, if you haven't got language, you can't be conscious.

—*Alan Moore*

Learning a native language is a relatively natural process for most children. The prelinguistic phase begins at birth, where early perceptions of an infant's native language are already present. In utero, the fetus beings to recognize the synchrony or melody of her language. From birth to 1 month, crying is the predominant sound. By 1 to 2 months, *cooing*, which are vocalizations involving only vowel sounds, begins. By 6 to 7 months, *babbling*, which involves consonant-vowel pairs, emerges.

There are specific stages that guide this process. *Receptive language*, or the ability to understand certain language (e.g., infants and toddlers learn labels for nouns before verbs), comes before expressive language. At 8 months, babies begin to store words in memory; by 9–10 months they can understand 20–30 words and by 13 months this understanding grows to about 100 words. *Expressive language* is the ability to produce meaningful language. A toddler's first words typically appear at around 12–13 months.

Generally, the first thing infants learn about their language is the *phonology*, which is the sounds that a language makes. *Phonemes* are the smallest units of sound in language; each letter of the alphabet has a corresponding sound. Infants are born attuned to the sounds of their native languages because, once their ears develop in utero, they can hear the muffled sound of their mothers' voices. There are different types of phonemes, like the onset and rhyme. The *onset* phoneme starts a word whereas the *rhyme* ends the word. In the word *cat*, there are two phonemes: "c," the onset, and "-at," the rhyme. There are two phonemes because, even though "a" has its own corresponding sound, when pronounce the word "cat" the "a" is blended with the "t" sound and not emphasized. The word is not pronounced "c/aa/t"; it is pronounced "c/at/."

When learning to read, children will use a strategy referred to as *phonological decoding*, or sounding out an unfamiliar word based on its letter composition. In order to implement this strategy effectively, it is important that children have a good grasp on the alphabet and letter-sound pairings. With that said, it is also important to note that not all words can be broken down phonetically; in fact, there are many words like this in the English language. *Sight words* are words that cannot be phonologically decoded when a child learns to read (e.g., the, does, were, are, by, could, each, was, use). These words must be taught using different strategies that mostly rely on a child's memory (e.g., flashcards, reading, writing, spelling exercises). As a child gains experience with reading, he must also employ strategies that help him read for comprehension. This involves using *metalinguistic awareness*, or the ability to think about language. There are several factors that contribute to how well children can implement metalinguistic awareness when learning to read (Torok, 2008). A larger discussion of these factors and how they contribute to reading acquisition appears later in this chapter.

The next thing infants learn about language is the *morphology*. *Morphemes* are the smallest meaning-bearing units in language. There are two types of morphemes: free morphemes and bound morphemes. *Free morphemes* can make sense and hold meaning on their own (e.g., dog, horse, cup). *Bound morphemes* need to be connected to a free morpheme and alter the meaning of that free morpheme in some way (e.g., "-s," "-ed," "-ing," "-es"). For example, if you take the word "dog" and change it to "dogs" you slightly alter the meaning of the word dog by making it plural.

Older infants and toddlers then begin to learn about *semantics*, which is the meaning of words (i.e., vocabulary). The one-word stage of semantics occurs between 12 to 20 months. When starting to speak, most toddlers only speak a word at a time, and these are usually nominal words, labels for objects or events. Then they move to action words, modifiers (e.g., dirty, happy), and social words (e.g., "please" and "thank you"). A toddler's first words typically refer to important people (e.g., mom, dad, doggie), or familiar objects (e.g., ball, milk, cookie). Toddlers' first words are also more likely to focus on things they can use (e.g., car, bottle, toy). The first 10 words are usually acquired a bit more slowly, but then toddlers start to add about one to three words a month. At 16 months, the first vocabulary spurt typically occurs, and toddlers have a speaking vocabulary of around 50 words. Around 18 months, toddlers typically experience another vocabulary spurt (sometimes referred to as a *naming explosion*), acquiring approximately 20 new words per week. At this point, children also begin to associate words with actions. By 24 months, toddlers typically have a vocabulary of 320 words. Interactions with parents, older children, and other adults in the toddler's life can definitely impact the rate and breadth of vocabulary acquisition in toddlers. The frequency and manner in which adults and older children address infants and toddlers can be referred to as *child-directed speech* (a.k.a. motherese or parentese). This type of speech is distinct because it is more melodic, repetitive, simple, and typically deals the toddler's direct experiences, unless the use of storytelling is being implemented. Child-directed speech has been found to be a universal across cultures.

Common errors in the one-word stage are typical. *Overextension* occurs when a toddler applies a label to a broader class of objects than the term signifies (e.g., calling a horse or a cow a "doggie" because the toddler has a dog at home and knows the verbal label for it but not the label for horses or cows, which also have four legs and tails). *Underextension* occurs when a toddler applies a label to a narrower class of objects than the term signifies (e.g., using the term "car" for all vehicles that look like station wagons but not sedans or pickup trucks).

Once they have acquired basic facility in learning the meanings and structures of words, toddlers and young children begin to learn about grammar (i.e., syntax), which involves the rules that govern how words are put together. *Holophrases* occur when toddlers combine a single word with gestures to make a complete thought; these are used between 12 and 18 months. Toddlers then graduate to using *stage 1 grammar* (a.k.a. telegraphic speech), which involves short, simple, sentences where grammatical markers like conjunctions and prepositions may be missing. This type of grammar consists of combos of verbs, nouns, and adjectives, and toddlers use very few morphemes to mark tense or plurals. *Pivot grammar* may be employed, meaning one word is used repetitively in a fixed position to generate several two-word phrases (e.g., "more juice, more read, more cookie"). These two-word sentences may reflect multiple meanings depending on context as well. *Stage 2 grammar* occurs around 23 months and involves sentences that are more complex, integrating the use of plurals, past tenses, auxiliary verbs, and prepositions. As children get older and enter formal educational settings, their grammar becomes more complex and they can better understand and integrate questions, the use of negatives, and jokes into their everyday conversation. During this stage of language learning, *overregularization* errors can occur. These involve the common tendency among children and second-language learners to apply regular and productive grammatical rules to words that are exceptions ("knew" age 2 1/2 = modeling vs. "knowed" age 3 1/2 = creative error vs. "knew" age 4 1/2 = establishes exceptions to specific language rules).

Finally, children acquire *pragmatics*, which are the social conventions of a language and culture. As early as three years old, children modify their speech based on who they are speaking to. For instance, they will become more polite when they are speaking to older people. Additionally, parents and older children can teach young children about social conventions in language (e.g., "Say please"). *Referential communication* is important in pragmatics as well. This involves communication in situations that require the speaker to describe an object to a listener or to evaluate the effectiveness of a message. Pragmatics also involves nonverbal cues like appropriate body language, facial expressions, and social norms (e.g., personal space when talking, turn-taking when talking, the volume and speed of speech, making eye contact with the other person in the conversation).

HOW LANGUAGE ACQUISITION FACILITATES READING ACQUISITION

The more that you read, the more things you will know. The more that you learn, the more places you'll go.

—Dr. Seuss

Vellutino and his colleagues identified the various cognitive skills that are necessary for proficiency in reading to occur (Vellutino, 2003; Vellutino, Fletcher, Snowling, & Scanlon, 2004; Vellutino & Scanlon, 2002; Wolf, Vellutino, & Berko Gleason, 1998). They pointed out that while language and reading development are complementary processes, the acquisition of skill in reading is a more deliberate procedure, requiring formalized and direct instruction as well as much cognitive exertion.

Permanent Memory

Permanent memory is needed to store and retrieve all the information processed during the act of reading. Information about the grapheme-phoneme pairings (e.g., letters and the constituent sounds they make either in isolation or paired with other letters, such as in the sequence "d-o-g"), the semantic value of printed words (e.g., the definition of the word "dog" as a four-legged furry creature that barks) and the syntactic properties of these words (e.g., the word "dog" is a noun and being such has certain properties that determine its placement in a sentence) are all pieces of information that are stored in permanent memory. Theoretically, certain fragments of this information such as basic grapheme-phoneme pairings, and alphabetic labels, measured by naming speed (Bowers & Wolf, 1993; Johnston & Anderson, 1998; Kail & Hall, 1994; Kail, Hall, & Caskey, 1999), should become automated in memory for the normally developing reader, thus requiring less energy to retrieve this information, allowing the reader to focus on the higher-order properties of written text that facilitate comprehension. The amount of general "world" knowledge and domain-specific knowledge an early reader possesses can determine the ease with which these processes become automated. The acquisition of this knowledge is determined by the reader's innate capabilities and experiences from the external environment, both of which allow the reader to assign semantic values to individual words.

Verbal Working Memory

Verbal working memory refers to the mental workspace in which recent environmental stimuli are briefly held in the form of linguistic codes, either for rehearsal and recall or for meaningful integration with other knowledge (Berko Gleason & Ratner, 1998). In other words, it acts as a conduit between permanent memory and general linguistic abilities. In processing spoken and written language, verbal working memory is especially important for integrating propositions (idea units) encoded linguistically, in the interest of language comprehension. Virtually all models of verbal working memory suggest that short-term memory has a limited capacity. This limited capacity can be overcome by rehearsal, which is said to require some form of subvocal articulation (Hulme & Roodenrys, 1995) such as the phonological loop (Baddeley, 1996; Baddeley, Gathercole, & Papagno, 1998; Gathercole & Hitch, 1993). This link between verbal working memory and phonological coding abilities has been well established (Shankweiler, Liberman, Mark, Fowler, & Fischer, 1979). Research has consistently found that poor readers typically perform worse than their normal counterparts on tests of verbal working memory and are impaired in their memory for digits, letters, words, and sentences, and on complex memory tasks (McDougall, Hulme, Ellis, & Monk, 1994; Muter, 1998).

General Linguistic Abilities

Permanent memory is not the only component needed for comprehension, however. In order for grapheme-phoneme pairings and other important pieces of information to become automated processes during reading, other skills must be in place. General linguistic abilities such as phonological, semantic, and syntactic/grammatical coding are the means by which we store information encoded in spoken and written text into permanent memory (Vellutino et al., 2004; Wolf et al., 1998). In turn, permanent memory assists verbal working memory by using stored phonological representations in reconstructing incoming verbal or written information (Hulme & Roodenrys, 1995).

Phonological coding is the ability to use speech sounds to represent concepts in the external environment. Phonological codes are mental representations of speech sounds that facilitate associations between spoken and written text. When learning to speak their native language, children are normally facile at implicitly analyzing the "rules" that govern the ways in which they combine phoneme strings. For instance, children soon learn that three consonant sounds together (e.g., "xgn") cannot be readily vocalized in spoken language and in learning to read; they soon come to recognize that combining the graphemic counterparts of such consonants is a violation of orthographic convention. If children are given enough exposure to written text and proper strategies for print decoding are modeled via interactions with parents and teachers, they will learn to generalize these strategies and implement them when they are reading independently. Phonological coding also helps children learn sight words and provides a framework for acquiring forms of sublexical knowledge (e.g., phoneme awareness) that allow them to acquire and implement letter-sound decoding strategies, which is the primary means of reducing the load on visual memory for beginning readers (Blachman, 2000; Vellutino, 2003).

Wolf et al. (1998) theorized that phonological coding also facilitates acquisition of morphophonemic rules, which serve two functions. First, morphophonemic rules enable children to decode derived words because the child can recognize similar morphemic structures between words despite slight variations in their grammatical form (e.g., sad *adj.* and sadness *n.*). Second, they enable children to attach the appropriate sounds to common letter strings (bound morphemes) to modify words for their tense and number (e.g., *-ing* and *-ed*) and syllables (*-ike* in *bike* and *spike*).

Another general linguistic ability is semantic coding. *Semantic coding* is the process whereby meaning is assigned to units of spoken and written language. Semantic codes are interconnected mental representations of the meanings given to individual words and groups of words. In order for children to form associations between a printed word and its meaning, they must make the association with the word in isolation and in context. They must also be able to distinguish between words that have similar referential meanings (e.g., *dog* and *puppy*) and similar functional meanings (e.g., *she* and *her*). Children make extensive use of semantic coding processes at the beginning stages of reading development, due to the fact that they are implicitly biased to rely heavily on word meanings when learning to identify written words for the first time (Vellutino & Denckla, 1991; Vellutino et al., 2004; Wolf et al., 1998).

Grammatical and syntactic coding are defined as the abilities to represent form classes (e.g., noun, verb, adjective, etc.) and the rules for ordering words in sentences, respectively. In order to perform these types of coding, children must have implicit knowledge of morphemes and the ability to segment sentences into smaller sub-units of meaning. Grammatical coding and syntactic coding function interdependently because grammatical coding employs knowledge about the parts of speech in a sentence while syntactic coding employs the rules of ordering these parts of speech to form meaningful units of language. Wolf et al. (1998) asserted that these forms of coding are also important in facilitating word identification skills. Syntactic and grammatical coding influence printed word identification in three ways: (1) by enabling a child to use context to anticipate which words should appear in a particular sentence, (2) by aiding the process of assigning function codes to noncontent words such as *if*, *the*, *from*, and *of*, and (3) by providing an opportunity for children to implement morphophonemic production rules.

Visual Coding

Another key cognitive process involved in learning to read is visual coding. *Visual coding* can be defined as the ability to encode, store, and retrieve visual-spatial stimuli. This process makes use of permanent memory and general linguistic abilities, especially phonological coding, in facilitating acquisition of visual representations of word-specific spellings (cat, rat, fat; mop, hop, top) and word-general spelling units that children come to recognize in print (-at in cat, rat, fat). The conjoint use of visual and linguistic coding skills facilitates reading by enabling beginning readers to encode, store, retrieve, and reproduce written text. For example, when children acquire phonological coding skills and come to realize that the sounds in spoken language have corresponding symbols in written language, they can begin to decode written text using strategies like recalling and implementing rules for letter ordering in words relative to a specific orthography. Furthermore, they can discriminate between subtle differences in words that appear similar and can implement morphophonemic rules such as using *-ing* and *-ed*. Ultimately children can combine all of their knowledge to identify new words they encounter in written text using letter-sound decoding strategies (Vellutino & Denckla, 1991; Vellutino et al., 2004; Wolf et al., 1998).

It is important to note that because of the heavy load on visual memory imposed by written English and by any orthography derived from an alphabet, visual encoding of printed words is necessarily mediated by the language systems, especially the phonological system. Spoken language provides a context in which to organize, integrate, and interpret the large amount of visual information encountered in written text. One result is gaining facility in word identification. The ease with which linguistic coding skills are acquired can affect children's abilities to implement meaning-based strategies for word identification and can account for individual differences in how they implement visual coding in learning to read (Vellutino et al., 2004; Wolf et al., 1998).

Metalinguistic Analysis

Metalinguistic analysis entails manipulating spoken and written text and analyzing the linguistic processes associated with both. According to Vellutino et al. (2004), metalinguistic analysis enables children to acquire the various forms of sublexical knowledge entailed in learning to read (e.g., phonological and orthographic awareness, alphabetic knowledge, and general orthographic awareness).

Phonological and orthographic awareness are defined as the ability to reflect on and manipulate the subunits of language, in terms of their structural relationships, specifically the phonemes, syllables, and words in spoken language, and their visual counterparts in written language. *Phonological awareness* refers to explicit knowledge and conceptual grasp of the speech-sound systems that govern a language. For example, phonemes are the smallest units of sound in a given language. Each language uses a small and finite set of phonemes to form words. Furthermore, each language uses different sets of rules for combining these phonemes. The ability to form an association between a grapheme (written symbol) and a phoneme (constituent sound for that symbol), as well as the ability to follow the correspondence rules for combining them are dependent partly on phonological awareness (Berko Gleason, 2001; Berko Gleason & Ratner, 1998). Phonological awareness is said to be an influential skill in learning to read and a strong predictor of subsequent reading achievement. Explicit training of phoneme segmentation and decoding have been used to differentiate poor and normally developing readers and have also been used to enhance phonological awareness in order improve reading achievement in young children (Blachman, Ball, Black, & Tangel, 1994; Hatcher, Hulme, & Ellis, 1994; Holligan & Johnston, 1988; Johnston, Anderson, & Holligan, 1996; Johnston & Watson, 1997; McDougall et al., 1994; Muter, 1998; Perfetti, Beck, Bell, & Hughes, 1987; Vellutino & Scanlon, 1987).

Orthographic awareness refers to the reader's sensitivity to the constraints of how letters in words are organized (zad = legal; dza = illegal) and to the regularities and redundancies in the writing system (-at in cat, fat, and rat). Thus whereas phonological awareness allows readers to detect and recognize that constituent speech sounds create the spoken and written language they use, orthographic awareness allows readers to detect and recognize the unique properties of the writing system (orthography) to which they are exposed. Furthermore, these forms of awareness facilitate the identification of constituent sounds and sound clusters encountered in all written and spoken words (Goswami & Bryant, 1990; Vellutino et al., 2004).

Syntactic awareness is defined as the ability to reflect on and manipulate the words in a sentence in terms of their structural relationships. Some scholars have supposed that awareness of syntactic constraints in spoken language[1] can prepare children to recognize the grammatical constraints of written text and enable them to identify and repair any errors they encountered in reading. Pratt, Tunmer, and Bowey (1984) tested this idea by asking children to employ their knowledge of syntax by having them correct sentences containing grammatical rule violations. They presented children with sentences that contained two types of violations. The first type of violation was a morpheme substitution (e.g., How *is* you?) and the second type was a word-order violation (How *you are*?). Children were able to correct sentences more when the type of violation involved morpheme substitution, which suggests that the type of violation can affect children's abilities to interpret the written text.

Pragmatic awareness is defined as the ability to reflect on, manipulate, and integrate individual propositions and themes encoded in sentences, in terms of the relationships between given sentences and the contexts in which they occur (e.g. prior text, prior knowledge, situational and social contexts). It allows speakers and readers to understand language in social contexts and thus aids language comprehension (Berko Gleason, 2001).

These forms of metalinguistic awareness are needed in order for children to combine the knowledge they possess about the alphabet and the orthography in general to eventually master the alphabetic code and thus facilitate word identification, reading comprehension, and writing skills.

Sublexical Knowledge

When children combine information acquired using general linguistic coding, visual coding, and metalinguistic analysis, they begin to acquire *sublexical knowledge*, which facilitates an awareness of the structural features of language. According to Vellutino and his colleagues, such knowledge includes phonological awareness, orthographic awareness, alphabetic knowledge, and general orthographic knowledge (Vellutino, 2003; Vellutino et al., 2004). Phonological awareness is an essential skill needed for letter-sound decoding, as it provides information about the sounds that make up an alphabetic system. Orthographic awareness is needed for gaining general orthographic knowledge and is an early form of knowledge about print concepts, as it provides information about the symbols that make up an alphabetic system. It allows children to distinguish between acceptable and unacceptable letter combinations in written text. For example, the string "zav" is acceptable because it has a consonant-vowel-consonant sequence versus "sbn," which would be considered unacceptable because it strings three consonants together consecutively.

Phonological awareness and orthographic awareness share a reciprocal relationship. By its very nature phoneme awareness forces children to implement letter-sound analysis, and thus introduces them to the phonemes that comprise common letter strings in word identification. For instance, children who possess phoneme awareness can identify a word based on the constituent sounds of the letter string it creates. In other words, children can identify the word "fat" by the sounds that the letters "f-a-t" make respectively. Implementing this strategy leads to orthographic awareness, which is an awareness of the structural regularities and redundancies in spoken and written language. For instance, the words "fat," "cat," "rat," and "pat" share the similar letter and sound pattern "-at." Once children have fully developed orthographic awareness, detection of more complex patterns, such as morphologically derived words (e.g., bomb, bombard, bombardier), can be deciphered. In addition, more mature distinctions between "regular" and "irregular" pronunciations of words having similar spellings (e.g., but, nut, cut vs. put) can be made (Bowers & Wolf, 1993; Vellutino, 2003; Vellutino & Scanlon, 2002).

Lexical Knowledge

Another cognitive component needed for reading is lexical knowledge. *Lexical knowledge* involves knowledge of whole words in spoken and printed contexts. In learning to read, acquiring lexical knowledge requires an awareness of print concepts and conventions in written text. Such concepts and conventions include an awareness that written words represent spoken language, that words are composed of letters, that words are read from left to right, and so forth (Vellutino et al., 2004).

Phonological Decoding

Phonological decoding refers to the ability to decode or sound out words using letter sounds. Research suggests that phonological decoding acts as a foundational strategy for reading novel words in text (Gough & Tunmer, 1986; Share, 1995; Treiman, Freyd, & Baron, 1984; Tunmer & Nesdale, 1985).

Decontextualized Word Identification

Word identification refers to the foundational ability to identify whole words at sight in written text. *Decontextualized word identification* refers to the ability to identify words without the aid of meaningful of context (Vellutino, Tunmer, Scanlon, Jaccard, & Chen, unpublished manuscript). According to Vellutino and Denckla (1991), in order to be successful at word identification, children must employ one or all of the general linguistic abilities (e.g., phonological coding, semantic coding, syntactic-grammatical coding).

Reading Comprehension

Reading comprehension refers to the ability to extract and construct meaning from written text. All of the models discussed in the current study have suggested that many different cognitive and linguistic factors can affect children's abilities to comprehend what they read.

General Analytic Ability

General analytic ability (which some call "general intelligence") refers to the ability to analyze, categorize, and relate information in an attempt to achieve a conceptual grasp of objects, events, and procedures that exist or occur in the external world. General analytic ability has been found to have links to reading comprehension skills even though it is not a reliable predictor of word identification and decoding skills (Fletcher et al., 1994; Share, McGee, & Silva, 1989; Share, McGee, McKenzie, Williams, & Silva, 1987; Siegel, 1989; Stanovich & Siegel, 1994; Vellutino, Scanlon, & Lyon, 2000; Vellutino, Scanlon, Small, & Fanuele, 2003). In a longitudinal study of impaired readers, Vellutino and Scanlon (2001) provided evidence to suggest that language-based measures, such as phonological measures, are better determinants of reading achievement than scores on an IQ test. Research indicates that skills such as letter and number naming speed and phonological awareness were better predictors of word reading in poor readers than measures of general analytic ability (Kail & Hall, 1994; McBride-Chang & Manis, 1996).

In summary, the cognitive processes and knowledge involved in learning to read are permanent memory, different forms of general linguistic ability, visual coding, sublexical and lexical knowledge, different forms of metalinguistic awareness, and general analytic ability. These processes work interdependently to facilitate word-level and text-processing skills so children can read for comprehension.

NOTE

1. Syntactic awareness indicates that emergent readers implicitly "know" the rules that order the words in written and spoken language (Gleitman, Gleitman, & Shipley, 1972). In spoken language, children, at a very early age, make use of implicit knowledge of syntax in generating their own sentences and spontaneously implementing the syntactic constraints of their language (Menyuk, 1963, 1964). Moreover, judgments about syntactic acceptability in spoken language can be made very early on by some children (Gleitman et al., 1972; de Villiers & de Villiers, 1972). These judgments may be facilitated by elliptical forms of the language to which infants are typically exposed, often called "motherese." High intonations, repetitiveness in phrasing and wording, melodic patterns, and short phrases are all characteristics of motherese. This form of language is intended to facilitate acquisition and comprehension in infants and toddlers. In a study conducted by Swanson and Leonard (1992), mother-child dyads were used to examine the role that motherese plays in children's abilities to recognize and differentiate parts of speech (e.g., content words $\cong$ nouns vs. function words $\cong$ articles). They recorded conversations between mothers and their children and mothers with other adults. They measured how long mothers pronounced content words and function words when speaking to their children and when speaking to other adults. They found significant differences between interactions with children and adults in pronunciations of content words; however, they found no differences in pronunciations of function words. On average, mothers spent more time pronouncing content words when speaking to their children. Swanson and Leonard asserted that children's grammar, as indicated by telegraphic speech, would be significantly influenced by their mothers' communications. They also asserted that the way in which children perceive their mothers' phonological pronunciations would facilitate syntactic bootstrapping.

REFERENCES

Baddeley, A. (1996). Exploring the central executive. *Quarterly Journal of Experimental Psychology, 49A*(1), 5–28.

Baddeley, A., Gathercole, S. E., & Papagno, C. (1998). The phonological loop as a language learning device. *Psychological Review, 105*(1), 158–173.

Berko Gleason, J. (2001). *The development of language* (5th ed). Boston, MA: Allyn & Bacon.

Berko Gleason, J., & Ratner, N. B. (1998). *Psycholinguistics*. Belmont, CA: Wadsworth.

Blachman, B. A. (2000). Phonological awareness. In M. L. Kamil, P. B. Mosenthal, P. D. Pearson, & R. Barr (Eds.), *Handbook of reading research* (vol. III, pp. 483–502). Mahwah, NJ: Lawrence Erlbaum.

Blachman, B. A., Ball, E. W., Black, R. S., & Tangel, D. M. (1994). Kindergarten teachers develop phoneme awareness in low-income, inner-city classrooms: Does it make a difference? *Reading and Writing: An Interdisciplinary Journal, 6*(1), 1–18.

Black, E. (2003). *War against the weak: Eugenics and America's campaign to create a master race.* Washington, DC: Dialog.

Bowers, P. G., & Wolf, M. (1993). Theoretical links among naming speed, precise timing mechanisms and orthographic skills in dyslexia. *Reading and Writing: An Interdisciplinary Journal, 5,* 69–85.

Cohen, A. (2017). *Imbeciles: The Supreme Court, American eugenics, and the sterilization of Carrie Buck.* New York, NY: Penguin.

DeLoache, J. S., & Todd, C. M. (1988). Young children's use of spatial categorization as mnemonic strategies. *Journal of Experimental Child Psychology, 46,* 1–20.

de Villiers, P. A., & de Villiers, J. G. (1972). Early judgments of semantic and syntactic acceptability by children. *Journal of Psycholinguistic Research, 1*(4), 299–310.

Fancher, R. E., & Rutherford, A. (2017). *Pioneers of psychology: A history* (5th ed.). New York, NY: Norton.

Flavell, J. H., Miller, P. H., & Miller, S. A. (1993). *Cognitive development* (3rd ed.). Upper Saddle River, NJ: Prentice Hall.

Fletcher, J. M., Shaywitz, S. E., Shankweiler, D. P., Katz, L., Liberman, I. Y., . . . Shaywitz, B.A. (1994). Cognitive profiles of reading disability: Comparisons of discrepancy and low achievement definitions. *Journal of Educational Psychology, 86* (1), 6–23.

Galton, F. (1869). *Hereditary genius: An inquiry into its laws and consequences.* London, England: Macmillan (Reprinted, Bristol: Thoemmes Press, 1999).

Gardner, H. (2011). *Frames of mind: Theories of multiple intelligences* (3rd ed.). New York, NY: Basic Books.

Gathercole, S. E., & Hitch, G. J. (1993). Developmental changes in short-term memory: A revised working memory perspective. In A. F. Collins, S. E. Gathercole, M. A. Conway, & P. Morris (Eds.), *Theories of memory* (pp. 189–208). Hillsdale, NJ: Lawrence Erlbaum.

Gleitman, L. R., Gleitman, H., & Shipley, E. (1972). The emergence of the child as a grammarian. *Cognition, 1,* 138–164.

Goswami, U., & Bryant, P. (1990). Phonological awareness and reading. *Phonological skills and learning to read* (pp. 1–28). Hove, England: Lawrence Erlbaum.

Gough, P. B., & Tunmer, W. E. (1986). Decoding, reading, and reading disability. *Remedial & Special Education, 7*(1), 6–10.

Greenwald, B. H. (2009). Commentary: The real "toll" of A. G. Bell: Lessons about eugenics. *Sign Language Studies, 9*(3), 258–265.

Hatcher, P. J., Hulme, C., & Ellis, A. W. (1994). Ameliorating early reading failure by integrating the teaching of reading and phonological skills: The phonological linkage hypothesis. *Child Development, 65,* 47–57.

Hergenhahn, B. R. (2014). *An introduction to the history of psychology* (7th ed.). Belmont, CA: Wadsworth.

Holligan, C., & Johnston, R. S. (1988). The use of phonological information by good and poor readers in memory and reading tasks. *Memory & Cognition, 16*(6), 522–532.

Hulme, C., & Roodenrys, S. (1995). Practitioner review: Verbal working memory development and its disorders. *Journal of Psychology & Psychiatry, 8*(3), 373–398.

Johnston, R. S., & Anderson, M. (1998). Memory span, naming speed, and memory strategies in poor and normal readers. *Memory, 6*(2), 143–163.

Johnston, R. S., Anderson, M., & Holligan, C. (1996). Knowledge of the alphabet and explicit awareness of phonemes in pre-readers: The nature of the relationship. *Reading and Writing: An Interdisciplinary Journal, 8*, 217–234.

Johnston, R. S., & Watson, J. (1997). Developing reading, spelling, and phonemic awareness skills in primary school children. *Reading, 31*(2), 38–41.

Kail, R. (1990). *The development of memory in children* (3rd ed.). New York, NY: Freeman.

Kail, R., & Hall, L. K. (1994). Processing speed, naming speed, and reading. *Developmental Psychology, 30*(4), 949–954.

Kail, R., Hall, L. K., & Caskey, B. J. (1999). Processing speed, exposure to print, and naming speed. *Applied Psycholinguistics, 20*, 303–314.

Lombardo, P. A. (2010). *Three generations, no imbeciles: Eugenics, the Supreme Court, and* Buck v. Bell. Baltimore, MD: Johns Hopkins University Press.

McBride-Chang, C., & Manis, F. R. (1996). Structural invariance in the associations of naming speed, phonological awareness, and verbal reasoning in good and poor readers: A test of the double deficit hypothesis. *Reading and Writing: An Interdisciplinary Journal, 8*, 323–339.

McDougall, S., Hulme, C., Ellis, A., & Monk, A. (1994). Learning to read: The role of short-term memory and phonological skills. *Journal of Experimental Child Psychology, 58*, 112–133.

Menyuk, P. (1963). Syntactic structures in the language of children. *Child Development, 34*, 407–422.

Menyuk, P. (1964). Syntactic rules used by children from preschool through first grade. *Child Development, 35*, 533–546.

Miller, G. A. (1956). The magical number seven, plus or minus two: Some limits on our capacity for processing information. *Psychological Review, 63*(2), 81–97. doi: 10.1037/h0043158

Muter, V. (1998). Concurrent and longitudinal predictors of reading: The role of metalinguistic and short-term memory skills. *Reading Research Quarterly, 33*(3), 320–336.

National Public Radio. (2019). Emma, Carrie, Vivian: How a family became a test case for forced sterilizations. Retrieved from https://www.npr.org/2019/02/17/695574984/emma-carrie-vivian-how-a-family-became-a-test-case-for-forced-sterilizations

National Research Council & Institute of Medicine. (2001). The development of delinquency. In J. McCord, C. Spatz Widom, & N. A. Crowl (Eds.), *Juvenile crime, juvenile justice* (pp. 66–106). Washington, DC: National Academy Press.

Perfetti, C. A., Beck, I., Bell, L. C., & Hughes, C. (1987). Phonemic knowledge and learning to read are reciprocal: A longitudinal study of first grade children. *Merrill-Palmer Quarterly, 33*(3), 283–319.

Pratt, C., Tunmer, W. E., & Bowey, J. A. (1984). Children's capacity to correct grammatical violations in sentences. *Journal of Child Language, 2,* 129–141.

Saxon, W. (1981). Dr. David Weschler, 85, author of intelligence tests. Retrieved from: https://www.nytimes.com/1981/05/03/obituaries/dr-david-wechsler-85-author-of-intelligence-tests.html

Shankweiler, D., Liberman, I. Y., Mark, L. S., Fowler, C. A., & Fischer, F. W. (1979). The speech code and learning to read. *Journal of Experimental Psychology: Human Learning and Memory, 5*(6), 531–545.

Share, D. L. (1995). Phonological recoding and self-teaching: Sine qua non of reading acquisition. *Cognition, 55,* 151–218.

Share, D. L., McGee, R., McKenzie, D., Williams, S., & Silva, P. A. (1987). Further evidence relating to the distinction between specific reading retardation and general reading backwardness. *British Journal of Developmental Psychology, 5,* 35–44.

Share, D. L., McGee, R., & Silva, P. A. (1989). IQ and reading progress: A test of the capacity notion of IQ. *Journal of the American Academy of Child and Adolescent Psychiatry, 28,* 97–100.

Siegel, L. S. (1989). IQ is irrelevant to the definition of learning disabilities. *Journal of Learning Disabilities, 22,* 469–479.

Stanovich, K. E., & Siegel, L. S. (1994). Phenotypic performance profile of children with reading disabilities: A regression-based test of the phonological-core variable-difference model. *Journal of Educational Psychology, 86*(1), 24–53.

Sternberg, R. J. (1985). *IQ: A triarchic theory of intelligence.* New York, NY: Cambridge University Press.

Swanson, L. A., & Leonard, L. B. (1992). Vowel duration in mothers' speech to young children. *Journal of Speech & Hearing Research, 35*(3), 617–626.

Torok, S. E. (2008). *Cognitive and metalinguistic precursors to emergent literacy: Revisiting the roles of metalinguistic awareness in reading instruction and remediation.* Saarbrücken, Germany: VDM Verlag Dr. Müller Aktiengesellschaft.

Treiman, R., Freyd, J., & Baron, J. (1984). Phonological recoding and use of spelling-sound rules in reading sentences. *Journal of Verbal Learning and Verbal Behavior, 22,* 682–700.

Tunmer, W. E., & Nesdale, A. R. (1985). Phonemic segmentation skill and beginning reading. *Journal of Educational Psychology, 77*(4), 417–427.

Vellutino, F. R. (2003). Literacy: Reading (Early stages). In *Encyclopedia of cognitive science* (pp. 922–930). London, England: Macmillan.

Vellutino, F. R., & Denckla, M. B. (1991). Cognitive and neuropsychological foundations of word identification in poor and normally developing readers. In R. Barr, M. K. Kamil, P. Mosenthal, & P. D. Pearson (Eds.), *Handbook of reading research* (vol. II, pp. 571–608). New York, NY: Longman.

Vellutino, F. R., Fletcher, J. M., Snowling, M. J., & Scanlon, D. M. (2004). Specific reading disability (dyslexia): What have we learned in the past four decades? *Journal of Child Psychology and Psychiatry, 45*(1), 2–40.

Vellutino, F. R., & Scanlon, D. M. (1987). Phonological coding, phonological awareness, and reading ability: Evidence from a longitudinal and experimental study. *Merrill-Palmer Quarterly, 33*(3), 321–363.

Vellutino, F. R., & Scanlon, D. M. (2001, April). Using early literacy intervention to improve our understanding of severe reading difficulties. Paper presented at the meeting of the *American Educational Research Association Special Interest Group/Basic Research and Literacy*, Seattle, WA.

Vellutino, F. R., & Scanlon, D. M. (2002). The Interactive Strategies approach to reading intervention. *Contemporary Educational Psychology, 27*, 573–635.

Vellutino, F. R., Scanlon, D. M., & Lyon, G. R. (2000). Differentiating between difficult-to-remediate and readily remediated poor readers: More evidence against the IQ-achievement discrepancy definition of reading disability. *Journal of Learning Disabilities, 33*(3), 223–238.

Vellutino, F. R., Scanlon, D. M., Small, S., & Fanuele, D. (2003, December). Response to intervention as a vehicle for distinguishing between reading disabled and non-reading disabled children: Evidence for the role of kindergarten and first grade intervention. Paper presented at the meeting of the *National Research Center on Learning Disabilities Symposium on Responsiveness to Intervention*, Kansas City, MO.

Vellutino, F. R., Tunmer, W. E., Scanlon, D. M., Jaccard, J. A., & Rusan, C. (unpublished manuscript). The components of reading ability: Multivariate evidence for a convergent skills model of reading development.

Williams, W. (1998). Are we raising smarter children today? School- and home-related influences on IQ. In U. Neisser (Ed.), *The rising curve: Long-term gains in IQ and related measures* (pp. 125–154). Washington, DC: American Psychological Association.

Wolf, M., Vellutino, F., & Berko Gleason, J. (1998). A psycholinguistic account of reading. In J. Berko Gleason & N. Bernstein Ratner (Eds.), *Psycholinguistics* (pp. 409–451). New York, NY: Harcourt Brace.

4

Developmental and Social Psychology in Educational Psychology

We cannot always build the future for our youth, but we can build our youth for the future.

—Franklin D. Roosevelt

The classroom environment is a complex one. There are many factors that can contribute to children's learning. Many of these factors involve qualities and experiences that they bring with them to the classroom environment. This includes their personalities, their self-concepts, aspects of their identities (e.g., gender, ethnic/racial, religious), and their attachments to family and teachers. These developmental and social aspects of a student's life can interact with the school environment in a number of ways.

ATTACHMENT THEORY

We do as we have been done by.

—John Bowlby

Children's attachments to their primary caregivers can also impact how they function in the school environment. The work of theorists like John Bowlby, Renee Spitz, Konrad Lorenz, and Mary Ainsworth had a strong theoretical influence on the understanding of infant-parent relationships. Their work was influenced by and further shaped the fields of evolutionary psychology, ethology, and psychanalytic theory.

British psychoanalyst John Bowlby's (1907–1990) attachment theory grew from his own personal experiences. Bowlby's parents had a cold and distance relationship with him, limiting their interaction to a mere hour a day, typically at high tea. His father was in the military and often absent from the home. At the young age of seven, Bowlby's parents sent him to boarding school; Bowlby recounted this as a traumatic experience. This may have impacted his choice to study psychology at Cambridge University. While there, he worked with delinquent students. Upon graduating from Cambridge, Bowlby volunteered at a school and worked with maladjusted children. This experience laid the groundwork for his future career as a child psychiatrist, leading him to study medicine at University College Hospital, psychiatry at Maudsley Hospital and psychoanalytic theory at the British Psychoanalytic Institute (Cherry, 2018).

He began his career as a psychoanalyst in 1937. Shortly thereafter, he enlisted in the Royal Army Medical Corps to fight in World War II. The following year he wed Ursula Longstaff, and they had four children. At the end of the war, Bowlby became director of the Tavistock Clinic, and in 1949 the World Health Organization (WHO) appointed Bowlby to write a report on the mental health of homeless children in Europe. Bowlby officially became a mental health consultant to the WHO in 1950 and in 1951 published a report entitled "Maternal Care and Mental Health." In his report he emphasized the role of the mother-child relationship, stating that it should be characterized by warmth, intimacy, and continuity, and be mutually enjoyable and fulfilling for the mother and the child (Bowlby, 1946, 1958; Cherry, 2018).

During the late 1940s and 1950s while Bowlby was working for the WHO, he was also conducting research on orphans with French psychoanalyst René Spitz (1887–1974). They studied institutionalized children and how their emotional attachments were negatively affected by their severed relationships with their mothers. The orphans often had their basic physiological needs met in the institutionalized setting (e.g., they were fed and changed and had a warm place to sleep) but they were rarely given any sort of emotional or social contact. This resulted in a pattern of behavior for the infants and children (Talbot, 1998). As a result of this research, Spitz identified symptoms of what he and Bowlby labeled *anaclitic depression*. They asserted this type of depression was characterized by symptoms that reflected psycho-emotional deprivation including social withdrawal, weight loss, insomnia, and an overall failure to thrive. Spitz also identified significant principles in attachment theory, including stranger anxiety that Bowlby and Ainsworth both elaborated on in their theories.

Thus, as a result of his own childhood experiences, studying psychoanalytic theory, and working with Spitz, Bowlby emphasized the significance of the earliest relationship between mother and child and made it the centerpiece of his theory. To this, he added important evolutionary and ethological concepts. In terms of the evolutionary and ethological value of attachment, he suggested the mother-child attachment is an innate function in all species that is necessary for survival. It serves to keep the human and animal infant close to the mother, who is a source of food, protection, and ultimately survival. *Ethology* is the systematic study of animal behavior, typically involving behavior that occurs in natural conditions and emphasizing the behavior's evolutionary value. Bowlby was influenced by the work of zoologist and ethologist Konrad Lorenz (1903–1989). He demonstrated that attachment was both innate and aided in survival in animals. In 1935, Lorenz conducted a study on *imprinting*, which involves a rapid and natural learning process that occurs early in the life of an animal and subsequently establishes an adaptive behavior pattern. These behaviors are specific to a particular species and aid in their survival. Lorenz was able to demonstrate goslings would imprint on attachment figures (e.g., a mother goose) in the environment within a certain critical period after hatching. Lorenz was even able to get newly hatched, orphaned geese to imprint on him and view him as a "mother" figure. His research revealed that attachment is an innate process and that there is a critical period during which the formation of attachment relationships is possible. A *critical period* is a specific time during development when the brain is primed for learning a particular behavior, skill, or piece of knowledge. Lorenz found that after a certain period (approximately 32 hours for geese), attachment was not likely to occur (Cherry, 2018).

Bowlby suggested that human infants also develop internal working models. *Internal working models* of attachment help infants form a cognitive blueprint of the workings of relationships. The earliest relationships between the infants and their mothers (or primary caregivers, in instances where the mothers are not available) may form the template for such a cognitive blueprint. Models shape and explain experiences and affect memory and attention. By age five, children have internal working models of their primary caregivers, themselves, and their immediate relationships. According to Bowlby children tend to re-create each new relationship in the pattern with which they are familiar, so if the relationship between them and their primary caregivers is positive, they will approach other relationships (e.g., with peers, teachers, and future romantic partners) in a positive way (Bowlby, 1946).

Bowlby suggested infants go through three phases of attachment formation to their primary caregivers within the first year. The first phase, *nonfocused orienting and signaling,* occurs within the first three months and there is no established attachment with the primary caregiver(s). Infants engage in *proximity-promoting behaviors,* which orient others toward them. Crying, cooing, and eye gaze are examples of proximity-promoting behaviors. The second phase, *focus on more than one figure,* occurs between three and six months. The proximity-promoting behaviors are targeted to specific people that infants come into regular contact with and who take care of the infants (e.g., mom, dad, daycare provider). During this phase, infants still respond relatively indiscriminately to anyone that tends to them, showing little stranger anxiety. The third phase, *secure base behavior,* occurs around six months, and if the infants have been provided with consistent care from their primary caregivers, genuine attachment begins to form. During this phase, infants have identified their primary caregivers as a *safe base,* which means that the infant will seek out and get physically closer to their primary caregiver in the face of fear or threat. Infants will also engage in *social referencing,* which occurs when infants take cues from other people in the environment, about how they should respond emotionally and behaviorally in a certain situation. Infants observe the behavior of their primary caregivers and imitate their actions and behaviors (Bowlby, 1969).

Bowlby believed that children show *separation anxiety,* or the distress of being separated from a primary caregiver. He also said infants experience *stranger anxiety,* which is the distress that occurs when infants are introduced to a stranger either in the presence or absence of their primary caregivers. These initially appear around the age of 7 to 9 months, peaking between 12 to 16 months and then declining around 24 months. There are factors that can impact how quickly children overcome separation and stranger anxiety, including their temperaments and the parenting styles they are exposed to. When an infant or child experiences a prolonged separation from their primary caregiver, Bowlby suggested they go through four phases: (1) the *protest phase,* where the child expresses anger about being separated, (2) the *despair/depression phase,* where the child transitions their anger into despair and sadness and eventual depression, (3) the *detachment phase,* where the child becomes detached from the primary caregiver through repressing their previous feelings about them, and finally (4) *anaclitic depression* (defined above), which occurs if the separation from the primary caregiver ultimately becomes permanent (Bowlby, 1973, 1980). See the Sidebar on the American Academy of Pediatrics Statement on the effects of family separation on young children for more discussion.

American-Canadian psychologist Mary Salter Ainsworth (1913–1999) was a colleague of John Bowlby. The developmental psychologist was born in Glendale, Ohio, in 1913 but her family moved to Toronto, Canada, five years later. Her family encouraged reading and scholarly activities while she was growing up as the oldest of three girls. At the age of 15 she encountered a book on psychology that set the path for her future career aspirations. She enrolled at the University of Toronto in 1929, being one of only four students to complete an honors degree in psychology. She went on to pursue graduate work and was subsequently introduced to security theory (i.e., attachment theory) for the first time, under the tutelage of William E. Blatz. After completing her graduate work, she eventually procured a teaching position at the University of Toronto in 1939 (Held, 2010).

Her tenure there was brief, as she enlisted in the Canadian Women's Army Corps in 1942. While serving, she procured a role as a clinician, administering tests, counseling, and taking histories of army recruits and other enlistees. After four years of this work, she returned to the University of Toronto as an assistant professor of psychology. It was during this time she met her husband, Leonard Ainsworth, who was a graduate student. They married in 1950 and eventually relocated to London, England, where she procured a research position working with John Bowlby at the Tavistock Clinic. In 1953, she travelled to Africa at the request of her husband. There, she arranged to be a research psychologist at the East African Institute of Social Research in Uganda. During her time at the institute, she conducted a two-year longitudinal, naturalistic study on the mother-infant relationship. She later published the results of this study after returning to America and becoming an instructor and clinical supervisor at Johns Hopkins University. She also opened her own private practice that focused on children. In 1963 she was finally granted the status of full professor (Held, 2010).

By that point she was a year into a longitudinal study that elaborated on Bowlby's concepts of separation and stranger anxiety between toddlers, young children, and their primary caregivers. She used both naturalistic observation in the home and created a laboratory setting, known as the *Strange Situation Paradigm*. The laboratory setting was a small room filled with toys and two chairs. There was a two-way mirror to observe the interactions and behaviors of the mother and children pairs. The procedure consisted of the following eight episodes (Connell & Goldsmith, 1982; Ainsworth, Blehar, Waters, & Wall, 1978).

- Caregiver and child are introduced to the experimental room.
- Caregiver and infant are alone. Caregiver does not participate while child explores.
- Stranger enters, converses with parent, then approaches child. Caregiver leaves inconspicuously.
- First separation episode: Stranger's behavior is geared to that of child.

- First reunion episode: Caregiver greets and comforts child, then leaves again.
- Second separation episode: Child is alone.
- Continuation of second separation episode: Stranger enters and gears behavior to that of child.
- Second reunion episode: Caregiver enters, greets child, and picks up child; stranger leaves inconspicuously.

Using this design, Ainsworth developed three attachment categories that classified the relationships between young children and their primary caregivers. The first and healthiest type of attachment was the *secure attachment*. With this attachment, children actively explore the laboratory room and play with available toys when their caregiver is present. When the caregiver leaves, the securely attached children become distressed and may cry or move around the room to regain proximity to their caregiver. The securely attached children are not consoled by strangers' attempts to comfort them in the absence of the caregiver. When the caregivers are finally reunited with the children, the children are comforted by them (Ainsworth et al., 1978; Carlson & Sroufe, 1995; Main & Solomon, 1990).

The second type of attachment is an *insecure detached/avoidant attachment*. With this type of attachment, children avoid contact with their caregivers when they are in the laboratory room (even after being separated and reunited) but may still play with toys and actively explore the room. They do not resist the caregiver's efforts to make contact but do not initiate contact either. These children also show no strong preference for their caregivers over the strangers and are not comforted by their caregivers when reunited after separation (Ainsworth et al., 1978; Carlson & Sroufe, 1995; Main & Solomon, 1990).

The third type of attachment is an *insecure resistant/ambivalent attachment*. With this type of attachment, children show little exploration of the laboratory room and are wary of strangers. They are upset when their caregivers leave the room but are not comforted when reunited. Children with this type of attachment both seek and avoid contact with their caregiver at various times. They may even show anger toward their caregiver when reunited, and resist both comfort and contact with the stranger (Ainsworth et al., 1978; Carlson & Sroufe, 1995; Main & Solomon, 1990).

The final type of attachment is *insecure disorganized/disoriented attachment*. The characteristics associated with this type of attachment do not fall neatly into any other category. This attachment is marked by dazed behavior, confusion, or apprehension on the part of children. They may show a contradictory behavior pattern simultaneously. For instance, they may move toward their caregiver when the stranger enters the room but may keep an averted eye gaze while doing so (Ainsworth et al., 1978; Carlson & Sroufe, 1995; Main & Solomon, 1990).

In 1975 Ainsworth left Johns Hopkins for a position at the University of Virginia and remained a professor there until 1984, when she retired. She continued to make professional contributions to the field until 1992. She received several accolades, including the Gold Medal Award for Life Achievement in the Science of Psychology from the American Psychological Foundation (Held, 2010).

The Strange Situation was criticized for not reflecting real-life situations, but Ainsworth's findings from her longitudinal and cross-cultural studies on parent-child relationships did have many applications to the real world. While the laboratory setting focused primarily on the responses of the children, Ainsworth found that there are distinct patterns of parenting that result in the different attachment types. For example, high levels of emotional availability, mutuality, and contingent responsiveness in caregivers correlate with more securely attached children. Low levels of emotional responsiveness are correlated with different types of insecurely attached children. It also should be noted that consistency in parenting behaviors is key to maintaining attachments. Children are able to recover from an insecure attachment or lose a secure attachment over time due to a variety of circumstances (e.g., divorce, death of a caregiver, addiction).

The developmental outcomes that result from a secure attachment are most beneficial. Securely attached children are more sociable, less clingy and dependent, function better in an academic setting, more empathetic, and more socially mature. Adolescence brings a change in the nature of the parent-child relationship. Even the most securely attached teenagers still wish to increase their autonomy from their parents while simultaneously maintaining a closeness with them. Even through the tumultuous times of adolescence, there are benefits to having a secure attachment. Securely attached teens are more likely to maintain intimate friendships, be rated as leaders by their peers, and have higher overall self-esteem (Bauminger, Finzi-Dottan, Chason, & Har-Even, 2008; Kobak, Zajac, & Smith, 2009). Insecurely attached adolescents are more likely to be sexually active at earlier ages and practice riskier sex (Carlson, Sroufe, & Egeland, 2004).

Social attachments can also play a role in the school setting. In early childhood, the quality of students' attachments with their teachers can impact long-term school adjustment. Birch and Ladd (1997) conducted a study using 206 kindergarten students and their teachers. They examined the interactions between school adjustment and three features of the student-teacher relationship: closeness to the teacher, dependency on the teacher, and conflict with the teacher. What they found is that clinginess, or dependency, was strongly correlated with difficulty in school adjustment, which was defined as poor academic performance, negative attitudes about school, and less positive engagement in the school environment. In addition, teacher-rated conflict was associated with teachers' negative ratings of how much they thought children liked school, how much the students avoided school or school-related activities, how self-directed their students were, and how willing their students were to engage in cooperative participation in the classroom. The degree of teacher-child closeness was positively linked with children's academic performance, teachers' ratings of how much they thought their students liked school, and their ratings of their students' self-directedness. In short, when children were able to build close, constructive relationships with their teachers, they used those teachers as a safe base to explore the rest of the classroom environment, were able to use their relationship with teachers to frame their expectations for relationships with their peers, and were able to be more open about how they were feeling at school in order to get appropriate assistance from teachers.

TEMPERAMENT AND THE DEVELOPMENT OF PERSONALITY

Children are not things to be molded, but are people to be unfolded.
—Jess Lair

Some aspects of a child's personality are evident at birth. Those aspects are referred to in developmental psychology as temperament. *Temperament*, broadly defined, refers to a child's habitual and enduring tendencies when approaching their external environments and the people in them. There are several theories that emphasize different aspects of temperament. One such theory involved the work of Thomas, Chess, and Birch, who conducted a longitudinal study in New York during the 1950s and 1960s involving Caucasian and Puerto Rican babies. Using previous research by Birch, Chess and colleagues identified nine dimensions of temperament: activity, regularity, initial reaction, adaptability, intensity, mood, distractibility, persistence, and sensitivity. Using these dimensions, they were able to classify approximately 65 percent of the infants in their study into three categories of temperament: difficult, easy, and slow-to-warm-up. *Easy babies* are highly adaptable to new experiences, have easily set schedules of eating and sleeping, and are receptive to new situations and people, generally displaying positive moods and emotions. *Difficult babies* are less adaptable to new experiences, display more negative emotionality, do not adapt well to change, are not consistent in patterns of eating or sleeping, and generally speaking are more irritable and fussy. *Slow-to-warm-up babies* are a combination of the easy baby temperament and the difficult baby temperament. They have a low activity level and tend to withdraw from new situations and people. They are slower to adapt to new experiences compared to easy babies, but eventually accept them if they are exposed to the experience more than once (Chess & Thomas, 1996).

Kagan (1997) suggests that a "slow-to-warm-up" baby also possesses higher levels reactivity and inhibition. For Kagan, *reactivity*, or the degree to which an infant reacted to a newly presented sensory stimuli, indicated her level of inhibition. In the context of his research on temperament, *inhibition* is a combination of shyness and fear of new and unfamiliar events.

Rothbart and Hwang (2005) suggested that there are three underlying dimensions of temperament: surgency/extraversion, negative affect, and effortful control. *Surgency/extraversion* involves qualities like impulsivity, eagerness, and a desire for sensation seeking. *Negative affect* involves qualities like fear, sadness, discomfort, and anger. In an infant, this might manifest as a fussy baby, not easily soothed. *Effortful control* involves qualities like the ability to self-regulate behavior, focus on tasks, and delay gratification.

From all of the theories on temperament, five key dimensions have risen to the surface (Caspi & Shiner, 2006; Kagan & Herschkowitz, 2005; Rothbart, 2007). *Activity level* involves the tendency to move often and vigorously, rather than to remain passive or immobile. *Approach/positive emotionality* involves the tendency to move toward new people, situations, or objects, usually accompanied by positive emotion. *Inhibition and anxiety* involves the tendency to respond with fear or to withdraw from new people, situations, or objects. *Negative emotionality/irritability/anger* involves the tendency to respond with anger, fussiness, loudness, or irritability, and a low threshold for frustration. *Effortful control/task persistence* involves the ability to stay focused and to manage attention and effort. A student's individual temperament can certainly interact with the school environment in a variety of ways. For example, a child with high levels of negative emotionality and low task persistence may not readily adapt to the demands of the classroom environment, like homework assignments, teacher's expectations about classroom rules, or appropriate communication with peers.

Teachers are tasked with accommodating a variety of temperaments in their classrooms. Some students' personalities will mesh better with the classroom environment than others, but there are some useful strategies for making every student feel engaged and a part of the learning environment. These strategies include techniques from social-emotional learning curriculums and include:

- Teaching students about proper emotional responses and provide them with constructive, age-appropriate strategies for expressing positive and negative emotions

- Providing a calming environment if students seem overstimulated (e.g., take a mindfulness meditation break)
- Being emotionally responsive and welcoming to emotionally inhibited students
- Teaching students how to self-regulate and control their own behaviors
- Providing opportunities for constructive social interactions for extroverted students (e.g., peer-to-peer learning activities)
- Keeping high energy students actively engaged using instructional strategies that involve some level of bodily-kinesthetic interaction (e.g., solving puzzles, learning games)
- Providing students with opportunities to adapt to changes in your classroom (e.g., new student, new teacher's aide)

SELF-CONCEPT AND IDENTITY FORMATION

There is in every child at every stage a new miracle of vigorous unfolding, which constitutes a new hope and a new responsibility for all.
—*Erik Erikson*

Self-concept involves a child's knowledge and thoughts about her own set of attributes or qualities. The self can be broken into two parts: the subjective self and the objective self. The *subjective self* involves developing (1) a sense of agency, or one's awareness that she is a separate entity and can act on the world, (2) a sense of permanency, or one's awareness that she will exist in the world for the long term, and (3) a sense of self-efficacy, or one's awareness that she is competent at acting on the world in a variety of ways. These things all initially begin to develop within the first year of life. The *objective self* is based on concrete characteristics a child can identify in herself. By age two, a child realizes she is a player in a social game with other actors (e.g., parents, siblings). By age three, a child knows her name, can describe her physical characteristics (e.g., "I have dark skin" or "My wheel chair helps me get around"). She also knows her size and age relative to others (e.g., "I am younger than my big brother"), and her biological sex and associated gender. She learns explicit roles based on gender by watching others (e.g., what a mommy does vs. what a daddy does). Learning these roles can inform her attitudes and ideas about others and also facilitate sociodramatic play. By the time a child is five, she can provide a description of what she is good at (e.g., "I am a very fast runner" or "I am great at math"). At this young age, children compartmentalize different aspects of their self-concepts, as if they were making separate lists for each aspect (Harter, 2006).

The objective self also involves the development of *self-awareness*, which involves being aware of one's one physical and psychological traits, behaviors, and feelings. Research suggests that self-awareness is evident in some infants as early as 21 months of age. Self-awareness is commonly assessed in young children using the *rouge-test*. During the rouge-test, a child is put in front of a mirror with a spot of paint/ink on their face. If the child touches his face during the test, that indicates self-awareness because the child recognizes that he has a spot of ink on his own face. If the child reaches for the image in the mirror and points to the spot of paint, that indicates that he does not yet recognized the image in the mirror as being himself, and thus he does not possess self-awareness (Lewis & Carmody, 2008; Lewis & Ramsay, 2004).

Self-awareness also facilitates emotional development. *Emotions* involve having an awareness of some standard of appropriate conduct in the social world. They serve three purposes: (1) they regulate overt actions, (2) they influence cognitive processing, and (3) they initiate, maintain, or terminate interactions with others. When a child is able to recognize these standards and compare her behavior to the behavior of others, and then modify her behavior to match that of those around her, then she is demonstrating her own *emotional regulation.* Emotional regulation is the foundation for social skills that develop later on in childhood. If a child has good emotional regulation early in life, the research suggests that they will have more positive social relationships into adolescence and adulthood (Srofe & Waters, 1976).

A child's ability to understand and control expressions of emotion involves impulse control and an awareness of social rules related to emotional expression. An early example of these social rules would be the "social smile" that is expressed beginning around the age of three years. A social smile is given when a child may not necessarily feel happy, but knows she is expected to look happy (e.g., smiling for annual school photos). Children also learn to conceal or suppress certain feelings in certain situations if they have been taught that is it not appropriate to express certain emotions in a given context (Srofe & Waters, 1976).

Gender can play a role in emotional regulation as well. In Western cultures, it is more common to socialize children to match gender stereotypes, which means that it is less acceptable for little boys to outwardly express emotions like sadness and for girls to outwardly express emotions involving anger. Children pick up on these messages from a very early age and will learn to adapt their emotional responses accordingly (Brody, 1985).

Nancy Eisenberg's research suggests that parents and teachers play a large part in shaping a child's emotional development. As the child gets older, control shifts from parent and teacher to the child with respect to emotional regulation. Parents and teachers need to model appropriate emotional responses by using appropriate physical controls and verbal communication when interacting with other adults and when disciplining or rewarding their children and students. This is because children observe these emotional reactions and subsequent behaviors that the adults around them are having and internalize these interactions for future use (Eisenberg, Fabes, Schaller, Carlo, & Miller, 1991). As referenced above in the section on attachment, an increasing number of social-emotional learning curriculums have been developed to assist children with their emotional regulation and social development (Jones et al., 2017).

Academic self-concept, or a child's perceptions of her academic abilities, begins to develop around school age. The school environment offers many sources of information that can be internalized into students' self-concepts. Teacher and coach expectations, parental expectations, academic performance, normative standardized assessments that rank students' performances (e.g., statewide, high-stakes tests), and social evaluations from peers can all contribute to academic self-concept. Because children spend so much time at school in their youth, at least in Western cultures, the school environment can contribute to their overall sense of self-worth, for better or worse. The way children integrate these sources of information into their self-concept becomes more complex and abstract as they get older.

During adolescence, academic self-concept and overall identity development evolves into abstract traits, and for some teens involves ideologies about specific aspects of their lives. *Identity* is a sense of personal continuity and uniqueness from others. Identity also involves aspects of group membership as well. Teenagers become increasingly aware of how their gender, religion, social class, race, and/or ethnicity have contributed to their overall self-concept. Identity becomes more differentiated based on the environment teens find themselves in. For instance, teens might present one aspect of their identities their teachers in the classroom, a different aspect to their friends at social gatherings, and another completely different aspect to their coworkers and boss while at work. Academic self-concept becomes more internalized, and teens may now have self-imposed standards of success and failure. Because they have spent a great time in school at this point in their lives, they may have set self-standards and compare their current performances to earlier successes or failures (Harter, 1988; Rosenberg, 1986). For example, a teen who used to succeed and find math courses easy and a source of accomplishment may now hate math class because he no longer excels at the subject. He may feel disappointed at his own declining performance and attribute that to a decreased level of competence in the subject area.

Changes in academic performance or other changes in a teen's life can potentially throw them into what Erik Erikson referred to as an adolescent identity crisis. Because adolescence involves so many physical, social, and emotional changes, teens can often feel overwhelmed and confused about who they are or where they are headed. Erikson defined an *identity crisis* as the brief uncertainty and confusion adolescents experience as they struggle with alternatives and choices presented to them during this period of life (Erikson, 1980). These choices could involve decisions about future schooling or careers, interpersonal relationships with friends and family, values related to religious and political beliefs, ethnic or racial identity, gender identity, and sexual orientation.

James Marcia (1966) elaborated on Erikson's original identity crises by expanding the possible identity statuses that teenagers could have during adolescence. Marcia looked at the interaction between two main components: (1) the level of crisis a teenager was experiencing with respect to occupation and ideology, and (2) the level of commitment a teenager was experiencing with respect to occupation and ideology. In the context of Marcia's theory, an *identity crisis* referred to a period of decision making during which old choices are reexamined and measured against new opportunities. *Identity commitment* referred to the adoption of a new ideology or aspiration. His study, involving 86 college males, determined the existence of four identity statuses: (1) *identity achievement*, when the crisis is resolved and the commitment has been made, (2) *moratorium*, when a crisis is in progress, but no commitment is yet made, (3) *foreclosure*, when a commitment is made based on parental or societal norms without a crisis occurring, and (4) *identity diffusion*, when a teenager is not in the midst of a crisis and has not made a commitment.

While Erikson and Marcia may have addressed the experiences of some teenagers, more contemporary research suggests that the identity crisis tends to take place later on in life, during college rather than high school. There are also a number of individuals that are foreclosed on their identity and do not experience a crisis at all. Gender, race, culture, and cognitive development can impact when a person goes through an identity crisis (Franz & White, 1985; Rothman, 1978; Ochse, 1986).

RACIAL AND ETHNIC IDENTITY IN THE SCHOOL ENVIRONMENT

We are, at almost every point of our day, immersed in cultural diversity: faces, clothes, smells, attitudes, values, traditions, behaviours, beliefs, rituals.

—Randa Abdel-Fattah

Differences in cultural norms can make a teenager's identity development more complex, especially when she is a member of a racial or ethnic minority. Teens with different ethnic and racial backgrounds must reconcile their own ethnic or racial identity within the mainstream culture while simultaneously establishing their own identity based on the overall culture's norms. For example, the United States values and promotes independence and individualism, but members of some ethnicities (e.g., Asian and Hispanic communities) may value familial and more collectivist approaches to development passed down from their cultural heritage. Teenagers with these backgrounds are tasked with trying to balance these two, seemingly opposing sets of values or choosing one set of cultural values and foreclosing on another. There are a number of theoretical models on racial, biracial, and ethnic identity development (Phinney, 1989; Berry, 2005; Cross, 1971, 1978, 1991; Nadal, 2011; Rockquemore & Laszloffy, 2005). Many of these models involve the process of becoming aware of one's ethnic and/or racial identity, making distinctions between this identity and where it falls in the mainstream (Caucasian-centric) culture, internalizing or rejecting the values associated with their the ethnic and/or racial identity, and reconciling the values of the mainstream culture with those of their own ethnic and racial group. Successful completion of this final step should result in a stronger sense of ethnic and/or racial identity and pride, and an integration of the values associated with their ethnic and/or racial group and the mainstream culture.

While theories of ethnic and racial identity may propose a relatively linear and clear-cut path for the integration of these identities with the mainstream culture, other research has suggested that members of ethnic and racial minorities can be impacted by these identities. In the classroom environment, cultural differences can emerge in apparent and subtle ways, which can result in misunderstandings, isolation, and alienation among minority students. Such differences include language and dialect barriers, differences in nonverbal communication (e.g., making eye contact), the types of questions students ask, the types of information students disclose about their personal lives, expectations about relationships with teachers and peers, attitudes about authority, and conflicts in cultural values. McClain and colleagues (2016), examined the impacts of racial and ethnic identity, imposter feelings, and minority status stress on the mental health of black college students. They found that ethnic identity was a positive predictor of mental health and that imposter feelings and minority status stress served as negative predictors of mental health.

Warikoo and Carter (2009) suggest that new approaches should be developed when discussing ethnic and racial differences in the context of academic achievement. They argue that for far too long, being an ethnic or racial minority in the classroom has been assumed to be problematic, and oftentimes results in members of those groups experiencing an achievement gap with their Caucasian counterparts when it comes to school readiness, test performance, high school completion rates, and college attainment. They found that on closer examination, certain ethnic minority groups (e.g., Chinese Americans, Korean Americans, South Asian Americans) fare better in the academic context than Caucasian students.

Warikoo and Carter (2009) also argue that peer-reviewed psychological and educational literature focusing on educational achievement oftentimes generalizes the underachievement of other minority groups like African, Native, and Chicano Americans. In essence, the educational research perpetuates a negative narrative about the academic performances of these ethnic and racial groups. They feel that it is important to recognize the constellation of factors that have led to skewed representation of these groups and that their underachievement is actually the result of interactions between racial and ethnic identity with social class, resulting in the stratification of the educational experience.

AMERICAN ACADEMY OF PEDIATRICS STATEMENT ON THE DETENTION OF IMMIGRANT CHILDREN

This chapter focuses on the social-emotional development of children and its relationship to the educational environment. As you read, attachment theory asserts that there is an innate tendency for infants and children to form deep social attachments to their primary caregivers. The quality and continuity of these attachments have lasting impacts on the psychological, physical, and educational well-being of the child. These are findings that have been empirically validated time and time again. Because of this established body of research, the American Academy of Pediatrics was compelled to issue a statement on the deleterious effects of the separation and detention of immigrant children. In their statement, Linton, Griffin, Shapiro, and the AAP Council on Community Pediatrics (2017) cite inadequate conditions for refugee children who are detained at the border and separated from their primary caregivers. They indicate that the Department of Homeland Security has not provided adequate or appropriate support services and their facilities "do not meet the basic standards for the care of children in residential settings" (p. 1). The report goes on to detail what means to be a child refugee fleeing a country of origin, the history of migrant children from Central America and immigrant law, current practices and terminology for processing migrant children and their families, how they are detained and processed by the U.S. Border Patrol, and the process for determining whether they will be sent back to their country of origin or be given the opportunity to seek safe haven in the United States. The arbitrary arrest and detention of children is considered a human rights violation by the United Nations Convention on the Rights of the Child. This is a legal framework for protecting children's basic rights. It has been recognized internationally and ratified by every country except the United States. It emphasizes the following:

- freedom from arbitrary arrest and detention (Article 37),
- the provision of special protection to children seeking asylum (Article 22),
- humane and appropriate treatment of children in detention (Article 37), and
- guidelines regarding maintaining family unity (Article 9) (as cited by Linton et al., 2017, p. 6).

The report continues by discussing the potential trauma these children have experienced in their countries of origin, during their migration to the United States, and while at the detention centers. They also discuss the lasting, negative developmental outcomes for these children, which include: "regressive behavioral changes in their children, including decreased eating, sleep disturbances, clinginess, withdrawal, self-injurious behavior, and aggression" (p. 6).

Regardless of political orientations, these documented consequences of family separation and forced detention should be addressed and the practices implemented by ICE and by U.S. Border Patrol should cease immediately. In addition to the physical and psychological trauma these children experience, there is often a lack of quality educational resources made available to these children in their country of origin. The long, dangerous trek to migrate to the United States and lengthy stays in detention facilities also result in extended lapses of schooling. Once migrant children are processed and it is determined that they can entered the United States as an undocumented immigrant, they have limited legal rights. However, they are eligible for a free public education regardless of their immigration status. While they are eligible, there are still several issues with accessing an appropriate educational experience. These children must be provided with trauma-informed care and educational services that match their cognitive, linguistic, and social development, and be provided with a culturally responsive environment for their learning.

—Sarah E. Torok-Gerard

They also make distinctions between those minorities who were native to the United States and forcibly displaced and marginalized in the educational system (e.g., African Americans, Native Americans, Puerto Ricans, and Mexicans) and those minorities whose families intentionally migrated to the United States for better educational opportunities (e.g., Chinese, Korean) and/or who were displaced by their countries of origin as a result of political or economic strife (e.g., Southeast Asian). They suggest that these groups have been perceived differently with respect to how they value formal education, with the former group taking on oppositional cultural attitudes towards schools and traditionally whitewashed curriculums and the latter group eager to take advantage of the new educational opportunities afforded to them by migrating to the United States.

Warikoo and Carter (2009) also take into account that most school's cultural environments encourage racial and ethnic minorities to assimilate to the mainstream Caucasian culture. School curricula often overlook the economic and historical realities of minority groups, which further alienates and disenfranchises them, ultimately increasing the risk that they will completely disengage from learning.

The goal of education should be to transmit knowledge in an inclusive way that provides voice and representation for a variety of groups. History is full of diversity, and that should be reflected in students' educational experiences. Providing a wide range of perspectives in the curricula will benefit students in their academic experiences and also potentially help them shape their ideas about their self-concepts and emerging identities. The National Association of Elementary School Principals produced "The Principal's Guide to Building Culturally Responsive Schools" (2018) based on the work of the NAESP Diversity Task Force, which was established with the goal of creating guidelines for best practices that principals and other school administrators can use to create school environments that promote diversity and multiculturalism. The report cites that, for the first time in history, the majority of K–12 students are students of color.

REFERENCES

Ainsworth, M. D. S., Blehar, M., Waters, E., & Wall, S. (1978). *Patterns of attachment*. Hillsdale, NJ: Lawrence Erlbaum.

Bauminger, N., Finzi-Dottan, R., Chason, S., & Har-Even, D. (2008). Intimacy in adolescent friendship: The roles of attachment, coherence, and self-disclosure. *Journal of Social and Personal Relationships, 25*, 409–428.

Berry, J. W. (2005). Acculturation: Living successfully in two cultures. *International Journal of Intercultural Relations, 29*, 697–712.

Birch, S. H., & Ladd, G. W. (1997). The teacher-child relationship and children's early school adjustment. *Journal of School Psychology, 35*(1), 61–79. doi:10.1016/S0022-4405(96)00029-5

Bowlby, J. (1946). Maternal care and mental health. Geneva, Switzerland: World Health Organization.

Bowlby, J. (1958). The nature of the child's tie to his mother. *International Journal of Psychoanalysis, 39*, 1–23.

Bowlby, J. (1969). *Attachment and loss, Vol. 1: Attachment*. New York, NY: Basic Books.

Bowlby, J. (1973). *Attachment and loss, Vol. 2: Separation, anxiety, and anger*. London, England: Penguin.

Bowlby, J. (1980). *Attachment and loss, Vol. 3: Loss: Sadness and depression*. New York, NY: Basic Books.

Brody, L. R. (1985). Gender differences in emotional development: A review of theories and research. *Journal of Personality, 53*(2), 102–149.

Carlson, E., & Sroufe, A. (1995). Contribution of attachment theory to developmental psychopathology. In D. Cicchetti & D. J. Cohen (Eds.), *Developmental psychopathology: Vol. 1. theory and methods* (pp. 581–617). New York, NY: Wiley.

Carlson, E., Sroufe, A., & Egeland, B. (2004). The construction of experience: A longitudinal study of representation and behavior. *Child Development, 75*, 66–83.

Caspi, A., & Shiner, R. L. (2006). Personality development. In N. Eisenberg, W. Damon, & R. Lerner (Eds.), *Handbook of child psychology: Vol. 3, Social, emotional, and personality development* (6th ed., pp. 300–365). Hoboken, NJ: Wiley.

Cherry, K. (2018). John Bowlby biography (1907–1990). Found of attachment theory. Retrieved from https://www.verywellmind.com/john-bowlby-biography-1907-1990-2795514.

Chess, S., & Thomas, A. (1996). *Temperament.* New York, NY: Routledge.

Connell, J. P., & Goldsmith, H. H. (1982). A structural modeling approach to the study of attachment and strange situation behaviors. In R. N. Emde & R. J. Harmon (Eds.), *The development of attachment and affiliative systems* (pp. 213–243). New York, NY: Plenum.

Cross, W. E., Jr. (1971). The Negro-to-Black conversion experience: Toward a psychology of Black liberation. *Black World, 20*, 13–27.

Cross, W. E., Jr. (1978). The Thomas and Cross models of psychological nigrescence: A literature review. *Journal of Black Psychology, 4*, 13–31.

Cross, W. E., Jr. (1991). *Shades of black: Diversity in African American identity.* Philadelphia, PA: Temple University Press.

Eisenberg, N., Fabes, R. A., Schaller, M., Carlo, G., & Miller, P. A. (1991). The relations of parental characteristics and practices to children's vicarious emotional responding. *Child Development, 62*(6), 1393–1408.

Erikson, E. (1980). *Identity and the life cycle.* New York, NY: W. W. Norton.

Franz, C. E., & White, K. M. (1985). Individuation and attachment in personality development: Extending Erikson's theory. *Journal of Personality, 53*(2), 224–256.

Harter, S. (1988). The construction and conservation of the self: James and Cooley revisited. In D. K. Lapsley & E. C. Power (Eds.), *Self, ego, and identity: Integrative approaches* (pp. 43–69). New York, NY: Springer-Verlag.

Harter, S. (2006). The self. In N. Eisenberg, W. Damon, & R. Learner (Eds.), *Handbook of child psychology: Vol. 3, Social, emotional, and personality development* (6th ed., pp. 505–570). Hoboken, NJ: Wiley.

Held, L. (2010). Profile of Mary Ainsworth. Retrieved from http://www.feministvoices.com/mary-ainsworth/

Jones, S., Brush, K., Bailey, R., Brion-Meisels, G., McIntyre, J., Kahn, J . . . Stickle, L. (2017). Navigating SEL from the inside out. Looking inside & across 25 leading SEL programs: A practical resource for schools and OST providers. Retrieved from https://www.wallacefoundation.org/knowledge-center/Documents/Navigating-Social-and-Emotional-Learning-from-the-Inside-Out.pdf

Kagan, J. (1997). Temperament and the reactions to unfamiliarity. *Child Development, 68*(1), 139–143. doi:10.2307/1131931

Kagan, J., & Herschkowitz, N. (2005). *A young mind in a growing brain.* Mahwah, NJ: Lawrence Erlbaum.

Kobak, R., Zajac, K., & Smith, C. (2009). Adolescent attachment and trajectories of hostile/impulsive behavior. Implications for the development of personality disorders. *Development and Psychopathology, 21,* 839–851.

Lewis, M., & Carmody, D. (2008). Self-representation and brain development. *Developmental Psychology, 44,* 1329–1334.

Lewis, M., & Ramsay, D. (2004). Development of self-recognition, personal pronoun use, and pretend play during the 2nd year. *Child Development, 75,* 1821–1831.

Linton, J. M., Griffin, M., Shapiro, A. J., & AAP Council on Community Pediatrics. (2017). Detention of immigrant children. *Pediatrics, 139*(4), e20170483. doi: 10.1542/peds.2017-0483

Main, M., & Solomon, J. (1990). Procedures for identifying infants as disorganized/disoriented during the Ainsworth Strange Situation. In M. T. Greenberg, D. Cicchetti, & E. M. Cummings (Eds.), *Attachment in the preschool years: Theory, research, and intervention* (pp. 121–160). Chicago, IL: University of Chicago Press.

Marcia, J. E. (1966). Development and validation of ego-identity status. *Journal of Personality and Social Psychology, 3*(5), 551–558. http://dx.doi.org/10.1037/h0023281

McClain, S., Beasley, S. T., Jones, B., Awosogba, O., Jackson, S. & Cokley, K. (2016). An examination of the impact of racial and ethnic identity, impostor feelings, and minority status stress on the mental health of Black college students. *Journal of Multicultural Counseling and Development, 44,* 101–117. doi: 10.1002/jmcd.12040

Nadal, K. L. (2011). *Filipino American psychology: A handbook of theory, research, and clinical practice.* New York, NY: John Wiley & Sons.

NAESP Diversity Task Force. (2018). *The principal's guide to building culturally responsive schools.* Retrieved from https://www.naesp.org/sites/default/files/NAESP_Culturally_Responsive_Schools_Guide.pdf

Ochse, R. (1986). Cross-cultural investigation of the validity of Erikson's theory of personality development. *Journal of Personality and Social Psychology, 50*(6), 1240–1252.

Phinney, J. S. (1989). Stages of ethnic identity development in minority group adolescents. *Journal of Early Adolescence, 9,* 34–49.

Rockquemore, K. A., & Laszloffy, T. (2005). *Raising biracial children.* Lanham, MD: Altamira.

Rosenberg, M. (1986). Self-concept from middle childhood through adolescence. In S. Suls & A. Greenwald (Eds.), *Psychological perspectives on the self* (vol. 3, pp. 107–135). Hillsdale, NJ: Lawrence Erlbaum.

Rothbart, M. K. (2007). Temperament, development, and personality. *Current Directions in Psychological Science, 16,* 207–212.

Rothbart, M. K., & Hwang, J. (2005). Temperament and the development of competence and motivation. In A. J. Elliot & A. C. Dweck (Eds.), *Handbook of competence and motivation* (pp. 167–184). New York, NY: Guilford.

Rothman, K. M. (1978). Multivariate analysis of the relationship of psychosocial crisis variables to ego identity status. *Journal of Youth and Adolescence, 7*(1), 93–105.

Srofe, L. A., & Waters, E. (1976). The ontogenesis of smiling and laughter: A perspective on the organization of development in infancy. *Psychological Review, 83*(3), 173–189.

Talbot, M. (1998). The disconnected; Attachment theory: The ultimate experiment. *New York Times Magazine.* Retrieved from https://www.nytimes.com/1998/05/24/magazine/the-disconnected-attachment-theory-the-ultimate-experiment.html

Warikoo, N., & Carter, P. (2009). Cultural explanations for racial and ethnic stratification in academic achievement: A call for a new and improved theory. *Review of Educational Research, 79*(1), 366–394. doi: 10.3102/0034654308326162

5

Profiles in Contemporary Research

In the previous chapters, the reader was introduced to the origins of educational psychology as a field of study. The following chapter highlights some researchers that have been influential to the field of educational psychology. Their work involves a variety of areas including theories related to cognitive psychology, the psychology of prejudice and discrimination, and clinical psychology.

JEROME BRUNER: COGNITIVE PSYCHOLOGY—LESSONS ON CHILDREN'S THINKING IN THE CLASSROOM

Education must be not only a transmission of culture but also a provider of alternative views of the world and a strengthener of the will to explore them.

—Jerome Bruner

Jerome Bruner (1915–2016) is an American psychologist who is credited with being a forerunner in the field of cognitive psychology and greatly contributing to the fields of developmental and educational psychology. The youngest of three, he was born in New York City to two Polish immigrants, Herman and Rose Bruner. They lived a modest life with Herman working as a watchmaker and Rose staying at home. Jerome was blind at birth, an issue that was corrected at the age of two after an experimental surgery to remove his cataracts. This early life experience with gaining vision after being blind would influence his desire to study perception and cognition. When he was 12 his father passed away and his mother moved the family to Florida (Carey, 2016).

After attending a series of high schools in Florida, he entered Duke University, earning a degree in psychology in 1937. He earned his doctorate in psychology at Harvard University in 1941, and then enlisted in the Army to serve as an expert on psychological warfare during World War II. In 1945, he returned to Harvard, becoming a professor of psychology in 1952. While at Harvard, he conducted research relating to cognitive psychology and educational psychology after getting frustrated with the theoretical perspective of behaviorism. Unlike theorists like Ivan Pavlov, John B. Watson, and B. F. Skinner, Bruner did not believe that the human behavior could simply be boiled down to a stimulus-response relationship. He thought that behavioral theories, which were primarily based on animals and solely based on observable and measurable interactions in the environment, did not take into account the complex internal workings of the human mind. He thought that behaviorism also ignored the broader social and cultural contexts. Instead, Bruner suggested that factors such as a person's motivation, memory, instincts, and intentions influence their thinking and perception. In 1956, Bruner published the book *A Study of Thinking*, which formally initiated the study of cognitive psychology. His research and feelings about behaviorism prompted him to start and direct Harvard's Center for Cognitive Studies from 1960 to 1972 (Carey, 2016).

He founded the Center for Cognitive Studies with his colleague, experimental psychologist and fellow forerunner of cognitive psychology George A. Miller (1920–2012). While at the center, Bruner and Miller demonstrated what became known as the "new look" in perception, which is an understanding of perception that emphasizes how a variety of nonobjective factors can systematically influence the process of perception. The center also provided Miller and Bruner with a platform to promote the constructivist ideas about cognition that Jean Piaget formulated (Fancher & Rutherford, 2017; Hergenhahn, 2014).

Their work at the center would continue to influence a paradigmatic shift away from behaviorism to the emerging field of cognitive psychology. *Cognitive psychology* is the scientific study of mental processes such as attention, language use, memory, perception, problem solving, creativity, and thinking, all of which are typically analyzed in terms of information processing. Research in cognitive psychology has been integrated into various other subdisciplines of psychology (e.g., educational psychology, social psychology, personality psychology, abnormal psychology, and developmental psychology). George Miller argued that a symposium on information theory sponsored by the Massachusetts Institute of Technology marked the beginning of modern cognitive psychology (Fancher & Rutherford, 2017).

In 1972 Bruner left Harvard to become professor of experimental psychology at the University of Oxford, where he remained until 1980. While there, he promoted the idea that cognitive psychology should be broadened to include narrative construction and culture, which, he asserted, also shape the strategies people use to make sense of the world. He returned to the states and during the 1980s continued his work on developmental psychology. He later taught at the New School for Social Research, New York City, and in 1991 joined the faculty at the New York University School of Law (Carey, 2016).

With respect to the fields of educational and developmental psychology specifically, Bruner's work made him a sought-after expert. As a result of advances that the Soviet Union made during the Space Race of the 1950s, the United States felt an urgent need to improve national standards for education, particularly in the sciences. In 1959 Bruner participated in a meeting of prominent scholars regarding this initiative for educational reform. While there, he ran a meeting that inspired a subsequent book *The Process of Education* (1960). This book influenced the field of education for years to come and served as a powerful spur to the curriculum-reform movement of the period (Carey, 2016; Fancher & Rutherford, 2017).

Influenced by both Piaget and Vygotsky, Bruner believed that students possess a natural curiosity that drives their thinking and motivation to learn a variety of different tasks. He also thought that students have a threshold for task difficulty that impacts their sustained level of interest in learning about it—if the task is too difficult, then the students will become uninterested in it. As a result, Bruner asserted that it is the teacher's responsibility to gauge the level of task difficulty to the age and ability of the student. Furthermore, Bruner suggested that the teacher present the task in a structured interaction with the child, one that makes use of and builds upon the child's actual level of ability. Bruner referred to these frameworks as *instructional scaffolding*, which is intended to facilitate learning by limiting the child's choices in the learning process to an adaptable realm for his ability.

Bruner also created three ways of conceptualizing or mentally representing material being taught. These modes of representation paralleled Piagetian stages of cognitive development, and were identified as the as enactive mode, iconic mode, and symbolic mode. The *enactive mode* is the first mode of representation in Bruner's theory, in which a student begins by doing something with the material under study, representing it and "getting to know it"; this would be prominent during Piaget's sensorimotor period. The *iconic mode* is Bruner's second mode of representation, in which things are "known" primarily in terms of their perceptual qualities; this would be prominent during Piaget's preoperational stage. Finally, the *symbolic mode* is Bruner's third and final mode of representation, in which the student appreciates the abstract qualities of the object of study; this parallels the last two operational stages—concrete operational and formal operational (Fancher & Rutherford, 2017).

Bruner argued that any subject could be taught to any child at any stage of development, if it was presented using age-appropriate educational strategies. Specifically, Bruner referred to the concept of the "spiral curriculum." The *spiral curriculum* involved teachers introducing students to topics early, in age-appropriate language, and revisiting the same topics in later years, adding depth and complexity as the students get older. This is a technique that became widespread in many school districts and was based on Piaget's theory of cognitive development (Carey, 2016).

Bruner's other contributions include his involvement in designing Head Start, the federal program introduced in 1965 to improve preschool development. Head Start programs are intended to provide young children with the social and academic skills and resources to ready themselves for the school environment. Over the course of his career, Bruner won a long list of awards in psychology and education. In the 1990s, he became an educational ambassador, visiting and working with preschools in Reggio Emilia, Italy. As a result, a number of preschools around the world now use the Reggio Emilia approach (Carey, 2016).

Bruner also published many works. Among these include *Mandate from the People* (1944), *A Study of Thinking* (1956, with Jacqueline J. Goodnow and George A. Austin), *On Knowing: Essays for the Left Hand* (1962), *Toward a Theory of Instruction* (1966), *Processes of Cognitive Growth: Infancy* (1968), *The Relevance of Education* (1971), *Communication as Language* (1982), *Child's Talk* (1983), *Actual Minds, Possible Worlds* (1986), *Acts of Meaning* (1990), *The Culture of Education* (1996), *Minding the Law* (2000), and *Making Stories: Law, Literature, Life* (2002).

JANE ELLIOTT: A CLASS DIVIDED, LESSONS ON IMPLICIT BIAS, PREJUDICE, AND DISCRIMINATION

You are not born racist. You are born into a racist society. And like anything else, if you can learn it, you can unlearn it. But some people choose not to unlearn it, because they're afraid they'll lose power if they share with other people. We are afraid of sharing power. That's what it's all about.

—Jane Elliott

Jane Elliott (1933–) is a former school teacher turned social justice activist, diversity trainer, and international speaker. She has travelled the globe, engaging audiences in her "blue-eyed, brown-eyed" exercise and speaking to the young and old on issues of racial discrimination and discrimination of other marginalized groups. She was first inspired to teach her lesson on race the day after Martin Luther King Jr. was assassinated, April 4, 1968. After watching biased news coverage of the assassination and having her students ask, "Why did they shoot that king?" she decided to create an age-appropriate way to explain the situation. She wanted to give her students a first-hand experience of discrimination. All of her Riceville, Iowa, students were white, so she decided to base the activity on eye color. She invented the "blue-eyed, brown-eyed" exercise. The lesson spanned two days and required the designated minority group to wear collars that she had sewn for them. During the first day, the students with blue eyes were deemed "superior" and given several privileges in the classroom, lunchroom, and on the playground (e.g., they could get a second helping of food during lunch; they also received five minutes of extra time at recess). Elliott also made subtle and obvious insults toward the students with brown eyes and revoked or restricted certain privileges (e.g., they could not use the same water fountain that the blue-eyed children used; she would make harsh comments and single them out if they did not properly follow directions during class).

Initially the students in the class were reluctant to engage each other in negative ways. Elliott manufactured a distinction between the superior group and the inferior group by explaining that melanin was the reason to the superior group's higher levels of intelligence and learning abilities. Her explanation quickly facilitated tension between the two groups of students. The blue-eyed group began to chastise their brown-eyed peers by taunting them, bossing them around, and self-segregating from them in the classroom and on the playground. Elliott made an unexpected observation with respect to the students' academic performances. On the days a group was deemed "superior" based on eye color, their scores on basic drills and tests were higher. The converse was true for those students who were labeled "inferior" due to their eye color, who acted timid, subservient, isolated, and less academically competent. This not only says something about the impact of the discrimination they were experiencing from their peers but also suggests that teacher expectations and stereotype threat played an influential role in their academic performances. After the blue-eyed students were deemed superior on the first day, it was their turn to become the inferior group the following day. The brown-eyed children became the superior students. The same behavior patterns in each group of children occurred when the dominant and subordinate groups were switched. Even the academic performance of the brown-eyed children improved when they became the superior group.

During the first year of the exercise (1968), Elliott's lesson was showcased in the local newspaper, the *Riceville Recorder*. In a piece called "How Discrimination Feels," her third grade students wrote about their experiences during the exercise. The story was soon picked up by the Associated Press, resulting in Elliott being invited onto the *Tonight Show Starring Johnny Carson*. Her appearance on the show put her and her students in the national spotlight. As a result, Elliott garnered both positive and negative feedback about her classroom lesson. While on the air, the *Tonight Show* received immediate feedback from angry viewers. One even stated that they thought the lesson was psychologically harmful to white children (Bloom, 2005).

Upon returning to Riceville, Elliott continued to receive a chilly reception. Some of her fellow teachers and parents of her students did not appreciate the attention the lesson brought to their small town. A few even feared that the publicity she received would draw African Americans and other outsiders to the town. Despite being isolated by many for conducting the lesson, Elliott continued to engage her third grade students in the blue-eyed, brown-eyed exercise until she left teaching in the mid-1980s. By that point her work had become very well known. After the 1968 appearance on the *Tonight Show* her lesson on discrimination would become the subject of several documentaries and books. The first of these documentaries was an ABC News documentary entitled *The Eye of the Storm*, which aired in 1970. The documentary thrust Elliott and her students further into the spotlight. William Peters then authored two books about her exercise, entitled *A Class Divided* and *A Class Divided: Then and Now* (Bloom, 2005).

The first of these books was turned into a subsequent documentary, also entitled *A Class Divided*, and produced by the PBS Frontline series. It aired in 1985 and featured the third grade students from the original 1970s documentary *The Eye of the Storm*. In addition to showing footage from the 1970s documentary, *Frontline* arranged a reunion of the students and Elliott. They reflected on how the lesson had changed their lives in subsequent years and also influenced the type of life partner they selected and how they parented their own children. The *Frontline* special also documented Elliott performing the exercise with adults during a diversity training at one of Iowa's state prisons. Their reactions to the blue-eyed, brown-eyed exercise paralleled those of her third graders (PBS, 2003).

Elliott left teaching to become a full-time public speaker and diversity trainer in the mid-1980s. She is credited with being a forerunner of diversity training in corporate settings (Watson, 2008). Her blue-eyed, brown-eyed exercise addressed issues of integrating multiculturalism in the workplace at a time when more people of color were entering corporate settings and companies were being mandated by federal policies to employ some sort of diversity initiatives among their employees.

There is some empirical research that calls into question the effectiveness of Elliott's methods. Stewart (2003) and Byrnes (1990) asserted that Elliott's exercise has proven moderately effective in reducing prejudice for the long term. There is research that calls into question the potential negative impact Elliott's exercise has on the psychological well-being of those who participate in it because of the emotional stress caused by the simulation (Byrnes & Kiger, 1992; Williams & Giles, 1992). Additional criticisms of the exercise include that Elliott did not provide informed consent to her young students, who were required to participate in the activity. She also did not procure consent from their parents (Bloom, 2005). There is other research on the effectiveness of Elliott's diversity training that suggests white participants experience differential outcomes in race reduction toward Asians and Latinos compared to African Americans. Overall, whites have more positive attitudes toward Asians and Latinos, but not African Americans, after experiencing the exercise (Stewart, 2003). Finally, research has indicated that people experience high levels of stress during the activity because they do not want to appear racist or biased. This can lead to negative emotional responses during and after the exercise (Byrnes, 1990; Mirza, 2005; Stewart, 2003).

Despite some of these criticisms, Elliott's lesson has resonated with many different groups, and her main message has continued to remain relevant in today's cultural context. Her work has earned her several accolades, including invitations to the White House, interviews on *Oprah*, and countless speaking opportunities at colleges and universities (Bloom, 2005). With heated debates about race, class, immigration, and the rights of same-sex couples and members of the trans community, the blue-eyed, brown-eyed exercise continues to provide direct experiences with bias and effectively engages children and adults in conversations about empathy, perspective taking, stereotype threat, and reducing their own prejudices against people who are different from them.

DR. PAULINE CLANCE AND DR. SUZANNE IMES: THE IMPOSTER PHENOMENON—LESSONS ON THE ROLE OF SELF-DOUBT IN SHAPING SELF-EFFICACY

What's talent but the ability to get away with something?
—*Tennessee Williams*

Dr. Pauline Clance and Dr. Suzanne Imes are two American clinical psychologists who coined the concept "imposter phenomenon" (Clance & Imes, 1978). The *imposter phenomenon* (also referred to as IP and the "imposter syndrome") occurs when a person experiences doubt about their own accomplishments and has a persistent, internalized fear of being exposed as a fraud. Those who experience IP attribute their success and achievement to external sources like luck and good social contacts, rather than to internal sources like intelligence or ability. Furthermore, imposters feel inadequate and thus they do not believe that they deserve their successes (Caselman, Self, & Self, 2006).

In 1985, Clance developed the Imposter Cycle. The cycle begins with an achievement-related task, like a major research paper. Once the task has been assigned, the student immediately begins to have feelings of anxiety, self-doubt, and worry. As a result of these feelings, one of two things can happen: the student will overprepare the task or procrastinate on completing it.

When responding with procrastination, the student's initial response will turn into a frantic effort to complete the task. In the event that the task gets completed, the student will experience a brief period of accomplishment and feeling of relief. If positive feedback is given once the work has been completed and turned in, the student will overlook the positive feedback and attribute their success to luck. Conversely, when responding to the task with overpreparation, the student will perceive this successful outcome as a result of hard work (Clance, 1985).

Unfortunately, when experiencing the impostor cycle, gaining success through hard work or luck is not interpreted as a matter of actual ability. To the student, it does not really matter if she completed her paper using hard work or procrastination, even when the outcome results in a positive response. The positive feedback the student receives from others (e.g., a high score on the paper from her teacher) essentially has no effect on her perceptions of her success. This results in the student discounting the positive feedback she receives, further reinforcing the idea that she is a fraud and continuing the imposter cycle. With every subsequent journey through the imposter cycle, the student's feelings of perceived fraudulence, increased self-doubt, depression, and anxiety increase. Furthermore, as the imposter cycle repeats, the student's increased success leads to more intense feelings of anxiety about being "exposed" for who she thinks she really is, which is someone not worthy of the success and recognition she is receiving (Clance, 1985).

While much of the research on imposter phenomenon focuses on high-achieving women in corporate settings and STEM fields, and women of color, there is other evidence that supports the assertion that IP exists in men too (Topping, 1983, as cited by Hoang, 2013). There is also empirical evidence that demonstrates the harmful effects of IP in social, romantic, and academic contexts. Specifically, previous research has shown an inverse relationship between a student's academic self-concept and IP. When academic self-concept increases, the symptoms of impostor phenomenon decrease, and vice versa (Royse-Roskowski, 2010). According to Hoang (2013), some of the ways that the impostor phenomenon can impact students include:

- They make frequent self-comparisons to their peers regarding their academic performance.
- They questioned their basis of being accepted into their respective graduate program.
- They attributed successes like positive recognition, awards, and good grades to external factors, not their own abilities or intelligence.
- Their feelings of self-doubt can undermine and directly impact their academic performance.

According to research from the University of Texas at Austin, students of color or other marginalized identities may attribute their inclusion in competitive programs as a result of affirmative action (Cokley, McClain, Enciso, & Martinez, 2013). McAllum (2016) also found that millennial students have been impacted by IP, which has contributed to higher levels of academic-related anxiety and depression. McAllum referenced previous research conducted by Twenge and colleagues (2012), who conducted longitudinal research between 1966 and 2009. The study involved surveying 6.5 million university students in the United States. They found that students responding in later years of the study were statistically more likely to view themselves in a favorable light, referring to themselves as more academically "above average" and identifying themselves as having more drive to achieve, and better leadership, public speaking, and writing skills.

McAllum (2016) points out that even though millennials rated themselves as having higher levels of ability compared to older generations in the Twenge, Campbell, and Gentile (2012) study, their perceptions of academic self-concept are more contingent on external constraints like standardized test scores, grades, and other academic "trophies" like scholarships and membership in extracurricular activities. They are used to performing and having to achieve certain benchmarks. These external constraints can make them more vulnerable to increased anxiety, depression, and feelings of fraudulence. Specifically, grade-related stress has impacted rates of depression in college-age students. This results in millennial students either compensating by studying too hard to prove their ability to themselves or becoming overwhelmed by feeling of incompetence, which leads to overanalysis paralysis.

There are several measures to assess IP. In 1985, Clance developed the Clance Imposter Phenomenon Scale (CIP). Two other scales also exist: one developed by Harvey (1981) called the Harvey Impostor Phenomenon Scale (HIP), and the one developed by Kolligan and Sternberg (1991) called the Perceived Fraudulence Scale (PFS). The CIP scale and PFS have been found to produce the most valid and reliable responses when compared to the HIP scale. The CIP specifically measures fear of evaluation, fear of not being able to repeat success, and fear of being less capable than others (Hoang, 2013).

McAllum (2016) argues that the prescriptive teaching and assessment strategies that provide formative feedback and specific and formulaic expectations, and micromanage students' thinking perpetuate IP. Students think that simply following instructions or what was on the rubric should result in a high score, and that they should be rewarded for simply following an assignment's instruction. McAllum argues that students lack the ability to use innovation and creativity when approaching assignments and, as a result, take fewer risks and have less ability to recover from criticism or failure. These experiences can perpetuate feelings of the imposter phenomenon especially in situations where there is ambiguity or flexibility in how an assignment or assessment is completed. If students are constantly given specific instructions on what to do and how to do it, they will not have enough confidence in their own abilities or intelligence to complete the assignment or assessment. Thus, teachers should, to the extent that they can, provide opportunities for students to use their own metacognitive and creative skills, challenge their students, and teach their students to interpret "failure" as a challenge to be reexamined, not an event that should undermine their own feelings of self-worth or terminate a learning experience.

REFERENCES

Bloom, S. G. (September, 2005). Lesson of a lifetime. *Smithsonian Magazine.* Retrieved from https://www.smithsonianmag.com/science-nature/lesson-of-a-lifetime-72754306/

Byrnes, D. A. (1990). The effect of a prejudice-reduction simulation on attitude change. *Journal of Applied Social Psychology, 20,* 341–356. doi:10.1111/j.15591816.1990.tb00415.x.

Byrnes, D. A., & Kiger, G. (1992). Prejudice-reduction simulations: Ethics, evaluations, and theory into practice. *Simulation & Gaming, 23*(4), 457–471.

Carey, B. (2016, June 8). Jerome S. Bruner, who shaped understanding of the young mind, dies at 100. *New York Times.* Retrieved from https://www.nytimes.com/2016/06/09/science/jerome-s-bruner-who-shaped-understanding-of-the-young-mind-dies-at-100.html

Caselman, T. D., Self, P. A., & Self, A. L. (2006). Adolescent attributes contributing to the imposter phenomenon. *Journal of Adolescence, 29,* 395–405.

Clance, P. R. (1985). *The impostor phenomenon: Overcoming the fear that haunts your success.* Atlanta, GA: Peachtree.

Clance, P. R., & Imes, S. (1978). The Imposter Phenomenon in high achieving women: Dynamics and therapeutic intervention. *Psychotherapy Theory, Research, and Practice, 15* (3), 1–8.

Cokley, K., McClain, M., Enciso, A., & Martinez, M. (2013). An examination of the impact of minority status stress and impostor feelings on the mental health of diverse ethnic minority college students. *Journal of Multicultural Counselling and Development, 41*(2), 82–95. doi:10.1002/j.2161-1912.2013.00029.x

Fancher, R. E., & Rutherford, A. (2017). *Pioneers of psychology: A history* (5th ed.). New York, NY: Norton.

Harvey, J. C. (1981). The imposter phenomenon and achievement: A failure to internalize success. Unpublished doctoral dissertation. Temple University, Philadelphia.

Hergenhahn, B. R. (2014). *An introduction to the history of psychology* (7th ed.). Belmont, CA: Wadsworth.

Hoang, Q. (2013). The impostor phenomenon: Overcoming internalized barriers and recognizing achievements. *Vermont Connection, 34*(6), 41–51. Retrieved from http://scholarworks.uvm.edu/tvc/vol34/iss1/6

Kolligan, J., & Sternberg, R. J. (1991). Perceived fraudulence in young adults. Is there an "Imposter Syndrome"? *Journal of Personality Assessment, 56*(2), 308–326.

McAllum, K. (2016). Managing the imposter syndrome among the "trophy kids" creating teaching practices that develop independence in millennial students. *Communication Education, 65*(3), 363–365. http://dx.doi.org/10.1080/03634523.2016.1173715

Mirza, M. (December 12, 2005). Ticking all the boxes. *BBC News Magazine.* Retrieved http://news.bbc.co.uk/2/hi/uk_news/magazine/4521244.stm

PBS. (2003, January 1). An unfinished crusade [Interview with Jane Elliott]. *Frontline: A Class Divided.* Retrieved from https://www.pbs.org/wgbh/frontline/article/an-unfinished-crusade-an-interview-with-jane-elliott/

Royse Roskowki, J. C. (2010). *Impostor phenomenon and counselling self-efficacy: The impact of impostor feelings.* Unpublished dissertation. Ball State University, Muncie, IN.

Stewart, T. L. (2003). Do the "eyes" have it? A program evaluation of Jane Elliott's "Blue-Eyes/Brown-Eyes" diversity training exercise. *Journal of Applied Social Psychology, 33,* 1898–1921. doi:10.1111/j.1559-1816.2003.tb02086.x.

Twenge, J. M., Campbell, W. K., & Gentile, B. (2012). Generational increases in agentic self-evaluations among American college students 1966–2009. *Self and Identity, 11*(4), 409–427.

Watson, J. (2008, January). When diversity training goes awry. Retrieved from https://diverseeducation.com/article/10543/

Williams, A., & Giles, H. (1992). Prejudice-reduction simulations: Social cognition, intergroup theory, and ethics. *Simulation & Gaming, 23*(4), 472–484.

PART 2

Practice

6

Applications in Equitable Educational Design and Instructional Development

I've learned that people will forget what you said, people will forget what you did, but people will never forget how you made them feel.
                                                        —*Maya Angelou*

Classroom teachers can do much to set the tone for learning in a classroom. According to a recent study, Goodboy, Bolkan, and Baker (2018) found that teacher "misbehaviors" can cause a reduction in learning. Teachers who are rude or sarcastic can impede the learning process. If students deem that a teacher does not like them, they may actively choose not to learn. Herbert Kohl devised the concept of "Not-Learning" to explain how students, consciously or not, resist learning from a teacher who they perceive as not respecting their identity, language, culture, gender, sexuality, and/or race. This chapter will begin with some background on issues facing teachers and students, followed by theoretical frameworks of learning, and then how teachers can apply these concepts within their planning and teaching.

In order to create truly equitable learning environments for students, teachers must understand the difference between *equity* and *equality*. On its face, equality sounds like a great idea for classroom planning: treating all students the same. However, nothing can be further from the truth. The concept of equity, of providing for the needs of each individual student, is actually more important for teacher planning. For example, not all students begin at the same point, in terms of prior knowledge, academic readiness, literacy, and so on. If teachers plan to instruct all students in the exact same way, then they are actually doing harm to some of their students. It is thus crucial that teachers differentiate their instruction to meet the needs of all of their students.

BACKGROUND: ISSUES OF THE FIELD OF TEACHER EDUCATION

The contempt for the profession of education in general has much to do with its historical feminine origins, which exacerbates and perpetuates the problem by limiting who enters the field and who will educate our future teachers. At the same time, schools are often viewed as a panacea for all of society's problems; when schools cannot fix poverty, racism, and miseducation (and other systemic problems) they are deemed as failing, and the onus is placed on teachers.

As Britzman (2003) argues, "The problem of conformity in teacher education stems in part from its emphasis on training" (p. 46). As a field, we are not collectively focused on knowledge creation per se, or on critical analysis of schools and institutions and the culturally irresponsive individual and systemic practices that occur within, but rather on the practitioner aspects of the field such as writing proper lesson plans and objectives, following state and national standards, and practicing classroom management.

The notion of caring is prominent within teacher education and K–12 teaching, but it is a concept that is not critically examined or theorized, and often lacks the quality of *authentic caring* for marginalized students because it lacks the component of action and an underlying unexamination of racial bias.

Issues with Students

In a variety of school settings, many nondominant students feel "isolation and alienation" and that they have to leave certain aspects of their identities at the school door in order to be successful (Carter Andrews, 2012, p. 1). According to Carter Andrews, "These feelings often result from structural features within the school (e.g., tracking, lack of culturally diverse curriculum, biased teacher attitudes and beliefs, negative stereotypical beliefs held by White peers, and discriminatory policies) that represent

ERIK ERIKSON

Erik Erikson is known worldwide as a psychologist who focuses closely on the formation of adolescent identity and social behaviors. He immigrated to America in the mid-1930s but struggled to form a career because he lacked the proper education and was not fully fluent in English (Weiland, 1993). Even though Erikson was not successful when he first came to America, he managed to become a psychoanalysis theorist and create the Eight Stages of Psychosocial Development, one of the most renowned analyses of human development.

In Erikson's Eight Stages of Psychosocial Development there are eight different age groups and 16 different psychosocial development traits. In each stage of development, a crisis occurs based on the psychosocial development traits (Knight, 2017).

Identity is one of Erikson's stages, for ages 13–21. "Erikson described identity as a fundamental organizing principal which develops constantly throughout the lifespan. Identity provides a sense of continuity within the self and in interaction with others ('self-sameness'), as well as a frame to differentiate between self and others ('uniqueness') which allows the individual to function autonomously from others" (Ragelienė, 2016). Erikson initiated the idea of the adolescent identity crisis; this happens in the years of adolescence for these individuals are focusing on their future readiness and the societal pressure they will face in preparation (Cote & Levine, 1989); they are confused about who they are, how prepared they are, and believe they must fit into the norms in which society places upon them. The adolescent identity crisis is the largest crisis to happen throughout all of Erikson's Eight Stages of Psychosocial Development, for identity is the largest factor in understanding one's self, building self-confidence, and forming relationships—it's fully who a person is and how they understand the world around them.

—*Courtney Cepec*

forms of institutional racism" (p. 5). However, these feelings are not often critiqued within teacher education programs, or even broached. Warikoo, Sinclair, Fei, and Jacoby-Senghor (2016) found that teachers do in fact treat students differently based upon their race, yet many teacher educators continue to endorse the notion of colorblindness and the associated myth that if we just treat everyone the same and be nice, that everything will work out fine. Teacher education programs are not paying enough attention to research on race in schools, for it is easier not to—but I ask, easier for whom?

The civil rights of Students of Color within all schools is a cause for concern for critical pedagogues and social justice educators, but it should be for all teachers and teacher educators: a disproportionate number of Students of Color are referred for special education services and disciplined more frequently and unfairly. White middle-class children are thus the "unmarked norm" against which the developmental progress of other children is measured (O'Connor & Fernandez, 2006). Further, O'Connor and Fernandez (2006) and Blanchett (2006) argue that the underachievement of Students of Color is exacerbated by their disproportionality in underfunded schools with unqualified or uncertified teachers lacking experience.

What Is Learning?

According to Merriam-Webster, learning is "knowledge or skill acquired by instruction or study" (Learning, n.d.). Although a common belief within the field of educational psychology is that every child can learn, this is not the reality. Although we have decades of research indicating best practices to improve learning for all students, we do not always follow what the research tells us.

The Mythical Norm

The mythical norm, as defined by Audre Lorde, consists of the "unmarked" groups within a particular society. The mythical norm represents all of the majority characteristics or identity characteristics that are assigned the most value, power, privilege. These are the characteristics that are perceived as "normal" in any given society.

What Is Curriculum?

A particular curriculum involves the subject, topics, and materials utilized in a particular course. According to Eisner (2001) there are various types of curriculum, including the explicit curriculum (or what is openly acknowledged and taught), the implicit or hidden curriculum (or what is taught unintentionally), and the null curriculum (or what is ignored or unacknowledged).

Eisner calls the hidden curriculum the "implicit" curriculum, because it is what students learn about the values of the school and the expectations of adults, both of which may be unintended, which are not included in the formal curriculum but which students learn during their school experience. Hidden or implicit curriculums can serve to reinforce existing social inequalities. Longstreet and Shane (1993) define the "hidden curriculum" as "the kinds of learnings children derive from the very nature and organizational design of the public school, as well as from the behaviors and attitudes of teachers and administrators." The hidden curriculum of a classroom or school informs students, implicitly or explicitly, what the teacher or the school values or does not value.

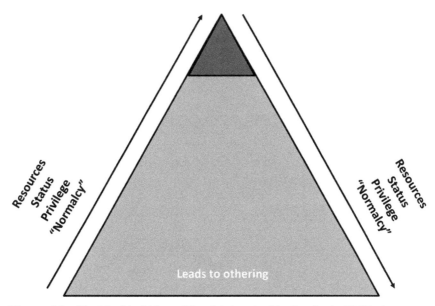

Group against which others are judged

Resources
Status
Privilege
"Normalcy"

Resources
Status
Privilege
"Normalcy"

Leads to othering

Figure 6.1 The Mythical Norm (Graphic inspired by Lorde, A. (1997). Age, race, class, and sex: Women redefining difference. *Cultural Politics*, 11, 374–380.)

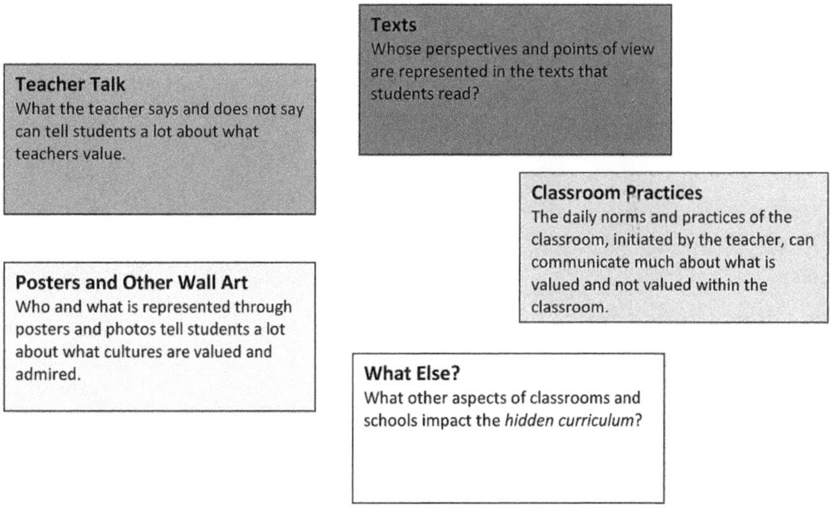

Texts
Whose perspectives and points of view are represented in the texts that students read?

Teacher Talk
What the teacher says and does not say can tell students a lot about what teachers value.

Classroom Practices
The daily norms and practices of the classroom, initiated by the teacher, can communicate much about what is valued and not valued within the classroom.

Posters and Other Wall Art
Who and what is represented through posters and photos tell students a lot about what cultures are valued and admired.

What Else?
What other aspects of classrooms and schools impact the *hidden curriculum*?

Figure 6.2 Keys to the Hidden Curriculum

How Do We Plan?

In our current educational milieu of standards and standardization, some teacher practitioners believe that the standards are the curriculum. However, it is important that teachers are intentional about their planning: designing lessons that are culturally relevant and sensitive to all cultures, attuned to various types of learning styles, student centered, and challenging.

THEORETICAL APPROACHES TO LEARNING

Although there are different theoretical approaches to learning, practitioners typically divide these into three types: behaviorist, cognitive constructivist, and social constructivist.

Behaviorism

John B. Watson (1878–1958) wrote "Psychology as the Behaviorist Views it" in 1913, an article considered to be the manifesto of behaviorism, outlining the basic principles of behaviorism:

> Psychology as the behaviorist views it is a purely objective experimental branch of natural science. Its theoretical goal is the prediction and control of behavior. Introspection forms no essential part of its methods, nor is the scientific value of its data dependent upon the readiness with which they lend themselves to interpretation in terms of consciousness. The behaviorist, in his efforts to get a unitary scheme of animal response, recognizes no dividing line between man and brute. The behavior of man, with all of its refinement and complexity, forms only a part of the behaviorist's total scheme of investigation. (p. 158)

Methodological Behaviorism

Ivan Pavlov's (1849–1936) study on dogs (1897) is likely the most famous experiment within the theoretical framework of behaviorism. Pavlov conditioned the dogs to salivate when they heard the ringing of a bell, after previously pairing the ringing of the bell with food. This is also known as *classical conditioning.*

Radical Behaviorism

Watson's approach to behaviorism suggests that at birth, the mind is a blank slate (tabula rasa). However, radical behaviorism views organisms as possessing both innate behaviors and behaviorally influenced by genes, biology, and environmental factors. B. F. Skinner (1904–1990) is considered to the founder of radical behaviorism and argued that the goal of the field of psychology should focus on predicting and controlling behavior. Skinner also believed that learning should be facilitated by positive reinforcement.

Skinner is perhaps best known for the "Skinner box," also known an *operant conditioning chamber.* This is an enclosed box containing a bar that an animal can press in order to obtain reinforcement, such as food or water. *Operant conditioning,* Skinner's best known theory, is based upon the idea that learning represents a change in overt behavior. Behavioral changes result from an individual's response to events occurring within their environment. Reinforcement is crucial in Skinner's Stimulus Response theory. A *reinforcement* is anything that strengthens the desired response, such as praise, grades, material goods, or a feeling of accomplishment. Negative reinforcements are anything resulting in the increased frequency of a response when the negative stimulus is withdrawn (this is different from punishment, which also results in reduced responses).

Skinner attempted to provide behavioral explanations for various cognitive phenomena. For example, he explained motivation in terms of deprivation and reinforcement schedules, and also attempted to account for verbal learning and language within the operant conditioning paradigm; this methodology was strongly rejected by linguists and psycholinguists such as Noam Chomsky.

Constructivism

Constructivism is the philosophical and scientific position that knowledge arises through a process of active construction.
—*Mascolol and Fischer*

Still one of the most popular educational theories, constructivism involves student-centered experiential and real-world learning. John Dewey (1859–1952) is often viewed as the philosophical founder of constructivism. Jerome Bruner (1915–2016) and Jean Piaget (1896–1980) are considered the chief theorists among the cognitive constructivists, while Lev Vygotsky (1896–1934) is the major theorist among the social constructivists.

Education is not preparation for life; education is life itself.
—*John Dewey*

John Dewey advocated for teaching in a manner that involves real-world, practical workshops where students can demonstrate knowledge through creativity and collaboration, rejecting the idea that schools should focus on repetitive tasks and rote memorization. Dewey felt that students should be provided with opportunities to think for themselves, participate in classroom curriculum development, and articulate their ideas, grounding education in authentic experiences.

John Dewey

Born in Burlington, Vermont, John Dewey (October 20, 1859–June 1, 1952) always had an affinity for learning. Dewey attended college at the University of Vermont, then going on to obtain his master's and doctorate in philosophy. Dewey would become a professor of philosophy and psychology at the University of Michigan.

John Dewey was a pioneer in the field of educational psychology. Unlike his predecessors, Dewey believed that education should not be a passive experience; rather, it should be active. Dewey believed that sitting in front of a teacher and listening to them lecture did not encourage critical thinking. Instead, he was an advocate for the philosophy of "learning by doing." Dewey theorized that humans too often attempt to conquer nature, rather than embrace it. Many attempt to tame nature into understandable and simple patterns. Dewey advocated for people to embrace the complexity of nature and learn from the lessons that it might teach.

Dewey was a founder of the pragmatism movement in education, which was a movement dedicated to the "learning by doing" philosophy. *Pragmatism* refers to the practical application of learned knowledge to real-world situations. Pragmatism encourages learners to take a step beyond the classroom in order to combine learned knowledge in order to synthesize new knowledge. Pragmatism encourages learners to scaffold their learning, while applying it to relevant problems and goals. Dewey believed that one many best learn from studying the patterns of different occurrences or objects. By connecting different ideas, theories, objects, and events, one may best discern the meaningful life lessons. One must experience the world and combine various approaches to fully understand a topic.

Dewey's work has left a profound impact on the education community. As a result of his works, many modern teachers seek to find practical applications to various lessons, so that students feel that the material is real, relevant, and rigorous. Prior to Dewey's word, education was often a rigid affair, in which lectures and books were often the sole method of educating pupils. Students did not interact with nature or the world within them; they stayed in their seats within the four walls of a classroom. Dewey and the Pragmatism Movement in education allowed for students to apply their knowledge in meaningful in memorable ways.

Throughout his lifetime, Dewey also worked to spread his educational theories and philosophies across the globe. Acting as a traveling lecturer, Dewey visited the Soviet Union, Turkey, China, and Mexico. According to Selcuk Uygun in his article, "The Impact of John Dewey on the Teacher Education System in Turkey" (2008) while Dewey was lecturing within each country, he also served as an advisor to each government regarding effective education strategies. Within Turkey, Dewey aided the National Ministry of Education as the organization sought to improve upon existing educational framework within the country. In order to provide the best possible education to all students, the National Ministry of Education incorporated Dewey's education into its curriculum.

Service learning is one such pedagogical strategy that has evolved out of the Dewey movement. Service learning seeks to provide students with the opportunity to push students out of the classroom and to work with the world around them. Students use the knowledge that they developed within the classroom in order to develop a service project to aid their community. Often, students are able to leave the classroom and work with their community members in order to resolve a relevant issue. This generates a meaningful and authentic learning experience.

Dewey's ideas revolutionized the ways in which education systems worked across the globe. Dewey's theories and educational philosophies had a profound impact on the field of education, and continue to inspire new pedagogical strategies that encourage students to gain practical skills through problem solving and interaction.

—Brianna Boehlke

Cognitive Constructivism

Cognitive constructivism is rooted in cognitive psychology and biology, emphasizing how learners create meaning and how knowledge is constructed or created. Piaget's theories are fundamental to constructivist education for they seek to explain how knowledge develops: mental structures are created from previous structures within individuals and do not develop directly from environmental stimuli. Thus, knowledge is not passively transferred from the environment to an individual. Piaget explicated three essential components to knowledge construction: equilibration, assimilation, and accommodation.

- *Equilibration* is the central learning mechanism and the motivation behind cognitive development.
- *Assimilation* and *Accommodation* are complementary processes to deal with the cognitive conflict.

These processes are linked, where the state of equilibrium is sought. The learner either applies previously acquired skills to a new situation in order to understand it or adjusts the skills or accommodates acquired skills to gain better understanding.

Table 6.1   Piaget's Developmental Stages

Stage	Age	Skill	Example
Sensorimotor stage	(0–2 years)	Intelligence takes the form of motor actions	Object permanence
Preoperation stage	(3–7 years)	Intuitive in nature	Egocentric thought
Concrete operational stage	(8–11 years)	Logical but depends upon concrete referents	Inductive logic begins
Formal operations stage	(12–15 years)	Thinking involves abstractions	Abstract thought emerges

Piaget rejected the idea that learning involved passive assimilation. Instead, Piaget argued that learning is a dynamic process comprising successive stages of adaption to reality, where learners actively construct knowledge by creating and testing their own theories of the world.

Piaget developed a model for understanding developmental and intellectual growth in children, helping us to understand how and in what stages children typically learn. These cognitive structures change through the processes of adaptation: assimilation and accommodation. *Assimilation* involves interpreting events in terms of existing cognitive structures; *accommodation* involves changing cognitive structures in order to make sense of the environment. In general, cognitive development is the constant effort to adapt to the environment through assimilation and accommodation.

While Piaget's stages of cognitive development are associated with specific age spans, they vary for every individual, and each stage has many detailed structural forms. For example, the concrete operational stage contains more than 40 distinct structures including classification and relations, spatial relationships, time, movement, chance, number, conservation, and measurement.

Social Constructivism

Social constructivism was developed by Lev Vygotsky (1896–1934). Vygotsky rejected Piaget's idea that it is possible to separate learning from its social context. Vygotsky believed that every function in a child's development is twofold: first, learning occurs on the social level and later on the individual level; second, between people (inter-psychological) and then inside the mind (intra-psychological). This applies equally to voluntary

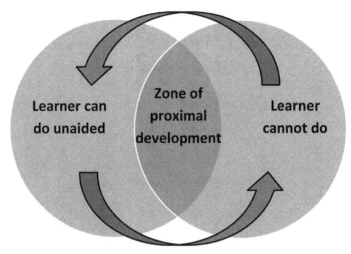

Figure 6.3   Vygotsky's ZPD

attention, logical memory, and the formation of concepts. All the higher functions originate as actual relationships between individuals.

When Vygotsky died in 1934, most of his publications had still not been translated into English and would not be until after 1960.

Vygotsky argues that social interaction plays a fundamental role in learning. Additionally, the potential for cognitive development depends upon the "zone of proximal development" (ZPD), a level of development attained when learners engage in social behavior. That is, when a learner is paired with another learner whose skills are more advanced, the initial learner is more likely to improve. Gains in learning through engaging in ZPD can be developed when adult guidance or peer collaboration exceeds what can be attained alone.

Influenced by Vygotsky, American psychologist Jerome Bruner (1915–2016) became convinced that students could usually learn more than had been traditionally expected as long as they were given appropriate guidance and resources. He called such support "instructional scaffolding"—that is, a temporary framework used to construct buildings allowing a much stronger structure to be built within. As Bruner argues, "We [constructivist educators] begin with the hypothesis that any subject can be taught effectively in some intellectually honest form to any child at any stage of development" (1960, p. 33). The concept of scaffolding was key to Bruner's statement—the importance of providing appropriate guidance at the proper time. When scaffolding is utilized, Bruner argued, students learn more.

Bruner initiated curriculum change based on the notion that learning is active and a social process where students build new knowledge based on

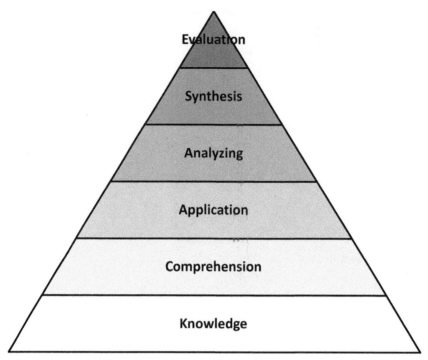

Figure 6.4   Bloom's Taxonomy, Original Version (Adapted from: https://www
.youtube.com/watch?v=__YdXxwBZ7Q)

their current knowledge. Bruner provides the following principles of constructivist learning:

- Instruction: concerned with the experiences and contexts that make
  students willing and able to learn (readiness).
- Instruction: structured so that it can be easily understood by the student (spiral organization).
- Instruction: designed to facilitate extrapolation (moving beyond the
  information given).
- Curriculum: should be organized in a spiral so students continually
  build upon what they have already learned.

Implications for Constructivist Teaching

Whether or not one identifies as a constructivist teacher, there are various effective strategies stemming from this theoretical tradition that are
effective in assisting students develop their thinking.

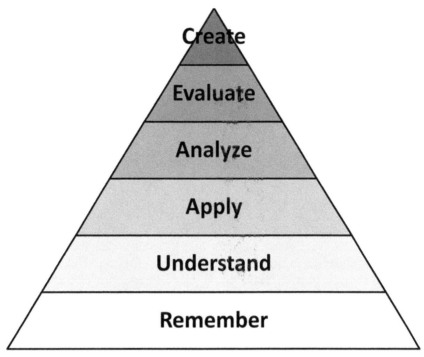

Figure 6.5   Bloom's Taxonomy, New Version (Adapted from: https://cft.vander bilt.edu/guides-sub-pages/blooms-taxonomy/)

Content organization is one of these strategies. Systematic content organization enables teachers to devise learning activities tailored to students' cognitive abilities, social interests, and so on. One of the most widely used frameworks for organizing content is Bloom's Taxonomy, designed by Benjamin Bloom (1913–1999). This schema can also help to ensure that teachers are planning lessons that tap into students' higher-level thinking skills (Bloom, 1956). Bloom's taxonomy describes six kinds of learning goals that teachers can expect in inspire in students, ranging from simple recall of knowledge to complex evaluation of knowledge.

Bloom's taxonomy makes useful distinctions among different types of knowledge, and potentially assists in selecting activities targeting students' ZPD. The original taxonomy consisted of nouns: the lowest level consisting of knowledge, which can represent rote memorization, and the highest level representing evaluation. (See Figure 6.4.)

The second iteration of the taxonomy consists of verbs, signifying a more action-oriented model. In this version, the highest level is creation—indicating creativity or the creation of new knowledge as the highest level. (See Figure 6.5.)

What Teachers Can Gain from Bloom's Taxonomy

No matter what grade or type of student, teachers should always be cognizant of the higher levels of Bloom's Taxonomy when lesson planning. If a teacher's lesson relies only on remembering and understanding (knowledge and comprehension), then that teacher is not adequately challenging their students—no matter the grade. It is crucial that teachers have high expectations for all of their students, and even, ideally, involve students in the actual planning and classroom instruction—that is truly higher-order thinking.

MULTIPLE INTELLIGENCES (HOWARD GARDNER)

Howard Gardner (1943–) devised his theory of multiple intelligences in the early 1980s. The theory suggests that there are a number of distinct forms of intelligence, or preferred learning styles, that each individual possesses to varying degrees. Gardner proposed seven primary intelligences: body-kinesthetic, interpersonal (e.g., social skills), intrapersonal (e.g., insight, metacognition), linguistic, logical-mathematical, musical, and spatial.

According to Gardner, teaching and learning should focus on the strengths of each learner. For example, if a student has strong spatial or musical intelligences, they should be encouraged to develop them. Additionally, the different intelligences represent not only different content domains but also learning modalities. Gardener argues that assessments should measure all forms of intelligence, not just linguistic and logical-mathematical—as standardized and high-stakes assessments typically do.

Gardner also stresses the cultural context of multiple intelligences. Different cultures emphasize particular intelligences. Gardner (1983) discusses the spatial abilities of the Puluwat people (Caroline Islands), who use these skills to navigate their canoes.

CONDITIONS OF LEARNING (ROBERT GAGNE)

Robert Gagne (1916–2002) argues that there are five different types of learning, each requiring different types of instruction: verbal information, intellectual skills, cognitive strategies, motor skills, and attitudes. Specific internal and external conditions are necessary for each type of learning. For example, with cognitive strategies, opportunities must be provided to the learner to practice developing solutions to problems.

Gagne suggests that learning tasks for intellectual skills can be organized hierarchically: stimulus recognition, response generation, procedure following, use of terminology, discriminations, concept formation, rule

Table 6.2 Bloom's Verbs for Planning

Level	Definition	Sample Verbs					Sample Behaviors
Creating	Students put together elements and form a working idea through planning, generating, or producing.	Design Compose Create Plan Formulate Negotiate Originate	Invent Hypothesize Write Compile Construct Propose Reorganize	Develop Integrate Modify Organize Prepare Simulate Structure	Produce Rearrange Rewrite Adapt Arrange Make Facilitate	Assemble Collaborate Devise Express	Students are at the highest order of thinking skills and can successfully design an organized plan to understand the educational objectives, combining cognitive, affective, and psychomotor domain.
Evaluating	Student forms an opinion based on criteria and standards through verification and critique.	Criticize Evaluate Order Appraise Judge Support	Decide Discriminate Recommend Assess Convince Defend	Measure Grade Rank Score Select Test	Argue Conclude Consider Critique Debate Distinguish	Editorialize Justify Persuade Rate Weigh Validate	Students will judge the effectiveness of a work product using Bloom's new taxonomy.
Analyzing	Student breaks down information into parts to determine the relationship between each part through differentiation, organization, and attribution.	Analyze Compare Classify Contrast Distinguish Test	Infer Separate Categorize Differentiate Discriminate Plan	Divide Order Subdivide Survey Advertise Organize	Conclude Correlate Deduce Devise Diagram Question	Dissect Estimate Illustrate Outline	Students will compare and contrast thinking and emotional learning.

(continued)

Table 6.2 (continued)

Level	Definition	Sample Verbs					Sample Behaviors
Applying	Student executes/implements a procedure.	Solve	Demonstrate	Predict	Act	Determine	Students follow a rubric utilizing each level of Bloom's new taxonomy to successfully complete a project.
		Apply	Experiment	Manipulate	Practice	Develop	
		Illustrate	Relate	Paint	Administer	Operate	
		Modify	Complete	Prepare	Articulate	Employ	
		Calculate	Construct	Produce	Chart	Explain	
		Change	Dramatize	Report	Collect	Interview	
		Simulate	Interpret	Teach	Compute	List	
Understanding	Student creates meaning of information through interpretation, exemplification, classification, summarization, explanation, comparison, and inferences.	Explain	Classify	Associate	Indicate	Translate	Students will explain the purpose of Bloom's taxonomy by evaluating the ethos of a lesson or situation.
		Describe	Compare	Convert	Infer	Cite	
		Interpret	Discuss	Demonstrate	Relate	Generalize	
		Paraphrase	Distinguish	Estimate	Restate	Group	
		Summarize	Predict	Express	Select	Order	
Remembering	Student recognizes and recalls information from long-term memory.	Define	Name	Memorize	Tell	Recite	Students can successfully define all six levels of Bloom's new taxonomy.
		Identify	State	Quote	Copy	Record	
		Describe	Match	Recall	Duplicate	Repeat	
		Label	Select	Reproduce	Enumerate	Retell	
		List	Locate	Tabulate	Omit		

Adapted from http://thepeakperformancecenter.com/educational-learning/thinking/blooms-taxonomy/blooms-taxonomy-revised/

application, and problem solving. The purpose of the hierarchical structure is to identify prerequisites that should be completed to facilitate learning.

Gagne also outlines nine instructional events and corresponding cognitive processes:

1. Gaining attention (reception)
2. Informing learners of the objective (expectancy)
3. Stimulating recall of prior learning (retrieval)
4. Presenting the stimulus (selective perception)
5. Providing learning guidance (semantic encoding)
6. Eliciting performance (responding)
7. Providing feedback (reinforcement)
8. Assessing performance (retrieval)
9. Enhancing retention and transfer (generalization) (Gagne, 1965)

The above should satisfy the necessary conditions for learning and serve as the basis for designing instruction and selecting appropriate curriculum.

CRITERION REFERENCED INSTRUCTION (ROBERT MAGER)

Robert Mager (1923–) developed Criterion Referenced Instruction (CRI), which is a comprehensive set of methods for the design and delivery of training programs. Some of the critical aspects include (1) identifying what should be learned through the creation of goals or tasks, (2) specifying the exact outcomes students are to accomplish and how they will be evaluated (the criterion) through written performance or behavioral objectives, (3) criterion referenced testing, the evaluation of learning using the knowledge and skills specified in the objectives, and (4) the development of learning modules tied to objectives. The positive thing about criterion referenced testing or assessment is that there is no bell curve. The assessment is not normed, thus all students can be successful, as they are not compared to one another but on their mastery of the content. CRI is based upon the ideas of mastery learning and performance-based instruction.

MASTERY LEARNING

First formally proposed by Benjamin Bloom in 1968 and originally called "learning for mastery," mastery learning is an instructional strategy and educational philosophy maintaining that students must achieve a level of mastery prior to moving on to other information.

For example, if a student does not achieve mastery on an assessment, they are given additional supports in learning and reviewing the information and then retested. This cycle continues until mastery. Mastery learning suggests that the focus of instruction should be the time required for different students to learn the same content and achieve the same level of mastery. This is in contrast with more traditional approaches to teaching, which focus more on differences in student ability, and where they are all given approximately the same amount of time to learn and in the same way.

In mastery learning, the onus is on the teacher to increase learning and, ultimately, mastery; student "failure" is deemphasized and viewed as due to some lack in instruction, and not necessarily the lack of student ability.

EXPERIENTIAL LEARNING (CARL ROGERS)

Rogers (1902–1987) distinguished two types of learning: cognitive (meaningless) and experiential (significant). *Cognitive learning* corresponds to academic knowledge such as learning vocabulary or memorizing multiplication tables, and *experiential learning* refers to applying knowledge such as learning about the building trades in order to build a house. Experiential learning addresses the desires of the learner. The characteristics of experiential learning include personal involvement, self-initiated, self-evaluation, evaluated by learner, and long-term impact on the learner.

According to Rogers, all humans possess a natural propensity to learn. The role of the teacher is to facilitate this learning, which includes setting a positive learning environment, clarifying the purposes of the learning, organizing and making learning resources available, balancing the intellectual and emotional components of learning, and providing feedback to learners without dominating the learning environment.

According to Rogers, learning occurs when students participate completely in the learning process and have buy-in for the task; curriculum is created using practical, social, personal, or relevant research problems; and self-evaluation is the primary method of assessment.

OTHER CONCEPTS RELEVANT TO PLANNING AND TEACHING: INTERSECTIONALITY

Intersectionality is the study of intersections between various forms or systems of oppression. Individuals may experience multiple forms of oppression simultaneously. For example, individuals who possess multiple statuses are often expected to rank their identity categories or are expected to identify with one identity status over another, such as gender versus race. However, the experience of identifying both as a woman and as another minority cannot be understood in terms only of race or gender, but must include the interactions between race and gender, which frequently reinforce one another (Crenshaw, 1993).

Intersectionality as a theoretical construct functions to describe the experience of individuals possessing interlocking oppressions and/or multiple minority statuses and is a depiction of the lived experience of individuals who possess identities that may or may not conflict in their political orientations. The concept presupposes that a single lens is inadequate in communicating the various and diverse oppressions that many face.

The concept of intersectionality is inherently culturally responsive, and we must be cognizant of our students' various and interlocking identities in order to truly meet their needs.

See: https://www.ted.com/talks/kimberle_crenshaw
_the_urgency_of_intersectionality

OTHER CONCEPTS RELEVANT TO PLANNING AND TEACHING: ATTRIBUTION ERROR

According to attribution theory, the personality characteristics (and personal accomplishments) of women and men are often explained differently (Kirchmeyer, 1998). For example, women's accomplishments may be attributed to luck or other external factors; likewise, women's advancement may be attributed to affirmative action and not to personal ability (as are men's accomplishments) (Kirchmeyer, 1998; Lyness & Thompson, 1997). Moreover, a woman's performance (on tasks traditionally conceived of as male) is often attributed to luck or to effort, and men's performance to skill (Greenhaus & Parasuraman, 1993). The reason for the former is because such successes violate people's (observers) sex role expectations; to avoid cognitive dissonance, observers attribute negative attributes to women, such that women are not responsible for their own successes—they just "got lucky." Similar attribution errors are made for other non-dominant identities.

OTHER CONCEPTS RELEVANT TO PLANNING AND TEACHING: CULTURAL MISMATCH

What Linda Darling-Hammond calls "cultural mismatch" (2010), or the gaps between students and teachers in terms of their racial, cultural, ethnic, social, and linguistic identities, can impact students' level of comfort in school as well as how successful they are in their learning. Students who, for example, speak nonstandard forms of English may experience language devaluation in school and may be more inclined to leave school (Charity Hudley & Mallinson, 2011). According to Salazar (2013), teachers should focus on student assets, as opposed to focusing on deficits, by utilizing students' prior knowledge and connecting it to new learning, thereby legitimizing students' home languages and cultures. In short, students are viewed as the experts.

Again, cultural mismatches within schools can contribute to misunderstanding that harms students. For example, differences in intonation when asking questions, responding to questions, and in other everyday interactions may be viewed as a lack of interest and enthusiasm, disrespect, or even lack of ability, and can account for the larger percentages of students of color receiving more behavioral referrals and referrals for special education services from white teachers (and standard English speakers) than their white counterparts (Charity Hudley & Mallinson, 2011). Schools with the highest populations of nondominant or minority students refer more students for special education services; this mislabeling affects African American children twice as much as white children (Smitherman, 2006).

REFERENCES

Blanchett, W. J. (2006). Disproportionate representation of African American students in special education: Acknowledging the role of white privilege and racism. *Educational Researcher, 35*(6), 24–28.

Bloom, B. (Ed.). (1956). *Taxonomy of educational objectives: Handbook #1: Cognitive domain.* Boston, MA: Addison-Wesley Longman.

Britzman, D. P. (2003). *Practice makes practice: A critical study of learning to teach.* New York, NY: State University of New York Press.

Bruner, J. (1960). *The process of education.* Cambridge, MA: Harvard University Press.

Carter Andrews, D. J. (2012). Black achievers' experiences with racial spotlighting and ignoring in a predominantly white high school. *Teachers College Record, 114*, 1–46.

Charity Hudley, A. H., & Mallinson, C. (2011). *Understanding English language variation in U.S. schools.* New York, NY: Teachers College Press.

Cote, J. E., & Levine, C. G. (1989). An empirical test of Erikson's theory of ego identity formation. *Youth & Society, 20*(4), 388.

Crenshaw, K. (1993). Mapping the margins: Intersectionality, identity politics, and violence against women of color. *Stanford Law Review, 43*, 1241–1299.

Darling Hammond, L. (2010). *The flat world and education: How America's commitment to equity will determine our future.* New York, NY: Teachers College Press.

Eisner, E. (2001). *The educational imagination: On the design and evaluation of school programs* (3rd ed.). Columbus, OH: Merrill//Prentice Hall.

Gagne, R. M. (1965). *The conditions of learning and theory of instruction*. Belmont, CA: Wadsworth.

Gardner, H. (1983). *Frames of mind: The theory of multiple intelligences*. New York, NY: Basic Books.

Goodboy, A. K. Bolkan, S., & Baker, J. P. (2018). Instructor misbehaviors impede students' cognitive learning: testing the causal assumption. *Communication Education, 67*(3). doi: 10.1080/03634523.2018.1465192

Greenhaus, J. H., & Parasuraman, S. (1993). Job performance attributions and career advancement prospects: An examination of gender and race effects. *Organizational Behavior and Human Decision Processes, 55*, 273–297.

Kirchmeyer, C. (1998). Determinants of managerial career success: Evidence and explanation of male/female differences. *Journal of Management, 24*(6), 673–692.

Knight, Z. G. (2017). A proposed model of psychodynamic psychotherapy linked to Erik Erikson's eight stages of psychosocial development. *Clinical Psychology & Psychotherapy, 25*(5), 1047–1058.

Longstreet, W. S., and Shane, H. G. (1993) *Curriculum for a new millennium*. Boston, MA: Allyn and Bacon.

Lyness, K. S., & Thompson, D. E. (1997). Above the glass ceiling? A comparison of matched samples of female and male executives. *Journal of Applied Psychology, 82*(3), 359–375.

O'Connor, C., & Fernandez, S. D. (2006). Race, class, and disproportionality: Reevaluating the relationship between poverty and special education placement. *Educational Researcher, 35*(6), 6–11.

Ragelienė, T. (2016). Links of adolescent's identity development and relationship with peers: A systematic literature review. *Journal of the Canadian Academy of Child & Adolescent Psychiatry, 25*(2), 97–105.

Salazar, M. (2013). A humanizing pedagogy: Reinventing the principles and practice of education as a journey toward liberation. *Review of Research in Education, 37*, 121–148.

Smitherman, G. (2006). *Word from the mother: Language and African Americans*. New York, NY: Routledge.

Uygun, S. (2008). The impact of John Dewey on the teacher education system in Turkey. *Asia-Pacific Journal of Teacher Education, 36*(4), 291–307.

Warikoo, N., Sinclair, S., Fei, J., & Jacoby-Senghor, D. (2016). Examining racial bias in education: A new approach. *Educational Researcher, 45*(9), 508–514.

Weiland, S. (1993). Erik Erikson: Ages, stages, and stories. *Generations, 17*(2), 17.

7

Classroom Management and Student Motivation: An Intersectional Perspective

Classroom teachers often struggle with classroom management, or managing student behavior to create a classroom that is optimal for learning. There are many psychological factors that play into the management of a classroom, including the personalities, learning preferences, and emotional development of the students and the teacher. Although there is not one magic bullet to manage a classroom, there are some empirically tested strategies found to be effective. Additionally, issues of classroom discipline can be subjective; perhaps the most subjective issue is behaviors that fall into the category of "student disrespect." Often, issues of perceived disrespect stem from racial and cultural differences and are impacted by implicit bias. This chapter will discuss current issues surrounding classroom management.

VOCABULARY TERMS

Applied Behavior Analysis (ABA)

Applied behavior analysis is a process designed to understand and change behavioral deficits and social skills, typically for special needs students. Applied behavior analysis is based upon the principles of positive reinforcement and discrete trial training, where skills are broken into smaller components, taught in order, and mastered over time.

Classroom Management

Classroom management is a complex process involving how a classroom is run, including rules/procedures/routines, furniture arrangement, discipline policies, expectations for interactions with others, lesson planning, and so on.

Corporal Punishment

Corporal punishment involves disciplining students in a physical manner when they break a rule. "Paddling," a form of spanking typically done with a wooden paddle, was a common form of corporal punishment. According to the civil rights data of 2014, black students are twice as likely as white students to experience corporal punishment (U.S. Department of Education Office for Civil Rights, 2014).

See below for the National Association of School Psychologists position on corporal punishment (2014):

> The National Association of School Psychologists (NASP) opposes the use of corporal punishment in schools and supports ending its use in all schools. Further, NASP resolves to educate the public about the effects of corporal punishment, to provide alternatives to its use, and to encourage research and the dissemination of information about corporal punishment's effects and alternatives. Corporal punishment of students is the intentional infliction of pain or discomfort and/or the use of physical force upon a student with the intention of causing the student to experience bodily pain so as to correct or punish the student's behavior (Bitensky, 2006). In the United States, the most typical form of school corporal punishment is striking a student's buttocks with a wooden paddle by a school authority because it is believed that the student has disobeyed a rule. Worldwide there are an increasing number of countries that have banned corporal punishment in schools (Zolotor & Puzia, 2010); however, the United States does not have any national policy concerning it (Robinson, Funk, Beth, & Bush, 2005). Within the United States, corporal punishment was first banned in the state of New Jersey in 1867. It is still currently allowed in schools across 19

states (Rollins, 2012); it has been banned in prisons and mental health institutions (Andero & Stewart, 2002). In 2011, a bill calling for an end to corporal punishment in all states (H.R.3027.IH—Ending Corporal Punishment in Schools Act of 2012) was proposed with 12 cosponsors in the House, but it did not make it out of the Early Childhood, Elementary, and Secondary Education subcommittee (Library of Congress, 2013).

Federal civil rights data indicate that students experienced corporal punishment in 21 states and more than 4,000 schools throughout the United States during the 2013–14 school year. In the 2013–14 academic year, Texas, Alabama, Mississippi, Arkansas, Georgia, Tennessee, and Oklahoma utilized corporal punishment the most, and it was most widespread in Mississippi, where over 50 percent of students attend a school that utilizes paddling or other forms of corporal punishment. Problematically, some students were physically disciplined in states that actually prohibit the practice.

CORPORAL PUNISHMENT

If a parent regularly uses forms of corporal punishment like spanking his child, then that child may be more likely use physical means when interacting with her peers to express certain emotions like anger or frustration. It is not enough to tell her not to hit someone; her parent needs to demonstrate other, more appropriate means of dealing with his anger and frustration with her when she does something that warrants punishment. *Corporal punishment* is defined as the use of physical force with the intent to cause pain. The pain is intended to reduce the existing behavior and subsequently lead to a change in behavior when a child is in a similar situation in the future. With parents, this typically takes the form of spanking with an open hand. In a school setting, corporal punishment is typically administered with a wooden paddle. Some states, like Texas, expand the definition of corporal punishment to include hitting, slapping, or other physical force as acceptable means to cause pain and control behavior (Gershoff & Font, 2016).

Unfortunately, research indicates that the intended impacts of using corporal punishment are limited and somewhat ineffective. Corporal punishment does not consistently work to immediately redirect negative behavior from occurring. It also fails to redirect the negative behavior to more appropriate behavior. Research indicates that children who are spanked for doing something may stop at the time the corporal punishment is administered but are likely to repeat that same negative behavior again and do so in a more vigorous and aggressive manner (Gershoff & Font, 2016).

When corporal punishment is used in school settings, it also has several negative effects including: impacting students' general self-concepts, increasing issues like anxiety and depression, disengaging students from their school work, poorer academic performance, higher risks of dropping out, negative impacts on relationships with teachers and peers, higher rates of aggression and defiance, and it has even been linked to future domestic violence in some students (Berlin et al., 2009; Gershoff, Lansford, Sexton, Davis-Kean, & Sameroff, 2012; Han, 2011; Rollins, 2012).

The American Academy of Pediatrics (AAP) recently reaffirmed their original 1998 policy statement regarding effective and ineffective uses of disciplining children. Reinforcing the findings of existing AAP research, the Council on Child Abuse and Neglect, Committee on Psychological Aspects of Child and Family Health found (1) forms of aversive punishment like spanking, yelling, or publicly shaming children are not effective long-term disciplinary strategies, and (2) these forms of aversive punishment have long-term negative impacts on children's behavior, cognitive, psychosocial, and emotional development. The policy statement also addressed the impacts of using punishments like spanking and yelling on special populations, including foster children and children with special physical and intellectual needs. The research explains how using corporal punishment can lead to aggressiveness in children and, in some instances, reflects a cycle of intergenerational abuse from parent to child to grandchild (Sege et al., 2018).

This AAP's recent policy statement also reiterates the research and the long-standing positions that many professional organizations hold regarding the use of corporal punishment. There are well over a hundred professional organizations that officially oppose the use of corporal punishment in the home, school, or any other facility that involves the care of children. These professional organizations include the American Psychological Association, the National Parent-Teacher Association, National Education Association, American Civil Liberties Union and Human Rights Watch, and National Association of School Psychologists.

In addition to these professional organizations opposing the use of corporal punishment, there is also federal legislation that exists to protect students. According to the National Association of School Nurses (2015) this legislation was prompted by a 2009 report from the U.S. Government Accountability Office (USGAO) that cited that states did not consistently implement laws regarding the use of seclusion and physical restraints in educational settings. As a result of these inconsistencies, there were cases where students incurred physical injury or death at the hands of untrained and unvetted school personnel. The report clarified what they meant by restraint and seclusion. The definitions included physical restraint (e.g., school personnel physically prohibiting movement in a student), mechanical restraint (e.g., devices used to restrict movement in a student, with exception of equipment that has been prescribed by medical professionals), and seclusion (e.g., forced solitary confinement of a student).

Upon the release of the USGAO report, the U.S. House of Representatives passed H.R. 4274, "The Preventing Harmful Restraint and Seclusion in Schools Act" in March 2010. This law was amended to the "Keeping All Students Safe Act" and extended the types of prohibited restraints to include chemical restraints (e.g., unprescribed drugs or medication that resulted in restriction of free movement) or anything else that restricted breathing. In order to provide protection for more vulnerable student populations the law also mandated that the use of physical restraint or seclusion should not be written into a student's IEP, although they could be written into a school's crisis plan. Further amendments came in October of 2010 when certain disability advocacy groups asserted that children with behavioral disorders could be disproportionately targeted by these policies. The bill was refiled as H.R. 1381 by the House of Representatives in 2011, under the same name. In 2012, the United States Department of Education published a document outlining guidelines entitled *Restraint and Seclusion: Resource Document*. A few years later, Congress passed the "Ending Corporal Punishment in Schools Act of 2014" defining corporal punishment as involving paddling students with a wooden paddle (National Association of School Nurses, 2015).

Despite the large body of substantiated research validating the negative effects of corporal punishment, as well as ample formal opposition including federal legislation, as many as 19 states still allow K–12 schools to implement forms of corporal punishment on students. According to Gershoff and Font (2016), who produced an extensive report on the status of corporal punishment across U.S. schools, 163,000 students were subjected to corporal punishment during the 2011–2012 school year. Additionally, more than half of the schools in southern states like Mississippi, Arkansas, and Alabama use corporal punishment.

Gershoff and Font (2016) also found that students of color, disabled students, and male students were disproportionately targets of corporal punishment. In states like Mississippi and Alabama, students of color—particularly African American males—were 51 percent more likely to be paddled or otherwise struck compared to their white counterparts in more than half of the state's districts. They also found that disabled students were more than 50 percent likely to experience corporal punishment compared to their nondisabled counterparts in states like Alabama, Arkansas, Mississippi, and Tennessee. Finally, male students were three times as likely as female students to receive corporal punishment in states like Alabama, Tennessee, Mississippi, and Louisiana.

—*Jennifer L. Martin*

Discrete Trial Training (DTT)

A component of applied behavioral analysis where a skill is broken down into basic components so that the components can be taught one at a time.

Functional Behavior Analysis (FBA)

A process describing a student's disruptive behaviors, potential reasons for these behaviors, and proposed interventions intended to teach new behaviors to replace undesired behaviors.

Locus of Control

The concept of *locus of control* developed out of social learning theory and is defined by Rotter (1990) as follows:

> Briefly, internal versus external control refers to the degree to which persons expect that a reinforcement or an outcome of their behavior is contingent on their own behavior or personal characteristics versus the degree to which persons expect that the reinforcement or outcome is a function of chance, luck, or fate, is under the control of powerful others, or is simply unpredictable. (p. 489)

Although the concept of locus of control is often defined as a personality characteristic, it is subject to change with a person's experiences. An individual's locus of control is not a static phenomenon. As Chubb, Fertman and Ross (1997) state, "An individual does not have a clearly defined internal or external locus of control, since locus of control is a continuous variable, not a dichotomous one, and can vary situationally" (p. 115). To summarize, an individual's locus of control can be altered.

Positive Behavior Support (PBS)/Positive Behavioral Interventions and Supports (PBIS)

An all-school approach to create more positive behaviors in students toward prosocial skills.

According to PBIS (2019):

> Funded by the U.S. Department of Education's Office of Special Education Programs (OSEP), the Technical Assistance Center on PBIS supports schools, districts, and states to build systems capacity for implementing a multi-tiered approach to social, emotional and behavior support. The broad purpose of PBIS is to improve the effectiveness, efficiency and equity of schools and other agencies. PBIS improves social, emotional and academic outcomes for all students, including students with disabilities and students from underrepresented groups. (para. 1)

PBIS has also published *A 5-Point Intervention Approach for Enhancing Equity in School Discipline* (McIntosh, Girvan, Horner, Smolkowski, & Sugai, 2018). This includes:

1. Collect, Use, and Report Disaggregated Discipline Data
2. Implement a Behavior Framework that is Preventive, Multi-Tiered, and Culturally Responsive
3. Use Engaging Instruction to Reduce the Opportunity (Achievement) Gap
4. Develop Policies with Accountability for Disciplinary Equity
5. Teach Strategies for Neutralizing Implicit Bias in Discipline Decisions

Token Economies

A *token economy* is a system of contingency management, which can be another name for operant conditioning and involves stimulus control and reinforcement in order to change behavior. The reinforcers in a token economy are tokens that can be exchanged for prizes, goods, rewards, and the like.

Zero-Tolerance Policies

Zero-tolerance policies in the United States became common in 1994, after federal legislation required states to expel students bringing firearms to school for one year, or lose all federal funding. After the mass shooting at Columbine High School on April 20, 1999, schools have attempted to ensure safety and control disciplinary policies fashioned after the zero-tolerance model has become standard (Lewis, Butler, Bonner, Fred, & Joubert, 2010; Lickel, Schmader, & Hamilton, 2003). Zero tolerance involves strict enforcement of rules and regulations, and bans undesirable behaviors or possession of certain items.

MOTIVATION AND LEARNING

Some issues of classroom management arise when teachers are frustrated by students' seeming refusal to learn, or their lack of motivation to learn. Self-regulation can be broadly defined as a psychological and behavioral function that facilitates adaptation to academic, social, and physical environments. It is important to our learning, as it requires the use of our metacognitive and motivational processes. Self-regulation does not necessarily lead to immediate expertise, but it can eventually facilitate effective knowledge and skills acquisition if one engages in it in a consistent way (Toering, Elferink-Gesmer, Jordet, & Visscher, 2009).

According to Hong and O'Neil's (2001; cited by Toering et al., 2009) trait self-regulation model, before self-regulated learners initiate actions to improve performance, they engage in the following processes:

1. They *compare* the demands of the task at hand with their own personal resources and then identify and align any matches between the two.

2. During the task performance they *monitor* their behaviors/strategies in relation to their ultimate goal and identify whether their behaviors/strategies are the best means for success.

3. Once the goal is attained, they *evaluate* their process for goal achievement and also set their own contingencies for success or failure. For

instance, if they did well, they decide to move onto the next goal or take a rest day; if not, they practice/correct their current strategy until they accomplish success.

Additionally, the research conducted by Toering et al. (2009) revealed that there are certain characteristics of successful *expert learners*. These include:

1. A heightened awareness of task-specific demands,
2. Flexibility and creativity in planning and strategizing,
3. Better use of metacognitive skills (e.g., planning, self-monitoring, and evaluation),
4. Reflective learning styles, that emphasize mastery learning rather than just performance-based outcomes,
5. Abilities to choose appropriate self-regulatory strategies in the face of task failure, and
6. Abilities to engage in a maximal amount of effort and persistence during their learning (they are consistent with the level of effort output, even over the course of several years).

THE ROLE OF MOTIVATION IN LEARNING

Broadly defined, *motivation* is the process of physical, cognitive, and/or emotional stimulation within a person that guides and sustains behaviors. *Intrinsic motivation* occurs when people engage in an activity for the sake of doing so. There are no additional intended consequences that are being sought. While people are engaged in intrinsically rewarding activities, they may experience enjoyment, excitement, and gratification. Furthermore, when people engage in behaviors/activities that they find intrinsically rewarding, the end result involves feelings of autonomy and volition (Deci, 1975).

In contrast, *extrinsic motivation* involves receiving distinct outcomes from engagement in activities or behaviors. These outcomes typically involve receiving a reward, avoiding a negative experience (e.g., guilt, embarrassment), or acquiring admiration and praise. Unlike intrinsic motivation, extrinsic motivation does not involve volition or autonomy. It operates under instrumentality, where the goal-directed behavior is the direct result of an external force (Deci & Ryan, 1996).

MOTIVATIONAL ORIENTATION

Bohlin, Durwin, and Reese-Weber (2010) identify two primary categories of motivational orientation in learning. The first is motivation for *mastery learning,* which is more intrinsically driven. This orientation is more focused on the process of learning rather than the product of learning. Learners with this orientation seek one of two goals. With a mastery approach goal, the learner is oriented toward setting goals that focus on mastery, improving intellectually (and/or athletically) and acquiring new skills and knowledge. Mastery-avoidance goals involve motivation to avoid a lack of mastery or the appearance of looking incompetent according to one's own internalized standards of performance. The second primary motivational orientation is for *performance outcomes.* This orientation is more extrinsically driven and focused on the product of learning rather than the process. Learners with this orientation possess one of two goals. Performance-approach goals involve motivation to demonstrate ability and do better than others at a task. Performance-avoidance goals involve motivation to avoid a lack of mastery or looking incompetent compared to the performance of peers.

MOTIVATION AND SELF-DETERMINATION THEORY

Self-determination theory (SDT) (Deci, 1975; Deci & Ryan, 1985) explores how self-regulation is integrally linked to motivation. According to SDT, the degree to which outcomes motivate people to engage in behaviors or activities influences the voracity with which they self-regulate for those behaviors or activities. Self-regulation for certain behaviors requires a significant amount of engagement on behavioral and cognitive levels. Thus, the more intrinsically motivating the outcome to engage is, the more self-regulation will occur.

According to Deci's (1975) seminal work, on some level every child is born with "undifferentiated intrinsic motivation" (p. 77). As children age and have differing life experiences that require the development of competencies (e.g., academic, social, familial, athletic) and self-determination, they develop more specific forms of intrinsic motives. Among these would include the need to achieve and the need to become self-actualized. These intrinsic motives are what facilitate the development of self-regulatory behaviors in certain contexts. For instance, if a child is inherently curious and they are put in an educational system (e.g., a Montessori school) where they are allowed to actively engage in their learning, the outcome of their experiences—learning more and satisfying their curiosity—should theoretically increase their intrinsic motivation and thus their desire to self-regulate the behaviors that resulted in their initial learning (e.g., questioning, reading, fact finding, critical thinking).

Self-determination theory (Deci, 1975; Deci & Ryan, 1980, 1985, 1991, 1996) classifies motivated behavior into two different types, controlled and

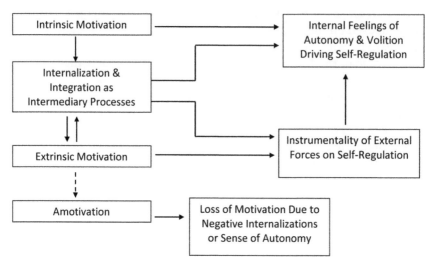

Figure 7.1   Interpretation of Deci & Ryan's Self-Determination Theory

autonomous; these vary with respect to how much self-determination is needed to engage in them. *Controlled* forms of motivated behavior (e.g., primarily externally motivated) do not require self-determined forces in order to be regulated, while *autonomous* forms of motivated behavior (primarily internally motivated) require self-determined processes. Between these two broad types of motivated behavior lies a continuum of five types of behavioral regulation that rely on varying degrees of intrinsic and extrinsic motivation (Lonsdale, Hodge, & Rose, 2008). It should be noted that amotivation, or a diminished sense of motivation, is also part of Deci and Ryan's (1985) model.

HOW SELF-REGULATION WORKS WITH MOTIVATION

While these constructs, in their truest form, seem to be opposites, Deci and Ryan (1996) suggest in that they fall along a continuum that influences the degree of self-regulation. Integration and internalization are the two intermediary processes involved in turning purely extrinsically regulated behaviors into more intrinsically regulated processes. See Figure 7.1 for an illustration.

Within the context of self-determination theory, *internalization* is a relatively natural and adaptive process that occurs when people internalize values and behaviors through witnessing and engaging in them and experiencing their outcomes. The more exposure people have to certain values and behaviors, the more refined their internalizations become. The more a value or behavior is internalized and subsequently *integrated* into a

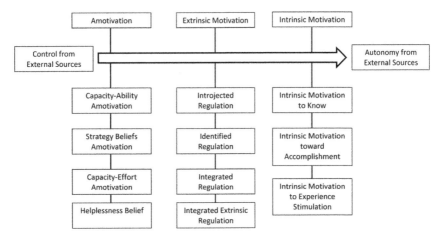

Figure 7.2   Continuum of Deci and Ryan's Extrinsic Regulation

repertoire, the better it can shape the regulation of its associated behaviors. Values and behaviors that are initially extrinsically motivated can undergo the process of internalization and integration and result in increased self-regulation. In instances where people only partially internalize the values and behaviors and full integration does *not* occur, an intermediary form of self-regulation occurs (Deci & Ryan, 1996).

Deci and Ryan (1996) discuss five types of extrinsic regulation that vary with respect to control and autonomy. Figure 7.2 provides an illustration of the continuum that they fall on. These include external regulation, introjected regulation, identified regulation, integrated regulation, and integrated extrinsic regulation. *External regulation* is most influenced by control from outside sources and involves the least amount of internalization. This sort of regulation involves the use of external motivators for engaging in an activity or behavior (e.g., avoiding punishment or receiving a reward).

Introjected regulation involves some degree of internalization; however, this internalization involves perceptions about an external set of consequences (Deci & Ryan, 1996). For example, a piano student may want to perform well and will train hard to do so, but if she is operating under introjected regulation, her training is the result of her thoughts about how her performance will be perceived by her instructor. The level of control that the external consequence has over the student's motivation and self-regulation is still high, but there is some level of internalization that takes place. This internalization can result in feelings of guilt or shame if the student falls short of what she perceives her teacher's expectations are. This, in turn, can undermine any intrinsic motivation she has to further engage in learning to play the piano.

Identified regulation may be used when accomplishing a short-term or sub-goal for a larger goal. With identified regulation, the behavior or activity is identified as personally relevant and a means of self-enhancement. The person sees value in engaging in the behavior or activity for their own gain, even if the gain is not for a more important goal (Deci & Ryan, 1996). For instance, a student who wants to be an environmental lawyer takes a chemistry class. The student struggles to do well on the chemistry exams and begins to dread the class. She knows that she must study to get passing grades if she wants to reach her ultimate career goal of being an environmental lawyer. Despite her stress and negative feelings about the chemistry class, she continues to study for her exams because she knows her performance on them will contribute to a larger end goal.

Integrated regulation is the most autonomous form of extrinsic motivation and involves a high level of internalization. When an identification has become fully integrated into a person's self-regulation, it leads that person to act with full volition and commitment. The volition of the self-regulatory behaviors may transfer to other domains and contribute to a person's more global sense of self (Deci & Ryan, 1996). For instance, a study sought to determine if there were links between athletic and academic self-regulation in runners. An assumption is made that if students are highly motivated to perform well in one domain, some of those sources of motivation may transfer to other skills in other domains.

Integrated extrinsic regulation falls at the end of the continuum and most closely resembles intrinsic motivation. Full autonomy and engagement occur with integrated extrinsic regulation. The main difference between this type of regulation and intrinsic regulation is how the self-regulation was initiated. With intrinsically self-regulated behaviors, the behaviors are usually the result of spontaneous encounter (e.g., when a student learns a new math skill and realizes that she really enjoys it). Thus, it involves the highest level of autonomy and volition. With integrated extrinsic regulation, a student may be required to engage in an activity that initially involves external consequences. Over time, the student realizes that she likes (or finds significant purpose) in engaging in this activity and begins to find intrinsically motivating aspects of it, which subsequently leads to autonomous self-regulation of the behaviors involved in performing the activity (Deci & Ryan, 1996).

MOTIVATION AND AMOTIVATION

Vallerand (2001) presents a hierarchical theory of motivation and regulation that builds on Deci and Ryan's original work. In earlier work Vallerand et al. (1992, 1993) identified three distinct forms of intrinsic motivation. These include intrinsic motivation to know, intrinsic motivation toward accomplishments, and intrinsic motivation to experience stimulation. *Intrinsic motivation to know* involves taking pleasure in the learning process that is associated with performing an activity. *Intrinsic motivation toward accomplishments* involves the gratification that takes place when accomplishing a goal related to an activity. Finally, *intrinsic motivation to experience stimulation* refers to the physical, psychological, social, or intellectual pleasure one receives when performing an activity.

In addition to types of extrinsic and intrinsic motivation, Vallerand and his colleagues include elaborated on Deci and Ryan's (1985) concept of amotivation. *Amotivation* is a lack of motivation that involves the perception that there is no point in engaging in an activity. Students may initially be interested in an activity, but after engaging in it and experiencing feelings of failure, incompetence, and/or helplessness, may determine that they no longer enjoy the activity. Unfortunately, this can happen in the classroom, especially when students are being evaluated with grades. According to Vallerand (1997) there are four types of amotivation. The first is *capacity-ability amotivation*. Here a student may not think she has the capacity or ability to perform a particular activity. If a student is assigned the task of writing a poem but has limited experience with writing in general or has previously received negative feedback on her writing from her teachers, she may be intimidated by the assignment and avoid it. The second is *strategy beliefs amotivation*, which means a student does not trust or have confidence in the strategies she may use to engage in an activity. Maybe the strategy her teacher is using during instruction is not working for her personally, so she stops using it or tries to disengage from the activity. The third is *capacity-effort amotivation*. This differs from *capacity-ability amotivation* in that the student perceives the activity as involving too much effort to participate in. For instance, a student is required to complete a summer reading list, but instead of actually reading the books during the summer months, decides to look up summaries of each book on YouTube and base her reports on the videos. Finally, the fourth type of amotivation, *helplessness belief*, occurs when a person perceives a task as being too grand relative to their abilities, strategies, or efforts. A student who struggles with basic algebra may avoid taking precalculus because she expects to fail.

THE ROLE OF SELF-REGULATION AND MOTIVATION IN NEURAL DEVELOPMENT

Neurological research provides empirical evidence to suggest that engaging in self-regulatory behaviors while in highly motivated states can lead to physiological changes in the brain. In his book, *The Talent Code*, Coyle (2009) investigated myelination theory. The theory suggests that those who engage in "deep practice" (a.k.a. self-regulatory behaviors) and who are "ignited" (a.k.a. motivated) to develop a specific skill set can achieve their goals apart from any influence from genetic endowment (for a more detailed review of the research refer to Fields, 2005, 2008a, 2008b; Pujol, 2006; Casey, Giedd, & Thomas, 2000).

The basic process of myelination can be summed up in the following modified adage: "Practice makes myelin, and myelin makes perfect" (Coyle, 2009, p. 44). The more a person practices a particular skill, the more frequently the neural circuits needed to engage in that skill are fired. The more the neural circuits are activated, the more myelin insulates them. The more myelin that insulates the circuits, the faster the electrical impulses travel through the neural circuit and the more automatic the connections become. As the myelin builds and automaticity results, the easier (and presumably better) the practiced skills become. Thus, self-regulatory behaviors (e.g., practicing a set of skills) facilitates myelin formation, which facilitates the successful execution of the skills. This automaticity that yields both neural and behavioral outcomes can also facilitate motivation to advance a skill set by engaging in increasingly more technical and complex skills.

Myelination theory identifies three sources of talent development. The first is *deep practice*, which involves elements of self-regulation and persistence in the face of failure. Deep practice involves struggling in certain goal-directed ways in order move from actual ability to potential ability. Thus, it requires a learner to operate at the edge of her ability. Because of this, mistakes will likely be made during the learning process, but those mistakes are intended to push the learner out of her comfort zone and make her better at the skill she is learning. This error-learning process occurs because the experience of deep practice requires the learner to slow down, make errors and correct them. The idea is that if these errors and corrections occur frequently and consistently enough, then the skills being learned will eventually become more automatic, making the learner more adept at performing them without any real conscious awareness of the process (Coyle, 2009).

Ignition is the process by which intrinsic motivation is created and sustained. It works with deep practice to create skill by providing the energy to engage in that skill; deep practice translates that energy into forward progress (e.g., myelination). Ignition is more spontaneous and intense, while deep practice requires conscious, deliberate thinking. The moment of ignition often goes unnoticed in those that experience it; however, this facilitates passion and persistence in the face of failure or difficulty. In terms of myelination theory, sustained ignition is needed in order to insulate larger neural networks for complex skills (Coyle, 2009).

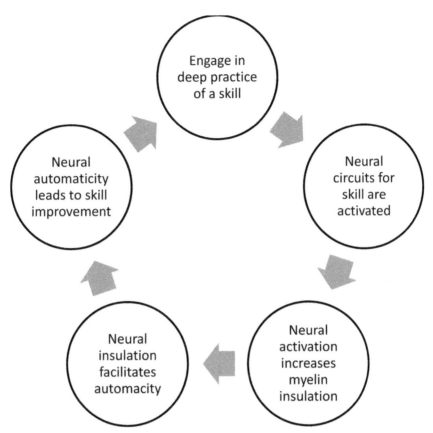

Figure 7.3   The Cycle of Deep Practice, Myelination, and Skill Development

Ignition also involves an emotional response and requires the detection of primal cues. When a learner can actively identify herself as an eventual expert in the skill she is learning (e.g., distance running) there is often an emotional response that is triggered in that she can see herself in the future engaging in the skills. This ability to visualize a future state of learning and knowing facilitates the motivation needed for deep practice and in doing such, subsequently facilitates progress (Coyle, 2009).

The third source of talent development is *master coaching.* Coyle describes master coaches as those who can foster talent and deep practice. He identifies eight characteristics of master coaches in his book. Among these are (1) they are mostly older and have taught for 30–40 years, (2) they are skilled at listening, (3) they are attuned to the instructional needs of those they are teaching, and (4) they individualized their coaching methods to each learner's personality.

CURRENT INTERSECTIONAL ISSUES IN
SCHOOL DISCIPLINE

The U.S. education system has a history of institutional racism, revealed in differential discipline which favors white students and disadvantages black and brown students (Black, 2016). In recent years, educational researchers have explicated the problem of the school-to-prison pipeline and its impact on urban populations, specifically its effects on African American boys. More recently, scholars such as Kimberlè Crenshaw (1993) and Monique Morris (2016) have raised the call to include African American girls in this conversation, because their social exclusion and pushout from schools is largely minimized and ignored by gendered policies and programs that focus primarily on boys. According to Morris (2016), "While boys receive more than two out of three suspensions, Black girls are suspended at higher rates (12%) than girls of any other race or ethnicity and most boys" (p. 13). Morris argues that the treatment of African American girls in schools is far more insidious, with much disciplining of and control over appearance, often done in informal ways, but with the end result being the punishment of black girl aesthetics, such as natural hair, dreadlocks, or braids, being deemed as "disruptive."

According to the U.S. Department of Education Office for Civil Rights (2014), African American students are 3.5 times more likely to be suspended or expelled. Although they make up only 18 percent of the overall student population, African American students make up 46 percent of those students suspended more than one time. One in 4 African American students are suspended at least once compared to 1 in 11 white students (U.S. Department of Education Office for Civil Rights, 2014). In the 60 years post-*Brown*, we have a resegregated educational system where students of color experience structural inequalities (Lee, 2003), and where African American girls are disproportionately disadvantaged by such segregation. Sharma, Joyner, and Osment (2014) found that segregation and racial isolation result in the decreased performance of minority students on standardized English and mathematics examinations, which serves to reinforce the stereotypical ideology that blacks are less intelligent than whites (Penner & Saperstein, 2013; Steele and Aronson, 1995), and subsequently, that black students are unable to perform as well as whites because of cultural deficits (Spencer, 2012) or inherent intellectual ineptitude (Goff, Jackson, Di Leone, Culotta, & DiTomasso, 2014).

In general, students who deviate from ascribed cultural norms are vulnerable to sanctioning, which has resulted in the misinterpretation of behavior by teachers and administrators and the subsequent sanctioning of students of color for subjective interpretations of infractions, e.g., loitering, excessive noise, and threat, as opposed to their white counterparts, who are punished for objective, measurable misconduct, e.g., smoking and vandalism (Monroe, 2005; Perry & Morris, 2014; Skiba, Michael, Nardo, & Peterson, 2002; Zion & Blanchett, 2011). Presumed disobedience, argumentation, and disrespect are frequently cited as reasons for disciplinary referral for students of color (Monroe, 2005); however, these supposed infractions are often subjective misinterpretations of critical cultural, linguistic, and behavioral patterns exhibited by young men in the African American community (Zion & Blanchett, 2011).

The perception of black students as deviant has severe implications for education, and school discipline is perhaps the area where this is most glaring. Students of color are referred for more arbitrary and subjective concerns and for less serious offences that may not result in a referral for a white student. The *perception* of a threat (by black students) is an issue (for white teachers). What is perceived as a threat when committed by a black student is commonly not considered a threat when the same behavior is committed by a white student (O'Connor & Fernandez, 2006, p. 9). Zion and Blanchett (2011) identify a second, latent, function of education: social control. The function of education as a mechanism of social control is manifest in the utilization of disciplinary techniques to manage and control students identified as disruptive (Skiba et al., 2002).

In an effort to ensure safety and control, particularly post-Columbine (Lickel, Schmader, & Hamilton, 2003), disciplinary policies fashioned after the zero-tolerance model have become standard (Lewis et al., 2010). Urban schools, often considered "apartheid" schools (Orfield & Frankenberg, 2004) are more likely subject to zero-tolerance policies, police intervention and surveillance, and strict discipline policies. These schools are also most often located in urban environments, employ underprepared teachers, lack resources, and often operate from deficit mindsets, low expectations, and less academic rigor (Milner, 2013a). In these apartheid schools, students are viewed as criminals or potential criminals; their lack of academic success is then blamed on them, their culture, or their families, as opposed to a system stacked against them. According to the African American Policy Forum (2015), "At-risk young women describe zero-tolerance schools as chaotic environments in which discipline is prioritized over educational attainment" (pp. 12–13).

Another discriminatory practice involves "subjective discipline"— imparted by teachers and motivated by implicit bias. For example, the concept of "disrespect" is inherently subjective. In fact, "disrespect" is in the eye of the beholder and difficult to prove. If one student receives no consequences for a conflict, when another student receives all of the consequences, implicit bias may play a role. Previous research suggests that disciplinary techniques not only are negatively associated with educational outcomes but may also target students of color, whether explicitly or implicitly (Casella, 2003; Monroe, 2005; Perry & Morris, 2014). Some discipline techniques that target African American girls, such as suspensions and informal pushouts, lead these girls to eventually drop out of school. We know that 7 percent of African American girls drop out, compared to 3.8 percent of white girls (Morris, 2016).

In a ground-breaking study, Goff and colleagues (2014) argue that black and brown children are perceived as older and thus more responsible for their actions than their white counterparts. These misperceptions (based on implicit bias) have grave consequences for nonhegemonic students, and contribute to their dehumanization and criminalization. The Goff et al. study found that teachers do not perceive black and brown students as possessing the "essence of innocence," as do their white peers. Rather, they are viewed as "little criminals" who are in need of discipline as opposed to education.

WHITE TEACHERS AND CULTURAL RESPONSIVENESS

Previous research has suggested that not only are disciplinary techniques negatively associated with educational outcomes, but also, they are inequitably levied toward Students of Color (Casella, 2003; Lewis et al., 2010; Monroe, 2005; Perry & Morris, 2014; Skiba et al., 2002). Is the problem that most teachers are white, and unaccustomed to working with populations different from them? Is it that they are operating from stereotyped notions of their students and thus deficit thinking? Can white teachers be prepared to work in culturally diverse settings? According to Milner (2006, 2008), for teachers to be prepared to work in diverse settings, they must be well versed in cultural and racial awareness, critical reflection, and the merging of theory and practice. They must also be committed to defying the notion that lack of student success, particularly in urban schools, is the fault of students, their parents, their home cultures, and their communities. To this end, we must advocate for teacher education programs that challenge and confront the dominant social order (Bolotin Joseph, Luster Bravmann, Windschitl, Mikel, & Stewart Green, 2000). However, this work is difficult, and some white students may tend to resist it (Martin, 2015; Milner, 2013b).

Teacher educators must advocate for asset perspectives when viewing all students in their respective communities: tapping into students' prior cultural knowledge when teaching new knowledge can help to establish dynamic mental models that network to the learners' existing schema, adding meaning to the new knowledge for the learner (Griner & Stewart, 2012; Moll & González, 1992). As teacher educators, we must provide our future educators with mindsets, dispositions, and practices aimed at closing opportunity gaps for all students, but for Students of Color in particular.

According to Akiba (2011), educators who value their students' opinions enabled a level of comfort within the classroom where students felt comfortable expressing themselves, when students were able to learn from one another, and where the educators created a learning community within the classroom. When these conditions are met, students are more likely to develop positive views on diversity. Being sensitive to students' own cultural backgrounds and presenting concepts in a constructivist environment are also effective techniques (Akiba, 2011).

Dover (2013) provides further suggestions for fostering positive views on diversity in teacher education. Preservice teachers must cultivate the following beliefs:

1. assume all students are participants in knowledge construction, have high expectations for students and themselves, and foster learning communities;
2. acknowledge, value, and build upon students' existing knowledge, interests, cultural and linguistic resources;
3. teach academic skills and bridge gaps in students' learning;
4. work in reciprocal partnership with students' families and communities;
5. critique and employ multiple forms of assessment; and
6. explicitly teach about activism, power, and inequity in schools and society (p. 90).

Finally, teacher education candidates and professors of education must:

1. Deconstruct white privilege and racism (Blanchett, 2006),
2. Defy colorblindness,
3. Confront stereotypes of Blackness,
4. Interrogate the notion that schools and neutral, fair, and equitable spaces, where all students are treated equally and can expect they be offered the same chance at success (Bartolome, 1994). (Dover, 2013)

Schools must change their policies, and teachers, their attitudes that success is a white domain (Carter Andrews, 2012). Carter Andrews (2012) argues that teachers must examine race, racism, whiteness, and how these concepts relate to teaching and learning. Finally, preservice and in-service teachers should utilize Gay's (2000) approach to culturally responsive pedagogy, where teachers are encouraged to utilize the "cultural knowledge, prior experiences, frames of reference, and performance styles of ethnically diverse students to make learning encounters more relevant to and effective for them" (p. 29).

STEREOTYPE THREAT

Stereotype threat is the fear of confirming the negative stereotypes held about one's group by others not possessing the same identities (Steele & Aronson, 1995). This heightened fear to "represent" for one's racial/ethnic/ gender (or other) group may result in higher stress and lower performance. For example, if a female is in a math class with a teacher who holds the stereotype that girls are not as good at math as their male counterparts, the females in the class may feel additional pressure to perform well in order to dis-confirm that stereotype that the teacher holds. This added pressure and stress may cause the stereotyped individuals to perform poorly, thus perpetuating said stereotypes. It becomes a vicious circle, and one that serves to reinforce stereotypes. According to Hill, Corbett, and St. Rose (2010), "Stereotype threat arises in situations when a negative stereotype is relevant to evaluating performance" (p. 39). Stereotype threat can impact individuals both psychologically and physiologically. Fortunately, stereotype threat can be counteracted by teaching students about it (Hill, Corbett, & St. Rose, 2010). Unfortunately, this is not often the case.

Students are susceptible to stereotype threat when they find themselves in situations where they feel at risk to confirm stereotypes about the racial, gender, or ethnic group to which they identity. The fear of confirming these negative stereotypes can result in stress and thus negative academic outcomes (Morris & Monroe, 2009). Both teachers and students are influenced by stereotypes. Teachers may ask students less challenging questions if they view said student's culture from a deficit perspective.

Likewise, pressures of representing a culture as a whole may derail students determined to defy the stereotypes held for their cultural group. As Morris and Monroe (2009) argue, "stereotype threat most affects young people who closely identify with their ethnicity or gender, are critically aware of societal stigmas, are accepting of stereotypes, and see intelligence as a relatively fixed enterprise" (p. 30). Most young people are not equipped to cope with or understand such injustices at an institutional level. Moreover, any questioning of the status quo may be viewed as deviance and exacerbate the already dangerous stereotypes of blackness.

Steele (2010) pinpoints the identity categories that are often rife for stereotype threat, including age, sexual orientation, race, gender, ethnicity, political affiliation, mental illness, and disability. Steele (2010) further illuminates the danger of stereotype threat: "We know what 'people think.' We know that anything we do that fits the stereotype could be taken as confirming it" (p. 5). Thus, the vicious circle is perpetuated. If teachers are unaware of their implicit biases and of the phenomenon of stereotype threat, they are likely to perpetuate it. According to Benjamin Bloom, "After forty years of intensive research on school learning in the United States as well as abroad, my major conclusion is: What any person in the world can learn, *almost* all persons can learn *if* provided with the appropriate prior and current conditions of learning" (Bloom, as cited in Dweck, 2007, pp. 65–66). However, Bloom's sentiment as well as knowledge and understanding of implicit bias and stereotype threat are not explicitly taught in many teacher education programs, and thus do not trickle down to classrooms and schools.

According to Dweck (2007) some teachers have "fixed mindsets," believing that the students who enter their classrooms with lower academic achievement levels are somehow different from their other students, and that this fact is unchangeable. On the other hand, other teachers possess "growth mindsets," and believe that all students can learn and develop their skills. As Dweck (2007) states, "The group differences had simply disappeared under the guidance of teachers who taught for improvement, for these teachers had found a way to reach their 'low-ability' students" (p. 66). Furthermore, according to Dweck (2007):

> The fixed mindset limits achievement. It fills people's minds with interfering thoughts, it makes effort disagreeable, and it leads to inferior learning strategies. What's more, it makes other people into judges instead of allies. Whether we're talking about Darwin or college students, important achievements require a clear focus, all-out effort, and a bottomless trunk full of strategies. Plus allies in learning. This is what the growth mindset gives people, and what's why it helps their abilities grow and bear fruit. (p. 67)

It is important for all teachers to possess growth mindsets in order to cultivate the abilities of all of their students.

Finally, the phenomenon on stereotype threat can affect the strongest and most capable students, indicating that the pressure from without (or "situational pressure") can impact student performance (Steele, 2010). According to Steele (2010), stereotype threat "causes rumination, which takes up mental capacity, distracting us from the task at hand—from the questions on the standardized test we're taking or from the conversation we're having with persons of a different race. So beyond the physiological reactions that identity threat causes, it also impairs performance and other actions by interfering with our thinking" (p. 121).

WHY WE SHOULD CARE PART 1: WHAT THE RESEARCH TELLS US

In a book based on his scholarly work, Page (2007) argues that diversity can lead to better problem solving. In his definition, "Diversity . . . means differences in how people see, categorize, understand, and go about improving the world" (p. xiv). In his research, Page found that diverse groups can often outperform groups of the best performers. He asserts that while ability is important, a group of high-ability problem solvers is often homogenous, and this homogeneity may prevent the sort of "out of the box" thinking necessary to solve a problem (Hong & Page, 2004). Diverse groups outperform homogenous high-ability groups under four conditions: (1) the problem must be difficult, (2) the individuals must have diverse problem-solving tools and perspectives, (3) there must be a large pool of individuals to choose from to form the group, and (4) the group of problem solvers cannot be too small (Page, 2007).

According to Asher (2007) preservice teachers, most of whom are white, often come into their teacher education programs with little to no exposure to multicultural education, diversity, or culturally responsive pedagogy. Perhaps more concerning, some students go through their entire teacher education programs without specific training in multicultural education or culturally responsive pedagogy, thus graduating unprepared for successful teaching of students unlike themselves. If preservice teachers are provided the opportunities to "explicitly and critically interrogate the historical and present-day intersections of race, culture, gender, and foster a self-reflexive engagement with difference" (Asher, 2007, pp. 65–66), teachers can uncover more significant and reflective ways to know themselves and their students in relation to race, power, and privilege.

Sharma, Joyner, and Osment (2014) found that such segregation and racial isolation results in the decreased performance of minority students on standardized English and mathematics examinations, which may serve to reinforce the stereotypical ideology that blacks are less intelligent than whites (Penner & Saperstein, 2013; Steele & Aronson, 1995), and subsequently, that black students are unable to perform as well as whites because of cultural deficits (Spencer, 2012) or inherent intellectual ineptitude (Goff et al., 2014).

Sharma, Joyner, and Osment (2014) also found that teachers can exacerbate these issues. For example, disparities in educational opportunities for black students involve teacher quality: the percentage of novice teachers increases as the percentage of black students increases, and segregated schools actually reduce the level to which black students meet their academic promise (Wildhagen, 2012). In schools where disciplinary climates are harsh, black students are less likely to reach their full potential, regardless of whether they were subject to discipline themselves. These students, whom Perry and Morris (2014) deem as "collateral consequences" of harsh disciplinary environments, showed reduced academic outcomes and were stunted in their educational attainment in general.

Understanding and navigating diversity is the key to success in our increasingly global and technological world. The proliferation of text-based communication technologies and increasing dependence on intercultural communication both nationally and internationally point to language as a key area of educational importance. As the United States loses its status as the main cultural influence on the world stage, our educational system is shortchanging many of our students who are attempting to prepare for this new multicultural world. By continuing to teach from a privileged, hegemonic worldview, we are leaving out a wide swath of students from true preparation for success. Access to language resources, as well as the discourses of power, through multicultural education, is crucial in preparing our students, poised to enter this changing workforce, to successfully navigate a global economy.

We must prepare our students to work with increasingly diverse populations in a social and political climate that is increasingly hostile to these endeavors and to forces that are resistant to global change. Because although the pre-K–12 student population in the United States is becoming increasingly diverse, the teaching force is increasingly hegemonic. According to the National Center for Education Information (Feistritzer, 2011), 84 percent of the teaching force in the United States is white. Without explicit training about—or at least recognition of—the cultural differences between teachers and students and how they can impact teachers' attitudes toward their multicultural students (and the languages they bring to school), this culture gap will continue to contribute what is known as the achievement gap.

Teachers are doing our students a disservice by not recognizing their language and culture. The cultural mismatch between a large portion of the student population and the majority of teachers greatly contributes to the achievement gap, leaving students without access to the discourses of power. The achievement/opportunity gap could realistically be considered a cultural and linguistic gap; this gap continues to negatively impact students the further they go in education and then into the working world.

Cultural assumptions play out particularly through language use, and this is especially true in the classroom. Most teachers feel it is their job to prepare students for success in a "standardized" world, where nonstandard language will most likely hinder workplace success. But allowing for diversity in language practices in the classroom helps students understand different ways of seeing the world and can only strengthen the ability of our students to succeed in an increasingly diverse workplace.

In the United States, the high school graduation rate is under 70 percent, the achievement gap has remained relatively stagnant since 1988, and socioeconomic factors greatly affect student outcomes (Carter & Welner, 2013). What Linda Darling-Hammond (2013) calls "cultural mismatch," or the gap between students and teachers in terms of their racial, cultural, ethnic, social, and linguistic identities, readily influences student disconnection from school. Students who speak nonstandard forms of English often may feel that their language is devalued in school and thus are more inclined to drop out, losing confidence in schools that make them feel devalued (Charity Hudley & Mallinson, 2011). According to Salazar (2013), a "humanizing pedagogy" is additive, as opposed to focusing on deficits; it utilizes students' prior knowledge and connects it to new learning, thereby legitimizing students' home languages and cultures. In such a pedagogy students are viewed as experts in their particular culture and language. The teachers' role is to impart "insider knowledge" that is necessary to succeed in the academic world.

Over the past 40 years, income inequality for children has risen in the United States, which is a strong contributor to the increasing achievement gap for U.S. children (Duncan & Murname, 2014). Students from low-income families often begin their academic careers already behind developmentally and cognitively. According to Jensen (2013), there are seven factors as to why impoverished students struggle with engagement in the classroom: health and nutrition, vocabulary, effort, hope and the growth mindset, cognition, relationships, and distress.

To combat these factors, Jensen (2013) recommends that teachers must be willing to get to know their students, make connections, and establish relationships to combat these issues. Strong teachers can help low-income students build bridges to success. Banks (2013) argues that what is necessary in today's schools is "transformative citizenship education," which includes challenging mainstream knowledge for the purpose of improving the human condition, recognizing and valuing diversity and social/community activism with the goal of producing a multicultural democracy, and developing cosmopolitan values. According to Appiah (2006), cosmopolitanism is a universal trait of humankind and an ethic that is both binding and commonsensical. Appiah views cosmopolitanism as a "rethink" of how we view the world and a moralistic interpretation of shared values (good and bad). However, this ethic of understanding and enacting in the cosmopolitan world requires a particular type of charge to its inhabitants. Although intended for all, cosmopolitans require sophisticated intelligence, critical and creative thinking skills, caring dispositions for self and others, and the need to look beyond tribal entities. Darling-Hammond (2013) argues that to meet the demands of the 21st century, we must establish equitable schools in order to prepare our students for this knowledge-based, global, and multicultural world economy. In order to do this, we must view diversity as a strength and not as a deficit (Apple, 2013). We must develop and nurture all students with the intention of embracing the ideal of global citizenship, and it begins with language.

REFERENCES

African American Policy Forum. (2015). *Black girls matter: Pushed out, overpoliced, and underprotected.* New York, NY: Center for Intersectionality and Social Policy Studies.

Akiba, M. (2011). Identifying program characteristics for preparing pre-service teachers for diversity. *Teachers College Record, 113*(3), 658–697.

Appiah, K. A. (2006). *Cosmopolitanism: Ethics in a world of strangers.* New York, NY: W. W. Norton.

Apple, M. (2013). Thinking internationally and paying our debts: Critical thoughts on diversity, globalization, and education. *Kappa Delta Pi Record, 49*(3), 118–120.

Asher, N. (2007). Made in the (multicultural) U.S.A.: Unpacking tensions of race, culture, gender, and sexuality in education. *Educational Researcher, 36*(2), 65–73.

Banks, J. (2013). Group identity and citizenship education in global times. *Kappa Delta Pi Record, 49*(3), 108–112.

Berlin, L. J., Ispa, J. M., Fine, M. A., Malone, P. S., Brooks-Gunn, J., Brady-Smith, C., & Bai, Y. (2009). Correlates and consequences of spanking and verbal punishment for low-income White, African American, and Mexican American toddlers. *Child Development, 80,* 1403–1420. doi: 10.1111/j.1467 -8624.2009.01341.x

Black, D. W. (2016). *Ending zero tolerance: The crisis of absolute school discipline.* New York, NY: New York University Press.

Blanchett, W. J. (2006). Disproportionate representation of African American students in special education: Acknowledging the role of white privilege and racism. *Educational Researcher, 35*(6), 24–28.

Bohlin, L., Durwin, C. C., & Reese-Weber, M. (2008). *Ed psych in modules.* New York, NY: McGraw Hill.

Bolotin Joseph, P., Luster Bravmann, S., Windschitl, M. A., Mikel, E. R., & Stewart Green, N. (2000). *Cultures of curriculum.* Mahwah, NJ: Lawrence Erlbaum.

Carter, P. L., & Welner, K. G. (Eds.). (2013). *Closing the opportunity gap: What America must do to give every child an even change.* New York, NY: Oxford University Press.

Carter Andrews, D. J. (2012). Black achievers' experiences with racial spotlighting and ignoring in a predominantly white high school. *Teachers College Record, 114*(10), 1–46.

Casella, R. (2003, November). Punishing dangerousness through preventive detention: Illustrating the institutional link between school and prison. *New Directions for Youth Development. Special Issue: Deconstructing the School-to-Prison Pipeline, 99,* 55–70.

Casey, B. J, Giedd, J. N., & Thomas, K. M. (2000). Structural and functional brain development and its relation to cognitive development. *Biological Psychology, 54,* 241–257.

Charity Hudley, A. H., & Mallinson, C. (2011). *Understanding English language variation in U.S. schools.* New York, NY: Teachers College Press.

Chubb, N. H., Fertman, C. I., & Ross, J. L. (1997). Adolescent self-esteem and locus on control: A longitudinal study of gender and age differences. *Adolescence, 32*(125), 113–129.

Coyle, D. (2009). *The talent code: Greatness isn't born. It's grown. Here's how.* New York, NY: Bantam Dell.

Crenshaw, K. (1993). Mapping the margins: Intersectionality, identity politics, and violence against women of color. *Stanford Law Review, 43*, 1241–1299.

Darling-Hammond, L. (2013). Diversity, equity, and education in a globalized world. *Kappa Delta Pi Record, 49*(3), 113–115.

Deci, E. L. (1975). *Intrinsic motivation.* New York, NY: Plenum.

Deci, E. L., & Ryan, R. M. (1980). The empirical exploration of intrinsic motivational processes. In L. Berkowitz (Ed.), *Advances in experimental social psychology* (Vol. 13, pp. 39–80). New York, NY: Academic.

Deci, E. L., & Ryan, R. M. (1985). *Intrinsic motivation and self-determination in human behavior.* New York, NY: Plenum.

Deci, E. L., & Ryan, R. M. (1991). A motivational approach to self: Integration in personality. In R. Dienstbier (Ed.), *Nebraska symposium on motivation: Perspectives on motivation* (Vol. 38, pp. 237–288). Lincoln, NE: University of Nebraska Press.

Deci, E. L., & Ryan, R. M. (1996). Need satisfaction and the self-regulation of learning. *Learning & Individual Differences, 8*(3), 165–183.

Dover, A. G. (2013). Getting "up to code": Preparing for and confronting challenges when teaching for social justice in standards-based classrooms. *Action in Teacher Education, 35*(2), 89–102.

Duncan, G. J., & Murnane, R. J. (2014). *Restoring opportunity: The crisis of inequality and the challenge for American education.* Cambridge, MA: Harvard Education Press.

Dweck, C. (2007). *Mindset: The new psychology of success.* New York, NY: Ballentine.

Feistritzer, C. E. (2011, July). *Profiles of teachers in the U.S. 2011.* National Center for Education Information. Retrieved from pot2011final-blog.pdf

Fields, R. D. (2005). Myelination: An overlooked mechanism of synaptic plasticity? *Neuroscientist, 11*(6), 528–531.

Fields, R. D. (2008a). White matter in learning, cognition, and psychiatric disorders. *Trends in Neurosciences, 31*(7), 361–370.

Fields, R. D. (2008b). White matter matters. *Scientific American*, 54–61.

Gay, G. (2000). *Culturally responsive teaching: Theory, research and practice.* New York, NY: Teachers College Press.

Gershoff, E. T., & Font, S. A. (2016). Corporal punishment in U.S. public schools: Prevalence, disparities in use, and status in state and federal policy. *Society for Research in Child Development, 30* (1), 2–26.

Gershoff, E. T., Lansford, J. E., Sexton, H. R., Davis-Kean, P. E., & Sameroff, A. J. (2012). Longitudinal links between spanking and children's externalizing behaviors in a national sample of White, Black, Hispanic, and Asian American Families. *Child Development, 83*, 838–843. doi: 10.1111/j.1467-8624.2011.01732.x

Goff, P. A., Jackson, M. C., Di Leone, B. A., L., Culotta, C. M., & DiTomasso, N. A. (2014). The essence of innocence: Consequences of dehumanizing black children. *Journal of Personality and Social Psychology, 106*(4), 526–545.

Griner, A. C., & Stewart, M. L. (2012). Addressing the achievement gap and disproportionality through the use of culturally responsive teaching practices. *Urban Education, 48*(4), 585–621.

Han, S. (2011) Probability of corporal punishment: Lack of resources and vulnerable students. *Journal of Educational Research, 104,* 420–430. doi:10.1080 /00220671.2010.500313

Hill, C., Corbett, C., & St. Rose, A. (2010). *Why so few? Women in science, technology, engineering, and mathematics.* Washington, DC: American Association of University Women. Retrieved from http://www.aauw.org/files /2013/02/Why-So-Few-Women-in-Science-Technology-Engineering-and -Mathematics.pdf

Hong, L., & Page, S. E. (2004). Groups of diverse problem solvers can outperform groups of high-ability problem solvers. *Proceedings of the National Academy of Sciences of the United States of America, 101*(46), 16385–16389.

Jensen, E. (2009). *Teaching with poverty in mind.* Alexandria, VA: Association for Supervision and Curriculum Development.

Lee, C. D. (2003). Why we need to re-think race and ethnicity in educational research. *Educational Researcher, 32*(5), 3–5.

Lewis, C. W., Butler, B. R., Bonner, I. I., Fred, A., & Joubert, M. (2010). African American male discipline patterns and school district responses resulting impact on academic achievement: Implications for urban educators and policy makers. *Journal of African American Males in Education, 1*(1), 7–25.

Lickel, B., Schmader, T., & Hamilton, D. L. (2003). A case of collective responsibility: Who else was to blame for the Columbine High School shootings? *Personality and Social Psychology Bulletin, 29*(2), 194–204.

Lonsdale, C., Hodge, K., & Rose, E. A. (2008). The Behavioral Regulation in Sport Questionnaire (BRSQ): Instrument development and initial validity evidence. *Journal of Sport & Exercise Psychology, 30,* 323–355.

Martin, J. L. (Ed.). (2015). *Racial battle fatigue: Insights from the front lines of social justice advocacy.* Santa Barbara, CA: Praeger.

McIntosh, K., Girvan, E. J., Horner, R. H., Smolkowski, K., & Sugai, G. (2018). *A 5-Point Intervention Approach for Enhancing Equity in School Discipline.* Retrieved from https://www.pbis.org/Common/Cms/files/pbisresources /A%205-Point%20Intervention%20Approach%20for%20Enhancing%20 Equity%20in%20School%20Discipline.pdf

Milner, H. R. (2013a). Analyzing poverty, learning, and teaching through a critical race theory lens. *Review of Research in Education, 37,* 1–53.

Milner, H. R. (2013b). *Start where you are, but don't stay there: Understanding diversity, opportunity gaps, and teaching in today's classrooms.* Cambridge, MA: Harvard Education Press.

Moll, L., & Gonzalez, N. (1994). Lessons from research with language minority children. *Journal of Reading Behavior, 26*(4), 23–41.

Monroe, C. R. (2005). Why are "bad boys" always black? Causes of disproportionality in school discipline and recommendations for change. *The Clearing House: A Journal of Educational Strategies, Issues and Ideas, 79*(1), 45–50.

Morris, J. E., & Monroe, C. R. (2009). Why study the U.S. south? The nexus of race and place in investigating black student achievement. *Educational Researcher, 38*(1), 21–36.

Morris, M. W. (2016). *Pushout: The criminalization of black girls in schools.* New York, NY: New Press.

National Association of School Nurses. (2015). *Use of restraints, seclusion and corporal punishment in the school setting (Position Statement).* Silver Spring, MD: Author.

National Association of School Psychologists. (2014). Corporal punishment (Position Statement). Bethesda, MD. Retrieved from https://www.nasponline .org/research-and-policy/professional-positions/position-statements

O'Connor, C., & Fernandez, S. D. (2006). Race, class, and disproportionality: Reevaluating the relationship between poverty and special education placement. *Educational Researcher, 35*(6), 6–11.

Orfield, G., & Frankenberg, E. (2004, spring). "Where are we now?" *Teaching Tolerance.* Southern Poverty Law Center.

Page, S. (2007). *The difference: How the power of diversity creates better groups, firms, schools, and society.* Princeton, NJ: Princeton University Press.

Penner, A. M., & Saperstein, A. (2013). Engendering racial perceptions: An intersectional analysis of how social status shapes race. *Gender & Society, 27*(3), 319–344.

Perry, B. L., & Morris, E. W. (2014). Suspending progress collateral consequences of exclusionary punishment in public schools. *American Sociological Review, 79*(6), 1067–1087.

Positive Behavioral Interventions and Supports. (2019). Retrieved from https:// www.pbis.org/

Pujol, J. (2006). Myelination of language-related areas in the developing brain. *Neurology, 66,* 339–343.

Rollins, J. A. (2012). 2012: Revisiting the issue of corporal punishment in our nation's schools: Editorial. *Pediatric Nursing, 38*(5), 248.

Rotter, J. B. (1990). Internal versus external control of reinforcement: A case history of a variable. *American Psychologist, 45*(4), 489–493.

Salazar, M. (2013). A humanizing pedagogy: Reinventing the principles and practice of education as a journey toward liberation. *Review of Research in Education, 37,* 121–148.

Sege, R. D., Siegel, B. S., Council on Child Abuse and Neglect, Committee on Psychological Aspects of Child and Family Health. (2018). Effective discipline to raise healthy children. American Academy of Pediatrics policy statement. *Pediatrics, 142*(6), 1–10. doi: 10.1542/peds.2018–3112

Sharma, A., Joyner, A. M., & Osment, A. (2014). Adverse impact of racial isolation on student performance: A study in North Carolina. *Education Policy Analysis Archives, 22*(14).

Skiba, R. J., Michael, R. S., Nardo, A. C., & Peterson, R. L. (2002). The color of discipline: Sources of racial and gender disproportionality in school punishment. *Urban Review, 34*(4), 317–342.

Spencer, J. P. (2012). "Cultural deprivation" to cultural capital: The roots and continued relevance of compensatory education. *Teachers College Record, 114*(6), 1–5.

Steele, C. M. (2010). *Whistling Vivaldi and other clues to how stereotypes affect us.* New York, NY: W. W. Norton.

Steele, C. M., & Aronson, J. (1995). Stereotype threat and the intellectual test performance of African Americans. *Journal of Personality and Social Psychology, 69*(5), 797–811.

Toering, T. T., Elferink-Gemser, M. T., Jordet, G., & Visscher, C. (2009). Self-regulation and performance level in elite and non-elite youth soccer players. *Journal of Sports Sciences, 27*(14), 1509–1517.

U.S. Department of Education Office for Civil Rights. (2014, March). Civil rights data collection data snapshot: School discipline. Retrieved from http://www2.ed.gov/about/offices/list/ocr/docs/crdc-discipline-snapshot.pdf

Vallerand, R. J. (1997). Toward a hierarchical model of intrinsic and extrinsic motivation. In M. P. Zanna (Ed.), *Advances in experimental social psychology* (pp. 271–360). San Diego, CA: Academic Press.

Vallerand, R. J. (2001). Deci and Ryan's self-determination theory: A view from the hierarchical model of intrinsic and extrinsic motivation. *Psychological Inquiry, 11*, 312–318.

Vallerand, R. J., Pelletier, L. G., Blais, M. R., Brière, N. M., Senécal, C., & Vallières, E. F. (1992). The Academic Motivation Scale: A measure of intrinsic, extrinsic, and amotivation in education. *Educational & Psychological Measurement, 52*, 1003–1019.

Vallerand, R. J., Pelletier, L. G., Blais, M. R., Brière, N. M., Senécal, C., & Vallières, E. F. (1993). On the assessment of intrinsic, extrinsic, and amotivation in education: Evidence on the concurrent and construct validity of the Academic Motivation Scale. *Educational & Psychological Measurement, 53*, 159–172.

Wildhagen, T. (2012). How teachers and schools contribute to racial differences in the realization of academic potential. *Teachers College Record, 114*(7), 1–27.

Zion, S. D., & Blanchett, W. (2011). (Re)conceptualizing inclusion: Can critical race theory and interest convergence be utilized to achieve inclusion and equity for African American students? *Teachers College Record, 113*(10), 2186–2205.

8

Educational Psychology and Special Education: An Issue of Civil Rights

ORIGINS

The origin of special education can be traced to the early 20th century. Parent advocates and reformers argued that the social isolation of individuals with disabilities, often in rural institutions without access to education, proper medical care, exercise, and other necessities that many of us take for granted in modern American society, were not only inappropriate but also harmful and even abusive. In the mid-20th century, disability advocacy groups gained more leverage.

- 1961: President John F. Kennedy creates the President's Panel on Mental Retardation, which recommended federal aid to states.

- 1965: President Lyndon B. Johnson signs the Elementary and Secondary Education Act, providing funding for primary education, viewed by advocacy groups as increasing access to public education for children with disabilities.

Despite these two advancements, by the early 1970s public schools were only educating a small percentage of students with disabilities. This would change in 1975, with the enactment of the Education for all Handicapped Children Act (EHA).

- 1975: President Gerald Ford signs into law the Education for All Handicapped Children Act. Considered a landmark civil rights legislation, the act opened public school doors to millions of children with disabilities.

The Education for all Handicapped Children Act established the right to public education for all students regardless of disability, reauthorized in 1990 as the *Individuals with Disabilities Education Act.* The overarching goal of IDEA is to provide students with disabilities the same opportunities for education as those without disabilities.

IDEA requires that schools provide individualized or special education for students with disabilities; additionally, the law requires that states that accept public funding for education must provide special education services to students with disabilities who qualify under the law.

Nearly 1.8 million students with disabilities were excluded from public education prior to 1975. Currently, public schools provide special education and other services to nearly seven million children with disabilities.

Today, over 60 percent of students with disabilities are in general education classes 80 percent of the time or more. And interventions are being provided to infants, toddlers, and their families with special needs prior to entering formal schooling.

Students with disabilities are also referred to as "differently abled," or "exceptional children." Future teachers and education professionals should be aware that our language is constantly evolving; terms that were once acceptable to refer to groups of persons are no longer palatable.

It is important to note that not all students with disabilities are considered special education students. There are very specific federal guidelines a school must meet in order for a student to qualify for special education services.

ELIGIBILITY FOR SPECIAL EDUCATION

In order to qualify for special education, a student must meet all three of the following:

1. The student must have a disability (or multiple disabilities)
2. The student's disability (or disabilities) adversely impact their education performance.
3. The student's unique needs cannot be met through general education alone (with or without accommodations), and necessitates special instruction.

Eligibility for special education is based upon a comprehensive initial evaluation, including all existing data used to evaluate the student through the special education referral process and any additional evaluations necessary in order to determine eligibility. The initial evaluation report is used to determine what specific special education (and related) services the student needs.

IDEA

The Individuals with Disabilities Education Act (IDEA) is a federal law that provides for free appropriate public education to eligible children with disabilities in the United States and ensures special education and related services to those children. It also governs how states and public agencies provide early intervention, special education, and related services to students with disabilities.

IDEA provides specific guidelines regarding Free Appropriate Public Education, including the notion that education must be tailored to meet the needs of students with disabilities, and that it must benefit students and prepare them for future education, and/or to prepare them to live and work as independent people. The law also requires that education be provided in the least restrictive environment and that school officials consider students' disabilities when enforcing discipline.

Later amendments have led to increased access to the general education curriculum of the school, services for early childhood interventions (birth–five years of age), transition planning, and accountability measures for the achievement of students with disabilities. In sum, IDEA protects the rights of "infants, toddlers, children, and youth with disabilities and their families" (IDEA, n.d.).

In the last four decades, the expectations for all students have been heightened. No longer do schools segregate all students with disabilities from the general education classroom. Classrooms and schools have and are becoming more inclusive.

Additionally, the IDEA authorizes Formula Grants, provided to states to support special education, related services, and early intervention services and support; and Discretionary Grants, provided to state educational agencies, colleges and universities, and nonprofit organizations in order to support research and dissemination of said research, technology, professional development, and parent training and information in order to support students with disabilities. Congress reauthorized IDEA in 2004 and most recently amended it through Public Law 114-95, the Every Student Succeeds Act, in December 2015. In the law, Congress states:

Disability is a natural part of the human experience and in no way diminishes the right of individuals to participate in or contribute to society. Improving educational results for children with disabilities is an essential element of our national policy of ensuring equality of opportunity, full participation, independent living, and economic self-sufficiency for individuals with disabilities. (IDEA, 2015)

INDIVIDUALIZED EDUCATION PROGRAM

An individualized education program (IEP) is a legal document created by a team of school officials, including the special education teacher, the general education teacher, and students; a parent or guardian; and other relevant stakeholders when warranted, such as a school psychologist or speech pathologist. The IEP defines specific objectives for a student with a disability and what special accommodations the child will receive to meet them. The purpose of an IEP is to assist students with disabilities to meet their educational goals more easily than without this support. The IEP is also intended to assist teachers and other education professionals (e.g., administrators, paraprofessionals) with whom the student will interact to understand the students, the disability, how the disability impacts learning, and the student's unique needs. The IEP details how the particular student learns, how the student can best demonstrate learning, and what schools/service providers must do in order to assist the student to learn more effectively. IEP development requires assessing the student in all areas related to the disability, while considering access to the general education curriculum, writing goals and objectives corresponding to the student's needs, and providing a placement for the student in the least restrictive environment.

The *least restrictive environment* is an issue of equity, and pertains to the right of students living with disabilities to be educated with nondisabled peers. For example, students with disabilities should not be segregated from their nondisabled peers for the entire school day. This segregation not only creates undue stigma but also presupposes that students with disabilities cannot keep pace with their nondisabled peers in all curricular areas. This is not the case.

In order to be placed on an IEP, there are two requirements:

1. A child must have one or more of the 12 specific disabilities listed in the IDEA. These include:
   1. Specific learning disability (SLD)
   2. Other health impairment
   3. Autism spectrum disorder (ASD)

4. Emotional disturbance

5. Speech or language impairment

6. Visual impairment, including blindness

7. Deafness

8. Hearing impairment

9. Deaf-blindness

10. Orthopedic impairment

11. Intellectual disability

12. Traumatic brain injury

13. Multiple disabilities

2. The disability must affect the child's educational performance and/or ability to learn and benefit from the general education curriculum, necessitating specialized instruction.

504 PLANS

504 plans stem from Section 504 of the Rehabilitation Act (1973), which was the first civil rights laws for individuals with disabilities. The law prohibits discrimination against people with disabilities in programs receiving federal financial assistance, and is the forerunner of the Americans with Disabilities Act. Section 504 covers students who do not meet the requirements for special education but who still require some accommodations in order to succeed academically. Students are eligible for 504 plans if they currently have a physical or mental impairment that adversely impacts their learning. For example, students with ADHD may qualify for 504 plans if their ADHD "substantially limits" their ability to learn.

504 plans are formal plans developed by school officials to provide students with disabilities the supports they need to succeed. 504 plans are not a part of special education, so they cannot provide individualized instruction. The purpose of 504 plans is to provide access for students with disabilities to the same education as nondisabled peers. One way in which 504 plans can assist students with disabilities is through "accommodations," such as being provided extended time on tests or permission to leave the classroom for breaks. Some 504 plans include speech therapy or specific study skills based upon student need. There are no hard-and-fast rules for what 504 plans should look like; schools often create written 504 plans, but they are not required to do so. However, schools are required to put in writing their formal policies for their 504 plan procedures.

Table 8.1   IEP and 504 Differences

Individualized Education Programs	504 Plans
An individualized plan for a student's special education experience at school.	An individualized plan providing a student access to learning at school.
Provides individualized *special education* and related services to meet the unique needs of the child.	Provides services and changes to the learning environment to meet the needs of the child as adequately as other students.
No cost to parents.	No cost to parents.
IEPs are a part of the Individuals with Disabilities Education Act (IDEA)	504 plans are part of Section 504 of the Rehabilitation Act of 1973.
This is a federal special education law for children with disabilities.	This is a federal civil rights law.
There are two requirements to obtain an IEP:	There are two requirements to obtain a 504 plan:
1. A student has one or more of the 13 specific disabilities listed in IDEA.	1. A student has any disability (including many learning or attention issues).
2. The disability must impact the student's educational performance and/or ability to learn from the general education curriculum, necessitating the need for specialized instruction.	2. The disability must interfere with the student's ability to learn in a general education classroom.
	IDEA funds cannot be used to serve students with 504 plans.

Adapted from https://www.understood.org/en/school-learning/special-services/504-plan/the-difference-between-ieps-and-504-plans

Students of educational psychology and even beginning teachers are often confused as to the differences between an IEP and 504 plans. The table below may assist with understanding these differences.

SPECIAL EDUCATION VOCABULARY[1]

Auditory Processing Disorder

Students experiencing auditory processing disorder typically have normal hearing but struggle to process and make sense from sounds—particularly if background noise is present. In short, students with auditory processing disorder can have trouble making sense of what people say.

Autism

Autism is a complex developmental disability that typically appears during the first three years of life and impacts an individual's ability to communicate and interact with others. Autism is defined by a certain set of behaviors that affect individuals differently and to varying degrees.

TEMPLE GRANDIN: BEST PRACTICES FOR AUTISM ADVOCACY

Born Mary Grandin and later nicknamed "Temple" to avoid confusion with a family maid who carried the same name, Temple Grandin (August 29, 1947–) had a challenging but bright childhood. Unable to speak until the age of three, Temple was able to overcome every obstacle put in her way and carve out a path of success. As a baby and toddler, Temple possessed a strong aversion to touch and showed no attachment to her mother, Eustacia. This greatly troubled Eustacia, as she already lacked confidence in her role as a mother. Eustacia possessed little experience with babies, and Temple was her first child. When Eustacia compared her interactions with Temple to the interactions of other children with their mothers, she felt insecure. As a result, Richard Grandin, Temple's father, and Eustacia sought help from a therapist.

After various tests and doctors, Temple was diagnosed with infant schizophrenia, what is now called autism, as a toddler and doctors strongly encouraged Temple's mother to institutionalize the child. Richard Grandin, as was custom of the time, supported such an endeavor, as he thought that Temple's behavior was too much for the family to handle. Eustacia, however, was passionately against such a move. Eustacia at just 19 took a stand against her husband, who was 20 years her senior. Eustacia vehemently argued against the institutionalization of her child, and instead worked to begin intervention programs to aid Temple. Eustacia strove to equip Temple with the tools of surviving within American society, assigning her a caregiver and teaching her manners. Eustacia personally mentored her daughter and pulled upon the support of various experts to best teach her daughter. By the age of four, Temple was able to speak full sentences and communicate her feelings. At the age of five, Temple would go on to attend private school, where she would have a fairly normal elementary school education.

Despite her easygoing elementary school days, junior high was tough for Temple. The change of scenery and the increased bullying of her peers took a toll on her. Temple was unable to read social cues from her peers, so she had a lot of trouble making friends. Coupled with that, many children ruthlessly teased her, which often led to violent outbursts from Temple. To cope, Temple often escaped to the barns on the school's property. She developed an affinity for the horses, and she could easily read the signals that animals gave off to showcase their fear. Often, Temple could calm the animals before their fear escalated into panic. This knack for calming animals would later greatly benefit Temple's research in cattle slaughter.

In high school, Temple developed obsessions with various subjects or objects. Mr. Carlock, Temple's beloved high school science teacher, in turn channeled these obsessions to benefit Temple. He assigned her science projects and extra work to further her love of science and provide her with a productive and healthy obsession. Mr. Carlock would become a lifelong mentor and supporter for Temple. With Mr. Carlock's guidance, Temple was able briefly to escape the judgement of her peers and bury herself in science work.

The summer after her senior year of high school, Temple was encouraged to stay at her Aunt Ann's cattle ranch. Temple was against the plans, as the change of scenery inspired anxiety within her; however, she eventually went and enjoyed herself immensely. There, Temple fell in love with cows and discovered the squeeze chute. The squeeze chute was utilized to calm cows when they became panicked. Temple found inspiration for herself in observing the cows. Temple often craved physical touch, but like most autistic children, could not cope with the sensory overload that human contact entailed. As a result, she sought a method of receiving the comfort of a hug without the human element. During this summer, she would invent the squeeze machine, which aided her in calming down when she began to panic. Temple would simply enter the machine, pull a lever, and the sides would collapse to comfort her. Temple's work and research would later impact both the cattle and autistic communities.

Throughout college, Temple began a more in-depth study into the treatment of cattle. Eventually, she would develop a method to herd cattle more calmly towards slaughter. This humane method would decrease panic levels of cattle, which would in turn decrease the likelihood of gruesome deaths. Temple developed a maze in which cattle would herd themselves around curves and bends. They would not be rushed, and they would go through the maze single-file, therefore decreasing the likelihood of a stampede. Temple observed that farmers would often leave shirts or bags hanging over the rails of the pens, causing cattle to panic and balk. In addition, cows were often led too quickly through the process and would injure themselves during the process. Temple revolutionized the farming industry and changed the ways in which cattle are led to slaughter. Because of Temple, cattle now peacefully approach their deaths without being harmed prior to being slaughtered.

In addition, Temple continues to be a strong advocate for autism awareness. Temple offers valuable insight to parents on the perspectives of autistic children. As Temple was growing up, autism was not even a term yet, and, as a result of the common practice of institutionalizing autistic people, many people never interacted with autistic people. People were never exposed to autism, so they simply did not understand autistic people. People pushed the problem away rather than tackling it head on. Temple continues to work to change that. Temple advocates against institutionalization and offers specific steps for parents in taking care of their autistic children. She also works to explain common tendencies of autistic children, such as sensory overload and aversion to change. Temple is working to shed new and valuable light on autism awareness.

—*Brianna Boehlke*

Autism Spectrum Disorder

Autism spectrum disorder is a developmental disability covering a wide range of symptoms and skills but mainly impacting an individual's social and communication skills. It can also impact behavior, and is characterized by difficulties in social interaction, verbal and nonverbal communication, and repetitive behaviors.

Deaf-Blindness

Individuals with this diagnosis have both hearing and visual impairments. Their communication and other needs are so vast that programs for the deaf or blind cannot meet them.

Deafness

Individuals with this diagnosis have a severe hearing impairment. They are not able to process language through hearing.

Dyscalculia

Dyscalculia involves learning challenges in math. Students with dyscalculia may struggle with quantities, or with binary differences. They may not make connections between the written words corresponding to numerical values (e.g., 2 versus two). Students with dyscalculia may also have difficulty recalling math facts, such as memorizing their times tables.

Dysgraphia

Dysgraphia involves issues with expressing one's self in writing. Students with dysgraphia may have difficulty holding a writing utensil, and writing in a straight line. Other issues include the aesthetic or standard appearance of handwriting.

Dyslexia

Dyslexia is the most common learning challenge and involves the difficulty in reading, a major indicator of which involves trouble decoding, breaking down words by syllable to their individual sounds, or phonemic awareness. Dyslexia involves problems with reading accuracy and fluency. Students with dyslexia may have problems comprehending what they have read, but they may comprehend what is read to them. Dyslexia can also involve issues with spelling, writing, and math.

Emotional Disturbance

Students with emotional disturbances, sometimes known as emotional impairments, involve mental health issues that can include anxiety disorders, bipolar disorder, behavioral conduct disorders, depression, eating disorders, obsessive-compulsive disorder, schizophrenia, and psychotic disorders.

Hearing Impairment

This impairment can refer to hearing losses not covered by deafness definition. These losses can change over time. Having difficulties with hearing is not the same as experiencing auditory processing issues.

Intellectual Disability (ID)

Students with intellectual disabilities possess below-average intellectual abilities. Students possessing intellectual disabilities may also exhibit poor communication skills, self-care skills, and social skills. ID has previously been referred to as *mental retardation*. As language has evolved, this term is no longer acceptable to use.

Multiple Disabilities

Students possessing multiple disabilities have more than one condition covered by IDEA. Possessing multiple disabilities creates educational needs that cannot be met in single programs designed for any single condition.

Nonverbal Learning Disability (NVLD)

Nonverbal learning disabilities involve deficits in social skills, which can impact student learning. Students with NVLD do not always communicate in socially appropriate ways; they may have particular difficulty with nonverbal communication such as body language, facial expressions, and tone of voice. Students with NVLD often miss social cues, so they may have difficulty making friends and cause misunderstandings with parents and teachers.

Orthopedic Impairment

An orthopedic impairment involves an impairment to a student's body, no matter the cause, involving deformities of bones or muscles (e.g., cerebral palsy). These physical disabilities can impact the learning process.

Other Health Impairment

Other health impairment is an umbrella term that covers conditions such as those that limit a student's strength, energy, or alertness (e.g., attention-deficit/hyperactivity disorder); diabetes; epilepsy; heart conditions; hemophilia; lead poisoning; leukemia; nephritis; rheumatic fever; sickle cell anemia, and Tourette syndrome.

Performance Deficit

A performance deficit pertains to a student's social or academic skills deficits, where students understand a specific skill but fail to practice it consistently.

Speech or Language Impairment

This is an umbrella that covers a number of communication issues, including stuttering, impaired articulation, and language or voice impairment.

Traumatic Brain Injury

Traumatic brain injuries are caused by accidents of physical force that can impact learning.

Universal Design for Learning

Universal Design for Learning (UDL) is a pedagogical approach intended to make curriculum accessible for all students, regardless of background, learning style, ability, and so on. Specifically, UDL is a framework addressing learning barriers including inflexible or "one-size-fits-all" curricula. Gifted learners and learners with disabilities are particularly vulnerable, but all learners may have unmet needs based upon poor curricular design. Often UDL is referred to as "curb cutting," or removing barriers so that all learners have equal access to learning. When curricula are designed to meet the needs of an imaginary "average," or "teaching to the middle," they do not address learner variability. "Teaching to the middle" does provide all individuals with fair and equitable learning opportunities for it excludes learners with different abilities, backgrounds, and motivations. The UDL framework encourages teachers to meet students where they are. For more information, see http://www.udlcenter.org/aboutudl/whatisudl.

Visual Impairment (Including Blindness)

Students with visual impairments can include both partial sight and blindness. If eyewear can correct this problem, then it does qualify under IDEA.

ADDITIONAL SPECIAL EDUCATION VOCABULARY

Accommodations

Accommodations are curricular changes made by the teacher in order to compensate for the learning challenges of students without modifying the curriculum. Students receiving accommodations experience the same curriculum and take the same tests as students without disabilities. Examples of accommodations include large print textbooks, additional time on assignments, space for movement or time for breaks, and use of a study carrel.

Assessment Plan

An assessment plan is a written description of the assessments used to evaluate a student's strengths, weaknesses, and progress in order to determine special education eligibility and the types of services necessary to help the student succeed. IDEA requires schools complete such as evaluation within 60 days from the time of parental consent to do so.

Attention Deficit Disorder (ADD)

Some consider ADD to be an outdated term used to describe students with difficulty paying attention without being hyperactive.

Attention Deficit/Hyperactivity Disorder (AD/HD)

Attention Deficit/Hyperactivity Disorder is a condition that can make it difficult for students to sit still, control their behavior, and pay attention. Students with AD/HD are sometimes eligible for special education services.

Behavior Intervention Plan (BIP)

A behavior intervention plan targets one to three of a student's undesirable behaviors with interventions specifically addressing a measurable, clearly stated targeted behavior. A BIP may include prevention strategies, which can stop the behavior before it begins, or replacement behaviors.

Behavior Management

Behavior management is a process of responding to, preventing, and/or deescalating disruptive behaviors.

Behavior Support Plan (BSP)

Behavior support plans are proactive action plans that address negative or disruptive student behaviors that are impeding the learning of others.

Developmental Delay

Developmental delays can pertain to delays in one or more of the following: cognitive development, physical development (including vision and hearing), communication development, social and/or emotional development, and adaptive development (including eating skills, dressing and toileting skills and other areas of personal responsibility).

Developmental Milestones

A set of age-specific tasks that most children can do within a certain age range.

Differentiated Instruction

Differentiated instruction involves teachers actively planning for differences in student learning. Teachers utilize varied methods and resources in order to meet the learning needs of students with varied backgrounds, readiness, skill levels, and interests within a classroom.

Inclusion, or Inclusive Classroom

Inclusion is a philosophy advocating for and securing opportunities for students with disabilities to learn inside traditional mainstream classrooms.

Individualized Education Program (IEP)

A legal document that defines the specific special education services provided for a student by the school district.

Individualized Education Program (IEP) Team

The team of qualified professionals, including a special education teacher, data analyst, district representative, and general education teacher, as well as parents/caregivers. This group makes all decisions related to the instructional program of students with special needs, including placement and services provided.

Individualized Family Services Plan

A written treatment plan mapping early intervention services a child (birth to three) will receive, and specifics on how and when these services will be administered. This plan also details the child's current levels of functioning, specific needs, and goals or outcomes for treatment.

Individuals with Disabilities Education Act (IDEA)

A federal law guaranteeing educational rights to students with disabilities, making it illegal for school districts to refuse education to any student because of disability.

Interventions

Interventions are teaching procedures used by teachers to assist struggling students to succeed. Interventions can be academic or behavioral.

Least Restrictive Environment

Least restrictive environment pertains to the environment in which students with disabilities are educated, mandated by IDEA, as a classroom setting that is as close as possible to the general education setting.

Modifications

Curricular adaptations that compensate for learners' weaknesses by changing or lowering expectations or standards. Modifications may include altered assignments, modified tests and grading, and modified expectations.

Monitoring

Part of the Response to Intervention processes, involving assessing, keeping accurate records, and monitoring student progress regarding responsiveness to instruction and intervention.

Occupational Therapist

An occupational therapist is a professional trained to treat patients with injuries, illnesses, or disabilities through the therapeutically practicing daily activities. Occupational therapists assist individuals develop, recover, and improve the skills needed for daily life.

Response to Intervention (RTI)

Response to Intervention is a process used by educators to help struggling students. If students do not respond to initial interventions, more focused interventions are developed. Effective interventions are apparent when learning is accelerated, and fewer students are at risk for academic failure, among other factors. There are three tiers of interventions within the RTI process. For example, all students in Tier 1 receive quality differentiated instruction; these students are periodically screened to identify struggling students who may need additional support. In which case, these students would move on to Tier 2 interventions where they are provided with intensive instruction paired with their needs and progress rates. Students receiving Tier 3 interventions receive individualized and intensive interventions targeting their learning needs and providing remediation.

Speech-Language Pathologist

A speech-language pathologist is a professional who diagnoses and treats communication and swallowing disorders (also known as a speech therapist).

"Stay Put" Law

A law indicating that a parent can request that a student stay in their current educational placement while an IEP is in dispute.

Student Baseline

Student baseline pertains to a student's academic starting point determined by data, used to measure a student's academic progress throughout the year.

Transition/Transition Plan

Transition is a term used to describe a change in a student's school or program. A transition plan is specific to an IEP. For example, a transition plan may pertain to how a student will transition to life after high school.

Widening Gap

The gap between what a student with a disability knows and what their peers know, which widens as they advance in grade level.

STEREOTYPE THREAT AND SPECIAL EDUCATION

Stereotype threat is the fear of confirming the negative stereotypes held about one's group by others not possessing the same identities (Steele & Aronson, 1995). This heightened fear to "represent" for one's group may result in higher stress and lower performance. For example, if a math teacher holds the stereotype that girls are not as good at math as their male counterparts, the females in the class may feel additional pressure to perform well in order to dis-confirm that stereotype that the teacher holds. This added pressure and stress may cause the stereotyped individuals to perform poorly, thus perpetuating said stereotypes. It becomes a vicious circle, and one that serves to reinforce stereotypes. According to Hill, Corbett, and St. Rose (2010), "Stereotype threat arises in situations when a negative stereotype is relevant to evaluating performance" (p. 39). Stereotype threat can impact individuals both psychologically and physiologically. Fortunately, stereotype threat can be counteracted by teaching students about it (Hill, Corbett, & St. Rose, 2010). Unfortunately, this is not often the case.

Steele (2010) pinpoints the identity categories that are often rife for stereotype threat, including age, sexual orientation, race, gender, ethnicity, political affiliation, mental illness, and disability. Steele (2010) further illuminates the danger of stereotype threat: "We know what 'people think.' We know that anything we do that fits the stereotype could be taken as confirming it" (p. 5).

BEST PRACTICES FOR EDUCATING UNDERGRADUATES TO WORK IN THE FIELD OF DISABILITY SERVICES

Autism spectrum disorder (ASD) is a developmental disability associated with communication, social, and behavioral challenges. In April 2018, the Centers for Disease Control and Prevention (CDC) reported that the current prevalence of autism is 1 in 59 (CDC, 2018). This is the most recent increase since 2000, when the CDC reported that 1 in 150 children have ASD. With the increased diagnosis comes an increase in the need for highly trained professionals to provide quality services to those with ASD. It's the mission of the Spectrum Education Center to give undergraduate students the opportunity to receive high-quality training.

I had two experiences that were instrumental in the vision for the Spectrum Education Center. The first was students' enthusiastic response to the creation of a new course, Introduction to Autism, at the University of Mount Union. I designed the course for students interested in gaining an understanding of the characteristics and incidence of autism, and the implications for children's learning, behavior, and ability to process information. Students filled the classroom the first time it was offered, and every semester since then.

My second experience was research I conducted on best practices for adults with autism. My research led to the recognition of the need for well-trained professionals in the field of disability services. The field has historically been underserved, requiring little more than a high school diploma and driver's license to meet hiring requirements. Without adequate training, service providers cannot effectively meet the needs of those with ASD.

Students' enthusiasm for coursework related to ASD and the growing need for professional training made an undergraduate program in disabilities service training ripe for development. The Spectrum Education Center at the University of Mount Union was founded in 2015. Spectrum offers a semester-long immersive program that pairs practical experience with coursework. Students accepted into the Spectrum Program work at clinical sites that serve people with ASD, while engaging in rigorous coursework on developmental disorders. In addition, students earn the credential of Registered Behavior Technician while enrolled in the program.

The Spectrum Program is rooted in best practice. The program is collaborative, as it supports the community by combining the efforts of clinical sites and academic institutions; efficient, as it reduces the burden of staffing and training for clinical sites; cyclical, as the efforts of the stakeholders are continually evaluated to maintain the quality of the program; and valuable, as it facilitates the creation and maintenance of services to those in the community with developmental disabilities.

The Spectrum Education Center serves the growing interest of highly motivated undergraduate students who want to engage in valuable work that benefits their long-term goals related to careers in autism intervention. Spectrum's internship program increases the visibility of its graduates, making them more desirable to graduate programs and potential employers.

—Dr. Kristine Turko

THE DISPROPORTIONALITY OF STUDENTS OF COLOR IN SPECIAL EDUCATION: STEREOTYPE THREAT?

Artiles (2011) argues that special education policies do nothing to dismantle the hierarchical structure of schools, which makes special education "complicit in the perpetuation of educational inequities for certain subgroups of students, most notably poor students and racial minority learners" (p. 433). White, middle-class children are the "unmarked norm" against which the developmental progress of other children is measured (O'Connor & Fernandez, 2006). Blanchett (2006) argues that, ironically after *Brown v. Board*, special education as a field has done much to resegregate students of color, which further limits their academic, psychological, and future employment potential.

For example, throughout the history of education, black students have been disproportionately placed in the most severe categories of special education diagnoses, are less likely to exit these programs once placed, and are less likely to be mainstreamed. Schools create mean differences that serve to increase minority special education referrals and more of these students being labeled as disabled because behaviors are perceived differently, which can also increase the likelihood of minority children being referred for special education services (O'Connor & Fernandez, 2006). However, if African American Language (AAL) were the norm within schools, then the speakers of AAL would be perceived as academically competent, literate, and successful. Thus, as O'Connor & Fernandez (2006) argue, "the underachievement of minority students is not a function of deficient parenting practices but is rooted in the 'arbitrary' standards of schools that are represented as if they were rational and culturally neutral" (p. 9).

Further, O'Connor and Fernandez (2006) argue that the underachievement of minority students is exacerbated by their disproportionality in underfunded schools with unqualified or uncertified teachers lacking experience. However, when those same students do attend predominantly white schools, "they are resegregated into basic and remedial courses, where their achievement suffers under low standards and poor instruction. . . . These inequities prevent minority students from performing competently on standard indexes of achievement" (p. 9). In sum, racism and white privilege serve to maintain the disproportionate numbers of students of color in special education through various means: insufficiently funded schools, culturally unresponsive curriculum, and underprepared teachers (Blanchett, 2006).

NOTE

1. For more information, see https://www.understood.org/en/learning-atten tion-issues/child-learning-disabilities

REFERENCES

Artiles, A. J. (2011). Toward an interdisciplinary understanding of educational equity and difference: The case of the racialization of ability. *Educational Researcher, 40*(9), 431–445.

Blanchett, W. J. (2006). Disproportionate representation of African American students in special education: Acknowledging the role of white privilege and racism. *Educational Researcher, 35*(6), 24–28.

Centers for Disease Control and Prevention (CDC). (2018, April 26). *Data and statistics.* Retrieved from https://www.cdc.gov/ncbddd/autism/data.html

Hill, C., Corbett, C., & St. Rose, A. (2010). *Why so few? Women in science, technology, engineering, and mathematics.* Washington, DC: AAUW.

IDEA. (n.d.). *Individuals with disabilities education act.* Retrieved from https:// sites.ed.gov/idea/

IDEA. (2015). *Public law 114-95.* Retrieved from https://www.congress.gov/114 /plaws/publ95/PLAW-114publ95.htm

O'Connor, C., & Fernandez, S. D. (2006). Race, class, and disproportionality: Reevaluating the relationship between poverty and special education placement. *Educational Researcher, 35*(6), 6–11.

Steele, C. (2010). *Whistling Vivaldi: How stereotypes affect us and what we can do.* New York: W. W. Norton.

Steele, C. M., & Aronson, J. (1995). Stereotype threat and the intellectual test performance of African Americans. *Journal of Personality and Social Psychology, 69*(5), 797–811.

ADDITIONAL RESOURCES ON SPECIAL EDUCATION

Allsopp, D., Lovin, L. H., & Van Ingen, S. (2017). Supporting mathematical proficiency. *Teaching Exceptional Children, 49*(4), 273–283.

Anastasiou, D., & Keller, C. E. (2014). Cross-national differences in special education coverage: An empirical analysis. *Exceptional Children, 80*(3), 353–367.

Bottge, B. A., Cohen, A. S., & Choi, H. (2018). Comparisons of mathematics intervention effects in resource and inclusive classrooms. *Exceptional Children, 84*(2), 197–212.

Breit-Smith, A., Busch, J. D., Dinnesen, M. S., & Ying, G. (2017). Interactive book reading with expository science texts in preschool special education classrooms. *Teaching Exceptional Children, 49*(3), 185–193.

Brock, M. E., Cannella-Malone, H. I., Seaman, R. L., Andzik, N. R., Schaefer, J. M., Page, E. J., . . . & Dueker, S. A. (2017). Findings across practitioner training studies in special education: A comprehensive review and meta-analysis. *Exceptional Children, 84* (1), 7–26.

Brownell, M., Kiely, M. T., Haager, D., Boardman, A., Corbett, N., Algina, J., Dingle, M. P., & Urbach, J. (2017). Literacy learning cohorts: Content-focused approach to improving special education teachers' reading instruction. *Exceptional Children, 83*(2), 143–164.

Burke, M. M., & Decker, J. R. (2017). Extended school year: Legal and practical considerations for educators. *Teaching Exceptional Children, 49*(5), 339–346.

Collins, L. W., Sweigart, C. A., Landrum, T. J., & Cook, B. G. (2017). Navigating common challenges and pitfalls in the first years of special education. *Teaching Exceptional Children, 49*(4), 213–222.

Council for Exceptional Children: https://wwwcec.sped.org/

Council for Exceptional Children. (2014a). Council for Exceptional Children: Standards for evidence-based practices in special education. *Teaching Exceptional Children, 46*(6), 206–212.

Council for Exceptional Children. (2014b). Evidence-based special education in the context of scarce evidence-based practices: The Council for Exceptional Children's Interdivisional Research Group. *Teaching Exceptional Children, 47*(2), 81–84.

Council for Exceptional Children. (2017). High-leverage practices in special education. *Teaching Exceptional Children, 49*(5), 355–360.

Coyne, M. D., & Koriakin, T. A. (2017). What do beginning special educators need to know about intensive reading interventions? *Teaching Exceptional Children, 49*(4), 239–248.

Dewey, J., Sindelar, P. T., Bettini, E., Boe, E. E., Rosenberg, M. S., & Leko, C. (2017). Explaining the decline in special education teacher employment from 2005 to 2012. *Exceptional Children, 83*(3), 315–329.

Francis, G. L., Haines, S. J., & Nagro, S. A. (2017). Developing relationships with immigrant families: Learning by asking the right questions. *Teaching Exceptional Children, 50*(2), 95–105.

Fuchs, L. S., Fuchs, D., Malone, A. S. (2017). The taxonomy of intervention intensity. *Teaching Exceptional Children, 50*(1), 35–43.

Gage, N. A., Cook, B. G., & Reichow, B. (2017). Publication bias in special education meta- analyses. *Exceptional Children, 83*(4), 428–445.

Harris, K. R., Graham, S., Aitken, A. A., Barkel, A., Houston, J., & Ray, A. (2017). Teaching spelling, writing, and reading for writing. *Teaching Exceptional Children, 49*(4), 262–272.

Justice, L. M., Logan, J. A. R., Kaderavek, J. N., & Dynia, J. M. Print-focused read-alouds in early childhood special education programs. *Exceptional Children, 81*(3), 292–311.

Leko, M. M., Brownell, M. T., Sindelar, P. T., & Kiely, M. T. (2015). Envisioning the future of special education personnel preparation in a standards-based era. *Exceptional Children, 82*(1), 25–43.

Lewis, T. J., Hatton, H. L., Jorgenson, C., & Maynard, D. (2017). What beginning special educators need to know about conducting functional behavioral assessments. *Teaching Exceptional Children, 49*(4), 231–238.

Mason-Williams, L. (2014). Unequal opportunities: A profile of the distribution of special education teachers. *Exceptional Children, 81*(2), 247–262.

Morgan, P. L., Farkas, G., Cook, M. Strassfeld, N. M., Hillemeier, M. M., . . . Schussler, D. L. (2017). Are black children disproportionately overrepresented in special education? A best-evidence synthesis. *Exceptional Children, 83*(2), 181–198.

Morgan, P. L., Farkas, G., Hillemeier, M. M., Hui L., Pun, W. H., & Cook, M. (2017). Cross-cohort evidence of disparities in service receipt for speech or language impairments. *Exceptional Children, 84*(1), 27–41.

Riccomini, P. J., Morano, S., & Hughes, C. A. (2017). Big ideas in special education: Specially designed instruction, high-leverage practices, explicit instruction, and intensive instruction. *Teaching Exceptional Children, 50*(1), 20–27.

Schulte, A. C., & Stevens, J. J. (2015). Once, sometimes, or always in special education: Mathematics growth and achievement gaps. *Exceptional Children, 81*(3), 370–387.

Scruggs, T. E., & Mastropieri, M. A. (2017). Making inclusion work with co-teaching. *Teaching Exceptional Children, 49*(4), 284–293.

Sweigart, C. A., & Collins, L. W. (2017). Supporting the needs of beginning special education teachers and their students. *Teaching Exceptional Children, 49*(4), 209–212.

Umansky, I. M., Thompson, K. D., & Díaz, G. (2017). Using an ever—English learner framework to examine disproportionality in special education. *Exceptional Children, 84*(1), 76–96.

Vaughn, S., & Swanson, E. A. (2015). Special education research advances knowledge in education. *Exceptional Children, 82*(1), 11–24.

Wood, A. (2016). *Temple Grandin: Voice for the voiceless.* New York, NY: Skyhorse Publishing.

9

Protections for Contemporary Student Minority Groups against Oppression

Teachers and other school employees must understand that there are various disenfranchised groups, historically and otherwise, within our schools; their status makes them more vulnerable to discrimination, harassment, and negative academic consequences.

Particularly relevant to today's schools and classrooms is protecting nonhegemonic students from bullying and harassment from peers, and potentially teachers and other school staff, as well as adequately preparing teachers to teach in a culturally responsive manner that inherently presupposes an equity-based pedagogy and asset-based mindset for all students.

In an educational context, there are some students who are more vulnerable than others. The further an individual is from the mythical norm (see Chapter 5), the more vulnerable they are to "othering." This othering can lead to external consequences, such as bullying and harassment, as well as internal consequences that result from external factors, such as suicidal ideation, suicide, depression, reduced academic performance, and alienation from peers and family.

MINORITY GROUP VOCABULARY

Asset-Based Mindset

Viewing students' interests and culture/race/ethnicity as strengths within the class, rather than something that must be "overcome."

Cultural Responsiveness

Respecting, valuing, and centering student culture in the classroom setting.

Curricularly Underserved Students

Students who do not see themselves within their curriculum. For the nonhegemonic student, counterstories and counterhistories can provide validation for and pride in one's own culture and increase engagement in school when they can relate to the curriculum as opposed to always being othered. For the hegemonic student, counterstories and counterhistories can work to undermine stereotypes that dominant students hold for minoritized populations with which they may have little contact, thereby potentially reducing implicit bias.

ELL Students

ELL is an acronym for English Language Learners, or students who are learning English as a second language.

Equity-Based Pedagogy

Making issues of equity the center of a classroom or school.

Immigrant Students

Immigrant students who students who have come to the United States from a different country.

LGBTQ+

An acronym for members of the Lesbian, Gay, Bisexual, Transgender, and Queer community. The + represents the other identities embedded under this label, such as Intersex, Questioning, and Ally, and the identities yet to be identified.

Nonhegemonic Students

Students who possess one or several historically marginalized identity categories, such as those of a nondominant/nonprivileged race, class, gender, sexuality, religion, ethnicity, or disability.

Undocumented Students

A relatively new and more culturally responsive term for students who were formally known as "illegals," also known as "Dreamers."

TITLE IX DEFINED[1]

Title IX of the Education Amendments of 1972 states, "No person in the United States shall, on the basis of sex, be excluded from participation in, be denied the benefits of, or be subjected to discrimination under any education program or activity receiving federal financial assistance." Title IX was named the Patsy T. Mink Equal Opportunity in Education Act on October 9, 2002.

Students' Rights under Title IX

Title IX protects students of all genders and sexual orientations from sex discrimination in schools. Students in federally funded institutions, public schools, colleges, and universities[2] have a right to an education free from discrimination on the basis of sex—including equitable access to all academic programs, activities, athletics, course offerings, admissions, recruitment, scholarships—and to be free from harassment (including assault) based upon sex, gender, gender identity and expression (real and perceived), and sexual orientation (real and perceived).[3] Title IX protects students in academic and nonacademic activities because of pregnancy, birth, miscarriage, and abortion. Title IX also protects faculty, staff, and whistleblowers from sexual harassment, sex discrimination, and retaliation.[4]

School policies must provide for prompt and equitable investigation and resolution, including time frames for resolution and an antiretaliation statement (Title IX prohibits retaliation against those who file complaints). School policies must specifically indicate that sexual assault, even a single incident, is covered under Title IX. Students have the right to file a complaint with the school if their rights under Title IX are violated. Victims may also file a complaint with the Department of Education's Office for Civil Rights if a school's policies or handling of a complaint are not compliant with Title IX. Victims may also recover monetary damages under Title IX if the school shows deliberate indifference in dealing with the discrimination or related retaliation.

Each federally funded institution (school district) must designate a Title IX coordinator to oversee compliance and grievance procedures. The identity and contact information of the Title IX coordinator must be made public and be readily available to students, staff, and parents.

LGBTQ+ STUDENTS

According to Sallee and Diaz (2013), individuals in more vulnerable identity classes (e.g., those possessing nonhegemonic identities, such as racial and ethnic minorities, sexual minorities, and women), while protected by civil rights laws, are more susceptible to bullying. For example, LGBTQ+ students are the most susceptible group of students to experience bullying and harassment in schools (GLSEN, 2017). It has been documented that LGBTQ+ students have been more exposed to harassment since the 2016 election (Turner, 2017). LGBTQ+ students are also the most vulnerable to suicide (GLSEN, 2017).

WOMEN AND GIRLS

Women are more likely to report being bullied—and more likely victims of bullying that takes on the form of sexual harassment (Sallee & Diaz, 2013). Bullies tend to target only those who are the most vulnerable, for a variety of reasons (Kohut, 2008), such as identity characteristics. Also, the degree of the bully's personal feelings of inadequacy, often in relation to the target, who is often high performing, is relevant.

ELL STUDENTS

In postelection 2016, ELL students may be more subject to increased harassment, particularly if they are perceived to be "undocumented." In our current milieu, there are increasing negative national sentiments toward immigrants, individuals speaking a first language other than

English, and individuals who are perceived to be in the United States "illegally," whether or not by their own choice.

STUDENTS EXPOSED TO TRAUMA

National estimates project that approximately 60 percent of school-aged children have experienced some form of trauma within the last year (National Survey of Children's Exposure to Violence, n.d.). These traumas can play out in school and impact how students react to others and how they learn. Forms of trauma that students can experience can include

---

CHILDHOOD TRAUMA AND TRAUMA-INFORMED CARE

Trauma is one or multiple events or circumstances that are physically or emotionally harmful to an individual and could result in long-term negative effects "on the individual's physical, social, emotional, or spiritual well-being" (SAMHSA as cited in Crosby, 2015, p. 223). Trauma that occurs in childhood may be specifically referred to as traumatic stress or adverse childhood experiences (ACEs). Approximately 60 percent of children witness some form of violence each year, and more than 25 percent of children report trauma from physically, sexually, or emotionally abusive experiences (Blitz, Anderson, & Saastamoinen, 2016; Crosby, 2015). ACEs can be caused by "child maltreatment, family stress or dysfunction, community violence, and natural disasters" (Van Der Kolk as cited in Blodgett & Lanigan, 2018, p. 137). Traumatic experiences can also occur in the school setting, such as bullying, harassment, school shootings, or other crisis events

Children who have experienced trauma are more likely to experience various emotional, behavioral, social, cognitive, and academic difficulties as they grow and develop (Blitz et al., 2016). Trauma can physically affect brain growth and maturation, nervous and endocrine system function, and the relationship between a person's cognition, emotion regulation, and behavior (Van der Kolk, 2003). Other negative impacts of trauma include: attention deficits, poor mental and physical health, disruptive behavior, impulsivity, poor social skills, and hindered academic experiences (Blitz et al., 2016; Blodgett & Lanigan, 2018; Crosby, 2015). Adverse childhood experiences (ACEs) are associated with not moving onto the next academic grade, low commitment to school, and purposefully avoiding school (Blodgett & Lanigan, 2018). Traumatic experiences can be appropriately overcome when children have numerous resiliency factors such as strong support systems, healthy parent or caregiver attachments, and safe living environments (Blodgett & Lanigan, 2018). However, without resiliency factors or assistance, childhood trauma can have long-lasting effects in adulthood. Exposure to childhood trauma is associated with symptoms of cardiovascular disease, changes in physical maturation, the development of psychotic disorders, hindered executive brain functioning, and lower cognitive performance (Lei, Beach, & Simons, 2018; Quidé et al., 2017).

Communities, families, and educators can all play a role in addressing the effects of childhood trauma by acknowledging that trauma has occurred, identifying how it is impacting the child's life, and working to resolve or meet the child's unique needs. Doing this through a culturally diverse lens can help identify trauma that individuals of diversity have experienced and then appropriately address these situations with multicultural interventions. Parents, guardians, and other caregivers should be aware of the resources, specialists, and interventions that are available and necessary to obtain if a child has experienced trauma. Trauma-informed practices such as counseling, yoga, and expressive arts are various options that may help individuals cope with the trauma they have experienced. Yoga has been found to reduce psychological and physiological symptoms following traumatic life events, and is specifically beneficial for individuals who experienced childhood trauma (Nguyen-Feng, Clark, & Butler, 2018; West, Liang, & Spinazzola, 2017). Therapy interventions using music, art, dance/movement, and drama can provide an outlet when speaking may not be enough, or even possible; these interventions have been empirically validated for use with individuals who have experienced trauma (Baker, Metcalf, Varker, & O'Donnell, 2018; Landis-Shack, Heinz, & Bonn-Miller, 2017).

Schools and educators are very influential in children's lives, and trauma-informed practices in the school setting are both beneficial and necessary for children who have experienced trauma. Educators should be appropriately trained to know what trauma and ACEs are; what the effects of these experiences look like; how these experiences may manifest in the classroom; and how to appropriately respond, care for, and assist the child (Blodgett & Lanigan, 2018). Educators should model healthy connections, be emotionally present for their students, and show them support and unconditional positive regard (Crosby, 2015). Students should be given clear academic and behavioral expectations, and classrooms should be structured, safe, and comfortable environments where students have the time, space, and tools to work through their emotions with adult and peer support (Crosby, 2015). Schools should have adequate mental health services and staffed professionals who can help address the difficulties and inequities that children are facing, teach students coping skills and resiliency factors, and promote children's overall well-being and achievement (Blitz et al., 2016). Trauma-informed schools show improvement in students' behavior, academic success, and future life outcomes; the overall school climate; and teacher satisfaction (Crosby, 2015).

—Caitie Boucher, Taylor Cook, Halle O. Devoe,
Evan Hopkins, Grace A. Moll

exposure to or being victims of crime, physical or mental abuse, and substance abuse by family members.

BULLYING OF MARGINALIZED GROUPS

Individuals possessing multiple minority statuses, because of their multiple marginalized identities, experience intersectional bullying. For these individuals, the experience of bullying cannot be understood in the context of only one of their identities. Rather, as suggested by Misawa (2010), the intersection of multiple stigmatized identities results in stacked experiences of bullying that serve to further marginalize the targets and sanction their differences.

Those individuals possessing minority or multiple minority statuses understand that they have to work harder to be taken seriously (Steele and Aronson, 1995). The relative positions of power of the target and the bully, and the bully's ability to harm the target without facing consequences, are pertinent to this conversation (Kohut, 2008). In sum, there are clear differences between bullying and harassment, particularly pertaining to protected classes. In fact, bullying may constitute implicit harassment, by the very nature of the identities of the targets.

Individuals who have experienced identity-based, intersectional, or general bullying indicate that it is a painful and devastating experience, leaving long-term scars, including post-traumatic stress disorder (Farrington, 2010), depression, difficulty concentrating, and lowered self-esteem (Lutgen-Sandvik, 2006).

BULLYING VERSUS HARASSMENT

The word *bullying* is often used as an umbrella term, particularly within K–12 schools, to explain various behaviors, some illegal, and to define perpetrator behaviors that serve to regulate the behaviors of victims in order to punish those who do not conform to some an ideal standard based upon gendered expectations, or other standards required by societal expectations based on hetero-patriarchy. Bullying is commonly conflated with harassment, particularly in schools.

Bullying should be defined as repeated and unwanted behavior used to intentionally ridicule, humiliate, or intimidate another person. However, bullying is not necessarily based upon the target's membership in a protected class or based on one's identification with a particular group, as is harassment in its many forms. Bullying behaviors are not necessarily illegal. By its very nature, gender-based bullying should be deemed as gender-based harassment or gender-based bullying/harassment because federal laws are in place to protect individuals from harassment based on gender. To be more specific, Title IX protects all students in federally funded institutions, public and private schools, and colleges and universities from harassment (including assault) based upon real and perceived conceptions of another's sex, gender, gender identity and expression, and sexual orientation. To deem said behaviors as bullying may prevent victims from legal redress. Title VII protects employees from sexual harassment. Sexual harassment in the form of sexual orientation harassment may be considered a form of sex discrimination under Title VII.

Bullying and harassment are often viewed as synonymous; their definitions overlap in terms of the behaviors they prohibit, but there are important differences. In instances of bullying, some state laws require proof that the perpetrator intended the harm. In instances of harassment, the intention of the perpetrator is almost always irrelevant and the victim's perception of the behavior is largely determinative. Another important difference between bullying and harassment is that the definition of harassment is fairly uniform among all 50 states while bullying laws vary widely. Finally, schools have little to no liability for violations of bullying laws, while they face multiple pathways of potential liability if they fail to comply with antiharassment laws.

GENDER ISSUES IN SCHOOL: TOXIC MASCULINITY AS A CAUSE FOR SCHOOL VIOLENCE

Sexism is harmful to all genders, and, more broadly, to all communities. According to Peacock and Barker (2014) rigid gender norms contribute to gender-based violence globally. *Hostile or toxic masculinity* (Rogers, Cervantes, & Espinosa, 2015) is an umbrella term encompassing ideologies such as dominance, hostility toward women and to feminism, rape myths, adversarial relationship beliefs, traditional/sexist views of gender roles, and sexually aggressive behavior. Toxic masculinity is a system of belief wherein women are viewed as objects/sexual objects, potentially causing a litany of dangerous and criminal behaviors:

> confusion regarding their [women's] behavior; misperception of platonic interest as sexual . . . suspicion, hostility, and mistrust of women; an adversarial approach to relationships, a belief that resistance to sexual overtures is mere "scripted refusal." . . . and even a sense of victimization when women refuse sexual consent, withdraw if once given, or express purely nonsexual interest; potentially justifying sexual assault within this distorted worldview. (pp. 745–746)

Rogers, Cervantes, and Espinosa (2015) found that the belief that women are sexually deceptive is a precursor to hostile masculinity and may predict future sexual aggressiveness.

The phenomenon of hostile masculinity was personified in May 2014, when a college student, Elliot Rodger, engaged in a shooting rampage and killed seven people, including himself. As the investigation unfolded, Rodger's motivation for the killings became clear. A series of YouTube videos compiled prior to the spree showed Rodger threatening to kill people, particularly women, on his college campus, the University of California at

Santa Barbara, for not being attracted to him and for not accepting his sexual and dating advances. Dana Feldman (2014), reporting for *Reuters*, provided an example of Rodger's manifesto. It read, in part, "You girls have never been attracted to me. I don't know why you girls aren't attracted to me. But I will punish you all for it. It's an injustice, a crime" (para. 15).

The concept of hostile masculinity directly relates to sexual terrorism theory. Coined by Carole Sheffield (1989), *sexual terrorism* serves to keep women in positions of fear and powerlessness. As Sheffield (1989) argues, "Sexual terrorism is a system that functions to maintain male supremacy through actual and implied violence. . . . Both violence and fear are functional" (p. 17). Sexual terrorism theory suggests that sexual harassment and other components of sexual terrorism including sexual objectification, sexual harassment, stalking, assault, and violent (rape) or coercive sexual assault function as tools to maintain the status quo where men enjoy the lion's share of power, autonomy, and economic opportunity. Male perpetrators of sexual terrorism likely adhere to some form of hostile masculinity and engage in sexual harassment, assault, stalking, and other forms of sexual terrorism based upon these beliefs.

INTIMATE PARTNER VIOLENCE

According to the Centers for Disease Control and Prevention (2018), "'intimate partner violence' [IPV] describes physical violence, sexual violence, stalking and psychological aggression (including coercive acts) by a current or former intimate partner" (para. 1). Approximately one in three students will be victims of IPV (Centers for Disease Control and Prevention, 2015). Approximately 10 percent of high school students have been intentionally physically harmed by an intimate partner, and 10 percent have been sexually coerced into engaging in unwanted sexual situations by an intimate partner (Centers for Disease Control and Prevention, 2015).

Teen victims of IPV can experience a multitude of negative personal and academic consequences, including depression, suicidal ideation, alcohol and drug abuse, body dysmorphia, unwanted pregnancy and sexually transmitted infections (STIs), identity issues, poor grades, increased absenteeism, and problems with future intimacy (Centers for Disease Control and Prevention, 2015).

WHAT EDUCATORS CAN DO

• Educate students about healthy relationships (at various/appropriate developmental stages).

- Educate community members about how they can help students with prevention and identification.
- Develop appropriate curricular materials and clear response plans to address IPV.
- Provide effective support to traumatized youth by curtained and appropriately trained counselors.
- Address the behavior and needs of perpetrators through education and restorative justice when requested by victims.

SEXUAL HARASSMENT

Sexual harassment is a complex phenomenon involving various inter-related factors such as gender, patriarchal norms (most specifically, hege-monic or hostile masculinity), and issues of power. Thus, sexual harassment possesses many accepted definitions and can lead to more violent behav-iors, including violence against the female body (rape, battery, incest, and harassment). The perpetuation of this fear and violence forms the basis of patriarchal power (Sheffield, 1989). Brandenburg (1997) defines sexual harassment as "unwanted sexual attention that would be offensive to a rea-sonable person and that negatively affects the work or school environ-ment" (p. 1).

Sexual harassment is defined by the American Association of University Women Educational Foundation as *"unwanted* and *unwelcome* sexual behavior that interferes with your life. Sexual harassment is *not* behaviors that you *like* or *want* (for example wanted kissing, touching, or flirting)" (2001/1993, p. 2). Research conducted by the American Association of Uni-versity Women (2001/1993) found that in students from 8th to 11th grade:

- 83% of girls have been sexually harassed
- 78% of boys have been sexually harassed
- 38% of the students were harassed by teachers or school employees
- 36% of school employees or teachers were harassed by students
- 42% of school employees or teachers had been harassed by each other (AAUW, 2001/1993)

In higher education, high rates of sexual harassment around the world have been reported (DeSouza & Solberg 2003; Paludi, Nydegger, DeSouza, Nydegger, & Dicker, 2006). The literature on sexual harassment suggests that over 90 percent of the time, males are the perpetrators of sexual harassment against females (Fineran & Bennett, 1999). Gender is a key fac-tor in enabling a culture of harassment according to Rospenda, Richman, and Nawyn (1998).

VIOLENT (RAPE) AND COERCIVE SEXUAL ASSAULT

In 2012, the Uniform Crime Report adjusted its definition of rape: "the penetration, no matter how slight, of the vagina or anus, with any body part or object, or oral penetration by a sex organ of another person, without the consent of the victim" (U.S. Department of Justice, 2012, p. 1). The definition was changed after public outcry (Bierie & Davis-Siegel, 2014) at the narrowly defined instance of rape that had previously been the standard. The previous definition limited rape to the "carnal knowledge of a female, forcibly and against her will," where "carnal knowledge" was defined as "the slightest penetration of the sexual organ of a female (vagina) by the sexual organ of the male (penis)" (Federal Bureau of Investigation, 2004, p. 19). In part, the change in definitions allowed for the inclusion of coercive sexual assault, which is defined as using threats, arguments, and pressure to compel sexual contact (Rubenfeld, 2013; Senn et al., 2013). While sexual assault is usually seen as rape, state statutes generally include any unwanted sexual contact, regardless of penetration (Miller, Markman, Amacker, & Menaker, 2011). According to Senn et al. (2013), approximately 25 percent of adult women will experience violent rape during their lifetimes. Incidences of coercive sexual assault increase the number of targets significantly, with striking numbers of victims noted on college campuses.

VICTIMIZATION PREDICTORS

In a study of undergraduate students, Banyard (2007) found that women reported higher rates of unwanted negative sexual experiences than did men. However, both women and men experience negative consequences because of sexual terrorism and have low disclosure rates. Despite the differential rates of reporting, Tjaden, Thoennes, and Allison (2002) found that younger and more educated women "are more likely to define assaultive behaviors as inappropriate and worthy of sanction" (p. 22). However, there are factors that, according to Waldron, Wilson, Patriquin, and Scarpa (2015), render individuals less able to identify and/or interpret real threats of sexual terrorism, and subsequently lead to an increased risk of victimization.

Previous research (Bernston, Cacioppo, & Quigley, 1991; Lovallo, Farag, Corocco, Cohoon, & Vincent, 2012; Simeon, Yehuda, Knutelska, & Schmeidler, 2008) suggests that women who experience childhood sexual abuse (CSA) exhibit blunted or numbed responses to cues of sexual danger. In their study investigating depression and physiological reactivity among college-age women who had been targets of CSA, Waldron et al. (2015) found that the numbing caused by childhood victimization actually led to later revictimization as adults.

Regarding the indicators associated with perpetrator risk of victimizing, Williams and Frieze (2005), who examined persistence or pre-stalking behaviors during early courtship in relation to future relationship violence, found that in relationships, persistence behaviors and behaviors of violence are related. Additionally, mild aggression performed at the beginning of relationship is associated with a greater likelihood of further violence during the course of the relationship. These behaviors include surveillance, intimidation, hurting the self, verbal aggression, and physical violence (Williams & Frieze, 2005). According to Bancroft (2002), abusers have a distorted sense of right and wrong: "Their value system is unhealthy, not their psychology" (p. 38). An abusive person justifies his actions by his sense of entitlement. He believes that he deserves rights and privileges that others do not (Bancroft, 2002). Bancroft typically uses the masculine pronoun in his discussion of the abusive personality because, in his experience, most abusive persons who terrorize their partners physically, psychologically, or both, are males, who learn these behaviors from a variety of sources, "including key male role models, peers, and pervasive cultural messages" (p. 113), i.e., hostile masculinity.

SELF-HARM IN ADOLESCENTS

Nonsuicidal self-injury (NSSI) refers to intentional harm that individuals do to themselves without suicidal intent. These behaviors include cutting, burning, biting, bruising, scratching, constricting, inhaling, picking, and scalding, of which cutting is the most common (Klonsky, Victor, & Saffer, 2014). Although the reasons for NSSI self-harm vary, the most common are to alleviate negative emotions, to punish themselves for engaging in behaviors they perceive to be shameful or regretful, and to create physical signs of their emotional distress (Klonsky, Victor, & Saffer, 2014).

The population most impacted by instances of NSSI is adolescents, and behaviors typically begins at ages 13 to 14—impacting anywhere between 15 to 23 percent of the adolescent population. However, recent research suggests that between 33 to 50 percent of the adolescent population engage in NSSI (Peter, Freedenthal, & Sheldon, 2008). NSSI is more prevalent among the LGBTQ+ student population (Project Aware Ohio, 2017). As with suicide, the LGBTQ+ population is the most vulnerable.

It conclusion, students who engage in NSSI do so neither for attention nor as a form of manipulation, contrary to popular belief. Most students who engage in NSSI do so in private and to curb negative emotions. Finally, about 50 percent of students who engage in NSSI do not have a diagnosed mental disorder (Project Aware Ohio, 2017).

NOTES

1. This section was developed by Jennifer L. Martin, Ph.D., with help from Wendy Murphy, New England Law, Boston.

2. Most private institutions are subject to Title IX regulation for their acceptance of federal funds.

3. Bullying, sexual harassment, and sexual assault are often conflated or used interchangeably. Such mislabeling does not alleviate schools from responding properly and enforcing Title IX provisions.

4. Schools may have the authority and responsibility to address sexual harassment even if the behavior occurs off campus, and/or in social media and other online venues.

REFERENCES

American Association of University Women Educational Foundation. (2001/1993). *Hostile hallways: Bullying, teasing, and sexual harassment in school.* Washington, DC: American Association of University Women Educational Foundation. Retrieved from https://www.aauw.org/files/2013/02/hostile -hallways-bullying-teasing-and-sexual-harassment-in-school.pdf

Baker, F. A., Metcalf, O., Varker, T., & O'Donnell, M. (2018). A systematic review of the efficacy of creative arts therapies in the treatment of adults with PTSD. *Psychological Trauma: Theory, Research, Practice, and Policy, 10*(6), 643–651. https://doi-org.ezproxy.uis.edu/10.1037/tra0000353.supp (Supplemental)

Bancroft, L. (2002). *Why does he do that? Inside the minds of angry and controlling men.* New York: Berkley.

Banyard, V. L. (2007). Unwanted sexual contact on campus: A comparison of women's and men's experiences. *Violence and Victims, 22*(1), 57–70.

Bernston, G. G., Cacioppo, J. T., & Quigley, K. S. (1991). Autonomic determinism: The modes of autonomic control, the doctrine of autonomic space, and the laws of autonomic constraint. *Psychological Review, 98*, 459–487.

Bierie, D. M., & Davis-Siegel, J. C. (2014). Measurement matters: Comparing old and new definitions of rape in federal statistical reporting. *Sexual Abuse: A Journal of Research and Treatment*, 1–17.

Blitz, L. V., Anderson, E. M., & Saastamoinen, M. (2016). Assessing perceptions of culture and trauma in an elementary school: Informing a model for culturally responsive trauma-informed schools. *Urban Review: Issues and Ideas in Public Education, 48*(4), 520–542.

Blodgett, C., & Lanigan, J. D. (2018). The association between adverse childhood experience (ACE) and school success in elementary school children. *School Psychology Quarterly, 33*(1), 137–146.

Brandenburg, J. B. (1997). *Confronting sexual harassment: What schools and colleges can do.* New York, NY: Teachers College Press.

Centers for Disease Control and Prevention. (2015). Youth risk behavior surveillance—United States, 2015. *Morbidity and Mortality Weekly Report, 65*(6).

Retrieved from https://www.cdc.gov/healthyyouth/data/yrbs/pdf/2015/ss 6506_updated.pdf.

Centers for Disease Control and Prevention. (2018). *Violence prevention.* Retrieved from https://www.cdc.gov/violenceprevention/intimatepartnerviolence /definitions.html

Crosby, S. D. (2015). An ecological perspective on emerging trauma-informed teaching practices. *Children & Schools, 37*(4), 223–230. https://doi.org /10.1093/cs/cdv027

DeSouza, E. R., & Solberg, J. (2003). Incidence and dimensions of sexual harassment across cultures. In M. Paludi & C. A. Paludi Jr. (Eds.), *Academic and workplace sexual harassment: A handbook of cultural, social science, management, and legal perspectives* (pp. 3–30). Westport, CT: Praeger.

Farrington, C. A. (2014). *Failing at school: Lessons for redesigning urban high schools.* New York, NY: Teachers College Press.

Federal Bureau of Investigation. (2004). *Uniform crime reporting handbook.* Retrieved from http://www2.fbi.gov/ucr/handbook/ucrhandbook04.pdf

Feldman, D. (2014). *Gunman kills six in drive-by shooting in California college town.* Reuters. Retrieved April 1, 2015 from http://www.reuters.com/article /2014/05/24/us-usa-shooting-california-idUSBREA4N05120140524.

Fineran, S., & Bennett, L. (1999). Gender and power issues of peer sexual harassment among teenagers. *Journal of Interpersonal Violence, 14*(6), 626–641.

GLSEN. (2017). 2017 national school climate survey. *GLSEN.* Retrieved from https://www.glsen.org/article/2017-national-school-climate-survey-1

Klonsky, E. D., Victor, S. E., & Saffer, B. Y. (2014). Nonsuicidal self-injury: What we know, and what we need to know. *Canadian Journal of Psychiatry, 59*(11), 565–568.

Kohut, M. R. (2008). *The complete guide to understanding, controlling, and stopping bullies and bullying at work.* Ocala, FL: Atlantic.

Landis-Shack, N., Heinz, A. J., & Bonn-Miller, M. O. (2017). Music therapy for posttraumatic stress in adults: A theoretical review. *Psychomusicology: Music, Mind, and Brain, 27*(4), 334–342. https://doi-org.ezproxy.uis .edu/10.1037/pmu0000192

Lei, M.-K., Beach, S. R. H., & Simons, R. L. (2018). Childhood trauma, pubertal timing, and cardiovascular risk in adulthood. *Health Psychology, 37*(7), 613–617. https://doi-org.ezproxy.uis.edu/10.1037/hea0000609

Lovallo, W. R., Farag, N. H., Sorocco, K. H., Cohoon, A. J., & Vincent, A. S. (2012). Lifetime adversity leads to blunted stress axis reactivity: Studies from the Oklahoma Family Health Patterns Project. *Biological Psychiatry, 71,* 344–349.

Lutgen-Sandvik, P. (2006). Take this job and . . . : Quitting and other forms of resistance to workplace bullying. *Communication Monographs, 73*(4), 406–433.

Miller, A. K., Markman, K. D., Amacker, A. M., & Menaker, T. A. (2011). Expressed sexual assault legal context and victim culpability attributions. *Journal of Interpersonal Violence, 27*(6), 1023–1039.

Misawa, M. (2010). Racist and homophobic bullying in adulthood: Narratives from gay men of color in higher education. *New Horizons in Adult Education and Human Resource Development, 24*(1), 7–23.

National Survey of Children's Exposure to Violence. (n.d). Retrieved from https://www.ojjdp.gov/research/national-survey-of-childrens-exposure-to-violence.html

Nguyen-Feng, V. N., Clark, C. J., & Butler, M. E. (2018). Yoga as an intervention for psychological symptoms following trauma: A systematic review and quantitative synthesis. *Psychological Services.* https://doi-org.ezproxy.uis.edu/10.1037/ser0000191

Paludi, M., Nydegger, R., DeSouza, E., Nydegger, L., & Dicker, K. A. (2006). International perspectives on sexual harassment of college students: The sounds of silence. *Annuals of the New York Academy of Sciences, 1087*(1), 103–120.

Peacock, D., & Barker, G. (2014). Working with men and boys to prevent gender-based violence: Principles, lessons learned, and ways forward. *Men and Masculinities, 15*(5), 578–599.

Peter, J., Freedenthal, S., & Sheldon, C. (2008). Non-suicidal self-injury in adolescents. *Psychiatry, 5*(11), 20–26.

Project Aware Ohio. (2017). *Non-suicidal self-injury: Information brief.* Retrieved from https://education.ohio.gov/getattachment/Topics/Other-Resources/School-Safety/Building-Better-Learning-Environments/PBIS-Resources/Project-AWARE-Ohio/Project-AWARE-Ohio-Statewide-Resources/Final-Non-Suicidal-Self-Injury-What-is-it-Why-does-it-happen-How-do-we-help-docx.pdf.aspx

Quidé, Y., O'Reilly, N., Rowland, J. E., Carr, V. J., Elzinga, B. M., & Green, M. J. (2017). Effects of childhood trauma on working memory in affective and non-affective psychotic disorders. *Brain Imaging and Behavior, 11*(3), 722–735. https://doi-org.ezproxy.uis.edu/10.1007/s11682-016-9548-z

Rubenfeld, J. (2013, December 1). Rape-by-deception: A response. *Yale Law Journal Online, 123,* 3, https://www.yalelawjournal.org/forum/rape-by-deceptiona-response

Rogers, D. L., Cervantes, E., & Espinosa, J. C. (2015). Development and validation of the belief in female sexual deceptiveness scale. *Journal of Interpersonal Violence, 30*(5), 744–761.

Rospenda, K. M., Richman, J. A., & Nawyn, S. J. (1998). Doing power: The confluence of gender, race, and class in contrapower sexual harassment. *Gender & Society, 12*(1), 40–60.

Sallee, M. W., & Diaz, C. R. (2013). Sexual harassment, racist jokes, and homophobic slurs. In J. Lester (Ed.), *Workplace bullying in higher education* (pp. 41–59). New York, NY: Routledge.

Senn, C. Y., Eliasziw, M., Barata, P. C., Thurston, W. E., Newby-Clark, I. R., Radtke, H. L., & Hobden, K. L. (2013). Sexual assault resistance education for university women: Study protocol for a randomized controlled trial (SARE trial). *BMC Women's Health, 13*(1), 25.

Sheffield, C. J. (1989). Sexual terrorism. In J. Freeman (Ed.), *Women: A feminist perspective* (4th ed., pp. 3–19). Mountain View, CA: Mayfield.

Simeon, D., Yehuda, R., Knutelska, M., & Schmeidler, J. (2008). Dissociation versus posttraumatic stress: Cortisol and physiological correlates in adults highly exposed to the World Trade Center attack on 9/11. *Psychiatry Research, 161*, 325–329.

Steele, C. M., & Aronson, J. (1995). Stereotype threat and the intellectual test performance of African Americans. *Journal of Personality and Social Psychology, 69*(5), 797–811.

Tjaden, P., Thoennes, N., & Allison, C. J. (2002). Comparing stalking victimization from legal and victim perspectives. In K. E. Davis, I. H. Frieze, & R. D. Maiuro (Eds.), *Stalking: Perspectives on victims and perpetrators* (pp. 9–30). New York, NY: Springer.

Turner, A. (2017). New survey of 50,000+ young people reveals troubling post-election spike in bullying & harassment. Human Rights Campaign. Retrieved from https://www.hrc.org/blog/new-survey-of-50000-young -people-reveals-troubling-post-election-spike-in-b

U.S. Department of Justice. (2012, January 6). Attorney General Eric Holder announces revisions to the Uniform Crime Report's definition of rape. *Justice News*. Retrieved from http://www.justice.gov/opa/pr/2012/January/12 -ag-018.html

Van der Kolk, B. A. (2003). The neurobiology of childhood trauma and abuse. *Child and Adolescent Psychiatric Clinics of North America, 12*(2), 293–317. doi:10.1016/s1056-4993(03)00003-8

Waldron, J. C., Wilson, L. C., Patriquin, M. A., & Scarpa, A. (2015). Sexual victimization, history, depression, and task physiology as predictors of sexual revictimization: Results from a 6-month prospective pilot study. *Journal of Interpersonal Violence, 30*(4), 622–629.

West, J., Liang, B., & Spinazzola, J. (2017). Trauma sensitive yoga as a complementary treatment for posttraumatic stress disorder: A qualitative descriptive analysis. *International Journal of Stress Management, 24*(2), 173–195. https://doi-org.ezproxy.uis.edu/10.1037/str0000040

Williams, S. L., & Frieze, I. H. (2005). Courtship behaviors, relationship violence, and breakup persistence in college men and women. *Psychology of Women Quarterly, 29*, 248–257.

10

Case Studies in Educational Psychology for Educational Equity

---

MARGINALIZATION OR NECESSARY PUSH-OUT? EDUCATING ELL STUDENTS

Introduction

This case is timely, as it illustrates how politics impacts education. The policies and legal issues raised in this case include English Only movements, the education of immigrant and ethic student populations, the third grade reading guarantee, and the banning of ethnic studies courses and programs in Arizona.

The banning of ethnic studies programs began in Arizona in 2010, which exacerbated the already contentious political climate in schools. Deemed to be anti-American by various right-wing politicians, although contributing to the general well-being and graduate rates of ethnic minorities in Arizona schools, such courses and programs were banned in 2010. Such legislation contributes to the alienation of various minority groups in the state. A foundational text in the field of education, *Pedagogy of the Oppressed* by Paulo Freire (1970), was among the books banned.

This case centers on Noemi, a recent immigrant to Arizona and an English language learner (ELL). Two laws impact Noemi: English-only and the third grade reading guarantee. The law requires that students falling far below grade level on the third grade reading assessment will not be promoted to the third grade, with two exceptions: (1) the student is an ELL or is deemed as limited English proficient, receiving less than two years of English instruction, or (2) is a student possessing a disability and possesses an individualized education plan (IEP).

Although Noemi is primarily Spanish speaking, the district policy of English Only permits her primary subjects be taught only in English. Additionally, if Noemi does not show that she is reading at a third grade level in English by the end of the year, she will be retained. This case asks the reader to reflect on the laws and policies that impact children, and to make determinations about how to best meet the interests of the child depicted in this case in light of or in spite of these provisions.

The Case

English language learners are the fastest-growing student population group in our schools. Providing them with high-quality services and programs is an important investment in America's future.

—*NEA president Dennis Van Roekel*

Noemi recently emigrated from a rural area in Honduras to Arizona and is an ELL. Although approximately 83 percent of the population in Honduras is literate, with bilingual (Spanish/English) and even trilingual (Spanish/English/Arabic, or Spanish/English/German) schools, the rural populations lack access to consistent schooling. The primary school completion rate is reported to be approximately 40 percent.

Arriving in the United States in May, Noemi had been in the country for five months prior to entering Jane Addams Elementary for third grade. She had little experience with English literacy prior to entering the United States. Arizona has two laws impacting Noemi: English-only and the third grade reading guarantee.

In general, ELL students are more likely to stay in school if they feel connected to their teachers (Catterall, 1998; De La Cruz, 2008; Englund, Egeland, & Collins, 2008). Teachers who provide extra attention and support can be transformational in the education and retention of ELL students. Teachers of ELL students who understand the importance of getting to know their students and their cultures can have a lasting impact.

Definitions

ELL Students

According to No Child Left Behind (NCLB) (2002):

NCLB uses the term Limited English Proficient (LEP) and defines an ELL student as an individual who (a) is age 3 to 21 years; (b) is enrolled or preparing to enroll in elementary or secondary school; (c) was not born in the U.S. or whose native language is not English; (d) is a Native American, Alaskan Native, or a resident of outlying areas; (e) comes from an environment in which a language other than English has had a significant impact on an individual's ELP; (f) is migratory and comes from an environment where English is not the dominant language; and (g) has difficulties in speaking, reading, writing, or understanding the English language that may deny the individual the ability to meet the state's proficient level of achievement, to successfully achieve in classrooms where English is the language of instruction, or to participate fully in society. (NCLB, 2002)

Third Grade Reading Guarantee in Arizona

Arizona law requires that students falling far below grade level on the third grade reading assessment will not be promoted to the third grade, with two exceptions: (1) the student is an ELL or is deemed to be Limited English Proficient, receiving less than two years of English instruction, or (2) the student possesses a disability and an individualized education plan (IEP), and the IEP team has decided, along with the parent or guardian, that promotion is appropriate and in accordance with the IEP (Arizona Revised Statute 15-701).

Starting in 2013–14, every third grade student in Arizona must demonstrate proficiency in reading; otherwise, they are not allowed to advance to the fourth grade. House Bill 2732, the high-stakes reading mandate, was modeled after a 2002 Florida law.

English Only

English Only is a movement that began in California in the late 1990s, arguing that traditional bilingual programs prevented immigrants from readily learning English and from valuing English as the primary spoken language.

English Only laws, including Proposition 227 (State of California, 1998), advocate against bilingual programs and link the poor academic performance of non-English speakers, most of whom are Spanish speakers, to their placement in bilingual education programs. This legislation sought to make English Only programs the standard education for ELL students. The first English Only law was passed in 1998.

ELL Teachers

The majority of general education teachers have little to no training in teaching ELL students (Hopkins, Lowenhaupt, & Sweet, 2015). Because teaching English as a second language is not considered to be an academic discipline, teachers of ELL students often find their expertise questioned or undervalued. This can lead to ELL student needs being unattended in general education classrooms (Hopkins, Lowenhaupt, & Sweet, 2015, p. 412).

Push Out

English as a Second Language (ESL) programs have traditionally utilized pullout programs, which remove ELL students from their regular classroom for an allotted period of time in order to provide these students with explicit language instruction in English. Conversely, push-in and coteaching models require teachers of ELL students and general education teachers to work in collaboration (Hopkins, Lowenhaupt, & Sweet, 2015, p. 411).

The classification of ELL students, as "English learner" to "fluent English proficient," is important, but not without controversy. When a student is deemed "fluent English proficient," the student is able to enter the educational mainstream. However, this reclassification has lasting implications for students.

According to Umansky and Reardon (2014):

> English learner status is designed to support students learning English with specially prepared teachers, content instruction taught with modifications to increase English learner accessibility, English language development classes, and regular monitoring and English language proficiency assessments. Once reclassified, students lose access to these specialized services but gain access to mainstream classes including the full breath of courses, teachers, and peers. (p. 880)

Arizona promotes reclassification after 1 year (Umansky & Reardon, 2014). However, research suggests that reclassification can take from between 4 to 10 years, and is slower for students living in or coming from poverty (Umansky & Reardon, 2014).

A National Problem

According to the National Education Association (2008):

Teachers lack practical, research-based information, resources, and strategies needed to teach, evaluate, and nurture ELL students, whether those students were born in this country or elsewhere, or whether they are the first, second, or third generation to attend an American public school. In too many cases, ELL students are being given reading and math tests in English before they are proficient in the language. (pp. 1–2)

The academic performance of ELL students is well below that of their peers. ELL students also have an excessively high dropout rate (NEA, 2008). In the 2005 National Assessment of Educational Progress, 29 percent of ELLs scored at or above the basic level in reading, compared with 75 percent of their peers (NEA, 2008).

Additional Political Battles in Arizona

In addition to the English Only movements, recent political battles in Arizona impact the education of immigrant and ethic student populations, most notably the banning of ethnic studies courses and programs. The banning of ethnic studies programs began in 2010, which exacerbated the political climate in schools.

Deemed to be anti-American by various right-wing politicians, although contributing to the general well-being and graduation rates of ethnic minorities in Arizona schools, such courses and programs were banned in 2010. Such legislation contributes to the alienation of various minority groups in the state.

Noemi has four hours of ELL instruction throughout each school day, but her core subjects—math, social studies, reading, and science—are all taught in English. Although Noemi was considered to be academically talented in her home country, despite her disparate instruction, her current teacher for her primary subjects as well as her peers perceive her to be less than average.

Some teachers view ELL students as similar to low-performing English-speaking students, leading to watered-down curriculums, including delivering reading instruction with materials well below the students' comprehension levels. These curricular and cultural mismatches contribute to the low academic performance levels of many ELL students (Coyne, Kami'enui, & Carnine 2010).

Because the United States is primarily a monolingual country, students and teachers often cannot see beyond language barriers. Noemi's teacher for her core subjects, Ms. Sanders, has little to no exposure to any language other than English. A recent transfer to the building, she also has had little exposure to ELL students.

Research indicates that novice teachers are more likely to be placed in ELL content-based courses (Blanca Dabach, 2015). According to Blanca Dabach (2015), "Low student status also became associated with teacher status within schools, and lack of teaching experience justified placing teachers with less experience into lower-track classes" (p. 248).

Noemi is a happy child and has made a few English-speaking friends in her primary subjects, despite the language barrier. However, Noemi is teased by her some of peers and taunted that she should "speak English." Her teacher, Ms. Sanders, does nothing to correct this behavior.

A common mistake with some teachers is assuming that ELL students are not intelligent because they may not participate or speak up in class. Many teachers are afraid to approach ELL students and do not take the opportunity to get to know them. Ms. Sanders is guilty of both of these mindsets.

She placed Noemi's desk at the rear of the classroom and diverts her attention from her. Noemi smiles at Ms. Sanders each morning as she enters the classroom and greets her with "Hola Señora Sanders." Ms. Sanders has never responded to Noemi's greetings, nor has she attempted to learn even rudimentary Spanish in order to communicate with or assist Noemi.

Because her school does not have enough ELL students to justify an entire class of same-aged peers (or similarly proficient English-speaking students), Noemi is in an ELL class with students in various grades and English proficiency levels ranging from kindergarten to sixth grade.

Because of this large range, the one ELL teacher in the building, Ms. Weller, struggles to meet all of her students' needs. Ms. Weller, a native English speaker, double majored in Spanish and early childhood education as an undergraduate, but had not used her Spanish in several years before being hired from within her district to direct the ELL program at Jane Addams Elementary.

Although not specifically trained to work with ELL students, Ms. Weller is committed to her students. When her Spanish fails her, she relies on Google Translate to help with her Spanish literacy and in sending notes home to parents with homework and suggestions on how parents can assist their children. Ms. Weller knows that she needs help in assisting these students.

In addition to taking free Spanish courses at her local community center in the evenings, she is also in the process of pursuing an ELL certification at her own expense. Although she has asked that the district reimburse her for her university fees, the district has declined her request.

Ms. Weller also attempts to communicate with parents through home visits to better meet the needs of her students. Upon her first visit to Noemi's home, Ms. Weller learned that Noemi felt very strange upon entering Jane Addams Elementary because she did not understand anything that was going on around her. She felt singled out.

She confided in Ms. Weller that she was often the target of teasing by her peers and often felt that her peers were talking about her. She also admitted that she believed her teacher, Ms. Sanders, witnessed some of this behavior, but failed to do anything to protect her. Noemi's parents expressed shock at these sentiments, for Noemi had never communicated these issues to them. Ms. Weller was comforted by the fact that Noemi had supportive parents: upon hearing of Noemi's struggles, her parents rushed to her side to provide hugs and words of assurance and support.

Upon subsequent home visits, Ms. Weller learned that Noemi felt that her parents were the most influential factors in her educational motivation and success; she desired to please them, for their primary reason for immigrating to the United States was so that Noemi could receive a good education. They felt this likely would not happen in their small rural village in Honduras.

Parental expectations and family relationships can shape student's perseverance and achievement in school (De La Cruz, 2008; Englund, Egeland, & Collins, 2008). Noemi's parents stressed homework completion and the importance of education, to which both Noemi was committed (Fulgini, 1997).

After several home visits and Ms. Weller's unrelenting attempts to communicate with the family, despite her own language barriers, both Noemi and her family began to trust Ms. Weller. Eventually, Ms. Weller learned of the failure of Ms. Sanders to communicate with Noemi. Noemi's tearful confession of her invisibility in Ms. Sander's class also left Ms. Weller in tears.

Upon Ms. Weller's return to school the next day, she knew she had to speak to Ms. Sanders to determine the best course of action. She saw her as she walked from the parking lot into the school. "Excuse me, Ms. Sanders?"

"Yes?" Ms. Sanders replied.

"I would like to speak to you about a student in your class, Noemi?"

Ms. Sanders rolled her eyes. "What about her?"

"Well," Ms. Weller began, "I have visited the home several times, and I understand that the family wants the best for Noemi. They help her every night as best they can, and I was just wondering. . . ."

Ms. Sanders cut her off: "I know you are just doing your job, but this student probably will not be here for long and because I cannot educate the parents, I cannot do much for her. Likely, she will be deported soon. I have 25 other students that I need to focus on. I do not have time for this. I have to get to class." And with that, Ms. Sanders rushed into the school.

Ms. Weller realized that she would be wasting her time trying to change the mind of Ms. Sanders on anything relating to Noemi from this point forward, but she was troubled by Ms. Sanders's assumption that Noemi and her family were undocumented. She wondered if she should report this conversation to her administrator.

As a new teacher, she was fearful of approaching her administrator with problems. Already overwhelmed with a large population of ELL students and other staff problems, the administrator maintained neither an open door policy for faculty nor any mentoring programs for new teachers.

Ms. Weller knew from her ELL certification program that teachers with no training in the area of ELL language development may create instructional and pedagogical styles largely governed by stereotypes, which she felt would likely be exacerbated by the current political climate of the contentious issue of the banning of ethnic studies in the state.

Ms. Weller knew that she would need to focus on institutional factors impacting Noemi and her family. However, Ms. Sanders's evaluation of Noemi would impact her potential retention or her continued educational progression at Jane Addams.

Another major problem that Ms. Weller saw in her district was a direct result of English Only policies. There were few books and instructional materials written in Spanish in the school, or written in both English and Spanish. Most books were written in English. The policy governing the district reads as follows, "Although teachers may use a minimal amount of the child's native language when necessary, no subject matter shall be taught in any language other than English, and children in this program learn to read and write solely in English" (Crawford, 2000).

With a relative lack of support from her district, Ms. Weller struggles, particularly in the current contentious political climate of how to best serve her students.

References

Arizona Revised Statute 15-701. (n.d.). Retrieved from http://www.azleg.gov/ars/15/00701.htm

Blanca Dabach, D. (2015). Teacher placement into immigrant English learner classrooms: Limiting access in comprehensive high schools. *American Educational Research Journal, 52*(2), 243–274.

Catterall, J. S. (Feb., 1998). Risk and resilience in student transition to high school. *American Journal of Education, 106*(2), 302–333.

Coyne, M. D., Kami'enui, E. J., & Carnine, D. W. (2010, July 20). Problems in current instruction of English language learners. Retrieved from http://www.education.com/reference/article/problems-instruction-english-learners/

Crawford, J. (2000). English-Only vs. English-Only. A tale of two initiatives: California and Arizona. Retrieved from http://www.languagepolicy.net/archives/203-227.htm

De La Cruz, Y. (2008). Who mentors Hispanic ELLs? *Journal of Hispanic Higher Education, 7*(1), 31–42.

Englund, M. M., Egeland, B., & Collins, W. A. (2008). Exceptions to high school dropout predictions in a low income sample: Do adults make a difference? *Journal of Social Issues, 64*(1), 77–93.

Freire, P. (1970). *Pedagogy of the oppressed.* New York, NY: Bloomsbury.

Fulgini, A. J. (1997). The academic achievement of adolescents from immigrant families: The role of family background, attitudes, and behavior. *Child Development, 68*(2), 351–363.

Hopkins, M., Lowenhaupt, R., & Sweet, T. M. (2015). Organizing English learner instruction in new immigrant destinations: District infrastructure and subject-specific school practice. *American Educational Research Journal, 52*(3), 408–439.

National Education Association (NEA). (2008). English language learners face unique challenges. Policy Brief. Retrieved from http://www.nea.org/assets/docs/HE/ELL_Policy_Brief_Fall_08_%282%29.pdf

NCLB. (2002). No child left behind: A desktop reference. Retrieved from https://www2.ed.gov/admins/lead/account/nclbreference/reference.pdf

State of California. (1998, June 2). Proposition 227: English language in public schools. Retrieved from http://www.smartvoter.org/1998jun/ca/state/prop/227/

Umansky, I. M., & Reardon, S. F. (2014). Reclassification patterns among Latino English learner students in bilingual, dual immersion, and English immersion classrooms. *American Educational Research Journal, 51*(5), 879–912.

Additional Resources

American Psychological Association. (2015). *The English-only movement.* Retrieved from http://www.apa.org/pi/oema/resources/english-only.aspx

Arizona Department of Education. (2014, December). *Structured English immersion models of the Arizona English language learners task force.* Retrieved from http://www.azed.gov/english-language-learners/files/2015/01/structured-english-immersion-models-revised-december-2014.pdf

Ballotpedia. (2006). *Arizona English as the official language, Proposition 103.* Retrieved from http://ballotpedia.org/Arizona_English_as_the_Official_Language,_Proposition_103_%282006%29

Fehr-Snyder, K. (2010, September 4). *New Arizona law: Future 3rd-graders to have to read to pass grade. Arizona Republic.* Retrieved from http://archive.azcentral.com/arizonarepublic/local/articles/20100904arizona-3rd-graders-must-pass-reading.html#ixzz3ei8ZlcrB

Great Pitch Media. (2010). Lawsuit filed against Arizona ethnic studies ban [Video file]. Retrieved from https://www.youtube.com/watch?v=0-a2q3Mq MOQ

Hamayan, E. V. (2012). Education policy and our perception of ELL performance. *Colorin Colorado.* Retrieved from http://www.colorincolorado.org/article /50359/

Huffington Post. (2015, July 2). *Arizona ethnic studies ban.* Retrieved from http:// www.huffingtonpost.com/news/arizona-ethnic-studies-ban/

Speaking in Tongues Film. (2010, July 20). How 'submersion' differs from immersion [Web log post]. Retrieved from https://speakingintonguesfilm.word press.com/2010/07/20/how-submersion-differs-from-immersion/

Three Sonorans News. (2011, October 8). Arizona's attack on Ethnic Studies in Tucson [Video file]. Retrieved from https://www.youtube.com/watch?v =76Y0Z8NmHyY

Wright, W. E. (2012). Beware of the VAM: Valued-added measures for teacher accountability. *Colorin Colorado.* Retrieved from http://www.colorincolo rado.org/article/50576/

BUS 57: LGBTQ+ HATE CRIME, OR AN ILL-FATED PRANK?

Introduction

Intimidation, bullying, and harassment that takes place in schools greatly impacts lesbian, gay, bisexual, transgender, and queer (LGBTQ) youth. LGBTQ students who experience school-based discrimination and harassment experience more negative academic outcomes and psychological struggles than their non-LGBTQ peers (Martin & Beese, 2016).

The Gay Lesbian Straight Education Network (GLSEN) conducted the National School Climate Survey in 2013 and identified schools as hostile environments for LGBTQ students, the majority of whom experience sexual harassment and discrimination at school because they do not conform to traditional gender roles. Although the rates of school-based discrimination and harassment for LGBTQ students have improved over the years, the overall school climate remains hostile for many (Martin & Beese, 2016).

This case is based on real incidents occurring in Oakland, California, in fall 2013 (Slater, 2015). The case was adapted to occur within a school setting, and the schools and district noted within are entirely contrived for the purposes of this case. However, the original bus number, 57, was retained to pay homage to the real victims.

Oakland is considered to be one of the most diverse cities in the United States. In fact, many residents pride themselves on multiculturalism and their tolerance for diversity. However, despite this sense of pride, there is much disparity. There are very wealthy areas with effective schools, low crime rates, and scenic views; on the other hand, East Oakland is rife with poverty, crime, and violence.

The Case

The Oak Ridge School District, covering a portion of Oakland proper and all of East Oakland, comprises many schools, which include several high school options, including two large traditional high schools, and two new schools opened within the last year: a smaller alternative school for students removed from the traditional schools for truancy, multiple suspensions, and academic distress, and an intervention high school. The latter was a federally funded program to assist juveniles who had previously been adjudicated in an attempt at rehabilitation and to prevent continued recidivism.

Statistical findings for the state include youth ages 10–19 comprise 14.5 percent of the total residents. A total of 15.4 percent live in poverty. Out of the families that are living below the poverty level, almost 53 percent are single-female-parent households. Out of the households who have had a child in the last 12 months, 40.1 percent are widowed, divorced, or never married, with 46.9 percent of children raised by a grandparent (U.S. Census Bureau, 2014).

The Alternative School

The Alternative School currently educates 138 students, providing academic and treatment services to nonadjudicated students who struggle academically or socially, behaviorally challenged students, and other at-risk youth ages 14 to 18 within the district. The daily operational programing of the school is designed with a therapeutic emphasis and is driven by a personalized Individual Service Plan (ISP) designed to encompass the specific mental, medical, and academic needs of each student.

The development of the ISP is the responsibility of the ISP team, made up of the parent, at least one of the student's general education teachers, at least one of the student's special education teachers, and a school district representative, and may include a school psychologist. The team is responsible for the ongoing review and revision of the plan. The ISP is developed in consultation with the parents or caregivers of the student.

In order to offer services, the school must maintain state licensure and certification, which are governed through legislative approval, granted through application with the state, and monitored by a state licensing agent. Caseworkers are assigned from the Department of Jobs and Family Services to oversee student placement and to ensure that all services are compliant with the student's ISP.

The Intervention School

The Intervention School provides academic and social services to adjudicated offenders, per district policy. The daily operational programing of the school is designed with an emphasis on academics, job preparation, and service to the community, and maintains a restorative justice discipline policy model. For example, if a student is sanctioned for a behavioral infraction, such as a physical conflict with another student, the students are required to sit together and resolve the conflict, along with staff and expert community members, in order to take responsibility for their part in the conflict, make apologies if necessary, work through positive conflict resolutions strategies, and effectively make the situation right.

All staff and community members involved in the restorative justice model are required to be trained in nonviolent conflict resolution and the restorative justice model in general. This year, the administration is piloting a program where a select group of students will be trained in this model so that a peer component can be added.

Additionally, students are often assigned a probation officer who acts as a legal representative of the court and subsequent joint decision maker for the county.

State school reform officials appointed Dr. Michael O'Donnell, superintendent, to oversee the low-performing schools in the Oak Ridge School District. He was hired two years previously when the district was found to be in "academic distress" by the state board of education. When a district when fails to make adequate yearly progress for four or more years it is placed in Academic Emergency status and a state commission becomes the governing board. O'Donnell was given full control over every district decision, and had the authority to limit the rights and roles of the board of education.

O'Donnell was given full authority over personnel and curriculum, with the expectation for him to show rapid turnaround in the schools, with student achievement reports due to the state office every eight weeks. It was O'Donnell's idea to create the two new high schools, and to revise the missions and curricula of the two traditional high schools: one became a performing arts school, the other, a STEM (science, technology, engineering, and math) school.

After the "incident" on Bus 57, a reporter from a prestigious national newspaper, Mei Chen, traveled to Oakland to investigate. Chen found that the two new schools were disproportionately populated with black and brown students when compared to the traditional two high schools in the district.

Additionally, she learned that there had been racial unrest and issues with bullying within the schools. Students informed her that some of the unrest was caused because students from different schools rode the same buses because, although they attended different schools, they lived in the same neighborhoods or in neighboring areas. She could find no evidence of training for students or staff, or any interventions devised by O'Donnell. Additionally, after interviewing the actors in this case, Chen also interviewed several teachers and students and found little commitment to diversity within the curriculum, and no attention to multicultural education, despite a diverse student population in terms of race, class, culture, and sexuality.

The Incident on Bus 57

At the end of a long week, a mix of students from the performing arts school and alternative school in the Oak Ridge School District rode Bus 57 home. These two schools were in close proximity of one another. Stacy Stern, a senior, self-identified as "agender": neither female nor male, they wore a T-shirt and a skirt, and dozed as the bus made its various stops.

As Stacy slept, three teen boys watched and snickered nearby. One boy, Leon, flicked a disposable lighter. Before anyone could think, Stacy's gauzy skirt went up in flames. Stacy stood and screamed, and two bystanders pushed Stacy to the ground and beat out the flames. The bus driver stopped the bus and called 911. The ambulance took Stacy to the nearby burn unit, where Stacy would spend nearly a month recovering from second- and third-degree burns over much of both legs—thighs to calves.

Leon, a 16-year-old African American male resident of East Oakland, was arrested the next day. There was much contention over whether Leon should be tried as an adult, but ultimately, he was charged with two felonies, both including a hate-crime clause. If convicted, Leon was faced with potentially serving life in prison.

Background

Stacy attended the performing arts school. Stacy was interested in art and exploring various aspects of gender identity and expression. Stacy also was attracted to the concept of "genderqueer," which to Stacy meant to question the concept of gender itself. Stacy self-identified as genderqueer because of its perceived gender neutrality, and preferred the pronoun "they" or the gender-neutral pronoun "xe."

Stacy's parents were aware of "trans kids" after watching a 20/20 special when Stacy was young. Because of Stacy's nontraditional gender expression, they were worried that Stacy would experience isolation and bullying in school. Thus, they opted to send Stacy to small alternative schools: at first a Montessori school from kindergarten to middle school, and later to the performing arts high school. Stacy's parents were surprised at how publicly Stacy, a shy and introverted child, eventually expressed gender in high school. Through Stacy's gender expression, they witnessed a profound confidence in their child that they had never seen previously.

Although supportive, Stacy's parents were worried about the potential violence that Stacy might encounter for openly transgressing gender norms. However, Stacy's parents only ever heard of or personally witnessed one negative comment about their child's gender presentation. While collectively riding public transportation, an elderly man looked at Stacy with a confused expression, and then loudly proclaimed, "You're a boy in a skirt!"

Leon attended the alternative school in East Oakland for students labeled "at risk" for school failure and for those who school officials feared would drop out. Leon was a junior at the alternative school, his third school in three years. The alternative school possessed one of the worst reputations of all the schools in the district, second only to the intervention high school. There were many troubled youths who had experienced traumatic events in their lives such as gang and domestic violence, drug-related problems, and poverty.

Leon lived with his mother, Julia; her second husband, Norman; his toddler brother, and three cousins whom his mother raised since the death of her sister during the birth of her third child.

Julia was aware that Leon had some developmental delays. He began walking and talking later than his peers, and she was worried that he struggled with reading and showed little interest in school. Although his elementary school recommended retention several times through the years, Julia felt that Leon should remain with his peers. Although academically delayed, Leon's teachers thought he interacted well socially. However, school counselors worried that the violence within the community left Leon emotionally stunted. For example, two of Leon's best friends during his elementary years were killed by stray bullets on two different occasions while walking home from school. The perpetrators were never found. Around this time, Leon expressed to his mother that he was afraid to attend school. Against his mother's express wishes, Leon began walking to a friend's house or to a local park to avoid school. Despite interventions from his parents and teachers, truancy would be a problem that would persist throughout Leon's life.

Leon's mother agreed to send him to the alternative school because she was assured that they would provide him with special programming. The policy for student admittance at the alternative school was intentionally vague. Parents who felt their children required special attention could apply for admittance, but the majority of student attendees came straight to the alternative school from behavioral dismissal from the two traditional schools in the district. Leon's mother hoped that he would not only graduate but also attend college and find a promising career.

According to Slater (2015),

> An investigation by the *San Francisco Chronicle* found that of some 600 black male students who start at Oakland high schools as freshmen each year, only about 300 end up graduating and fewer than 100 graduate with the requirements needed to attend a California state college or university. The odds of landing in the back of a police cruiser, on the other hand, are much better. African-American boys make up less than 30 percent of Oakland's under-age population but account for nearly 75 percent of all juvenile arrests. And each year, dozens of black men and boys are murdered within the city limits.

Leon had seen the violence that plagued his community from a young age, losing many friends and family members to gun violence. But his mother thought the alternative school could save him. They had summer internships, where Leon excelled, his supervisors reporting his high level of effort. However, when the academic year began, Leon struggled. When he realized he was falling behind his peers, Leon began skipping class. When questioned by the counselor and truancy officer, Mr. Simkins, Leon readily agreed to continue to come to school.

Mr. Simkins, a lifelong resident of East Oakland, was a self-proclaimed "reformed troubled youth." Although he came from a stable home, Mr. Simkins was attracted to the youth gangs of the 1970s. Although at first merely "hanging out" and trying to gain acceptance from older peers, he was initiated into a gang after the murder of his father by police who mistook him for a gang leader in a traffic stop. Mr. Simkins acknowledges that he did not channel his anger in the most productive way. Charged for his initiation crime as a juvenile, which he never discussed, he spent several years in a lock-up facility where he met a man who would change his life: Mr. Smith. Mr. Simkins never revealed the true identity of Mr. Smith, just that he had counseled him and helped him to complete his high school education and get into college. When Mr. Simkins was released from the juvenile facility, he vowed that he would for the rest of his life help the youth of East Oakland.

Mr. Simkins, surprised by Leon's amiable demeanor, invited him to be a part of a special program for chronically truant students at the intervention school. Although Mr. Simkins did not know at that time if Leon would qualify, he knew that he wanted this student in his program, as he saw something in Leon that he saw in his own teenage self: he felt Leon would be a positive influence on other students, as students did not readily volunteer to be a part of such a strict program. Mr. Simkins remembered Leon stating, "I want to be successful. I am just not sure how to do that. If you are offering help, I will take it."

Leon's program included additional counseling and more accountability. If students in the program missed more than 10 days in a semester, they were dismissed from the program and sent back to the traditional alternative program sans the additional counseling and other supports, or worse: some attendees of this special program within the intervention high school, depending upon their personal situation, often ended up in juvenile detention centers.

Leon used the office of Mr. Simkins daily. Although Mr. Simkins had many duties around the district, he tried to spend most of his time where he perceived the greatest need existed. For Mr. Simkins, that was at the intervention school. So committed was he, he gave students his cell phone number in case he was not on school grounds when students were in crisis. Leon would visit Mr. Simkins's before and after school and in between classes. If Mr. Simkins was not there, Leon would leave him notes. Leon offered help and hugs to other students when needed or requested and asked Mr. Simkins to call his mother often to provide her with updates or suggestions on what she could do at home to better help him succeed. His only desire was to graduate and to make his mother proud.

However, Leon was not without his issues. He was having trouble with his coursework. He and his mother requested that he be tested for special education.

During this time, Leon was faced with further violence. A neighborhood friend was killed, and soon after he and his cousin were robbed at gunpoint. Although Leon never told anyone, he considered one of the assailants a friend. Leon was torn between survival and homework. Betrayed and vulnerable, he knew not whom to trust—except for his mother and Mr. Simkins.

Seemingly counterintuitive, this sense of betrayal caused him to turn away from his one safe place: school. Leon felt vulnerable anywhere he went. In his mind, his safest place was alone in his bedroom, so he again began skipping. After being absent from school for one week, and when he could no longer dodge the multiple daily calls from Mr. Simkins, Leon returned to school to receive welcomes and congratulations from fellow students and teachers. He felt proud, and even happier when we saw his cousin waiting for him outside of the school doors. His cousin George, a student at the STEM school, entered the Bus 57 to travel home with Leon.

The Video

The bus camera video depicts Leon and his cousin George entering the bus, where they meet another seeming acquaintance, who is later identified as Joe. Joe was an older boy that both Leon and George knew from the neighborhood. Neither knew Joe very well, but both respected him as possessing great personal power and confidence.

Soon into the bus ride, Joe visibly points toward the sleeping Stacy and says something inaudible. Joe then passes a lighter to Leon.

Leon later reveals to authorities that "the incident" was meant to be a prank, and that he had absolutely no intention of harming Stacy.

The video reveals Leon flicking the lighter several times, before the clothing worn by Stacy actually ignites. Leon's two cohorts appear to egg him on, although the dialogue is inaudible. The video shows the three laughing between lighter flicks.

When the fire starts, George is seen standing and yelling for the bus driver to stop the bus. The three boys exit from the rear emergency door, with Leon leading the way, as Stacy's skirt disintegrates in flames.

The Aftermath

The next day, Leon was alone in the office of Mr. Simkins waiting for him to arrive when he was arrested. Mr. Simkins walked into his office to meet Leon in handcuffs. "I tried to call you," Leon stated. Nothing seemed to register with Leon. He neither appeared shaken by the events, nor did he seem to understand what was about to happen to him.

At the police station, two officers questioned Leon. They were friendly, providing him with lunch. They asked him questions about his life, about friends, school, and family. Leon admitted to being on Bus 57, and witnessing a "man's skirt catch fire."

The officers then asked Leon what he thought about men who wear skirts. Leon indicated that although he is homophobic, he does not hate gay people. After more probing from the officers, Leon stated, "They don't need to make it known to everyone that they are 'like that.'"

The officers repeatedly asked Leon to recall the events that occurred on the bus several times, and ultimately revealed that they possessed the tape of Leon's actions on Bus 57, and that they knew he had started the fire that ignited Stacy's skirt. They then asked Leon to tell them why he did it.

"I was just being stupid," Leon responded in almost a whisper. "I thought it was a joke. I didn't think anyone would get hurt."

Eventually, Leon was charged with assault with intent to cause great bodily injury, a felony, and a hate-crime clause that could potentially add an additional one to three years to his sentence. If convicted, Leon would face a maximum sentence of life in prison.

Leon would not have faced such a punishment were he charged as a juvenile. Joe, who handed Leon the lighter, was not interviewed, arrested, or charged.

After the Arrest

Soon after the arrest and of his own accord, Leon wrote Stacy, his victim, a letter entitled "Dear Victim." Leon apologized to Stacy for his actions and for the pain he had caused. He asked for forgiveness and apologized for his actions. He signed the letter, "Love Leon."

Two days later, Leon wrote a second letter to Stacy, this time even more contrite, and asked to meet face-to-face so that he could apologize in person. Leon then detailed the allegations against him, conceding all but the hate crime charges. Although he had expressed homophobic statements in the past, he indicated in his letter that he too had faced hurtful treatment in his life, both physical and mental, and expressed sorrow at perpetrating that same hurt upon another individual.

Leon's letters were riddled with misspellings and errors in grammar, indicating his level of literacy and his continued need for education.

The prosecutor in the case obtained the letters because they contained admissions of guilt. Stacy did not receive the letters for more than after a year after Leon originally penned them.

Stacy's Recovery

Stacy arrived home from the hospital almost one month after the attack, to a crowded street of well-wishers. Marches had occurred daily along the Bus 57 route since the attack, replete with rainbow flags and representation from local and national LGBTQ+ organizations. Stacy was met with cards and gifts from a national audience, including a medical fund to help with rehabilitation costs upwards of $30,000. All of the high schools in the district sponsored "skirt wearing days" and, at George's school, the football team sported shirts with Stacy's name along with the slogan "No hate" during game play. The alternative and intervention schools did not offer organized sports of any kind.

Stacy's parents, later interviewed, indicated that they desired that Leon be tried as a juvenile. When questioned, Stacy conceded that teenagers do "dumb things," but remained confused as to what they felt should happen to Leon.

The Aftermath

The reporter, Chen, indicated that Leon had a close gay friend and a family member who identified as trans, and that he was not truly homophobic; rather, he was trying to impress older peers who had a certain degree of influence over him. Leon's teachers and Mr. Simkins argued that

Leon did not possess the emotional maturity to stand up to his older peers.

However, the district attorney, Marsha Decon, did not agree. Decon felt that this was indeed a hate crime, and that Leon should serve as an example that such behavior would not be abided. She further indicated that members of protected classes are just that, and likened hate crimes to segregation.

According to Slater (2015):

> Until the mid-1980s, the law made no distinction between crimes motivated by bigotry and crimes motivated by money, passion or boredom. Murder was murder; vandalism was vandalism. The term "hate crime" arose in response to what was described at the time as an "epidemic" of neo-Nazi and skinhead violence, although in retrospect it's unclear whether any such epidemic existed.

Research indicates that many offenders are not necessarily biased toward their victims, but instead were influenced by a more powerful and biased peer (Criminal Justice Research, n.d.).

A national LGBTQ+ rights group went on record to support Leon being tried as a juvenile, and expressed the same sentiment to the office of the district attorney. This organization worried about the implication of imposing adult sanctions on a teen.

The Trial

Prior to the trial, Leon was held at the juvenile hall, where he was in school, getting good grades, and caused no trouble. His main concern was still pleasing his mother and staying out of trouble. Leon did not seem to understand the seriousness of the situation, and the trouble he was already facing.

Leon agreed, after consulting with his mother and his attorney, Darius Levine, to take a plea bargain, admitting to a charge of mayhem. In so doing, the hate-crime charge would be dropped. This deal meant that Leon would serve a five-year sentence, less with good behavior. If all went well, Leon would be released just prior to his 21st birthday, serving all of this time in juvenile facilities.

However, on the day Leon's plea was to be entered, District Attorney Decon changed the terms of the plea from five to seven years, effectively solidifying that Leon would serve time in an adult prison. Leon was advised to take the revised deal, or the case would go to trial.

Attorney Levine was distraught. He understood that the seven-year sentence could be commuted to five years, but that was only if Leon met certain conditions—including education and rehabilitation, the terms of which were not indicated at sentencing—and if he stayed out of trouble. Levine understood that one could not be assured of a clean record, despite concerted effort, because there was always conflict in prison, especially with younger and vulnerable inmates—those who could not protect themselves, those who were susceptible to negative influences by peers, those like Leon. Additionally, this longer sentence made it more likely that Leon would be transferred to an adult prison when he turned 18. Levine questioned whether justice was truly served in this case, and for whom. Was Leon truly a threat to his community? Levine was in the process of getting Leon tested for intellectual disabilities, and hoped that the findings would have an impact on Leon's case. Although the school district had been in the process of having Leon tested for special education services, this process was not completed because of Leon's arrest.

Mr. Simkins felt what was happening to Leon was a travesty. He did not feel that Leon's actions were intended to harm Stacy. In fact, Leon really did not understand what the consequences for his actions were, or how his life was about to change. Mr. Simkins wished he would have fought harder to have him tested for a learning disability sooner so there was something the attorney could use on Leon's behalf.

Teaching Notes

Violence and aggressive behavior are not new issues facing schools. However, researchers continue to explore relational causes and long-term effects violence exposure may have on educational and social outcomes. Psychologist Patricia Sullivan from the Center for the Study of Children's Issues at Creighton University documents school bullying, institutional violence, child abuse, neglect, community violence, and domestic violence in her research. Her main concern is that violent reports to officials can often go unnoticed and fall on deaf ears because children with disabilities are often deemed unbelievable (Sullivan, 2009).

Children exposed to violence can impose educational and social challenges for themselves as well as their peers. According to Carrell and Hoekstra (2008), "One more troubled peer in a classroom of 20 students reduces student test scores by 0.67 percentile points and increases the number of student disciplinary infractions committed by students by 16 percent" (p. 17). Additionally, victimization can be significantly associated with depression and substance abuse (Luk, Wang, & Simons-Morton, 2010, figures 1 & 2). It has become common in current studies to detail, by survey, the types of violent behaviors children are exposed to. Behavioral scientists Juvonen and Graham (2001) acknowledge that there are many misunderstandings about the effects school violence have on schooling, but note more evaluation is needed to help students with disabilities have positive school experiences.

School safety is a fundamental issue for school leaders. The issue of removing disruptive students because of violent behavioral characteristics can contribute to a dysfunctional cycle where many children experience dual roles as both victim and bully (Carter & Spencer, 2006). Significant exposure to violence can lead to detrimental factors in educational, emotional, and social competency.

Adverse childhood experiences (ACEs) can dramatically affect the mental, physical, and socio-emotional development of individuals and families for a lifetime (Crawford, 2013; Erikson, 1968; Felitti, 2009; Hughes, Lowey, Quigg, & Bellis, 2016; Schimmenti & Bifulco, 2015; Schore & Schore, 2008). Exploration of injurious effects of trauma on adolescents provides a more comprehensive understanding of the mechanisms linking childhood trauma, social attachment, life satisfaction, and resiliency.

Early childhood traumatic events stem from a host of devastating interpersonal experiences ranging from physical, emotional, and sexual abuse, to include community violence, loss of a caregiver, physical or emotional neglect, maltreatment, or experiencing trauma vicariously. The U.S. Government Accountability Office (2011) reported that in the fiscal year 2009 over 1,770 children died from maltreatment.

In 2009 the Children's Bureau produced an Issue Brief entitled: *Understanding the Effects of Maltreatment on Brain Development*. This report provided basic information on the effects of childhood abuse and neglect on brain development and assisted professionals to "understand the emotional, mental, and behavioral impact of early abuse and neglect in children who come to the attention of the child welfare system" (Children's Bureau, 2009, p. 1). The brief further indicated how an environment with nurturing caregivers and supportive professionals can play a significant role in helping abused and neglected children through the development of intervention strategies that strengthen families and provide needed services.

This evidence indicates that abuse and neglect during infancy and early childhood result in altered brain functioning. Early traumatization affects the ability to learn, form healthy relationships, and live healthy and positive lives. Utilizing this evidence provides significant information that will aid in prevention, treatment, and effective intervention of childhood adversity leading to dysfunction.

Biomedical research has revealed that childhood abuse and emotional trauma adversely alters the structural development of the brain, affecting the neuroregulatory systems that determine behavior and physical illness from early childhood, to adolescence, and well into adulthood. The long-term effects on the body contribute to the processes of disease and aging compromising the immune system (Moffitt, 2013).

As neuroscience investigates the development of the brain at a molecular level, the link between early childhood adversity, delinquency, and adult disease can be more readily understood (Felitti et al., 1998). Childhood adversity is an inhibiting mechanism in brain development that serves as a neurobiological pathway to dysfunction. Understanding the correlation between childhood adversity, delinquency, and institutionalization further demonstrates the need for institutions to cultivate a greater awareness of the effects of childhood adversity.

The cumulative effects are staggering. In one of the largest research studies of its kind, Anda and colleagues (2006) assessed 17,337 adult HMO members for having any of eight adverse childhood experiences (ACEs), which included physical, sexual, and emotional abuse; physical or emotional neglect; witnessing domestic violence; and household substance abuse or mental illness. With many of the adverse childhood experiences occurring together, they have cumulative effects. The findings showed that cumulative exposure of the developing brain to repetitive stress response resulted in impairment in multiple brain structures and functions.

According to Putnam (2006), the expenditures associated with maltreatment place childhood adversity are among the costliest health problems in history. Adams (2010) discovered that between 75–93 percent of youngsters entering the juvenile justice system have experienced some degree of childhood trauma.

The connection between childhood adversity, delinquency, and at-risk students further demonstrates the need for schools to cultivate a greater internal awareness and subsequent development of more effective and appropriate protocol for at-risk students. Children exposed to adverse childhood experiences often function in a constant state of fight-or-flight and are unable to focus in school. A study by the Area Health Education Center of Washington State University found that students with at least three ACEs are more likely to experience academic failure, chronic absenteeism, or behavioral problems, where punishment is often ineffective and better results can be achieved with positive reinforcement (Stevens, 2012).

Students with ACEs are often misdiagnosed with attention deficit hyperactivity disorder because they appear impulsive, acting out with strong emotions or anger. Identifying students with childhood adversity, implementing pathways for them to build relationships with compassionate adults, and providing a caring, safe environment would increase student outcomes.

There are internal and external factors that lead to violent behaviors in children. Current research tackles the complex causes and attempts to provide treatment resolutions leading to further development of safety policies. Educators and classified staff who are unfamiliar with traumatic events that affect their students and families can participate in trauma-informed care training that involves recognizing, understanding, and responding to different types of trauma. The training helps school employees look at student behavior through the lens of trauma, emphasizing physical, psychological, and emotional safety for students. The relationships school employees build with students can make a difference in a child's life.

References

Adams, E. J. (2010). Healing invisible wounds: Why investing in trauma-informed care for children makes sense. *Justice Policy Institute, 2.*

Anda, R. F., Felitti, V. J., Bremner, J. D., Walker, J. D., Whitfield, C. H., Perry, B. D., . . . Giles, W. H. (2006). The enduring effects of abuse and related adverse experiences in childhood. *European Archives of Psychiatry and Clinical Neuroscience, 256*(3), 174–186. http://dx.doi.org/10.1007/s00406-005-062 4-4

Carrell, S., & Hoekstra, M. (2008). Externalities in the classroom: How children exposed to domestic violence affect everyone's kids. *NBER WORKING PAPER SERIES*, 14246.

Carter, B., & Spencer, V. (2006). The fear factor: Bullying and students with disabilities. *International Journal of Special Education, 21*(1), 11–23.

Children's Bureau. (2009). *Understanding the effects of maltreatment on brain development* [Issue brief]. Retrieved from https://www.childwelfare.gov /pubs/issue_briefs/brain_development/brain_development.pdf

Crawford, S. (2013). *Life satisfaction among those who experienced trauma in early childhood: A qualitative study* (Doctoral dissertation). Retrieved from http://repository.asu.edu/attachments/125883/content/Crawford_asu _0010E_13499.pdf

Criminal Justice Research. (n.d.). Hate crime perpetrators. Retrieved from http:// criminal-justice.iresearchnet.com/crime/hate-crime/4/

Erikson, E. H. (1968). *Identity: Youth and crisis.* New York, NY: Norton.

Felitti, V. J. (2009). Adverse childhood experience and adulthood. *Academic Pediatrics, 9*(3), 131–132. http://dx.doi.org/10.1016/j.acap.2009.03.001

Felitti, V. J., Anda, R. F., Nordenberg, D., Williamson, D. F., Spitz, A. M., . . . Marks, J. S. (1998). Relationship to childhood abuse and household dysfunction to many of the leading causes of death in adults: The adverse childhood experiences (ACE) Study. *American Journal of Preventative Medicine, 14*(4), 245–258. Retrieved from http://www.acestudy.org/yahoo_site_admin /assets/docs/RelationshipofACEs.12891741.pdf

Hughes, K., Lowey, H., Quigg, Z., & Bellis, M. A. (2016). Relationships between adverse childhood experiences and adult mental well-being: Results from an English national household survey. *BMC Public Health, 16*(1), 1–11. http://dx.doi.org/10.1186/s12889-016-2906-3

Juvonen, J., & Graham, S. (2001). *Peer harassment in school: The plight of the vulnerable and victimized.* New York, NY: Guilford.

Luk, J., Wang, J., & Simons-Morton, B. (2010). Bullying victimization and substance use among U.S. adolescents: Mediation by depression. *Prev Sci, 11*, 355–359.

Martin, J., & Beese, J. (2016). *Teaching for social justice: Practical case studies for professional development and principal preparation, Volume 1.* Lanham, MD: Rowman & Littlefield.

Moffitt, T. E. (2013). Childhood exposure to violence and lifelong health: Clinical intervention science and stress-biology research join forces. *Development and Psychopathology, 25*(4).

Putnam, F. W. (2006). The impact of trauma on child development. *Juvenile and Family Court Journal, 57*(57), 1–11.

Schimmenti, A., & Bifulco, A. (2015). Linking lack of care in childhood to anxiety disorders in emerging adulthood: The role of attachment styles. *Child and Adolescent Mental Health, 20*(1), 41–48. http://dx.doi.org/10.1111/camh .12051

Schore, A., & Schore, J. (2008). Modern attachment theory: The central role of affect regulation in development and treatment. *Journal of Clinical Social Work, 36*(9), 9–20. http://dx.doi.org/10.1007/s10615-007-0111-7

Slater, D. (2015, January 29). The fire on the 57 bus in Oakland. *New York Times Magazine.* Retrieved from http://www.nytimes.com/2015/02/01/magazine /the-fire-on-the-57-bus-in-oakland.html?_r=0

Stevens, J. E. (2012). Lincoln high school in Walla Walla, WA, tries new approach to school discipline—Suspensions drop 85%. *ACEs Too High!* Retrieved from   https://acestoohigh.com/2012/02/28/spokane-wa-students-child -trauma-prompts-search-for-prevention/

Sullivan, P. (2009). Violence exposure among children with disabilities. *Clinical Child Family Psychology Review, 12*, 196–216.

U.S. Census Bureau. (2014, September 14). *Community Facts.* Retrieved from http://factfinder2.census.gov/faces/nav/jsf/pages/index.xhtml

U.S. Government Accountability Office. (2011). *Child maltreatment: Strengthening national data on child fatalities could aid in prevention* (GAO-11-599). Washington, DC: Government Printing Office.

"HE LOOKS LIKE A TERRORIST!" SPECIAL EDUCATION AND STEREOTYPE THREAT

Introduction

The key here is not the kind of instruction but the attitude underlying it. When teachers do not understand the potential of the students they teach, they will underteach them no matter what the methodology.
                                        —*Lisa Delpit (1995, p. 175)*

In 1975, the Education for All Handicapped Children Act (EAHCA) established the terms *disability* and *high risk*, and new requirements were established for educators. EAHCA was considered landmark federal legislation that secured and protected access to general and individualized education services for K–12 students identified with cognitive and/or physical disabilities (Ballard & Zettel, 1978; EAHCA, 1975; Keogh, 2007). Consequently, schools were required to administer diagnostic assessments to identify and to create individualized educational service plans for students with disabilities (Ballard & Zettel, 1978).

In 1990, the U.S. Congress reauthorized EACHA and changed the title to the Individuals with Disabilities Act (IDEA) (Pub. L. No. 94-142). IDEA is composed of six main elements: the Individualized Education Program (IEP), Free and Appropriate Public Education (FAPE), Least Restrictive Environment (LRE), appropriate evaluation, parent and teacher participation, and procedural safeguards with additional consideration given to confidentiality of information, transition services, and discipline (Hulett, 2009). IDEA expanded operational definitions, including additional disability identifications authorizing research to continue to define disabilities and propose recommendations to Congress (Aleman, 1991; Alexander & Alexander, 2008; Alexander, 2012).

Nine years after EAHCA was implemented, there was a 16 percent increase in students identified with handicaps and a 119 percent increase in students identified with learning disabilities (Wang, Reynolds, & Walberg, 1986). These data suggest that specific groups of students that may demonstrate gaps in learning or learning challenges, as opposed to learning disabilities, were being misidentified as learning disabled and inappropriately receiving special education services (Keogh, 2007).

The No Child Left Behind Act of 2001 (NCLB) raised the issue of accurate identification of students who do, and do not, possess a learning disability. However, discerning students with disabilities as opposed to students with learning deficiencies was not operationally defined until the passage of the Every Student Succeeds Act (ESSA, 2015). ESSA defined the achievement gap as the discrepancy between students who do, and do not, meet state academic standards and students who are identified as at risk for failure (2015, p. 52). This new guidance will hopefully alleviate some of the mischaracterizations of students with learning needs being referred for special education services.

We hope that new interventions will be created for these students who are caught in this achievement gap and fall behind their students academically, but not necessarily because of identified learning disabilities. Rather, the students impacted by the achievement gap may be attending failing schools with underprepared teachers, may have missed instructional time because of family transience or illness, or a variety of other reasons. In the continuum of student performance, there are at-risk students who face gaps in learning or learning challenges alongside students who have been appropriately identified as possessing learning disabilities.

The Case

Mr. Vincent Robbins was hired at a middle school in a large urban school district in the South to teach special education. Mr. Robbins is a Muslim man of Pakistani descent. He has lived in the United States his entire life. After receiving his teaching degree, he worked as a middle school English teacher for six years and recently finished his master's degree in special education. In his new position, he was hired to assist students with IEPs in traditional academic courses, as full inclusion was the law in the state.

Upon his hire at Lincoln Middle School, Mr. Robbins was given one week to observe other special education teachers as they made their rounds to their various classes. His first observation was that team teaching was not the norm.

Team teaching is an instructional strategy where two teachers collaborate to teach a group of students or a specific class. There are a number of different types of team teaching that can be used in both special education and general classroom settings. A few examples are the tag-team format, where two teachers deliver instruction together; the one teach, one assist method, where one teacher provides instruction while the other teacher walks around the room and assists students; and a method of grouping where one teacher works with a small group based upon their learning needs, and the other with the larger group (Vanderbilt University Center for Teaching, 2016). Some of the benefits of team teaching are that low-performing students receive individualized attention and small-group time, students experience different teaching styles that may better match their learning styles (Coffey, 2008), and the co-planning process produces stronger and more creative lessons (Kaplan, 2012). Team teaching requires teachers to coordinate their schedules to make time to engage in collaborative, interdisciplinary planning.

As Mr. Robbins noted during his observations, the special education teachers typically sat at the back of the classroom and waited for students to come to them if they needed assistance, which was rare. He did not notice any effective methods of team teaching. In fact, he was concerned that for students to approach the special education teacher would be to single themselves out as deficient or "less than" their noncertified peers. Mr. Robbins never witnessed the general education teacher consulting with or bringing in the special education teacher on any lesson in any classroom—and he observed many classes: math, science, language arts, and social studies.

Mr. Robbins also was allowed to observe the "discipline room": the room in which students who were disruptive in class were sent for a "time out," prior to interventions from the administration. Mr. Robbins noticed that the vast majority of the students sent to the discipline room were minority students; however, minority students made up only half of the overall student population. Likewise, most of the minority students were also certified for special education services. Mr. Robbins wondered if the implicitly held biases of the teachers were contributing to this disparity.

According to the U.S. Department of Education Office for Civil Rights (2014), African American students are 3.5 times more likely to be suspended or expelled. Although they make up only 18 percent of the overall student population, African American students make up 46 percent of those students suspended more than one time. One in 4 African American students are suspended at least once compared to 1 in 11 white students (U.S. Department of Education Office for Civil Rights, 2014). New data show inequitable discipline practices enacted upon minority children in general beginning in preschool (U.S. Department of Education Office for Civil Rights, 2014).

Mr. Robbins's observations led him to ask the administration for discipline records and special education referrals for the last five years. He did so on the presumption that this would better allow him to do his job. The administration freely divulged the records. Upon examination, Mr. Robbins learned that minority students were not only disproportionately being referred for special education services but also that they were disproportionately disciplined, and at greater risk for retention, suspension, and expulsion.

Mr. Robbins was aware of the research on the overrepresentation of students in special education who are not learning disabled, as many special education determinations were simply learning deficits that are misdiagnosed as learning disabilities, or *false positives* (Kavale, Kauffman, Bachmeier, & LeFever, 2008, p. 139). He personally wanted to successfully navigate any learning challenges or gaps in learning that students possessed through instructional interventions.

During this time, the district and the school were in jeopardy of being taken over by the state for underperformance. Thus, they were in need of making institutional changes that would lead to student success.

Upon his first day of teaching, Mr. Robbins was given a strict schedule: he was to "team teach" in two language arts classes with Ms. Porter and two social studies classes with Mr. Bishop; he would manage the resource room for one hour; and the final hour of the day would be his planning hour. The resource room was a space where special education students were sent, whether by their own or teacher request, in order to receive special academic or social attention and support. Mr. Robbins's planning hour was the same as the two teachers with whom he was to collaborate, and the presumption was that this common planning time would be used to create team-based lessons.

Mr. Robbins attempted to communicate with veteran teachers Ms. Porter and Mr. Bishop, who had taught at the school for five and seven years respectively, several times in person and via e-mail to meet as a team. Ms. Porter, a 33-year-old white woman, and Mr. Bishop, a 42-year-old white male, collectively indicated to Mr. Robbins in person that they were too busy grading papers to meet with him, and that things would be just fine as they were—with him assisting when needed and as requested by students.

Immediately following this conversation, Mr. Robbins sought out the principal, Mr. Horgan, to communicate his situation. Mr. Horgan, a white male with 42 years of experience in education, began his career as a math teacher in a suburban district where he taught for eight years; during the last three of those years he earned his master's degree in educational administration and principal licensure. It was almost 34 years ago when he decided to move to an urban setting so that he could make a difference in the lives of inner city children. However, Mr. Horgan has been increasingly disillusioned by the high turnover rate of his teachers, a common occurrence in urban schools. He knows that he probably should have retired years ago, lacking the energy it takes to lead a staff, particularly one that requires so much training and professional development on how best to serve a current student population that is rapidly becoming more diverse.

Mr. Robbins indicated to Mr. Horgan that he desired to be an integral part of the team, and asked for his advice on how to do so. Mr. Horgan, although too exhausted to fight with teachers, sympathized with Mr. Robbins; on the spot, he devised a plan.

"I mean no disrespect Mr. Robbins, but I am going to assume that you are of the Muslim faith." Mr. Robbins wondered why Mr. Horgan would assume this, for he had neither made no proclamations of his faith, nor did he wear any religious symbols. He wondered ironically if Mr. Horgan were so concerned and assured of his faith, why he did not provide a location for him to adhere to the Muslim call to prayer, but he readily dismissed these negative thoughts and listened to what Mr. Horgan had to say.

Mr. Horgan continued, "We have a student, Adeeb, who wears a religious headdress. He has been teased by other students, and some faculty feel that since he is now in America that he should not be allowed to wear this to school—citing the dress code policy of 'no hats' in school. I am wondering if your open planning time may be a blessing in disguise. How about you spend this time with Adeeb?" Mr. Horgan still faced ill will from staff members who lost the dress code battle over Adeeb's turban during the previous school year. Word traveled fast, and Mr. Horgan navigated many angry meetings with concerned staff members and phone calls from parents.

Mr. Robbins, a bit surprised, replied, "Well, I am happy to help, but what about this student's academics? Won't he be missing a class if he is with me during last period?"

"Well, yes," Mr. Horgan replied, "but we attempt to educate the whole child here, and I think Adeeb would benefit from some one-on-one time with another male to whom he can relate during the school day."

Mr. Robbins quickly agreed, not wanting to alienate himself from the administration in his brand new job. He asked to review the file on Adeeb, and Mr. Horgan enthusiastically provided it.

From his file, Mr. Robbins quickly learned that Adeeb Singh was a recent immigrant from India, who spoke both English and Punjabi. Mr. Robbins determined to seek him out the next day prior to the start of classes.

Upon first glance, Mr. Robbins recognized that Adeeb was a Sikh. Per his religious tradition, Adeeb was permitted to wear his turban to school, despite many previous protestations from parents and staff. Turbans are worn by males of the Sikh religion because it is seen as their commitment to their own higher consciousness and is a symbol of spirituality and holiness.

Many staff members, students, and parents confused Adeeb with being Muslim, and feared that he may be a terrorist. Mr. Robbins was concerned not only that his colleagues and his community would automatically assume that any Muslim would be a terrorist but also that they could not differentiate a Sikh from a Muslim and did not seem to care about the obvious religious differences.

Mr. Horgan was worried that Adeeb would be subject to bullying by other students and differential treatment by his teachers. Mr. Horgan felt that special attention from Mr. Robbins might be an additional source of support for a vulnerable student. After meeting Adeeb, Mr. Robbins asked Mr. Horgan if he could become more involved with Adeeb's case by checking in with his teachers, and overseeing his grades and overall academic progress. Mr. Horgan readily accepted Mr. Robbins's offer. However, Mr. Robbins was troubled by the fact that there was no training for staff or even the slightest recognition of Adeeb's faith and the unique challenges he may face within the school because of it.

When Mr. Robbins met with Adeeb again at the end of his first day, he was confused about why Adeeb was a special education student, which he had learned from reading his file. "This student is fluent in two languages, and likely proficient in more. Why is he in special education?" he wondered to himself after speaking with Adeeb for five minutes.

Mr. Robbins was also aware of the disproportionate number of English Language Learners (ELLs) classified in special education, a national trend (Sullivan, 2011). Their learning needs, based on rudimentary exposure to or proficiency in the English language, were often perceived to be a language learning disability. However, this did not pertain to Adeeb, for he was proficient in English.

Mr. Robbins spent his first planning hour engaging in conversation with Adeeb and simply getting to know him. He learned that Adeeb and his family had been in the United States for about six months, and that this was his first experience with schooling in the United States. His family had moved here because his father was a biochemist whose company had transferred him to their home office in the United States.

Mr. Robbins asked what subjects Adeeb struggled with. Adeeb stated that he did not have many struggles with the academics, but rather with the customs in the United States. On his first day, when called upon by one of his teachers to answer a question, he stood—as is the custom in India. When he did so, the teacher looked confused and commanded Adeeb to sit down. Adeeb did so, and subsequently put his head down on the desk in deference. The teacher took this to be an additional act of disrespect and sent Adeeb down to the principal's office, as opposed to the discipline room—bypassing a step in the required discipline policies and procedures. She also requested that Adeeb be tested for special education services, and requested that he be removed from her class.

For years, Mr. Horgan had been unsettled by the number of negative comments he heard from his staff about immigrant children from Eastern and Middle Eastern countries. His teachers had made negative assumptions regarding the overall intelligence of these students, and that these students were not as invested in their academics as their white counterparts. After years of trying to combat these stereotypes and their corresponding mindsets, Mr. Horgan gave up and stayed quiet. The battle over the dress code took quite a toll on him.

Mr. Horgan was deeply troubled when Mr. Robbins came into his office with his concerns. Mr. Robbins wanted answers about and validation for his feelings when he heard a stereotypical comment made by one of Adeeb's teachers, that "Arab American students are underachievers and receiving special needs services will be a support to Adeeb and others like him."

Mr. Robbins attempted to indicate to this teacher that Adeeb was not, in fact, Arab American, but his protestations fell on deaf ears. It was as if this teacher did not want to become educated about Adeeb, or any other student who was not white, Christian, and native born. Mr. Robbins wondered why this teacher went into the education profession in the first place, if he was unwilling to become educated himself.

For Mr. Robbins, this statement, and others like it, were highly offensive. Mr. Robbins engaged Mr. Horgan in a discussion of the school's overidentification (for special education) of some subgroups within the student population. Mr. Robbins asked, "Why are so many minority students identified as having disabilities? If you look at the data, it is not an anomaly, as a district it appears that either our minority kids are identified as special needs more frequently than their white counterparts or, there is a societal or evaluative bias at work in the identification process. The observable behaviors, which may very well be linked to cultural differences or a lack of dialogue, are used to attribute disability."

Mr. Robbins continued, "Why? Why are minority students overrepresented in our special education population? Why are they appearing at a more frequent rate in our test data when we look at the scores of our failing students?"

Mr. Horgan questioned the results of the process that resulted in Adeeb, and others, being referred for special education services, but he felt compelled to adhere to the results because of pressure from his staff. Most of the staff seemed afraid to deal with Adeeb.

Teaching Notes

According to Steele and Aronson (1995), stereotype threat is the fear of being judged by negative stereotype from others not possessing the same identities that are often subject to stereotypes in society, and/or the fear of acting in such a way to confirm that preexisting stereotypes that exist for one's particular identity or group. This heightened fear to "represent" for one's racial/ethnic/gender (or other) group may result in higher stress and lower performance. For example, if a math teacher holds the stereotype that girls are not as good at math as their male counterparts, the females in the class may feel additional pressure to perform well in order to dis-confirm that stereotype that the teacher holds. This added pressure and stress may cause the stereotyped individuals to perform poorly, thus perpetuating said stereotypes. It becomes a vicious circle, and one that serves to reinforce stereotypes. According to Hill, Corbett, and St. Rose (2010), "Stereotype threat arises in situations when a negative stereotype is relevant to evaluating performance" (p. 39). Stereotype threat can impact individuals both psychologically and physiologically. Fortunately, stereotype threat can be counteracted by teaching students about it (Hill, Corbett, & St. Rose, 2010). Unfortunately, this is not often the case.

Steele (2010) pinpoints the identity categories that are often rife for stereotype threat, including age, sexual orientation, race, gender, ethnicity, political affiliation, mental illness, and disability. Steele (2010) further illuminates the danger of stereotype threat: "We know what 'people think.' We know that anything we do that fits the stereotype could be taken as confirming it" (p. 5). Thus, the vicious circle is perpetuated. If teachers are unaware of their implicit biases, and of the phenomenon of stereotype threat, they are likely to perpetuate it. According to Benjamin Bloom, "After forty years of intensive research on school learning in the United States as well as abroad, my major conclusion is: What any person in the world can learn, *almost* all persons can learn *if* provided with the appropriate prior and current conditions of learning" (Bloom, as cited in Dweck, 2006, pp. 65–66). However, Bloom's sentiment as well as knowledge and understanding of implicit bias and stereotype threat are not explicitly taught in many teacher education programs, and thus do not trickle down to classrooms and schools.

According to Dweck (2006) some teachers have "fixed mindsets," believing that the students who enter their classrooms with lower academic achievement levels are somehow different from their other students, and that this fact is unchangeable. On the other hand, other teachers possess "growth mindsets," and believe that all students can learn and develop their skills. As Dweck (2006) states, "The group differences had simply disappeared under the guidance of teachers who taught for improvement, for these teachers had found a way to reach their 'low-ability' students" (p. 66). Furthermore, according to Dweck (2006):

> The fixed mindset limits achievement. It fills people's minds with interfering thoughts, it makes effort disagreeable, and it leads to inferior learning strategies. What's more, it makes other people into judges instead of allies. Whether we're talking about Darwin or college students, important achievements require a clear focus, all-out effort, and a bottomless trunk full of strategies. Plus allies in learning. This is what the growth mindset gives people, and what's why it helps their abilities grow and bear fruit. (p. 67)

It is important for all teachers to possess growth mindsets in order to cultivate the abilities of all of their students.

Finally, the phenomenon on stereotype threat can affect the strongest and most capable students, indicating that the pressure from without (or "situational pressure") can impact student performance (Steele, 2010). According to Steele (2010), stereotype threat "causes rumination, which takes up mental capacity, distracting us from the task at hand—from the questions on the standardized test we're taking or from the conversation we're having with persons of a different race. So beyond the physiological reactions that identity threat causes, it also impairs performance and other actions by interfering with our thinking" (p. 121).

References

Aleman, S. R. (1991). Education of the Handicapped Act Amendments of 1990, PL 101-476: A Summary. CRS Report for Congress.

Alexander, K., & Alexander, M. D. (2008). *American public school law.* Cengage Learning.

Alexander, M. (2012). *The new Jim Crow: Mass incarceration in the age of color-blindness.* New York, NY: New Press.

Ballard, J., & Zettel, J. J. (1978). The Managerial Aspects of Public Law 94–142. *Exceptional Children, 44*(6), 457–462.

Coffey, H. (2008). Team teaching. University of North Carolina School of Education. Retrieved from http://www.learnnc.org/lp/pages/4754

Delpit, L. (1995). *Other people's children: Cultural conflict in the classroom.* New York, NY: W.W. Norton.

Dweck, C. S. (2006). *Mindset: The new psychology of success.* New York, NY: Ballantine.

Education for All Handicapped Children Act (EAHCA), Pub.L. No. 94-142 § 6 (1975).

Every Student Succeeds Act of 2015, Pub. L. No. 114-95 § 114 Stat. 1177 (ESSA). (2015–2016).

Hill, C., Corbett, C., & St. Rose, A. (2010). *Why so few? Women in science, technology, engineering, and mathematics.* Washington, DC: AAUW.

Hulett, K. E. (2009). *Legal aspects of special education.* Upper Saddle River, NJ: Pearson Education.

Individuals with Disabilities Education Act of 1990, Pub. L. 94-142, U.S.C. 20 § 1400 *et seq.*

Kaplan, M. (2012). Collaborative team teaching: Challenges and rewards [Web log post]. Retrieved from http://www.edutopia.org/blog/collaborative-team -teaching-challenges-rewards-marisa-kaplan

Kavale, K. A., Kauffman, J. M., Bachmeier, R. J., & LeFever, G. B. (2008). Response-to-intervention: Separating the rhetoric of self-congratulation from the reality of specific learning disability identification. *Learning Disability Quarterly, 31*(3), 135–150. doi: 10.2307/25474644

Keogh, B. K. (2007). Celebrating PL 94-142: The Education of All Handicapped Children Act of 1975. *Issues in Teacher Education, 16*(2), 65–69.

No Child Left Behind Act of 2001, Pub. L. No. 107-110, § 115, Stat. 1425 (2002).

Steele, C. M. (2010). *Whistling Vivaldi and other clues to how stereotypes affect us.* New York, NY: W. W. Norton.

Steele, C. M., & Aronson, J. (1995). Stereotype threat and the intellectual test performance of African Americans. *Journal of personality and social psychology, 69*(5), 797.

Sullivan, A. (2011). Disproportionality in special education identification and placement of English language learners. *Exceptional Children, 77*(3), 317–334.

U.S. Department of Education Office for Civil Rights. (2014, March). *Civil rights data collection data snapshot: School discipline.* Retrieved from http://www2.ed.gov/about/offices/list/ocr/docs/crdc-discipline-snapshot.pdf

Vanderbilt University Center for Teaching. (2016). Team/Collaborative teaching. Retrieved from https://cft.vanderbilt.edu/guides-sub-pages/teamcollaborative-teaching/

Wang, M. C., Reynolds, M. C., & Walberg, H. J. (1986). Rethinking special education. *Educational Leadership, 44*(1), 26–31.

"WHAT ARE WE GOING TO DO ABOUT THE BATHROOMS?" TRANSGENDER STUDENTS: CIVIL RIGHTS OR LOCAL CONTROL?

Introduction

According to Orr, Baum, Brown, Gill, Kahn, and Salem (2015),"Transgender describes a person whose gender identity is different from what is generally considered typical from their sex assigned at birth" (p. 6). Because of a lack of knowledge about transgender individuals and the concept of gender in particular on the part of many teachers and administrators, the idea of making accommodations for transgender students can create legal problems for schools. Although the population of transgender students is a very small percentage of the overall student population, a growing acceptance of gender fluidity has encouraged many students to "come out" at younger ages than in past years. The culture seems to be progressing faster than schools and school policies.

Federal decisions affecting transgender students in public schools are becoming more common. The Obama administration's position on allowing transgender students to use the restrooms and locker rooms that correspond to their gender identities has been asserted in legal briefs and civil rights agreements in school districts in recent years (Blad, 2016). However, many state and local policy makers, as well as local school district officials, have disagreed with the Obama administration's stance on transgender school policies, and schools have recently been found in violation of federal civil rights guidance because, for example, they did not allow a transgender student access to the restroom corresponding to their gender identity.

There is a recent trend of state courts and civil rights panels siding with transgender students on questions of access to school facilities. While schools can lose federal funding for noncompliance, civil rights guidance does not carry the full force of law. Because of this, schools and districts sometimes bide their time in making these accommodations for transgender students and thus do not have policies in place to protect them. As federal civil rights officials put pressure on districts to accommodate transgender students, many districts continue to question their responsibilities to students whose gender identities do not match the genders they were assigned at birth.

This dilemma may be reduced to one ethical question: Should school districts do the bare minimum to reach civil rights compliance, or should they go above and beyond, and do as much as they possibly can to accommodate and protect all of their students? School districts often wait until they experience legal problems, such as being sued by families for civil rights violations, instead of getting ahead of lawsuits by creating policies protecting the civil rights of all students. Teachers and administrators should in fact accommodate the rights of transgender students by, for example, using their preferred name whether or not the students have had their names legally changed. Some districts create a two-tiered system, with the legal name of the student in a computer system, and the preferred name of the student on classroom documents to ensure that the student is not "outed," which may put them at risk for harassment. Districts should have policies in place for this, and for other issues facing transgender students.

However, some district leaders are often at a loss about what they are legally required to do for their transgender students. This is not because the information is not there; they are just not seeking it out or do not know where to look. This case examines the nuances of accommodating transgender student needs, while examining the legal requirements for schools as well as the practical implications of these requirements.

The Case

Robert (Bobby) Gonzalez, formerly Susan Gonzalez, is a gifted student at Shirley Chisholm High School in the Springfield Heights School District. The gifted coordinator, Heather Keenly, did not know Bobby personally yet, as he was a new transfer student, but she did recognize a mismatch with Bobby's name on the course rosters (Robert) and the official computer system (Susan). After some investigating, Ms. Keenly learned that Bobby's gender was listed as female (F) in the computer system as well. As the school typically used a student's name and gender as listed in the computer system when mailing information home, which relied upon recorded birth certificate information as their source, Ms. Keenly was unsure what to do. She did not know if this was a mistake: Was this student mixed up with another with the same last name? Or, was this a transgender student? She quickly searched the Internet to find if there was a standard for transgender student name change policies, because she wanted to be informed. She learned that when a transgender student transitions, there are many opportunities for a student's previous name or sex assigned at birth to inadvertently appear on documents generated by school systems (Orr et al., 2015), which can have negative consequences for the student. She also learned that although there are ideal standards to which schools can adhere in order to protect transgender students, such as using their preferred name and preferred pronouns, there is not a universal standard.

New to the school and unfamiliar with all of the district and school policies, she decided to consult the school administrator, Principal Romeo. Ms. Keenly asked for the story on this student. Principal Romeo replied,

"Bobby's gender identity is male. Everyone in the school is aware of Bobby's gender identity and expression: that he is male. However, simple things like taking attendance or enrolling in classes often can compromise a student's privacy. We do what we can, but these legal documents still pose a problem for us."

Principal Romeo indicated that since Bobby's name was never legally changed, she could not place the name "Robert" on the forms; instead, she had to use the student's legal name of Susan. Ms. Kennan ruminated on this. An issue such as this was something that she had never thought of. On the one hand, she thought, "What's the big deal? It is only a letter, M or F, and it is only the paperwork that is mailed home. How bad can that be?" On the other hand, she thought about the logical extension of this issue. She wondered, "What is the worst case scenario here?" She thought about a teacher inadvertently calling a student by the wrong name (and thus gender) when taking attendance; she thought about teachers unintentionally outing students in front of their peers; she thought about bullying. What she did not think about was the intentional outing of a student by a teacher. She then came to the following conclusion: "We should always think about the worst case scenario when making decisions impacting our students."

Ms. Kennan shared this idea with Principal Romero, and he nodded. They both verbally agreed that they would need to seek district support to create better and more inclusive policies to protect transgender students.

Ms. Kennan was not happy Principal Romeo's direction for her to use the student's legal name for home mailings, but she complied, understanding that this was a case of policy lagging behind rapidly changing social norms. She expected that more of these issues would present themselves.

As Ms. Kennan took her leave, another thought occurred to her. She stopped in her tracks and turned around to face Principal Romeo. "This is my first experience working with a transgender student," Ms. Kennan began. "This is my first experience as well," Principal Romeo concurred. "So . . ." Ms. Kennan paused. "What are we going to do about the bathrooms?"

District History with Transgender Students: John F. Kennedy High School

Two years previously, a very outspoken high school student new to John F. Kennedy High School in the Springfield Heights School District, Trevor Martin, who was born a biological female but identified as male, indicated that it is discriminatory to force him to use the girls' bathroom or locker room at school. After moving to the Springfield Heights School District at the end of his eighth grade year, Trevor's parents, Fred and Joann Martin, were in frequent communication with Principal McAfee over the summer to discuss Trevor's name change, his registration as a male student, his access to the boys' restrooms and locker rooms, and his eligibility for boys' sports teams.

However, at this time, Principal McAfee had no experience with transgender students, and no training. Although he consulted with other building principals in his district and in the surrounding area, and with his own central office administration, he found no easy solutions. The central office administration in the Springfield Heights School District dictated that this student would use the bathrooms and locker rooms for "her" biological sex, and that "she" would be referred to by "her" name per the legal documents.

Fred and Joann Martin respected Principal McAfee, and they knew that he was trying his best, but they also needed to advocate for their child. They pleaded with Principal McAfee to devise a solution that would benefit everyone. Principal McAfee thought about it, and thought he could "get around" the district mandates without getting anyone into trouble.

Prior to the beginning of the school year, Principal McAfee met with all of Trevor's teachers and explained the situation. He indicated that although Trevor's name would appear as Brittany on the class rosters, they should always refer to him as Trevor and using the male pronoun, as he preferred. Most of the teachers were sympathetic and readily agreed, except one.

Mr. Ward said nothing as Principal McAfee explained Trevor's situation. But the look on his face made his opinion about the situation more than clear. However, no one looked at him. Mr. Ward had a reputation for being stern, traditional, and hard on students. He had previously been taken to task by the union for proselytizing Evangelical religious views in class.

On the first day of school, all went well for Trevor, until the last period of the day: Mr. Ward's social studies class. When Mr. Ward took attendance, he called for Brittany Martin over and over. When no one responded to this name, Mr. Ward walked over to Trevor's desk. He stood in front of the desk, looked Trevor in the eye, and stated, "I know you go by Trevor now, but your legal name is Brittany, so I need you to respond when I call you. Otherwise, I will mark you absent."

At this stage, Mr. Ward did nothing else. He simply continued taking attendance, and then he went on with the first day's lesson.

Trevor ran home that day. When his parents arrived home from work that evening, he explained what happened, and they called Principal McAfee, but he was already gone for the day.

The next day, Trevor did not experience any fallout from Mr. Ward's confrontation in sixth hour, yet he still dreaded attending that class. He considered hiding in the bathroom instead, or ducking out a side door and walking home early. But, instead, he steeled himself and walked into Mr. Ward's class early, ready and willing to educate his teacher.

Trevor entered the class at 1:01 pm on Tuesday. There were still four minutes before the bell would ring signifying the start of class. Trevor figured that he had two minutes to speak to Mr. Ward before his classmates began filing in. Trevor found Mr. Ward at his desk, organizing papers that he presumably collected from the previous class.

"Excuse me, Mr. Ward. Can I talk to you before class starts?" Trevor began. Mr. Ward looked up at Trevor over the top of his glasses. He sighed. "Yes?"

"I am not sure what you think of me, but my name is Trevor. I would appreciate it if you could call me Trevor. If you have any questions about anything, I will answer them. I am not sure if now is the best time, but I will tell you anything to help you understand. Just please call me by my name." Appearing brave in his stance and in his words, Trevor was crumbling inside. He had never had to speak to a teacher like that before. At his previous school, all of his teachers complied with his request in name change. Trevor transitioned in middle school. His problem was not with his teachers. On the contrary, they were sympathetic and supportive. He had problems with some students who knew him as Brittany and could not or would not understand his transition, and therefore made his life hell. Such experiences pushed the Martins to move districts.

"Hon," Mr. Ward began, "I am sure you think you know who you are, but you're just a kid. You're in ninth grade. I am going to do my job as I always have. I am going to read off my roster, which is a legal document, by the way, just as I always have. If you do not respond to your name, you will be marked absent."

As Trevor stood in front of Mr. Ward's desk in disbelief, the one-minute warning bell rang. It was 1:04 pm. Trevor contemplated whether to run out or to sit down. As the seconds clicked by, students began to file in. Trevor felt as if he could feel their stares, as assuredly as he could hear the ticks of the clock's second hand. He chose to sit, so as not to draw any more attention to himself.

At 1:05 pm the bell rang, and Mr. Ward began to call roll. When he heard the name Brittany Martin, Trevor again was silent. But Mr. Ward was not.

"Class," Mr. Ward began, "I want you to know that we have a student who will not respond to her name." Mr. Ward approached Trevor's desk as he continued, "This student, a girl, named Brittany Martin, thinks she's a boy named Trevor." Now Mr. Ward was standing in front of Trevor's desk, facing him. "I guess I am not allowed to, what do they call it these days?" Mr. Ward paused for a moment. "I have it! I guess I am not allowed to 'out' this student," he continued sarcastically, "but what about my rights? Our rights? What about free speech? What about the bathrooms? This is a slippery slope folks. If I am made to call a girl a boy, what's next?" Mr. Ward looked around as if to gain support from the students, but he found none. The students appeared dumbfounded.

As if by divine intervention, Principal McAfee's voice sounded from the intercom speaker on the wall, "Mr. Ward, please send Trevor Martin to my office immediately."

Mr. Ward smiled. "Brittany, you heard him. Go!"

Trevor left the classroom at 1:10 pm, never to return.

Principal McAfee had finally returned the Martins' call just prior to the start of sixth period. Attempting to do his due diligence based upon the Martins' claims of what Trevor experienced the previous day, Principal McAfee called Trevor down to the office, listened to what Trevor experienced both on Monday and on Tuesday, and subsequently transferred him to another social studies class.

Principal McAfee silently praised the students in the class for not taking Mr. Ward's bait. Recently, he had become aware of the suicide rates of transgender students, and continued to check on the health and well-being of Trevor in his interactions with peers.

Principal McAfee felt he dodged a bullet here. He made a pledge to himself to be cognizant of the needs of transgender students, and to always err on the side of caution. He also pledged to himself that he would provide training for all of his staff and students on LGBTQ+ students and their needs, including their legal rights and the school's legal responsibilities. He was willing to fight central office administration if need be. He was now committed.

His first charge was to report Mr. Ward's inappropriate behavior to the district administration. By Friday of the same week, Mr. Ward was suspended pending an investigation. After much legal wrangling, Mr. Ward was relieved of his duties, and Principal McAfee considered himself a full-fledged advocate for LGBTQ+ students.

Now, at the start of each school year, Principal McAfee conferenced with each transgender student and their family to discuss any possible issues or concerns the family and student might have. Principal McAfee knew how difficult transgender situations can be because as the administrator, he is not permitted to tell anyone about the student. That would be considered "outing" someone. He had to rely on the parents and students to share their situation with teachers.

During the conference, students are provided the choice of using the bathroom and locker room of their birth gender or a private bathroom locker room set aside for their use. Students had always preferred to use a private bathroom. Because these issues are addressed in an honest and open manner, and students are provided choices, Principal McAfee had not faced any issues up to this point.

Current Situation: Shirley Chisholm High School

Shirley Chisholm High School honored Bobby's request to be treated as a male in all respects except access to the boys' restrooms and boys' locker room at the school. However, Shirley Chisholm High School did not have a principal advocate like JFK had in Principal McAfee. Because of this, the school and the district relied on a board decision and subsequently offered Bobby a single-stall unisex restroom and a private changing station in the locker room, which, according to Superintendent Brown, "appropriately serves the dignity and privacy of all students in our educational environment." Anne and Frank Gonzalez expressed dissatisfaction with that arrangement, stating, "This will ostracize our son and draw attention to the fact that he must change separately." They also complained about the lack of access to the boys' locker room as a student in a gym class.

The Gonzalez family expressed their dissatisfaction with the board's decision with Principal Romeo and Superintendent Brown. They also consulted an attorney, and wrote an appeal to the decision that they submitted to Principal Romeo and Superintendent Brown as well as to the board. However, the decision remained firm. At this point, the Gonzalez family filed a formal complaint with the civil rights office in their region.

The civil rights office subsequently filed suit on behalf of the Gonzalez's claim of discrimination based on gender. The issue was tied up in court for the rest of the academic year, and it was not until Bobby's sophomore year in high school that he was finally permitted access to the boys' locker room and restroom.

Soon after that, some parents and a minority of board members staged a protest of Bobby Gonzalez's use of the boys' locker room. A board member was overheard saying that transgender students suffer from a "mental disorder" and that it's not "a real thing." The board member stepped down in the aftermath of his comments. Despite all of this, the district still had not formulated a policy addressing transgender issues. Although district leaders were pressured by national LGBTQ+ groups and sympathetic parents and students to support transgender students, they also felt challenged by some parents, students, and community groups who argued that issues related to transgender bathroom and locker room use threatened the rights of other students.

This conflict caused many students, parents, teachers, and community members to take a side. What could have remained a private issue between the Gonzalez family and the school became a political issue, which led to the outing of Bobby's transgender status. Bobby then faced teasing and harassment on the part of several students, which caused him severe anxiety, stress, and decreased academic performance.

Additionally, in the wake of this policy wavering, the U.S. Justice and Education departments sent letters to the Springfield Heights School District instructing that transgender students should be allowed to use the bathrooms, showers, and locker rooms of their choice (matching their gender identity). Violations of this dictate could result in the loss of federal education funding.

The district ignored this guidance and, instead, sued for an injunction preventing the U.S. Department of Education from enforcing the rule allowing students to access bathrooms and other facilities based on gender identity. The Gonzalez family elected to sue on the side of the government indicating that the Springfield Heights School District discriminated against Bobby and violated his right to privacy.

The Gonzalez family argued that the "drop your trousers" policy," which would result if these informal and discriminatory policies would be allowed to continue, was ridiculous and unconstitutional. As Mr. Gonzalez argued in the press, "No one would know anything about biology unless they got down and peeked under the stall divider. What about the right to privacy?"

Despite protests from Principal McAfee, the Springfield Heights School District submitted a brief with the Supreme Court to find that the U.S. Department of Education does not possess the authority to dictate their bathroom policies (i.e., that they should not be compelled to allow transgender students to use the bathroom of their choice). The Springfield Heights superintendent was well aware that districts across the country were struggling with how to accommodate transgender students, so he desired to attempt to benefit from this confusion so as to appease his board. He was also well aware that some state legislatures passed laws requiring bathroom usage to accord to biological sex. He also desired to ride that wave.

The Springfield Heights board decided that its policies require them to treat students based on the gender recorded at birth. They decided that they would sue the U.S. Department of Education if they were found in violation of Title IX, which prohibits sex discrimination (including sexual harassment based upon gender identity and expression) in any education program or activity receiving federal funds.

Teaching Notes

Educators may have concerns about their own abilities to support their transgender students, or become hesitant because of personal feelings or from fear of negative reactions from the community. Similarly, families and caregivers are sometimes unsure of the support their child needs in school, or they may question the school's commitment to their child's well-being (Ott et al., 2015). This dynamic can create adversarial relationships between schools and families who must work together to meet students' needs. Finally, transgender students often struggle with fears of social rejection, bullying, and harassment from peers.

When transgender students are bullied or harassed, learning becomes less important than feeling safe in school and on the way home from school. Students who are bullied or face harassment are less likely to be successful in school (Kosciw, Greytak, Palmer, & Boesen, 2014). Harassment resulting from stereotyping and bias increases the risk of school absences (Kosciw, Greytak, Palmer, & Boesen, 2014), substance use, emotional distress, and suicide (Toomey et al., 2010). A school climate survey conducted by the Gay, Lesbian, and Straight Education Network found that students who experienced high levels of victimization based on gender expression face long-lasting negative effects on their mental health and life satisfaction as young adults (Toomey, Ryan, Diaz, Card, & Russell, 2010).

According to the National Transgender Discrimination Survey (Grant et al., 2011), 78 percent of the 6,450 respondents indicated that they had been harassed in school because of their transgender status. Thirty-five percent report being physically attacked, and 12 percent reported being sexually assaulted. Research indicates that clear school policies help to ensure that transgender students are protected (Grant et al., 2011).

Bullying, harassment, and discrimination against transgender students is covered by Title IX, a federal law, which prohibits sex discrimination in schools (National Center for Transgender Equality, 2016). The U.S. Department of Education, through the Office for Civil Rights (OCR), enforces Title IX, which applies to all K–12 and postsecondary schools that accept federal funds.

Further, many states such as California, Colorado, Connecticut, New Jersey, Oregon, Vermont, and Washington have laws and school district policies that prohibit discrimination in schools based on gender identity or expression as well as sexual orientation. Other laws that offer protection for transgender and nonconforming students are:

- The Equal Access Act requires all school affiliated student organizations, such as a Gay Straight Alliance, to be treated equally.

- The Family Educational Rights and Privacy Act protects personal information about students in school records, and in most circumstances prohibits the release of information without consent.

- The First Amendment of the U.S. Constitution protects the right of students to free speech and freedom of expression, including of one's gender identify.

The student, family, and school must work together to establish the most positive scenario for the student—planning is essential. The plan may include professional development for students or faculty.

References

Blad, E. (2016, June 1). Transgender students and bathrooms: What should schools do? *Education Week.* Retrieved from http://www.edweek.org/ew/articles /2016/05/27/transgender-students-and-bathrooms-what-should-schools .html

Grant, J. M., Mottet, L. A., Tanis, J., Harrison, J., Herman, J. L., & Keisling, M. (2011). *Injustice at every turn: A report of the national transgender discrimination survey.* National Council for Transgender Equality. Retrieved from http://www.thetaskforce.org/static_html/downloads/reports/reports /ntds_full.pdf

Kosciw, J. G., Greytak, E. A., Palmer, N. A., & Boesen, M. J. (2014). *The 2013 national school climate survey: The experiences of lesbian, gay, and transgender youth in our nation's schools.* New York, NY: GLSEN.

National Center for Transgender Equality. (2016). Transgender and gender nonconforming students: Your rights at school. Retrieved from http://www .transequality.org/sites/default/files/docs/kyr/KYR-Schools-May-2016.pdf

Orr, A., Baum, J., Brown, J., Gill, E., Kahn, E., & Salem, A. (2015). Schools in transition: A guide for supporting transgender students in K–12 schools. *Human Rights Campaign Foundation.* 1–68. Retrieved from https://www.gender spectrum.org/staging/wp-content/uploads/2015/08/Schools-in-Transi tion-2015.pdf

Toomey, R. B., Ryan, C., Diaz, R. M., Card, N. A., & Russell, S. T. (2010). "Gendernonconforming lesbian, gay, bisexual, and transgender youth: School victimization and young adult psychosocial adjustment." *Developmental Psychology, 46*(6), 1580–1589.

PART 3

Research and Looking Ahead

11

Classic Research

There are many studies that have contributed to the field of educational psychology. The two classic studies featured in this chapter illustrate the important roles of peer group conflict and internalizing aspects of identity in children's development and learning.

MUZAFER SHERIF AND CAROLYN WOOD SHERIF: THE ROBBER'S CAVE STUDY—LESSONS ON INTERGROUP CONFLICT AND REALISTIC CONFLICT THEORY

I don't like that man, I must get to know him better.

—Abraham Lincoln

Muzafer Sherif (1906–1978) was a Turkish-American psychologist and is considered one of the founders of the field of social psychology. He was born in the İzmir province of Turkey, specifically in the town of Ödemiś, to a wealthy family during the remaining days of the Ottoman Empire. He attended İzmir International College, earning a BA in 1926, and then earning an MA from Istanbul University in 1928. Upon receiving his first master's degree he was invited to Harvard University in 1929, where he studied psychology under psychologist and founding figure in the study of personality Gordon Allport (1897–1967). He earned his second master's degree in 1932 (Harvey, 1989).

After receiving his degree from Harvard in 1932, Sherif travelled to Germany to study in Berlin under German-American Gestalt psychologist Wolfgang Köhler (1887–1967). While there, he was exposed to the emerging Nazi regime and was disgusted by the effects it was having on German culture. During his time in Europe, he began teaching at the Gazi Institute in Ankara, Turkey. The work and research he engaged in there would eventually be the inspiration for his dissertation. In 1934 he returned to the United States, eventually landing at Columbia University in 1935, where he earned his PhD on social norms and perception under the tutelage of psychologist Gardner Murphy (1895–1979). Sherif's dissertation research would ultimately turn into the book *Psychology of Social Norms* (Harvey, 1989).

Sherif retuned to the Gazi Institute in 1937, where he was named assistant professor. Two years later, he moved again to Ankara University in Ankara, Turkey. While there, he started a research laboratory that focused on social psychology, specifically on social judgement. He was successfully promoted to professor in 1944. Unfortunately, by that point he had earned a reputation both on and off of Ankara University's campus for being an outspoken opponent of the Nazi racial doctrine that asserted biologically dictated differences between Aryan and Jewish, Germans and Turks. In 1944 he was arrested and sent to prison without a trial or any formal charges. He was sentenced to solitary confinement, where he lingered for four months (Harvey, 1989).

The U.S. Department of State petitioned for Sherif's release at the urging of his U.S. graduate students and colleagues. He returned to the United States in 1945 as a guest in the Blair House in Washington, DC. He then moved to Princeton as a Fellow of the U.S. State Department from 1945 to 1947. He met and married Carolyn Wood in 1947, who would become an esteemed research colleague. In 1947, Muzafer became a Rockefeller Research Fellow at Yale University, continuing his influential research in social psychology. In 1949, the Sherifs moved to Oklahoma where Muzafer would teach until 1966. It is here that he founded the Institute for Group Relations and published several influential works on group relations and intergroup conflict, including the infamous research at Robbers Cave State Park (Harvey, 1989).

During his many observations in Germany and Turkey, Sherif determined that competition over scarce resources could make people hostile toward others. However, he also noted that if you place a common obstacle in their way, they will cooperate to overcome it. In his earlier years, Sherif witnessed the interethnic violence between Turks, Greeks, and Armenians that ultimately led to thousands of deaths. Sherif was influenced to research the causes of such conflicts and seek solutions to solving them.

Carolyn Wood Sherif (1922–1982) was the youngest of three children born into a well-educated family in Indiana. Her father was the supervisor of teacher training at Purdue University. Carolyn's parents encouraged her and her siblings to get an education. She earned her bachelor of science from Purdue University in science and was awarded her degree with the mark of Highest Distinction (George, 2011).

She ultimately moved to Princeton, New Jersey, after earning a master's degree from the University of Iowa. While in New Jersey she briefly worked for Audience Research, Inc. Her experiences at her place of employment were unfulfilling to her and included an incident with sexual harassment. As a result, she quit her job and sought advice about graduate studies from a professor at Princeton University, social psychologist Hadley Cantril. Cantril offered her a position working with Muzafer Sherif, which excited Wood because she had was familiar with Sherif's research in social psychology (Alger-Feser, 2018; George, 2011).

Wood was not allowed to enter the graduate program at Princeton because she was a woman. She did, however, complete postgraduate coursework at nearby Columbia University while remaining Sherif's research colleague. Wood Sherif would go on to collaborate on many important research studies and publications with Muzafer. Unfortunately, due to her husband's notoriety in the field, her contributions were often overlooked, including her role in the Robbers Cave Study (Alger-Feser, 2018; George, 2011).

In 1958, she resumed her doctoral studies at the University of Texas, with the encouragement of her husband. By this time, she was a mother of three daughters. She successfully earned her PhD in 1961. While at the University of Texas, she also headed up a large project involving the U.S. Office of Vocational Rehabilitation. Eventually Wood Sherif would return to Oklahoma and join her husband at the Institute for Group Relations. After a two-year stay in Oklahoma, the Sherif family moved to Pennsylvania where they both settled into tenure-line positions at Penn State University (Alger-Feser, 2018; George, 2011).

In the early 1960s, Wood Sherif shifted her focus to the psychology of gender. Much of her work during the 1960s influenced her involvement in feminist psychology and led her to found Division 35 of the American Psychological Association. This became known as the Society for the Psychology of Women. She served as the seventh president of Division 35 between 1979 and 1980 and was also involved with the launching of the group's publication *Psychology of Women Quarterly* in 1976 (Alger-Feser, 2018; George, 2011).

Wood Sherif received many distinctions and honors for her work in the fields of social and gender psychology. She passed away from cancer at the young age of 60 in 1982 (George, 2011).

The Robber's Cave Study

In 1954, Sherif and his research associates set out to test his assertions about intergroup conflict. They defined a group as a social unit having two main qualities: (1) a number of individuals who share a sense of interdependence, and (2) a number of individuals who share a common set of values and norms that regulate their behaviors. The researchers also defined *intergroup relations* as the relationship between two or more groups and their respective members (Sherif, 1958).

The "Robbers Cave" study was staged at a Boy Scouts of America camp located in Oklahoma's 200-acre Robbers Cave State Park. The remoteness of the park ensured that the study remained free from external influences and that the true nature of conflict and prejudice could be studied. The participants were 22 Caucasian boys who all came from Protestant, two-parent, middle-class families. They were all approximately 11 years old at the time of the study. The boys were strangers to each other before coming to the camp. The researchers randomly divided the boys into two different groups and assigned them cabins far apart from each other. During this first phase of the study, the researchers provided opportunities for building group cohesion within groups. The boys from each group did not know about the other group's existence. The boys developed an attachment to their own groups throughout the first week of the camp by doing various activities together like hiking and swimming. They even chose names for their groups—"The Eagles" and "The Rattlers"—and created emblems that they put on flags and T-shirts (Sherif, 1958).

During the second phase of the study researchers created conflict between the groups by designing a four-day series of competitions (e.g., tug-of-war) pitting one group against the other. There were high stakes for winning, including trophies, medals, and camping knives. As the competition waged during this phase, prejudice began to become apparent between the two groups. At first, this prejudice was only expressed verbally, through taunting or name calling. As the competition wore on, this expression of prejudice took a more direct route: the Eagles burned the Rattlers' flag. This act led to more conflict the following day when the Rattlers sought retribution by ransacking the Eagles' cabin, overturning beds and stealing some of their private effects. Ultimately, the groups became so aggressive with each other that the researchers had to physically separate them (Sherif, 1958).

This phase ended with a period of two days where the groups did not come into contact with each other. During this break in contact, the boys were asked to list characteristics of their group and the other group. The boys tended to characterize their group in highly favorable terms and the other group in very unfavorable terms (Sherif, 1958).

The interactions in this phase demonstrated the idea of the *minimal group paradigm*, a standard set of research procedures that creates artificial ingroups and outgroups based on minimally important, or artificial, differences between groups (like which group the boys belonged to at camp in the Sherifs' study). *Ingroup bias* is people's bias in favor of members of their own group. This bias was created during the first phase of the Robbers Cave study when the boys engaged in positive group-building activities in their separate groups. Two hypotheses explain the ingroup bias effect. The *categorization-competition hypothesis* asserts that simply categorizing oneself and others into an ingroup and an outgroup is sufficient to generate intergroup competition. This hypothesis assumes the *outgroup homogeneity effect* that occurs when people tend to see members of their own group as very different from one another but underestimate the differences between members of other groups. For instance, members of the Eagles assumed that all of the members of the Rattlers shared similar personality characteristics and abilities. This outgroup homogeneity effect results in an "us versus them" perspective and can generate feelings of competition. This ultimately leads to an ingroup favoritism effect. However, intergroup bias decreases as the number of other groups increases, because feelings of competition are diluted across more outgroups (Kite & Whitley, 2016).

In the third phase of the study, the researchers attempted to reduce the prejudice between the two groups. They determined that simply increasing the contact of the two groups only made the situation worse. The researchers tried integrating the boys after the two-day "cooling off period" by providing opportunities for social interaction in more neutral settings (e.g., watching a movie). The boys in each group still demonstrated intense animosity towards members of the other group, engaging in name-calling and physical aggression. Ultimately, the researchers determined that forcing the groups to work together to reach subordinate (common) goals would ease the prejudice and tension among the groups. The boys from each group had to come together to find sources of water after both groups were impacted by a water shortage, and they also had to work together to transport food back to the camp (Sherif, 1958).

The Robbers Cave Study confirmed many ideas that Sherif and his colleagues asserted, including ingroup bias, the outgroup homogeneity effect, and *realistic conflict theory*, which proposes that people dislike members of outgroups because their ingroup in competing with the outgroup for resources. People are motivated by a desire to maximize the rewards they receive in life, even if that means taking those away from other people. Thus, competition leads to conflict between groups, which results in prejudice against members of competing groups (Kite & Whitley, 2016).

Intergroup conflict in the context of education can arise between groups of students, between groups of students and groups of teachers, between groups of teachers and administrators, and even between school districts. A perceived imbalance of social, economic, or political power can fuel this conflict. Chapter 6 discusses some educational strategies and applications for identifying and preventing intergroup conflict, including building classrooms that are more welcoming for students from stereotypical outgroups (e.g., racially or ethnically diverse, sexual and gender minorities).

MAMIE PHIPPS CLARK AND KENNETH CLARK: THE DOLLS TEST—LESSONS ON INTERNALIZING RACISM

A racist system inevitably destroys and damages human beings; it brutalizes and dehumanizes them, blacks and whites alike.
—*Kenneth Clark*

In Chapter 4, we discussed theories related to the development of self-concept and identity formation. Mamie Phipps Clark and Kenneth Clark influenced the study of racial identity formation as well as implicit racial bias. Mamie Phipps Clark (1917–1983) is best known for her research conducted with husband Kenneth B. Clark (1914–2005). Using her master's thesis, which provided the groundwork for their famous Doll Test study, the pair presented this research in the *Brown vs. Board of Education of Topeka* segregation case in 1954. Their research on self-esteem and self-concept in African American children boosted the case for Brown and would ultimately lead to desegregation in schools (Fancher & Rutherford, 2017).

Phipps Clark was born in Arkansas in 1917 to Harold Phipps, a physician, and Katy Florence Phipps, a homemaker. Despite growing up during the Depression and living in the Deep South, where racial oppression was ever-present, Phipps Clark recalled having a relatively happy childhood. She graduated from high school with several scholarships to study at two renowned black universities. In 1934 she began her college career at Howard University as a physics and math major. It was there that she met her future husband, Kenneth Bancroft Clark. He was a master's student in psychology and eventually persuaded Mamie to switch her major to psychology because the field provided more professional opportunities for women compared to math and physics. Pursuing psychology also allowed her to explore her interests in developmental psychology.

She graduated with a BA in psychology from Howard in 1938, magna cum laude, and immediately enrolled in the master's program. That summer she took a job in the law office of Charles Houston, an influential lawyer instrumental in the early planning of civil rights cases, working with the NAACP. He also worked with other prominent African American lawyers like Thurgood Marshall. This job helped Mamie learn more about the psychological effects of segregation in the South, informed her own research endeavors on racial self-concept in children, and gave her hope that an end to racial oppression and desegregation laws were attainable in her lifetime (Karera, 2010).

Phipps Clark earned her MA degree at Howard in 1939. Her master's thesis was entitled "Development of Consciousness of Self in Negro Preschool Children." This research was done 15 years before the *Brown* case. It paved the way for studying the development of self-esteem and self-concept in racial minority children, who up to this point had been relatively ignored in psychological research. In her thesis she coined the term "race consciousness," which she defined as "a consciousness of self as belonging to a specific group which is differentiated from other groups by obvious physical characteristics" (Clark & Clark, 1939 p. 594). Her research determined that children of color became aware of their racial identities as young as four years of age (Karera, 2010).

Phipps Clark received her PhD from Columbia University in 1943 and was the only African American student in the psychology program. Her dissertation advisor, Henry E. Garrett (1894–1973), was a well-known statistician, eugenicist, and segregationist. He was the chair of Psychology at Columbia from 1941 to 1955 and served as president of the American Psychological Association in 1946. His views on race, race mixing, and the intellectual inferiority of African American children were well known (Winston, 1998). In fact, later in her career, Phipps Clark would have to testify under oath against Garrett in a related desegregation case in Virginia that was linked to the decision in *Brown v. Board of Education* (Karera, 2010).

Although Phipps Clark was successful in earning her PhD despite facing adversity from her own mentor, she had a difficult time finding work as a psychologist in New York City once she graduated. Her husband had procured a teaching position at the City College of New York, but she did not find a home in academia. After several failed experiences, she found a position at the Riverdale Home for Children in New York. While there she worked with African American youth, specifically homeless African American girls. Her experiences made her aware that psychological and social services were lacking for impoverished children of color. This work would be seminal to her career as a developmental psychologist (Karera, 2010).

In 1946, she established the Northside Center for Child Development in a Harlem apartment basement. The center provided a homelike environment for children. Services were provided by social workers, psychologists, psychiatrists, and physicians. Due to the stigma of being mentally ill, most parents wouldn't seek help for their children. The people of Harlem accepted the center because of the frustration parents had with the public school system. Mamie had long suspected that many of the African American children who were tested and told they were retarded, or had some other learning disability, were in fact not retarded. The I.Q. tests were racially and economically biased toward white children. The center eventually grew into a place that provided psychological, behavioral, and educational resources for these children and their parents. It is also where Phipps Clark would build and expand her legacy as a psychologist and advocate until her retirement in 1979 (Karera, 2010).

Kenneth Clark (1914–2005) was born in the Panama Canal Zone to Arthur Bancroft Clark and Miriam Hanson Clark. His father was an agent for the United Fruit Company. When he was five, his parents divorced. His mother took him and his younger sister to live in Harlem in New York City. Clark's mother worked as a seamstress in a sweatshop, which led her to organize a union and become a shop steward for the International Ladies Garment Workers Union (Jones & Pettigrew, 2005).

Clark moved to New York City when Harlem was becoming less diverse. His school was populated by mostly African American students. Like most African American students of the time, Clark was trained to learn a trade. Wanting more for her son, Miriam transferred Kenneth to George Washington High School in Upper Manhattan, where he would graduate from high school in 1931 (Jones & Pettigrew, 2005).

Clark attended Howard University, where he first studied political science with professors including Ralph Johnson Bunche (1904–1971). He soon switched majors to psychology and worked under with mentor Francis Cecil Sumner (1895–1954), the first African American to receive a doctorate in psychology. Clark returned to Howard in 1935 for a master's in psychology. After earning his master's degree, on Sumner's direction Clark went to Columbia University to work with another influential mentor, Canadian social psychologist Otto Klineberg (1899–1992). While completing his doctorate in psychology, Clark collaborated with Swedish economist Gunnar Myrdal (1898–1987), who wrote *An American Dilemma* in 1944. Their research focused on the study of race relations. Clark earned his PhD in 1940, making him the first African American to earn a doctorate in psychology from Columbia University (Jones & Pettigrew, 2005).

The Coloring Test and The Doll Test

The Clarks conducted influential research on self-concept and racial identity in African American children. Their research stemmed from Mamie Phipps Clark's master's thesis, which would lead to the Coloring Test and the Doll Test. For the Coloring Test, three-year-old African American children were given a sheet of paper with the drawings of an apple, a leaf, an orange, a mouse, a boy, and a girl. They were also given a box of 24 crayons with the colors brown, black, yellow, white, pink, and tan. Mamie would then ask them to pretend that the little girl or boy was them, and to color the picture the same color they were. After the child responded, Mamie would ask the child to color the opposite gendered picture the color they want it to be. The results proved Mamie's suspicions: All African American children with very light skin colored the picture correctly. Most of the darker skinned children colored the picture with yellow or white crayons. Some children even used red or green. Mamie concluded that the children's choice of inappropriate colors indicated emotional anxiety in terms of the color of their own skin; that because they wanted to be white, they pretended to be (Clark, 1944).

In the Doll Test, 253 African American children between the age of three and seven years participated. Of the 253 children, 134 were categorized as "Southern" and resided in different towns in Arkansas. They attended segregated nursery schools and had no experiences with racial integration in school. The rest of the 119 children were categorized as "Northern" and resided in towns in Massachusetts. These children were exposed to racial integration in schools (Clark & Clark, 1947).

Children were shown four dolls clothed in diapers that were identical in every aspect except skin tone and hair color (two were white with yellow hair and two were brown with black hair). Half of the children were presented with a white doll first, then a black doll, then another white doll, and then another black doll. The other half of the children were shown the dolls in reverse order. The positions of the dolls' bodies, as they were presented to the children, were all the same. Children were put in a room alone with the experimenter, who asked each child the same set of questions. They asked the child to show them which doll:

1. she liked to play with best,
2. was the nice doll,
3. looked bad,
4. was a nice color,
5. looked like a white child,
6. looked like a colored child,

7.   looked like a "Negro" child, and

8.   looked like "you" [the child].

The first four questions were intended to assess the children's preferences, while questions five through seven assessed the children's knowledge of racial differences, and the final question assessed the children's
abilities to self-identify their own racial category. A majority of children
(94 percent) were able to correctly identify the races of the dolls, demonstrating their awareness of racial differences. Fewer children (72 percent)
were familiar with the term "Negro" when asked to identify the "Negro"
doll, but the Clarks determined that label of "Negro" was more abstract
to young children than terms like "white" and "colored" (Clark & Clark,
1947).

When children were asked to self-identify as colored by identifying
which doll looked like them, only 66 percent of the children chose the "colored" doll, while 33 percent chose the white doll. Clark and Clark concluded that just because children were aware of racial differences at a
young age did not mean that they had internalized their own racial identity yet. The Clarks did see increases in correct racial self-identification in
the older children in their sample, suggesting that by age seven, they had
developed a stronger awareness of racial identity. The Clarks did not find
any statistically significant differences between the responses of the
Northern and Southern children. They did note that more Northern children self-identified with the white dolls but attributed this to the fact that
more of them had a lighter skin tone compared to the Southern children
(Clark & Clark, 1947).

With respect to racial preferences, the Clarks found that a majority of
the children in their original study preferred the white dolls to the colored
dolls. They found that two-thirds of their sample preferred to play with the
white doll or perceived the white doll as a "nice" doll. Furthermore, 53 percent of these children identified the colored doll as the doll that looked
"bad" while only 17 percent thought that of the white doll. Only 38 percent
thought that the brown doll was a "nice" color, in contrast to 60 percent
indicating that the white doll was a "nice" color. They did find some differences between the preferences of the younger children and older children.
There was a marked decrease in preferences and positive perceptions of
how nice the white doll was as children approached seven years of age.
Regarding the perceptions of the how bad the skin color of the dolls looked,
and whether the color of the dolls was a "nice" color, the Clarks found that
the majority of children showed preferences for dolls with white skin tone,
although this preference was even more pronounced in lighter-skinned
children. There were some differences between Northern children and

Southern children in their preferences. While the majority still indicated they would prefer to play with the white doll and think it was nice, more Southern children showed preferences on these two points for the colored doll. Furthermore, a significantly larger percentage of Northern children perceived the brown dolls to be "bad" (Clark & Clark, 1947).

Finally, the Clarks reported some additional reactions from the children when asked to self-identify with the colored dolls. They noted that some children cried and ran from the room, while others provided unsolicited reasons why they self-identified with the white doll (e.g., they were white, but looked dark due to getting a suntan). The negative reactions tended to occur more with the Northern students, although some Southern students seemed disturbed by having to pick the brown dolls when asked what doll looked like them (Clark & Clark, 1947).

Because the Doll Study focused on stereotypes and children's self-perception in relation to their race, the results were used to support the assertion that school segregation was distorting the minds of young African American children, causing them to internalize negative stereotypes about their racial identity to the point of making them hate themselves. In 1954, at the request of Thurgood Marshall who had met and worked with Mamie Phipps Clark earlier in her career, the Clarks testified in *Brown v. Board of Education in Topeka*. Their research helped to persuade the U.S. Supreme Court that "separate but equal" schools for blacks and whites were anything but equal in practice and should be deemed illegal. Ironically, on their travels to testify before the Supreme Court, the Clarks experienced discrimination when trying to eat at certain restaurants or procure accommodations (Benjamin, 2006).

The Doll Study has been criticized on a few different points. First, there was no control group for comparison. The presence of African American researchers may have skewed the results. The experience of integration with white students may have actually had a more negative impact on Northern students' perceptions of their racial identity and influenced more negative reactions to the colored dolls, compared to their Southern (segregated) counterparts. While the study was used in the *Brown* case, it was not the only study or the most influential study to determine the ultimate ruling leading to desegregation in public schools. Finally, the study was replicated several times by the Clarks as well as other researchers. It has been replicated on film as recently as 2010, when *CNN* produced a segment on implicit racial bias. What more recent versions of the study have found is that while white bias still appeared in white and African American children who complete the test, fewer African American children have negative self-perceptions about the dolls with darker skin compared to those children tested in the 1940s (Desmond-Harris, 2014).

REFERENCES

Alger-Feser, S. (2018). Carolyn Wood Sherif: Founder of the Society of the Psychology of Women. Retrieved from https://psychmuseum.uwgb.org/social/carolynwoodsherif/

Benjamin, L.T. (2006). *A history of psychology in letters* (2nd ed). Malden, MA: Wiley-Blackwell.

Clark, K. B., & Clark, M. K. (1939). The development of consciousness of self and the emergence of racial identification in Negro preschool children. *Journal of Social Psychology, S.P.S.S.I. Bulletin, 10,* 591–599. Retrieved from https://psychclassics.yorku.ca/Clark/Self-cons/

Clark, K. B., & Clark, M. P. (1947). Racial identification and preference in Negro children. In T. M. Newcombe & E. C. Hartley (Eds.), *Readings in social psychology* (pp. 169–178). New York, NY: Holt.

Clark, M. (1944). Changes in primary mental abilities with age. *Archives of Psychology, 291.*

Desmond-Harris, J. (2014). The doll test for racial self-hate: Did it ever make sense? *The Root.* Retrieved from https://www.theroot.com/the-doll-test-for-racial-self-hate-did-it-ever-make-se-1790875716

Fancher, R. E., & Rutherford, A. (2017). *Pioneers of psychology: A history* (5th ed). New York, NY: Norton.

George, M. (2011). Profile of Carolyn Wood Sherif. Retrieved from http://www.feministvoices.com/carolyn-wood-sherif/

Harvey, O. J. (1989). Obituaries: Muzafer Sherif. *American Psychologist, 44*(10), 1325–1326.

Jones, J. M., & Pettigrew, T. F. (2005). Kenneth B. Clark (1914–2005). *American Psychologist, 60*(6), 649–651.

Karera, A. (2010). Profile of Mamie Phipps Clark. Retrieved from http://www.feministvoices.com/mamie-phipps-clark/

Kite, M. E. & Whitley, B. E., Jr. (2016). *Psychology of prejudice and discrimination* (3rd ed.). New York, NY: Routledge.

Sherif, M. (1958). Superordinate goals in the reduction of intergroup conflict. *American Journal of Sociology, 63*(4), 349–356.

Winston, A. S. (1998). Science in the service of the far right: Henry E. Garrett, the IAAEE, and the Liberty Lobby. *Journal of Social Issues, 54*(1), 179–210.

12

Emerging Research on Teaching and Learning

Many of us taking courses in educational psychology either will become teachers or will do other work within schools. It is thus crucially important for us to understand the scholarship of teaching and learning. Often, teachers teach how they were taught, or in the styles that best suit them personally. However, scholarship in teaching and learning has informed us of best practices for how students can better learn and retain material.

According to Edgar Dale, we remember:

- 10 percent of what we read
- 20 percent of what we hear
- 30 percent of what we see
- 50 percent of what we see and hear
- 70 percent of what we discuss with others

- 80 percent of what we personally experience
- 95 percent of what we teach others

The above quotation summarizes what is known as Dale's Cone of Experience (see Lee & Reeves, 2007). The age-old "sage on the stage" model of teaching, where the teacher stands at the front of the class and lectures for the entire class, does not work for everyone. However, there is something to be said for an engaging lecture or speech, but it is not the "end all, be all" model.

Although a continuing subject of empirical debate, Dale's Cone of Experience presents us with an entry point into how we should best deliver content and skills to our students. Those who become teachers were often good students in school themselves; some do not understand that they need to deliver material in differential ways in order to meet the learning needs of all of their students. As a reminder, differentiated instruction involves teachers actively planning for differences in student learning. Teachers utilize varied methods and resources in order to meet the learning needs of students with varied backgrounds, readiness, skill levels, and interests within a classroom.

To wit, Freire (1970) critiques the banking model of education, or the method of teaching where students are considered to be empty vessels, i.e., the teacher as disseminator of knowledge and the students as passive recipients, where students are not active in knowledge production/creation. Good pedagogy is the antithesis of this: the ideal is for students to become knowledge producers, where students engage with higher-level intellectual skills, such as those articulated in Bloom's taxonomy (i.e., comprehension, application, analysis, synthesis, and evaluation), and focuses less on the knowledge level, or simple rote memorization (Herreid, 2007; Yadav, Vinh, Shaver, Meckl, & Firebaugh, 2014). Teachers who encourage teamwork and reflective practice, while providing a relevant and conceptual understanding of the topics at hand (Bilica, 2004; Yadav et al., 2014), are engaging in best practice.

The use of case study in the classroom (as we have attempted in this text) encourages students to begin to transfer the concepts they have learned from course materials and prior experiences to solve new problems; as such the method of case study pedagogy provides relevancy and meaning to the course content and curriculum and can in fact extend and deepen curricular goals (Kolodner et al., 2003; Yadav et al., 2014). The use of case study can assist students in concept-based problem solving by placing them in realistic scenarios and authentic roles. By situating the learning process within authentic contexts, students are able to not only learn but also apply concepts and theory from their disciplines to real world

Paulo Freire

Paulo Freire (1921–1997) was a theorist from Brazil. His focus in the field of education was on creating a pedagogy for students experiencing poverty and oppression. He wrote many books contributing to the education field, but *Pedagogy of the Oppressed*, written in 1968, is his most used in educating teachers. *Pedagogy of the Oppressed* focuses on educating future and current educators about forming relationships between students, teachers, and society. According to Neumann (2016), "Freire's focus may be considered 'the critical intellectual,' meaning students will 'work to adopt a curious, investigative, probing, searching, restless attitude toward the world,' making the role of the teacher then to teach students to address problems from multiple different points of view outside of their own" (p. 640). As an educator, Freire emphasizes the importance of respecting views opposing to their own, and also "actively simulating engagement with alternative discourses" (Neumann, 2016, p. 640). If an educator is able to respect the views of their students and encourage them to think from another's perspective, this educator is in the process of mastering the pedagogy of the oppressed.

There are of course, many steps to mastering the pedagogy of the oppressed. Many critics and scholars write about Freire's liberatory pedagogies, in which dialogue is essential in the classroom. According to Beckett (2013), "through dialogue, the teacher-of-the-students and the student-of-the-teacher cease to exist and a new term emerges: teacher-student with students-teachers . . . they become jointly responsible for a process in which all grow" (p. 50). In this process, teachers learn as much from students as the students do the teachers. There is a mutual feeling of respect and safety in the classroom, and everyone's ideas are welcomed, making the classroom a safe space for problem solving and, as Beckett calls it, coinvestigating as students and teacher in order to problematize the student's world and look at the world as it really is—helping students to optimize reality (p. 51). Overall, the beliefs of Paulo Freire, specifically in *Pedagogy of the Oppressed*, is for the educator to not only be respectful of the student's beliefs but to educate them on their own reality, be open to students discussion topics, and to help them investigate their realities, making the best out of all situations.

—Courtney Cepec

applications (Brown, Collins, & Duguid, 1989; Kolodner, 1997). Cases can be designed for many educational purposes: to provide practice or reinforce concepts (Min, VanLehn, Litman, & Jordan, 2011), to hear others' points of view, to confront differences, to become aware of the complexity of a situation (Argyris, 1980), and/or to develop judgment or the ability to deal with ambiguity (Libby, 1991). One of the most important uses of case studies is for students to gain an understanding of the real world (Libby,

1991) by increasing their sense of empathy for others. That being said, by struggling with the facts of a case, case study pedagogy can encourage students to engage in ethical dilemmas and to create the best course of action in order to forge a just outcome.

Case study pedagogy has been found to "sharpen problem-solving skills and to improve the ability to think and reason rigorously" (Harvard Graduate School of Education, 2013, n.p.) because there is neither one "clear path" to the solution nor one correct answer. Moreover, well-written cases can hold students' attention and increase interest, for students are required to do more than listen: they must actively engage with the material. Effective cases require the learner to look beyond the facts of the narrative by providing guidance on current research and legal/policy guidelines, and by providing the learner with additional information that will assist them in making informed decisions.

As individuals living in contentious times, we face social, cultural, economic, and ethical issues on a daily basis. Students are able to relate to and apply relevant knowledge to current issues and unfamiliar situations that students might face in their careers (Mayo, 2002, 2004; Yadav et al., 2014).

BEST PRACTICES FOR TEACHING AND LEARNING

According to Lang (2016), the following strategies can contribute to increased learning.

Building Relationship with Students (Showing You Care) Can Increase Learning

If students do not feel they are cared about by the instructor, their motivation to learn can decrease. We saw this earlier in this text with Herbert Kohl's concept of "not learning" (see Chapter 6, this volume; Kohl, 1994). As we have argued throughout this text, building relationships with students, and engaging in culturally responsive pedagogical practices are crucial to student learning (Kohl, 1994).

Learn What Students Already Know

Then, the instructor can connect new content to existing knowledge. Empirical research indicates that the brain connects new information with existing knowledge; thus, new learning can become solidified when connected to something already there (Lang, 2016).

Inform Students of the Purpose of What Is Happening in the Classroom

Students often wonder, and sometimes ask, "Why are we doing this?" Frontloading the class by informing the students of the purpose of content, pedagogies, and instructional methodologies can increase student motivation to learn. Always provide reminders of the larger and overall purpose of the learning.

Present All Learning Objectives for the Course Ahead of Time So Students Know Where They Are Going in Terms of Content Progression

This strategy will enable students to keep track of what they learned, the knowledge they have gained, and the goals they still need to attain. This can promote a sense of accomplishment within students, and can continue to inspire motivation to learn more.

Lang (2016) also shares strategies to add memory and facilitate retention. We add our own knowledge and expertise after years of teaching at various levels to this information: Use periodic and low-stakes assessments throughout a course to determine what students are learning and what they struggle with, so that the instructor can retool instruction to provide students the knowledge and skills that they need to be successful in the course.

Provide students with insights into how to study and best practices for learning. For example, contrary to many student opinions, cramming for an exam is not the best way to prepare. Rather, studying a little material over a longer period of time will better prepare students for exams and other high stakes assessments. Some best practices for studying include encouraging students to create questions in anticipation of an exam or assessment; making predictions on important content that will be assessed can contribute to learning and retention. Also, making predictions when reading, whether or not these predictions turn out to be correct, can contribute to heightened learning. Furthermore, predictions can point out gaps in learning.

Use technology to aid in learning. Social media and apps that students can access from their phones can be fun and exciting ways to engage students and motivate them to learn.

Practice. Practice. Practice. Providing students with opportunities to practice the skills they need to learn with opportunities to make mistakes and to learn from them is key. Opportunities for rehearsal for high stakes assessments is also paramount to students success.

Use opening questions: anticipation triggers memory from previous learning/classes to this one. As previously stated, connecting new content to previous learning is key to new learning and retention.

Use closing questions: for example, what are the main takeaways of today's lesson? Closing questions serve to connect what was learned to new learning students will do on their own, perhaps within their next course reading; making connections is paramount to learning.

Use focus questions. Focus questions can be used during class to help students make connections with important information.

What we call *active participation* can encourage students to consciously think during class, as opposed to passively listening. This technique involves asking the class a question, and then providing time for everyone to write down an answer—prior to opening the floor to discussion and response. Also, this technique can encourage the more introverted students to speak, because they will already have a response written down.

Use enough wait time. Wait time is the silence that occurs after a teacher asks a question. Some students need more time to think and process a question than others. If the teacher simply calls on the first raised hand, this can limit the participation, thinking, and learning of other students, and the overall class in general.

If using a textbook, teach students how to use it. Again, many teachers were good students, and many were not first-generation college students and may not even realize that students have not been previously trained to read or how to use a textbook. This is an issue of equity. Ensure that all students understand the differences between and purposes of the table of contents, index, glossary, and so on.

Teach students how to take good notes (on lectures, class discussions, and on reading): include paraphrasing and making predictions in note-taking instruction.

Feedback is important. Teachers should provide feedback to students *and* allow students to engage with the feedback, such as making revisions to papers. Immediate feedback is ideal. If students are not provided the opportunity to engage with teacher feedback, as a mechanism to learning, then opportunities for learning are lost. Lang argues that teachers should attempt to "induce reflection" (2016, p. 59) in students. Providing students to reflect on teacher feedback, and to make additional reflections on what they learned from making revisions can contribute to even further learning. According to McGuire (2015):

> When their work is returned to them with a much lower grade than expected, most students cannot process the cognitive dissonance. If our courses are telling these students that they're not smart, competent individuals they believed themselves to be, what do they do? Their normal psychological self-defense mechanisms activate. They begin withdrawing psychologically; they might sit further back in the classroom or lecture hall; worse, they might start missing class. (p. 17)

Lang (2016) suggests teaching with the technique of *interleaving*: "The argument I am making here is not to eliminate blocked practice but to use interleaving to require students to return continuously, in different contexts, to material they have learned already" (p. 73). In other words, Lang argues that circling back to previous content and relating it to new learning can improve memory and retention of information.

Additional instructional tips from Lang include the following.

Inspiring intellectual struggle is important. When students grapple with concepts in a safe and affirming environment, engagement and motivation are activated. Peer interaction can do much to contribute to learning; students should be encouraged to teach and to help their fellow students. Both can contribute to deeper learning.

How to motivate students to learn: increase subjective value of the learning. Emotions can drive motivation (to the positive and to the negative). Our emotions can help us "capture the attention of our students" (p. 173); "when we feel strong emotions, our attention and cognitive capacities are heightened" (p. 174).

Self-transcendent motivation, or believing self-engagement in a particular activity, has the potential to change the world, in contrast with self-oriented motivation, and can increase deep learning. Creating self-transformative experiences where students feel they are making a difference in the world and moving beyond the self—service-learning projects—are instrumental for this type of learning.

Finally, according to Lang, telling a good story is important, because "the best stories invoke emotions" (p. 182). Being enthusiastic and communicating this through the telling of good stories can increase heighten student emotion, which can lead to increased motivation, engagement, and, ultimately, to learning.

According to McGuire (2015), who echoes Lang in large part, it is important for teachers to actually teach students *how* to learn, not just to teach the content. McGuire also argues that it is important for students to do the nonrequired homework because practice with concepts is important.

One of the main points McGuire makes in her 2015 text is that *metacognition* is key to learning. In other words, teaching students to think about how they think, and, in turn, how and what they learn can transform student success in the classroom. McGuire argues that in order to improve student learning, teachers must shift their focus to learning instead of teaching. She argues that it is important for teachers to show students their expectations for reading. For example, recommended reading is not helpful for student learning. Rather, required reading with a specific focus and accompanying assignments or low stakes assessments can improve learning and retention. McGuire (2015) additionally argues that actually teaching Bloom's Taxonomy to students can be helpful for learning and retention.

For example, according to McGuire, teachers should teach learning as opposed to studying: "Studying is focusing on the 'whats,' but learning is focusing on the 'hows,' 'whys,' and 'what ifs'" (p. 31), and this can be done through the application of Bloom's taxonomy in the classroom.

McGuire (2015) suggests 10 metacognitive strategies for learning:

1. Previewing
2. Preparing for active reading
3. Paraphrasing
4. Reading actively
5. Using the textbook even if it is not required
6. Going to class and taking notes by hand
7. Doing homework *without* using solved examples as a guide
8. Teaching material to a real or imagined audience
9. Working in pairs or groups
10. Creating practice exams (p. 44)

McGuire argues that "familiarity breeds active learning" (p. 25); when the brain is trying to learn new information, it attempts to connect to previously learned information. According to McGuire, "If we do not take the time to discover that our students already know and help them relate what they are learning to their prior knowledge, then they cannot learn in the most efficient ways" (p. 26).

McGuire also argues that mindset matters. She is a critic, and we agree, of gifted programs, which present a fixed label of intelligence on select students. As McGuire argues, "If we label our students as gifted, it encourages them to take on a fixed mindset, and consequently they become terrified to do anything that might contradict the idea that they are smarter than their peers" (p. 65). Instead, she advocates for a deprogramming of students from negative self-talk, such as, "I am not good at math." She also advocates that teachers inform students about brain plasticity, or the brain's ability to change throughout the life span. This key information may contribute to the development of a more growth mindset for students, which is key to learning, especially for learning information that students may feel is challenging, difficult, or incomprehensible.

MINDSET, PERSISTENCE, AND GRIT

Mindset is a term coined and extensively researched by Dweck and her colleagues. It can be defined as the way individuals think about and approach accomplishments and failures. In her book, *Mindset: The New*

MEMORY: A PROFESSOR TELLS HER STORY

When I was an undergraduate student, I had my first course in linguistics. The one thing I retained from the course is something my professor said that struck me: "Anything goes in informal English, as long as you are understood." I do not remember his name, and other than that one quotation, I only remember how he, and that course in general, made me feel: stupid.

I experienced exactly what McGuire argues students experience when they enter college, and find that what had worked for them in high school may not work as well in college. I experienced cognitive dissonance because my self-perceptions did not meld with my results in this course.

One of the building blocks of the course was phonics, and understanding the different vowel sounds (far beyond long vowels). I just could not understand or memorize the content. The professor was also mean. I remember one student, typically shy in class, standing up for another student who he berated in front of the whole class (the reason for which I no longer remember).

The professor did not take attendance. We only had to show up for exams. I stopped attending class, and just came for the exams. I was not learning anyway, I figured. I could not learn from this professor. I did not fail the class, but I did not master the material either.

I still have nightmares about this class, 20+ years later: about missing exams, and not graduating with my undergraduate degree. I eventually learned linguistics, even the phonetic components. But I learned a lot about how not to teach, and how negative experiences with learning can last a lifetime.

—Jennifer L. Martin

Psychology of Success, Dweck (2008) suggests that mindset shapes an individual's personality to a large extent, which prevents or facilitates success in various aspects of life.

According to Dweck (2008) mindset can operate in one of two ways: it can be fixed or it can be growth based. The mindset individuals adopt will subsequently affect the way they lead their lives. With a fixed mindset, individuals believe that their qualities are unchangeable. Because of that, they typically have a feeling of urgency to prove themselves to everyone on a regular basis. For instance, an individual may feel that she has to present herself as being smart, funny, or as friendly as possible to others. If she cannot present herself that way in a certain context, then she will avoid those situations. According to Dweck, some people are trained to have a fixed mindset early on. Some of these influences come from teachers, parents, and peers.

Individuals with a fixed mindset look at failure as an all-or-nothing experience. They internalize their failure to be the result of something that is inherent and thus unavoidable. They are less willing to take risks and leave their comfort zone for fear of being perceived as a failure. Furthermore, they do not feel the need to persist in the face of failure because they attribute their failures to something unchangeable. To them "risk and effort are two things that might reveal your inadequacies and show that you were not up to the task" (Dweck, 2008, p. 10).

On the other hand, Dweck (2008) has found that some people have a growth mindset. This mindset is based on the idea that a person's basic qualities are simply starting points for growth: that there is always room for improvement through effort, and that improvement can be achieved in most situations. Growth mindset individuals are neither afraid to stretch themselves beyond their current limits, nor are they afraid to fail. Unlike those with fixed mindsets, they welcome failure because they perceive it as an opportunity to learn and grow. Just like fixed mindset, a growth mindset can be taught. Thus, once the perspective is changed to a growth mindset, perceptions of the value of effort and persistence change.

Dweck (2008) also discusses the Low Effort Syndrome, which is a strategy people with fixed mindsets use to avoid getting bruised egos. They do this by not putting forth any effort at all when "engaged" in a task. This way when they fail or fall short of a goal, they can blame their lack of effort, not their innate abilities. In her years of research, Dweck found that students with a fixed mindset are primarily concerned with looking smart while exerting as little effort as possible. Those individuals with a growth mindset do not see a point in stopping their efforts, even if they do not perceive themselves to initially be successful at a task.

Dweck argues that the most common misconception of her work is equating growth mindset simply with student effort. Dweck argues that although the role of effort is important, it is not the only key to student achievement. Students need to access new learning strategies and they must have the opportunity to apply feedback from others when they come to an impasse in their learning. They need a "repertoire of approaches" in order to learn and to improve.

Duckworth and "Grit"

In Dweck's research, the role of persistence in the face of adversity seemed to be tantamount to successfully adopting a growth mindset. Persistence has been researched by others who have found similar results with respect to its influence in cognitive, physical, and social contexts. Duckworth, Peterson, Matthews, and Kelly (2007) targeted a specific type of persistence in their research. They define "grit" as passion and perseverance for long-term goals. They suggest that "grit" requires hard work, sustained effort, and interest in the face of difficult challenges. This "grit" is required for the long term, even when the challenge is difficult, results in failure, or plateaus in performance. In some respects, "grit" could also be likened to a combination of Coyle's (2009) "deep practice" and "ignition."

Whether they refer to motivation and self-regulation, deep practice and ignition, growth mindset, or "grit," the research that has been done by Deci and Ryan (1985), Vallerand (1997, 2001), Vallerand et al. (1992, 1993), Coyle (2009), Dweck (2008), and Duckworth et al. (2007), suggests that these qualities should be considered to be more influential to high achievement and talent development than inherent qualities like intelligence.

Critique of Grit

Angela Duckworth's 2013 TED talk, *Grit: The Power of Passion and Perseverance*, presents many problematic concepts as fact. After leaving corporate America, Duckworth entered the teaching profession as a middle school math teacher in New York City. She argues that her students "could learn the material if they worked hard enough and long enough." Fair enough, but then she argues, "In education. The thing we know how to measure best is I.Q." We could not disagree more with this premise. Duckworth defines "grit" as passion plus perseverance. Duckworth then studied grit in Chicago public schools. She found that "grittier" students were more likely to graduate. Duckworth argues that a lack of grit implies a lack of follow through.

A few of Duckworth's premises are problematic. First, her assertion that the thing educators know how best to measure best is I.Q. is patently false. The veracity of I.Q. tests has been debated for decades, and many scholars have argued that such tests privilege hegemonic students (Young, 2013). Second, Duckworth's argument about grit does much to "blame the victim," placing the onus of success on students. Duckworth worked in some of the most high-need areas in the country; did inequitable educational funding, lack of school resources, and inexperienced teachers (ubiquitous in urban schools) not figure into her assessments? We argue that schools are neither a panacea, fixing all of the society's ills, nor the vehicle through which students can "pull themselves up by their bootstraps." All schools and students deserve equitable funding, and well-prepared, experienced, culturally responsive, and caring teachers who know how to inspire all students and equip them to learn.

IMPLICIT BIAS

Educators should be aware that the expectations they hold of their students can be influenced by their own racial bias (Kirwin Institute, 2012; Steele & Cohn-Vargas, 2013). Aversive racist and stereotypical attitudes activated unconsciously or involuntarily are also known as *implicit bias* (Cohn-Vargas, 2015). Implicit racial bias "can affect a student's self-esteem, motivation, and academic performance" (Kirwin Institute, 2012, p. 15).

Implicit biases are pervasive in that they are widely held by persons in our society, often without their knowledge. Persons who see themselves as unprejudiced and nondiscriminatory are oftentimes guided in their interactions by these implicit biases—even as they generally believe themselves to be just and fair in their dealings with others. This is especially problematic behavior in persons who hold positions of authority and/or power.

Implicit and explicit biases are related to each other, in that what we actively think about and how we actively interact with others is rooted in deep-seated notions of stereotypes and feelings about them. Explicit biases are those deep-seated notions that we actively acknowledge, and implicit biases are those that we either do not acknowledge or do not understand that we hold. Because we are unaware of our beliefs, we sometimes take action based on them without realizing it. A teacher may state and believe that they hold equal expectations for all students, but in truth, "implicit bias lowers expectations for students of color and stimulates subtle differences in the way the teacher behaves toward these students for example less praise and recognition and more discipline" (Kirwin Institute, 2012, p. 15).

Implicit racial bias fuels racial stereotypes. Stereotype threat is an unconscious response to a prevailing negative stereotype about an identifiable group by a member of that group (Rudd, 2012). There is evidence of systematic bias in the use of exclusionary discipline. Black students are disproportionately represented in office referrals, suspensions, and expulsions and for less serious and more subjective reasons than white students who commit the same offenses (Lewin, 2012).

Implicit biases actually may be entirely different than our stated positions. We may *say* that we believe that certain persons are "good" or "equal"; however, our internalized understandings of them and subsequent internalized belief systems about them (implicit bias) do not reinforce our stated beliefs. Once we are able to analyze and reflect on our own beliefs, we can understand the truly negative impact they have on others and we can take steps to change those beliefs into something more constructive.

Working through Our Implicit Bias

Nieto (2005) argues that in order to become effective teachers for all students, educators must do the following:

1. Connect learning to students' lives.
2. Have high expectations for all students, even for those whom others may have given up on.

3. Stay committed to students in spite of obstacles that get in the way.

4. Place a high value on students' identities (culture, race, language, gender, and experiences, among others) as a foundation for learning.

5. View parents and other community members as partners in education.

6. Create a safe haven for learning.

7. Dare to challenge the bureaucracy of the school and district.

8. Are resilient in the face of difficult situations.

9. Use active learning strategies.

10. Are willing and eager to experiment and can "think on their feet."

11. View themselves as lifelong learners.

12. Care about, respect, and love their students.

Readers can take the Harvard Implicit Bias Test here: https://implicit.harvard.edu/implicit/takeatest.html

GROWTH MINDSET AND IMPLICIT BIAS

People possessing growth mindsets do not judge others only by first impressions; rather, they allow others to recover from mistakes within each setting. Those possessing growth mindsets are less like to operate by stereotyping others, believing that people can change, situations might drive behavior, and people deserve more than one chance before a "first impression" should be formed. Conversely, individuals possessing *entity mindsets* believe one has little potential for change; one situation can define a person forever, and these individuals will avoid information that might change their initial reaction to a person. Bias is best addressed through education or exposure to difference. If individuals possess entity mindsets, it is likely that they will be seeking validation of their initial, singular impression of others. As educators, we need to recognize mindsets within ourselves, our colleagues, and our students, and interact in deliberate ways to help each other "unlearn" our biases.

Carol Dweck's research on stereotypes and bias encourages educators to consider how we develop our perceptions of individuals unlike ourselves (2013). An individual with an entity perspective will judge others quickly and firmly based on the fixed traits they observe and even act on those stereotypical theories, whereas individuals with incremental perspectives recognize that any one group is composed of a variety of individuals with different traits and behaviors (Dweck, 2013). Incremental mindsets are developed through a wide variety of experiences with individuals who have different backgrounds and beliefs. Similarly, the concept of colorblindness nurtures the entity perspective by ignoring historical and current forms of discrimination, dehumanization, and implicit bias, and encourages deficit-minded and stereotyped thinking. As Samuels (2014) indicates, colorblindness, "also known as oppression-blindness . . . or identity-blindness is rampant in U.S. society. . . . Many white Americans believe that if they pretend not to see a person's race, then they cannot be racist" (p. 12).

MULTICULTURAL EDUCATION

The concept of multicultural education is also relevant to our discussion of teaching and learning. If a curriculum is strictly hegemonic, it may alienate some students from learning. Likewise, it is important for hegemonic students to understand nondominant points of view, issues of power and privilege, and the importance of embracing diversity in general.

James Banks is considered to be the father of multicultural education, and he devised the Five Stages of Multicultural Curriculum Transformation.

Stage 1: Curriculum of the Mainstream

This stage represented the traditional, canonized curriculum, best represented by many of our traditional textbooks. This curriculum represents the point of view of Western Europe and is male dominated. This curriculum does not make room for indigenous voices or nondominant cultures or perspectives. Banks (1993) argues that this curricular approach is harmful to all students because it "reinforces their [the dominant group] false sense of superiority, gives them a misleading conception of their relationship with other racial and ethnic groups, and denies them the opportunity to benefit from the knowledge, perspectives, and frames of reference that can be gained from studying and experiencing other cultures and groups" (p. 195). This curriculum also has negative consequences for nondominant students, failing to address their identities, experiences, and points of view. According to Banks (1993), it further alienates students who already struggle to survive in a school culture that differs from their home cultures.

Stage 2: Heroes and Holidays

This curricular stage represents as "ethnic additive approach," where teachers supplement the traditional curriculum with special events highlighting the accomplishments of minorities at certain times of the year. Cultural exemplars are highlighted who are not too threatening to the majority culture. Teachers "celebrate diversity" by introducing students to food of other cultures, for example, or by hosting events for Black History Month or Women's History Month. Although this approach is more culturally responsive that the curriculum of the mainstream culture, it does not truly address the real experiences of nondominant groups, instead focusing on the accomplishments of a few heroic and nonthreatening characters. The struggles of nondominant groups are still at the curricular periphery, which serves to trivializes the contributions, struggles, and voices of nondominant or "othered" groups.

Stage 3: Content Integration

At this stage, teachers add substantial materials and knowledge about nondominant groups to the traditional curriculum. Teachers add to their collections of books by nondominant authors to be more inclusive, but this approach is more individual as opposed to systemic and does not yet problematize the curriculum of the mainstream as a whole.

Stage 4: Structural Reform

Indigenous and nondominant materials, points of view, and voices are combined with existing knowledges to provide new levels of understanding in order to create a more accurate curriculum. Teachers are dedicated to continuously expanding their knowledge base by researching source material representing diverse perspectives. Students will experience curriculum through various cultural lenses. For example, "American History" would include African American History, Women's History, Asian American History, Latina/o American History, and all other previously differentiated fields of knowledge, and teachers consciously problematize the curriculum of the mainstream.

Stage 5: Multicultural, Social Action, and Awareness

In addition to the changes made in Stage 4, important social issues, including racism, sexism, and economic injustice, are explicitly addressed within the curriculum. The voices, ideas, and perspectives of the students regarding these and all other topics are moved to the center of the learning experience—the students become a key resource in curriculum development. The textbook is seen as only one perspective among many, and the relevance of its limitations, along with those of other educational materials, are problematized and critiqued.

—Jennifer L. Martin

One strategy to negate the entity mindset and even nurture individuals to adapt to a more incremental mindset might be to deemphasize specific stereotypes and focus on multiculturalism with the goal of a more holistic message of equality and tolerance. Schools are typically champions of multicultural experiences, but not of multicultural immersion. Multicultural immersion and antiracist pedagogy with explicit instruction on implicit bias for both teachers and students must occur in order to achieve true education equity. According to Singleton and Linton (2006), "Antiracism can be defined as conscious and deliberate efforts to challenge the impact and perpetuation of institutions of White racial power, presence, and privilege.... To be anti-racist is to be active" (p. 45). Antiracist schools do not ignore the history of oppressed peoples, as do so many of our schools.

Samuels (2014) provides eight transformative steps to building cultural inclusiveness:

1. Discover our own biases.

2. Reflect on our (systemic) socialization.

3. Challenge our assumptions.

4. Reflect on our own identities.

5. Contemplate our emotions.

6. Reflect on our own behavior.

7. Consider our purpose.

8. Commit to this work.

REFERENCES

Argyris, C. (1980). Some limitations of the case method: Experiences in a management development program. *Academy of Management Review, 5,* 291–298.

Banks, J. (1993). Approaches to multicultural curriculum reform. In J. Banks and C. Banks (Eds.), *Multicultural education: Issues and perspectives.* Boston, MA: Allyn & Bacon.

Banks, J. (2013). Group identity and citizenship education in global times. *Kappa Delta Pi Record, 49*(3), 108–112.

Beckett, K. S. (2013). Paulo Freire and the concept of education. *Educational Philosophy and Theory, 45*(1), 49–62.

Bilica, K. (2004). Lessons from experts: Improving college science instruction through case teaching. *School Science and Mathematics, 104*(6), 273–278.

Brown, J. S., Collins, A., & Duguid, P. (1989). Situated cognition and the culture of learning. *Educational Researcher, 18*(1), 32–42.

Cohn-Vargas, B. E. (2015). Tackling implicit bias. *Teaching Tolerance.* Retrieved from http://www.tolerance.org/blog/tackling-implicit-bias

Coyle, D. (2009). *The talent code: Greatness isn't born. It's grown. Here's how.* New York, NY: Bantam Dell.

Deci, E. L., & Ryan, R. M. (1985). *Intrinsic motivation and self-determination in human behavior.* New York, NY: Plenum.

Duckworth, A. L., Peterson, C., Matthews, M. D., & Kelly, D. R. (2007). Grit: Perseverance and passion for long-term goals. *Journal of Personality and Social Psychology, 92* (6), 1087–1101. doi: 10.1037/0022–3514.92.6.1087

Dweck, C. (2008). *Mindset: The new psychology of success.* New York, NY: Ballentine.

Dweck, C. (2013). *Self-theories: Their role in motivation, personality, and development* (Essays in Psychology). Hove, England: Psychology Press.

Freire, P. (1970). *Pedagogy of the oppressed.* New York, NY: Continuum.

Harvard Graduate School of Education (2013). Women in education leadership. *Programs in professional learning.* Cambridge, MA: Harvard Graduate School of Education.

Herreid, C. F. (2007). Case studies in science: A novel method of science education. In C. F. Herreid (Ed.), *Start with a story: The case study teaching method of teaching college science* (pp. 29–39). Arlington, VA: National Science Teachers Association Press.

Kohl, H. (1994). *I won't learn from you and other thoughts on creative maladjustment.* New York, NY: New Press.

Kolodner, J. L. (1997). Educational implications of analogy: A view from case-based reasoning. *American Psychologist, 52,* 35–44.

Kolodner, J. L., Camp, P. J., Crismond, D., Fasse, B., Gray, J., . . . Ryan, M. (2003). Problem-based learning meets case-based reasoning in the middle-school science classroom: Putting learning by design™ into practice. *Journal of the Learning Sciences, 12*(4), 495–547.

Lang, J. M. (2016). *Small teaching: Everyday lessons from the science of learning.* San Francisco, CA: Jossey-Bass.

Lee, S. J., & Reeves, T. C. (2007). Edgar Dale: A significant contributor to the field of educational technology. *Educational Technology, 47*(6), 56.

Lewin, T. (2012, March 6). Black students face more discipline, data suggest. *New York Times.* Retrieved from http://www.nytimes.com/2012/03/06/education/black-students-face-more-harsh-disciplinedata-shows.html

Libby, P. (1991). Barriers to using cases in accounting education. *Issues in Accounting Education, 6*(2), 193–213.

Mayo, J. A. (2002). Case-based instruction: A technique for increasing conceptual application in introductory psychology. *Journal of Constructivist Psychology, 15,* 65–74.

Mayo, J. A. (2004). Using case-based instruction to bridge the gap between theory and practice in psychology of adjustment. *Journal of Constructivist Psychology, 17,* 137–146.

McGuire, S. Y. (2015). *Teach students how to learn.* Sterling, VA: Stylus.

Min, C., VanLehn, K., Litman, D., & Jordan, P. (2011). Empirically evaluating the application of reinforcement learning to the induction of effective and adaptive pedagogical strategies. *User Modeling and User Adapted Interaction, 21*(1), 137–180.

Neumann, J. W. (2016). A limited, apolitical, and open Paulo Freire. *Educational Philosophy and Theory, 48*(6), 634–644.

Nieto, S. (Ed.). (2005). *Why we teach.* New York, NY: Teachers College Press.

Rudd, T. (2012). *A quick look at standardized testing and stereotype threat.* Columbus, OH: Kirwan Institute for the Study of Race and Ethnicity.

Samuels, D. R. (2014). *The culturally inclusive educator: Preparing for a multicultural world.* New York, NY: Teachers College Press.

Singleton, G. E., & Linton, C. (2006). *Courageous conversations about race: A field guide for achieving equity in schools.* Thousand Oaks, CA: Corwin.

Steele, D. M., & Cohn-Vargas, B. E. (2013). Identity safe classrooms: Places to belong and learn. Thousand Oaks, CA: Corwin.

Vallerand, R. J. (1997). Toward a hierarchical model of intrinsic and extrinsic motivation. In M. P. Zanna (Ed.), *Advances in experimental social psychology* (pp. 271–360). San Diego, CA: Academic.

Vallerand, R. J. (2001). Deci and Ryan's self-determination theory: A view from the hierarchical model of intrinsic and extrinsic motivation. *Psychological Inquiry, 11*, 312–318.

Vallerand, R. J., Pelletier, L.G., Blais, M. R., Brière, N. M., Senécal, C., & Vallières, E. F. (1992). The Academic Motivation Scale: A measure of intrinsic, extrinsic, and amotivation in education. *Educational & Psychological Measurement, 52*, 1003–1019.

Vallerand, R. J., Pelletier, L. G., Blais, M. R., Brière, N. M., Senécal, C., & Vallières, E. F. (1993). On the assessment of intrinsic, extrinsic, and amotivation in education: Evidence on the concurrent and construct validity of the Academic Motivation Scale. *Educational & Psychological Measurement, 53*, 159–172.

Yadav, A., Vinh, M., Shaver, G. M., Meckl, P., & Firebaugh, S. (2014). Case-based instruction: Improving students' conceptual understanding through cases in a mechanical engineering course. *Journal of Research in Science Teaching, 51*(5), 659–677.

Young, E. (2013). Intelligence testing: Accurate, or extremely biased? Retrieved from http://www.theneuroethicsblog.com/2013/09/intelligence-testing-accurate-or.html

Glossary

Academic self-concept
Children's perceptions of their academic abilities; begins to develop once children reach school age.

Accommodation
Accommodations are curricular changes made by the teacher in order to compensate for the learning challenges of students without modifying the curriculum. Students receiving accommodations experience the same curriculum and take the same tests as students without disabilities. Examples of accommodations include large print textbooks, additional time on assignments, space for movement or time for breaks, or use of a study carrel. In Piaget's theory, a process to aid in cognitive organization that requires a child to change a scheme as a result of new information she is taking in.

Action potentials
Electrical signals that travel down the axon in the neuron.

Activity level
One of five key dimensions in contemporary research on temperament. It involves the tendency to move often and vigorously, rather than to remain passive or immobile.

Anaclitic depression
A type of depression identified by Bowlby and Spitz. They asserted this type of depression was characterized by symptoms that reflected psycho-emotional deprivation including social withdrawal, weight loss, insomnia, and an overall failure to thrive.

Analytical intelligence
One aspect of Robert Sternberg's triarchic theory of intelligence that includes abilities such as planning, organizing, and remembering facts and applying them to new situations.

Animism
Involves assigning real-life qualities to inanimate objects.

Approach/positive emotionality
One of five key dimensions in contemporary research on temperament. It involves the tendency to move toward new people, situations, or objects, usually accompanied by positive emotion.

Assessment plan
An assessment plan is a written description of the assessments used to evaluate a student's strengths, weaknesses, and progress in order to determine special education eligibility and the types of services necessary to help the student succeed. IDEA requires schools complete such as evaluation within 60 days from the time of parental consent to do so.

Asset-based mindset
Viewing students' interests and culture/race/ethnicity as strengths within the class, not something that must be "overcome."

Assimilation
In Piaget's theory, a process to aid in cognitive organization that involves absorbing some new event or piece of information to make it part of an existing scheme; requires children to be selective and to pay attention to cognitive schemes that already exist in their knowledge base.

Attention deficit disorder (ADD)
Some consider attention deficit disorder to be an outdated term used to describe students with difficulty paying attention without being hyperactive.

Attention deficit/hyperactivity disorder (AD/HD)
Attention deficit/hyperactivity disorder is a condition that can make it difficult for students to sit still, control their behavior, and pay attention. Students with AD/HD are sometimes eligible for special education services.

Auditory processing disorder
Students experiencing auditory processing disorder typically have normal hearing but struggle to process and make sense from sounds—particularly if background noise is present. In short, students with auditory processing disorder can have trouble making sense of what people say.

Autism (AUT)
Autism is a complex developmental disability that typically appears during the first three years of life and impacts an individual's ability to communicate and interact with others. Autism is defined by a certain set of behaviors that affects individuals differently and to varying degrees.

Autism spectrum disorder (ASD)
Autism spectrum disorder is a developmental disability, covering a wide range of symptoms and skills but mainly impacting an individual's social and communication skills. It can also impact behavior, and is characterized by difficulties in social interaction, verbal and nonverbal communication, and repetitive behaviors.

Automaticity
The more a person engages in a task, the more accurate and efficient they can become at performing the task because the behavior becomes somewhat automatic to perform.

Axon terminal
Located at the end of the neuron; intended to transmit a neurotransmitter from one neuron to another.

Axons
Part of the neuron that is responsible for carrying electrical signals, called action potentials, away from the cell body. Some are coated with a protective layer of cells known as glial cells.

Babbling
Vocalizations that infants make during the prelinguistic stage involving consonant-vowel pairs.

Behavior genetics
a group of theories that examine how the inherited qualities of a person interact with his environment to create certain psychological and behavioral characteristics.

Behavior intervention plan (BIP)
A behavior intervention plan targets one to three of a student's undesirable behaviors with interventions specifically addressing a measurable, clearly stated targeted behavior. A BIP may include prevention strategies, which can stop the behavior before it begins, or replacement behaviors.

Behavior management
Behavior management is a process of responding to, preventing, and/or deescalating disruptive behaviors.

Behavior support plan (BSP)
Behavior support plans are proactive action plans that address negative or disruptive student behaviors that are impeding the learning of others.

Binet-Simon Intelligence Scale
First accepted standardized test of intelligence created by Alfred Binet and Théodore Simon in 1905; the test was intended to help diagnose children who were academically and intellectual "subnormal" so they could be filtered into special education programs rather than be deemed sick or too ignorant for school; it became the standard template for modern-day intelligence tests. It was revised in 1916 by Lewis Terman and would become known as the Stanford-Binet Intelligence Scale.

Bound morphemes
Morphemes that need to be connected to a free morpheme and alter the meaning of that free morpheme in some way (e.g., "-s," "-ed," "-ing," "-es").

Brain lateralization
Certain skills become more localized in their functioning and are subsequently attributed to either the right or left hemisphere of the brain. Lateralization is linked to many skills including language learning, handedness, spatial perception, facial recognition, higher-order thinking, and artistic ability.

Brain maturation
The older children get, the more neural connections they make, and the more refined parts of their brains become.

Brain plasticity
The ability of the brain to reorganize itself due to experience. Because many of its synapses are not yet established, the brain is more plastic during the first few years of life than at any later time. Early flexibility in neuronal development allows children to adapt to their environments better.

Brown v. Board of Education of Topeka
This marked the first time that social science research was used in Supreme Court deliberations, which would ultimately lead to the racial desegregation of public schools. The research used was the "Doll Studies" conducted by Drs. Kenneth Clark and Mamie Phipps Clark. These studies examined the racial identities in black and white children.

Categorization-competition hypothesis
Asserts that simply categorizing oneself and others into an ingroup and an outgroup is sufficient to generate intergroup competition.

Cell body
Sometimes referred to as the soma; contains the nucleus of the neuron. The cell body is responsible for (1) creating proteins to develop other parts of the neuron, and (2) determining whether the neuron should transmit an electrical signal within the neuron.

Centration
According to Piaget this is a tendency to think of the world in terms of a single aspect of a problem at a time. Children in the preoperational stage of cognitive development demonstrate this when performing conservation tasks.

Cerebral cortex
Least developed part of the brain at birth; the largest site of neural integration in the central nervous system. It plays a key role in memory, attention, perception, awareness, thought, language, and consciousness.

Child Study Movement
This movement would eventually reshape the field of educational psychology beginning in the 1920s. The primary intent of the movement was to establish empirically researched pedagogy, by using experimental psychology as a means of studying aspects of children's development including their sensory-perceptual development, physical development, ideas about religion, the role of play in their development, and the development of their memories and attention spans. The idea behind this research was for formal education to become more systematic and structured in a way that suited a wider range of learners.

Child-directed speech
(a.k.a. motherese or parentese) This type of speech is distinct because it is more melodic, repetitive, simple, and typically deals the toddler's direct experiences, unless the use of storytelling is being implemented; has been found to be a universal across cultures.

Chronological age
How old a person is from the time of his birth.

Class inclusion
The understanding that an object is part of a subset included within a hierarchical set (e.g., both robins and blue jays belong to a larger category of animal, birds).

Classification
The ability to structure objects hierarchically; develops for more complex categories.

Cognition
A mental process that help us acquire knowledge and understand the world we live in through our thinking. It involves a variety of abilities like sustaining attention, forming memories, using judgement to make decisions, problem solving, comprehending and producing language, and using existing knowledge to create new knowledge.

Cognitive disequilibrium
A term used by Piaget to explain a state of cognitive imbalance.

Cognitive psychology
The scientific study of mental processes such as attention, language use, memory, perception, problem solving, creativity, and thinking, all of which are typically analyzed in terms of information processing.

Concrete operations stage

Piaget's third stage of cognitive development; occurs between 6 and 12 years. During this stage children get better at thinking logically. They are less limited by the constraints of the preoperational child and can perform conservation tasks with better accuracy. With that said, they have a better chance at solving these when they are being asked to think about them in concrete, tangible terms.

Conditioning memory

Type of implicit long-term memory that involves some sort of automatic response to an external stimulus that is learned from previous experience or associations.

Conservation

The ability to understand that the quantity or amount of substance remains the same even when there are external changes in its shape or arrangement. Piaget and Inhelder had a series of tasks that measured conservation of liquid, mass, area, length, and volume.

Cooing

Vocalizations that infants make during the prelinguistic stage involving only vowel sounds.

Creative intelligence

One aspect of Robert Sternberg's triarchic theory of intelligence, which measures how well a person can see new connections between things, is insightful about experiences, and is able to "think outside the box" about various kinds of problems.

Critical period

A specific time during development when the brain is primed for learning a particular behavior, skill, or piece of knowledge (e.g., attachment formation, language acquisition).

Cross-modal transfer

Transfer of information from one sense to another.

Cultural responsiveness

Respecting, valuing, and centering student culture into the classroom setting.

Curricularly underserved students

Students who do not see themselves within their curriculum. For the nonhegemonic student, counterstories and counterhistories can provide validation for and pride in one's own culture and increase engagement in school when they can relate to the curriculum as opposed to always being "othered." For the hegemonic student, counterstories and counterhistories can work to undermine stereotypes that dominant students hold for minoritized populations with which they may have little contact, thereby potentially reducing implicit bias.

Deaf-blindness

Individuals with this diagnosis have both hearing and visual impairments. Their communication and other needs are so vast that programs for the deaf or blind cannot meet them.

Deafness
Individuals with this diagnosis have a severe hearing impairment. They are not able to process language through hearing.

Decentration
According to Piaget this is a tendency to think about a variety of aspects of a problem. This begins to be demonstrated by children during the concrete operations stage of cognitive development.

Decontextualized word identification
The ability to identify words without the aid of meaningful of context.

Deductive logic
Involves reasoning from the general to the particular, from a rule to an expected instance or from a theory to a hypothesis.

Deferred imitation
Occurs when an infant imitates a behavior that she has watched at an earlier time; Piaget suggested it begins around 18 months.

Dendrites
Part of the neuron that are the branchlike structures on the receiving end of the synapse that carry incoming signals from synapses to the next neuron's cell body.

Developmental delay (DD)
Developmental delays can pertain to delays in one or more of the following: cognitive development, physical development (including vision and hearing), communication development, social and/or emotional development and adaptive development (including eating skills, dressing and toileting skills and other areas of personal responsibility).

Developmental milestones
A set of age-specific tasks that most children can do within a certain age range. Hall and Gesell helped to establish these in psychological research.

Differentiated instruction
Differentiated instruction involves teachers actively planning for differences in student learning. Teachers utilize varied methods and resources in order to meet the learning needs of students with varied backgrounds, readiness, skill levels, and interests within a classroom.

Difficult babies
Classification from Thomas and Chess regarding infant temperament. These babies are less adaptable to new experiences, display more negative emotionality, do not adapt well to change, are not consistent in patterns of eating or sleeping, and generally speaking, are more irritable and fussy.

Doctrine of Formal Disciplines
An idea that the mind can be trained to learn by studying some fields first (e.g., Latin, philosophy, mathematics) that will make is easier to learn others; not widely believed anymore.

Dyscalculia
Dyscalculia involves learning challenges in math. Students with dyscalculia may struggle with quantities, or with binary differences. They may not make connections between the written words corresponding to numerical values (e.g., 2 versus two). Students with dyscalculia may also have difficulty recalling math facts, such as memorizing their times tables.

Dysgraphia
Dysgraphia involves issues with expressing oneself in writing. Students with dysgraphia may have difficulty holding a writing utensil and writing in a straight line. Other include the aesthetic or standard appearance of handwriting.

Dyslexia
Dyslexia is the most common learning challenge and involves the difficulty in reading, a major indicator of which involves trouble decoding, breaking down words by syllable to their individual sounds, or phonemic awareness. Dyslexia involves problems with reading accuracy and fluency. Students with dyslexia may have problems comprehending what they have read, but they may comprehend what is read to them. Dyslexia can also involve issues with spelling, writing, and math.

Easy babies
Classification from Thomas and Chess regarding infant temperament. These babies are highly adaptable to new experiences, have easily set schedules of eating and sleeping, and are receptive to new situations and people, generally displaying positive moods and emotions.

Echoic sensory memory
Memory for auditory stimuli; it has a larger capacity and a shorter duration, but it is said to last a bit longer than iconic memory, fading after 3 to 4 seconds.

Educational psychology
The scientific study of theories and principles related to human learning.

Effortful control
According to Rothbart and Hwang's research on temperament, this involves qualities like the ability to self-regulate behavior, focus on tasks, and delay gratification. One of five key dimensions in contemporary research on temperament. Combined with task persistence, it involves the ability to stay focused and to manage attention and effort.

ELL students
ELL is an acronym for English Language Learners, or students who are learning English as a second language.

Emotional disturbance (ED)
Students with emotional disturbances, sometimes known as emotional impairments, involve mental health issues that can include anxiety disorders, bipolar disorder, behavioral conduct disorders, depression, eating disorders, obsessive-compulsive disorder (OCD), schizophrenia, and psychotic disorders.

Emotional regulation
Occurs when a child is able to recognize standards of appropriate conduct, compare her behavior to the behavior of others, and then modify her behavior to match that of those around her.

Emotions
Involve having an awareness of some standard of appropriate conduct in the social world; Serve three purposes: (1) regulating overt actions, (2) influencing cognitive processing, and (3) initiating, maintaining, or terminating interactions with others.

Enactive mode
The first mode of representation in Bruner's theory, in which a student begins by doing something with the material under study, representing it and "getting to know it."

Encoding
Involves modifying information in a way that makes sense, in order to help store it in long-term memory and retrieve it at a later time.

Episodic memory
Type of explicit long-term memory, which involves memories for personal experiences.

Equilibration
According to Piaget, an innate tendency to achieve cognitive balance.

Equity-based pedagogy
Making issues of equity the center of a classroom or school.

Ethology
The systematic study of animal behavior, typically involving behavior that occurs in natural conditions, and emphasizing the behavior's evolutionary value. Bowlby's theory of attachment was influenced by the work of ethologist Lorenz.

Eugenic sterilization
Forced reproductive sterilization of those deemed mentally and intellectually "unfit."

Eugenics
Ideology promoted by Sir Francis Galton and others that asserted the human race could evolve to be a highly intelligent species through selective breeding.

Evolutionary theory
Theory proposed by Charles Darwin and others that asserts animals and humans would eventually adapt and evolve their physical characteristics to meet the needs of their environments over a period of time.

Explicit memories
(a.k.a. declarative memories) Type of long-term memories that involve memories for facts, figures, and personal experiences; they require conscious recall and include semantic memory and episodic memory.

Expressive language
The ability to produce meaningful language; comes after receptive language.

False belief principle
The understanding that another person might have a false belief and the ability to determine what information might cause the false belief.

False belief task
A task that measures theory of mind and is based on the false belief principle. It requires a child to infer that another person possesses the level of knowledge about a task that they do.

Focus on more than one figures
According to Bowlby, this is the second phase of attachment that occurs between three and six months. The proximity promoting behaviors are targeted to specific people that infants comes into regular contact with and who take care of the infants (e.g., mom, dad, daycare provider). During this phase, infants still respond relatively indiscriminately to anyone that tends to them, showing little stranger anxiety.

Foreclosure
One of Marcia's identity statuses; occurs when an identity commitment is made based on parental or societal norms without an identity crisis occurring.

Formal operational egocentrism
Occurs when teenagers are unable to separate their own abstract logic from the perspectives of others. This also often involves disregarding any sort of practical implications to their thinking.

Formal operations stage
Piaget's fourth stage of cognitive development; occurs at age 13 years and older; teenagers develop the ability to manipulate hypothetical concepts and think logically using abstract concepts. They engage in systematic and complete approaches to problem-solving, are better at using strategies and implement more organization to problem solve. Teenagers at this stage also are better at formulating and testing hypotheses, as well as separating and controlling variables. They can implement both hypo-deductive reasoning and proportional reasoning.

Free morphemes
Morphemes that can make sense and hold meaning on their own (e.g., dog, horse, cup).

Full scale IQ
Fifteen tests that comprise the Weschler Intelligence Scale for Children; include the scores from the verbal scales and performance scales; in the Weschler scales, scores are not intended to measure a person's quantity of intelligence, but instead measure their intellectual performance.

Gardner's Theory of Multiple Intelligences
Theory of intelligence created by Howard Gardner that asserts there are eight distinct types of intelligence: linguistic, logical/mathematical, musical, spatial, bodily

kinesthetic, interpersonal (understanding other people), intrapersonal (understanding oneself), and naturalistic (recognizing patterns in nature).

General analytic ability
The ability to analyze, categorize, and relate information in an attempt to achieve a conceptual grasp of objects, events, and procedures that exist or occur in the external world.

Genetic epistemology
The idea that as humans, we have a framework and timeline for developing how we think and what we think about. This influenced Piaget's theory.

Gestalt Psychology Movement
This approach to psychology viewed sensory, perceptual, and cognitive functions in a holistic manner and asserted that the whole of these experiences was greater than the sum of their parts.

Glial cells
The glial cells surround neurons and provide support for and insulation between them.

Guided participation
Another derived concept from Vygotsky's sociocultural theory. It is the tendency for adults to provide scaffolding to children so they can engage in mature activities (e.g., learning to mow the lawn or bake). Rogoff and colleagues assert that parents, teachers, coaches, and other adults that interact with younger, and/or more novice individuals, naturally engage in the process of guided participation as a means for social transmission of everyday knowledge.

Head Start Program
The federal program introduced in 1965 to improve preschool development; intended to provide young children with the social and academic skills and resources to ready themselves for the school environment.

Hearing Impairment
This impairment can refer to hearing losses not covered by deafness definition. These losses can change over time. Having difficulties with hearing is not the same as experiencing auditory processing issues.

Holophrases
Occur when toddlers combine a single word with gestures to make a complete thought; these are used between 12 and 18 months.

Horizontal decalage
The ability to apply new kinds of thinking to new kinds of problems, begins to occur more frequently.

Hypothetical reasoning
Involves deriving logical outcomes after considering hypotheses or hypothetical premises.

Iconic mode
Bruner's second mode of representation, in which things are "known" primarily in terms of their perceptual qualities.

Iconic sensory memory
Memory of visual stimuli in its exact original form. Its capacity is very large, but its duration lasts less than a second.

Identity achievement
One of Marcia's identity statuses; occurs when the identity crisis is resolved, and the identity commitment has been made.

Identity commitment
According to Marcia, this referred to the adoption of a new ideology or aspiration when forming aspects of identity.

Identity crisis
According to Erikson, this is the brief uncertainty and confusion adolescents experience as they struggle with alternatives and choices presented to them during this period of life. These choices could involve decisions about future schooling or careers, interpersonal relationships with friends and family, values related to religious and political beliefs, ethnic or racial identity, gender identity, and sexual orientation. According to Marcia, this referred to a period of decision making during which old choices are reexamined and measured against new opportunities.

Identity diffusion
One of Marcia's identity statuses; occurs when a teenager is not in the midst of an identity crisis and has not made an identity commitment.

Imaginary audience
Elkind's concept; occurs when teenagers believe that everyone is focused on them or some small flaw of theirs.

Imitation
Occurs when infants can performance something they see or hear someone else do.

Immigrant students
Immigrant students who students who have come to the United States from a different country.

Implicit memory
(a.k.a., nondeclarative memory) Type of long-term memory that influences behaviors but does not require conscious recall; includes procedural memory and conditioning memory.

Imposter phenomenon
(also referred to as IP and "imposter syndrome") Occurs when a person experiences doubt about their own accomplishments and has a persistent, internalized fear of being exposed as a fraud.

Imprinting
Involves a rapid and natural learning process that occurs early in the life of an animal or mammal and subsequently establishes an adaptive behavior pattern. These behaviors are specific to a particular species and aid in their survival. An example of this is when the young goslings imprinted on Lorenz after being orphaned.

Inclusion, or inclusive classroom
Inclusion is a philosophy advocating for and securing opportunities for students with disabilities to learn inside traditional mainstream classrooms.

Individualized education program (IEP)
A legal document that defines the specific special education services provided for a student by the school district.

Individualized education program (IEP) team
The team of qualified professionals, including special education teacher, data analyst, district representative, and general education teacher as well as a parent/caregiver. This group makes all decisions related to the instructional program of students with special needs, including placement and services provided.

Individualized family services plan (IFSP)
A written treatment plan mapping early intervention services a child (birth to three) will receive, and specifics on how and when these services will be administered. This plan also details the child's current levels of functioning, specific needs, and goals or outcomes for treatment.

Individuals with Disabilities Education Act (IDEA)
A federal law guaranteeing educational rights to students with disabilities, making it illegal for school districts to refuse education to any student because of disability.

Inductive logic
Involves reasoning from the particular to the general, from experience to broad rules.

Information processing theories
A set of theories that focus on the way people process information using internal mechanisms like cognition, attention, and memory.

Ingroup bias
People's bias in favor of members of their own group.

Inhibition
According to Kagan's research on temperament, this is a combination of shyness and fear of new and unfamiliar events; one of five key dimensions in contemporary research on temperament. Combined with anxiety, it involves the tendency to respond with fear or to withdraw from new people, situations, or objects.

Inner speech
According to Vygotsky, this is intended to serve the same purpose as private speech, but for older/adult learners and is internalized. For example, a high school student may be reciting the equation needed to solve his calculus problem in his head, during an exam.

Insecure detached/avoidant attachment
One of Ainsworth's attachment classifications. In the Strange Situation Experiment, children avoid contact with their caregivers when they are in the laboratory room (even after being separated and reunited) but may still play with toys and

actively explore the room. They do not resist the caregiver's efforts to make contact but do not initiate contact either. These children also show no strong preference for their caregivers over the strangers and are not comforted by their caregivers when reunited after separation.

Insecure disorganized/disoriented attachment
One of Ainsworth's attachment classifications. The characteristics associated with this type of attachment don't fall neatly into any other category. In the Strange Situation Experiment, this attachment is marked by dazed behavior, confusion, or apprehension on the part of children. They may show a contradictory behavior pattern simultaneously. For instance, they may move toward their caregiver when the stranger enters the room but may keep an averted eye gaze while doing so.

Insecure resistant/ambivalent attachment
One of Ainsworth's attachment classifications. In the Strange Situation Experiment, children show little exploration of the laboratory room and are wary of strangers. They are upset when their caregivers leave the room but are not comforted when reunited. Children with this type of attachment both seek and avoid contact with their caregiver at various times. They may even show anger toward their caregiver when reunited, and resist both comfort and contact with the stranger.

Instructional scaffolding
The process by which one structures the zone of proximal development so that a child can achieve problems on their own. Through this process, cognitive skills required for success in each culture are socially transmitted from generation to generation.

Intellectual disability (ID)
Students with intellectual disabilities possess below-average intellectual abilities. Students possessing intellectual disabilities may also exhibit poor communication skills, self-care skills, and social skills. ID has previously been referred to as mental retardation (MR). As language evolves, this term is no longer acceptable to use.

Intelligence
The general capacity to use all of the mental processes associated with cognition. Three broad definitions represent the varied ways in which psychological theorists have conceptualized this construct: (1) individual differences in how people process information or think, (2) the magnitude, pattern, origins, or stability of individual differences in mental functioning, and (3) acting or thinking in ways that are goal-directed and adaptive.

Intergroup relations
The relationship between two or more groups and their respective members.

Internal working models of attachment
These help infants form a cognitive blueprint of the workings of relationships. The earliest relationships between the infants and their mothers (or primary caregivers, in instances where the mothers are not available), may form the template for such a cognitive blueprint.

Interneurons
Relay signals between motor and sensory neurons.

Interventions
Interventions are teaching procedures used by teachers to assist struggling students to succeed. Interventions can be academic or behavioral.

Invulnerability fallacy
Occurs when teens' false sense of security lead them to believe that they cannot get hurt, even when engaging in high risk behaviors.

Law of Effect
Thorndike's law that asserted if an animal or person received a pleasant or rewarding outcome after performing a behavior, then that animal or person would be more likely to perform the behavior again, in anticipation of the pleasant outcome. He proposed that the type of outcome that occurred as a result of a behavior determined how it became "stamped" into memory.

Law of Exercise
Thorndike's law that asserted the more an animal or person is compelled to complete an action to receive a pleasant outcome, the stronger the connection between the behavior and the outcome becomes. This law validated a longstanding philosophical notion of associationism, (a.k.a. associative learning).

Learner-Centered Psychological Principles
This APA presidential taskforce recognized a need for a paradigmatic shift in how to design and deliver educational content. The principles addressed the multiple roles that teachers serve in their students' learning experiences and highlighted the complexities of the learning environment, including the myriad of characteristics that the learners themselves, bring to the classroom. They also emphasize diversity and the active and reflective nature of learning.

Learning
Involves many components including changes in the brain, changes in behavior, memories of previous experiences, adaptations to new environments, and problem-solving skills.

Least restrictive environment (LRE)
Least restrictive environment pertains to the environment in which students with disabilities are educated, mandated by IDEA, as a classroom setting that is as close as possible to the general education setting.

Lexical knowledge
Knowledge of whole words in spoken and printed contexts. In learning to read acquiring lexical knowledge requires an awareness of print concepts and conventions in written text.

LGBTQ+
An acronym for members of the Lesbian, Gay, Bisexual, Transgender, and Queer community; the + represents the other identities embedded under this label, such as Intersex, Questioning, and Ally, and the identities yet to be identified.

Long-term memory
In the three-store memory model, this is the final memory store and is considered to have a limitless capacity and duration, at least theoretically; different types of long-term memories include explicit memories and implicit memories.

Maintenance rehearsal
Rehearsal that is done to hold information in short-term memory.

Meaningful learning
Involves making connections between new information and prior knowledge; includes elaboration, organization, and visual imagery.

Means-end behavior
Behavior that is intended to have a specific purpose and lead to a specific result.

Medulla
Cone-shaped, neuronal (nerve cell) mass in the hindbrain, which controls a number of autonomic (involuntary) functions, like regulating heartbeat and breathing as well as attention, sleeping, waking, elimination, and movement of the head and neck.

Memory span tasks
Tests for the capacity of short-term memory by giving a series of items one at a time in a given order.

Mental age
Represents the age that a person should function intellectually, compared to average intellectual performance for that actual age.

Mental reversibility
According to Piaget this involves the knowledge that reversing a transformation brings about the conditions that existed before the transformation.

Mental schemas
Basic units of knowledge about objects, events, and actions. According to Piaget, schemas are built on a small group of sensory and motor skills that we utilize during the very first stage of our cognitive development, the sensorimotor stage.

Metacognition
Involves beliefs about one's own cognitive processing and the strategies used to regulate thinking; thinking about thinking.

Metalinguistic awareness
The ability to think about language.

Midbrain
Serves important functions in motor movement, particularly movements of the eye, and in auditory and visual processing.

Miller's Magic Number
Refers to the capacity of short-term memory, which is 7 +/- 2 units of information; George Miller (1920–2012) conducted studies testing the short-term memory using memory span tasks

Minimal group paradigm
A standard set of research procedures that creates artificial ingroups and out-groups based on minimally important, or artificial, differences between groups.

Modifications
Curricular adaptations that compensate for learners' weaknesses by changing or lowering expectations or standards. Modifications may include: altered assignments, modified tests and grading, and modified expectations.

Monitoring
Part of the Response to Intervention (RTI) processes, involving assessing, keeping accurate records, and monitoring student progress regarding responsiveness to instruction and intervention. (See RTI.)

Moratorium
One of Marcia's identity statuses; occurs when an identity crisis is in progress, but no identity commitment is yet made.

More Knowledgeable Other (MKO)
Vygotsky's asserted that knowledge was acquired through social interactions with individuals who knew more and had experienced more in life and in the cultural context.

Morphemes
are the smallest meaning-bearing units in language; there are two types: bound morphemes and free morphemes.

Motor neurons
Carry information from the central nervous system to organs, glands, and muscles.

Multiple disabilities
Students possessing multiple disabilities have more than one condition covered by IDEA. Possessing multiple disabilities creates educational needs that cannot be met in single programs designed for any single condition.

Myelin sheath
Sleeves of fatty tissue that protect your neurons; facilitates the speed of the electrical impulse that travels through the axon.

Myelination
The process of wrapping myelin sheath around neural circuitry, and results in more efficient firing of neural impulses. It is rapid during first two years of life and continues through adolescence.

Myelination theory
Asserts that the more a child practices a particular skill set, the more myelin will wrap around his neural circuitry involved in executing that skill set. This is a process that happens naturally and facilitates neurological development from infancy into adulthood.

Naïve idealism
Elkind's idea that suggests adolescents think about solutions and beliefs that are very optimistic and positive but not realistic or well thought out.

Negative affect/emotionality
According to Rothbart and Hwang's research on temperament, this involves qualities like fear, sadness, discomfort, and anger. In an infant, this might manifest as a fussy baby, not easily soothed; one of five key dimensions in contemporary research on temperament. Combined with irritability/anger, it involves the tendency to respond with anger, fussiness, loudness, or irritability, and a low threshold for frustration.

Neurotransmitter
Neurochemicals released between neurons to stimulate neighboring neurons or muscle or gland cells, allowing electrical impulses to be passed from one cell to the next throughout the nervous system.

"New look" in perception
An understanding of perception that emphasizes how a variety of nonobjective factors can systematically influence the process of perception.

Nonfocused orienting and signaling phase of attachment
According to Bowlby, this is the first phase of attachment that occurs within the first three months. There is no established attachment with the primary caregiver(s). Infants engage in proximity-promoting behaviors, which orient others toward them. Crying, cooing, and eye gaze are examples of proximity-promoting behaviors.

Nonhegemonic students
students who possess one or several historically marginalized identity categories, such as those of a nondominant/privileged race, class, gender, sexuality, religion, ethnicity, or disability.

Nonverbal learning disability (NVLD)
Nonverbal learning disabilities involve deficits in social skills, which can impact student learning. Students with NVLD do not always communicate in socially appropriate ways; they may have particular difficulty with nonverbal communication, such as body language, facial expressions, and tone of voice. Students with NVLD often miss social cues, so they may have difficulty making friends and cause misunderstandings with parents and teachers.

Norms
Test scores that accurately represent a group; these scores are typically used as a standard against which subsequently collected data is compared; provides insight into the distribution or prevalence of the characteristic being assessed in the larger population.

Numeration
The acquisition of numerical concepts like ordinal sequencing, addition, and subtraction.

Object permanence
Term coined by Piaget; occurs during the sensorimotor stage; the infant's realization that things continue to exist even though they are not in her immediate field of vision.

Objective self
Aspects of the self-concept that are based on concrete characteristics a child can identify in herself and can use as the basis of comparisons to other people (e.g., physical attributes, age, abilities).

Occupational therapist (OT)
An occupational therapist is a professional trained to treat patients with injuries, illnesses, or disabilities through the therapeutically practicing daily activities. Occupational therapists assist individuals develop, recover, and improve the skills needed for daily life.

Organization
In Piaget's view refers to an inborn mental process that helps us to derive generalizable schemes from specific experiences.

Orthographic awareness
Refers to the reader's sensitivity to the constraints of how letters in words are organized (zad = legal; dza = illegal) and to the regularities and redundancies in the writing system (-at in cat, fat, and rat).

Orthopedic impairment (OI)
An orthopedic impairment involves an impairment to a student's body, no matter the cause, involving deformities of bones or muscles, e.g., cerebral palsy. These physical disabilities can impact the learning process.

Other health impairment (OHI)
Other health impairment is an umbrella term that covers conditions that limit a student's strength, energy or alertness, e.g., attention-deficit/hyperactivity disorder, diabetes, epilepsy, heart conditions, hemophilia, lead poisoning, leukemia, nephritis, rheumatic fever, sickle cell anemia and Tourette syndrome.

Overextension
Occurs when a toddler applies a label to a broader class of objects than the term signifies (e.g., calling a horse or a cow a "doggie" because the toddler has a dog at home and knows the verbal label for it but not the label for horses or cows, which share similar physical qualities such as four legs and a tail.

Overregularization errors
These involve the common tendency among children & second language learners to apply regular and productive grammatical rules to words that are exceptions ("knew" age 2 1/2 = modeling vs. "knowed" age 3 1/2 = creative error vs. "knew" age 4 1/2 = establishes exceptions to specific language rules).

Outgroup homogeneity effect
Occurs when people tend to see members of their own group as very different from one another but underestimate the differences between members of other groups.

Paradigm
The entire collection of beliefs, values, and techniques shared by a group of scientists and research practitioners.

Partnership for 21st Century Learning's (P21) Framework
Content learning is still a relevant and valuable focus for student outcomes, but it has evolved beyond the basics of reading, writing, arithmetic, and history. It includes teaching mastery in skills like global awareness, and literacy in the domains of finance, civics, health, and the environment.

Performance Deficit
A performance deficit pertains to a student's social or academic skills deficits, where students understand a specific skill, but fail to practice it consistently.

Performance IQ scales
(a.k.a., performance comprehension index) Ten of the tests 15 tests that comprise the Weschler Intelligence Scale for Children; they assess performance skills like perceptual reasoning, processing speed, and working memory.

Personal fable
Elkind's concept; occurs when teenagers think that they are unique and no one else understands them.

Phonemes
The smallest units of sound in language; each letter of the alphabet has a corresponding sound.

Phonological decoding
When learning to read, children will use this strategy to sound out an unfamiliar word based on its letter composition.

Pivot grammar
Occurs when a toddler uses one word repetitively in a fixed position to generate several two-word phrases.

Practical intelligence
One aspect of Robert Sternberg's triarchic theory of intelligence; sometimes called "street smarts."

Pragmatics
In the study language these are the social conventions of a language and culture.

Pragmatism
A termed coined by one of James's friends and fellow scholars, Pierce; the view that scientific ideas and knowledge are constantly evolving based on the temporal, social, and cultural context.

Preoperational egocentrism
Occurs when a child displays the inability to distinguish personal perceptions, thoughts, and feelings from those of others. In other words, a preoperational child is unable to think about another person's perspective.

Preoperational stage
Piaget's second stage of cognitive development; occurs from 18 months to 6 years. During this stage, young children become more adept at using symbolic thinking to communicate. They continue to develop their language skills and use symbolic

representation through drawing, storytelling, and make-believe play, and their imaginations.

Primary circular reaction
Substage of Piaget's sensorimotor stage that involves the infant coordinating bodily sensations and new cognitive schemas.

Private speech
According to Vygotsky, this is audible speech used to guide children through solving a problem or engaging in an activity.

Procedural memory
Type of implicit, long-term memory that involves memory for some sort of physical process (e.g., playing the piano, kicking a ball, driving a car).

Progressive education
Differs from the traditional educational training model. It emphasizes the role of a student's experience over rote learning of facts and figures. It shifts the focus from simply training and testing students to teaching students how to use critical thinking skills, creativity, and social-emotional skills. Active engagement, experiential learning, and exploring the goals of learning are hallmarks of this approach.

Proportional reasoning
Involves understanding proportions (e.g., fractions, decimals, ratios) well enough to apply them to mathematical concepts.

Proximity-promoting behaviors
Behaviors that infants and young children engage in to orient others toward them. These behaviors include crying, cooing, and eye gaze. As infants get older, they more intentionally direct these behaviors at their primary caregivers.

Puzzle boxes
Thorndike's invention to test his principles of operant conditioning. These were elaborately redesigned fruit crates intended to test the ability of cats and dogs to press a lever or pull a loop to escape and find a reward (e.g., food).

Race consciousness
A term coined by Mamie Phipps Clark that she defined as "a consciousness of self as belonging to a specific group which is differentiated from other groups by obvious physical characteristics."

Reactivity
The degree to which an infant reacts to a newly presented sensory stimuli; Kagan would suggest it indicates the infant's level of inhibition.

Reading comprehension
The ability to extract and construct meaning from written text.

Realistic conflict theory
Proposes that people dislike members of outgroups because their ingroup in competing with the outgroup for resources.

Receptive language
The ability to understand certain language (e.g., infants and toddlers learn labels for nouns before verbs), comes before expressive language.

Referential communication
This is important in pragmatics; involves communication in situations that require the speaker to describe an object to a listener or to evaluate the effectiveness of a message.

Rehearsal
A cognitive strategy that involves repeating information over and over repeatedly as a means of keeping it in memory and learning it.

Reliability
The stability of a test score; yields scores that are stable over time.

Remedial age
In calculating intelligence scores for the Binet-Simon Intelligence Scales, this occurred when a child's mental age was less than their chronological age.

Response to Intervention (RTI)
Response to Intervention is a process used by educators to help struggling students. If students do not respond to initial interventions, more focused interventions are developed. Effective interventions are apparent when learning is accelerated, and fewer students are at-risk for academic failure, among other factors. There are three tiers of interventions within the RTI process. For example, all students in Tier 1 receive quality differentiated instruction; these students are periodically screened to identity struggling students who may need additional support. In which case, these students would move on to Tier 2 interventions where they are provided with intensive instruction paired with their needs and progress rates. Students receiving Tier 3 interventions receive individualized and intensive interventions targeting their learning needs and providing remediation.

Retrieval
The process of remembering previously stored information.

Rote learning
Learning primarily through repetition and practice, with little or no attempt to make sense of what is being learned; does not require as much effortful processing as other learning strategies.

Rouge test
Test of self-awareness in which a child is put in front of a mirror with a spot of paint/ink on their face. If the child touches her face during the test, that indicates self-awareness because the child recognizes that she has a spot of ink on her own face.

Safe base
A term in attachment theory; occurs when the infant seeks out and gets physically closer to their primary caregiver in the face of fear or threat.

Secure attachment
One of Ainsworth's attachment classifications. In the Strange Situation Experiment, children actively explore the laboratory room and play with available toys when their caregiver is present. When the caregiver leaves, they become distressed and may cry or move around the room to regain proximity to their caregiver. They are not consoled by strangers' attempts to comfort them in the absence of the caregiver. When finally reunited with their caregivers, they are comforted by them.

Secure base behavior phase of attachment
According to Bowlby, this is the third phase of attachment that occurs around 6 months, and if the infants have been provided with consistent care from their primary caregivers, genuine attachment begins to form. During this phase, infants have identified their primary caregivers as a "safe base" and engage in social referencing.

Self-awareness
Involves being aware of one's one physical and psychological traits, behaviors, and feelings; it is evident in some infants as early as 21 months of age.

Self-concept
A child's knowledge and thoughts about her own set of attributes or qualities.

Semantic memory
Type of explicit long-term memory, which involves factual knowledge that is universal for everyone (e.g., facts and figures from a book).

Semantics
In the study of language, this refers to the meaning of words (a.k.a., vocabulary)

Semiotic function
Piaget's term for forms of symbolic thinking and representation that emerges in the preoperational stage (e.g., language, drawing, storytelling, imaginary play).

Sensorimotor stage
Piaget's first stage of cognitive development; occurs from birth to 18 months and is characterized by thought that is based in physical action.

Sensory memory
Memory store in the three-store memory model where information from the external environment is processed via the body's sensory registers (eyes, ears, mouth, nose, and skin).

Sensory neurons
Sends information to the central nervous system from internal organs or from external stimuli.

Separation anxiety
A term in attachment theory that describes when an infant becomes distressed by being separated from her primary caregiver.

Seriation
This involves sorting objects or situations according to any characteristic, such as size, color, shape, or type.

Short-term memory
In the three-store memory model, this is where information that is consciously recognized and interpreted from sensory memory enters the mind and when information that has been successfully stored in long-term memory is retrieved to; it requires intentional, conscious cognitive processing and it is where humans actively rehearse information in order to process it for the next memory store, long-term memory; also known as *working memory*.

Sight words
Words that cannot be phonologically decoded when a child learns to read; must be taught using different strategies that mostly rely on a child's memory.

Slow-to-warm-up babies
Classification from Thomas and Chess regarding infant temperament. These babies are a combination of the easy baby temperament and the difficult baby temperament. They have a low activity level and tend to withdraw from new situations and people. They are slower to adapt to new experiences compared to easy babies, but eventually accept them if they are exposed to the experience more than once.

Social referencing
A term in attachment theory; tendency for the infants to take cues from other people in the environment, about how they should respond emotionally and behaviorally in a certain situation. Infants observe the behavior of their primary caregivers and imitate their actions and behaviors.

Speech or language impairment (SLI)
This is an umbrella that covers a number of communication issues, including stuttering, impaired articulation, and language or voice impairment.

Speech-language pathologist (SLP)
A speech-language pathologist is a professional who diagnoses and treats communication and swallowing disorders (also known as a speech therapist).

Spiral curriculum
Involves teachers introducing students to topics early, in age-appropriate language, and revisiting the same topics in later years, adding depth and complexity as the students get older.

Stage 1 grammar
(a.k.a. telegraphic speech) Involves short, simple, sentences where grammatical markers like conjunctions, prepositions may be missing. This type of grammar consists of combos of verbs, nouns, and adjectives, and toddlers use very few morphemes to mark tense or plurals.

Stage 2 grammar
Occurs around 23 months and involves sentences that are more complex, integrating the use of plurals, past tenses, auxiliary verbs, and prepositions.

Stage theories
Theories that break down development into distinct periods of development. Each stage is assumed to be somewhat culturally universal, chronologically fixed, and qualitatively different from the other stages.

Standardization
In testing this requires (1) that all test takers answer the same questions or complete the same set of tasks, (2) these questions or tasks are administered to the test-taker in the same way, and (3) the questions or tasks are scored in a "standard" manner; these requirements make it possible to compare relative performances of individual students or groups of students and yield normative data.

"Stay Put" Law
A law indicating that a parent can request that a student stay in their current educational placement while an IEP is in dispute.

Storage
The acquisition of new knowledge and involves the process of putting what is learned into memory initially.

Strange Situation Paradigm
Ainsworth's laboratory setting used to study and identify attachment classifications. It consisted of a small room filled with toys and two chairs. There was a two-way mirror to observe the interactions and behaviors of the mother and children pairs. There are eight steps in the experimental procedure that indicate the type of attachment the infant shares with their primary caregiver.

Stranger anxiety
A term in attachment theory that describes when an infant becomes distressed after being introduced to a stranger, either in the presence or absence of her primary caregiver. Subjective self: Begins within the first year of life and involves developing (1) a sense of agency, (2) a sense of permanency, and (3) a sense of self-efficacy.

Structuralism
Titchener's approach to psychology, which emphasized the discovery of the basic structure of mental phenomena as collections of sensations and feelings, before considering their functions.

Student baseline
A student's academic starting point determined by data and used to measure a student's academic progress throughout the year.

Sublexical knowledge
When children combine information acquired using general linguistic coding, visual coding, and metalinguistic analysis, they begin to acquire sublexical knowledge, which facilitates an awareness of the structural features of language.

Surgency/extraversion
According to Rothbart and Hwang's research on temperament, this involves qualities like impulsivity, eagerness, and a desire for sensation seeking.

Survival of the fittest
Asserts those animals and humans with physical features that were most evolved to match the constraints of their current environment would survive and reproduce, but those who did not possess such features would eventually die off.

Symbolic mode
Bruner's third and final mode of representation, in which the student appreciates the abstract qualities of the object of study.

Synapse
The space between neurons that permits a neuron to pass an electrical or chemical signal to another neuron or to the target effector cell.

Synaptic pruning
Natural neurological process that involves periods of removal of synaptic connections.

Synaptogenesis
Natural neurological process that involves periods of growth of synaptic connections.

Synchrony
The melody or sound of a language.

Syntactic awareness
The ability to reflect on and manipulate the words in a sentence in terms of their structural relationships.

Temperament
A child's habitual and enduring tendencies when approaching their external environments and the people in them.

Theory of mind
Involves an awareness of what others are thinking and the realization that it may differ from what you are thinking; perspective-taking.

Three-Mountain Task
Developed by Piaget and Inhelder in the 1940s to study children's ability to coordinate spatial perspectives.

Three-stage memory model
Information processing theories likened the human brain to a computer that involves three memory stores that take in information from the external environment, make sense of it, and then retain it; these stages include sensory memory, short-term/working memory, and long-term memory.

Title IX
Title IX of the Education Amendments of 1972: No person in the United States shall, on the basis of sex, be excluded from participation in, be denied the benefits of, or be subjected to discrimination under any education program or activity receiving federal financial assistance. Title IX was named the Patsy T. Mink Equal Opportunity in Education Act on October 9, 2002.

Transfer of training
Concept studied by Woodworth and Thorndike; involved the ability of a person to apply a behavior, knowledge, and skills acquired in one learning context to a different learning context.

Transition/transition plan
Transition is a term used to describe a change in a student's school or program. A transition plan is specific to an IEP. For example, a transition plan may pertain to how a student will transition to life after high school.

Transitive inference
A type of inferential reasoning that involves the ability to compare two objects via a transitional object. A common example is the statement: A > B and B > C and C > D and D > E.

Traumatic brain injury
Traumatic brain injuries are caused by accidents of physical force that can impact learning.

Trial-and-error learning
According to Thorndike, this occurred when the process of exhibiting chance behavior that was sporadically successful, gradually became more precise and intentional. An animal learning to navigate a maze and getting quicker with each successive trial is an example. Substage in Piaget's sensorimotor stage, which involves experimentation that results in infants trying out new ways of playing with or manipulating objects.

Triarchic Theory of Intelligence
Theory of intelligence created by Robert Sternberg, which asserts that there are three aspects of intelligence: analytical intelligence, creative intelligence, and practical intelligence.

Underextension
Occurs when a toddler applies a label to a narrower class of objects than the term signifies using term "car" for all cars that look like station wagons but nothing else.

Undocumented students
A relatively new and more culturally responsive term for students who were formally known as "illegals," also known as "Dreamers."

Universal Design for Learning
Universal Design for Learning (UDL) is a pedagogical approach intended to make curriculum accessible for all students, regardless of background, learning style, ability, and so on. Specifically, UDL is a framework addressing learning barriers: including inflexible, or "one-size-fits-all" curricula. Gifted learners and learners with disabilities are particularly vulnerable, but all learners may have unmet needs based upon poor curricular design. Often UDL is referred to as "curb cutting," or removing barriers so that all learners have equal access to learning. When curricula are designed to meet the needs of an imaginary "average," or "teaching to the middle," they do not address learner variability. "Teaching to the middle" does provide all individuals with fair and equitable learning opportunities for it excludes learners with different abilities, backgrounds, and motivations. The UDL framework encourages teachers to meet students where they are. For more information, see http://www.udlcenter.org/aboutudl/whatisudl

Use It or Lose It Principle
In neurological development, the idea that those neurons that are engaged on a regular basis will remain functional, while those that are not used regularly will be pruned away. This pruning is important because it allows for more efficiency of the synaptic connections that remain and makes room for future synaptic connections as we acquire different skills over our lifetime.

Validity
Indicates whether a test is measuring what it is intended to measure.

Verbal IQ Scales
(a.k.a., verbal comprehension index) Five of the 15 tests that comprise the Weschler Intelligence Scale for Children; they assess verbal skills.

Verbal working memory
Refers to the mental work space in which recent environmental stimuli are briefly held in the form of linguistic codes, either for rehearsal and recall or for meaningful integration with other knowledge

Visual coding
The ability to encode, store, and retrieve visual-spatial stimuli; process makes use of permanent memory and general linguistic abilities, especially phonological coding, in facilitating acquisition of visual representations of word specific spellings

Visual impairment (including blindness)
Students with visual impairments can include both partial sight and blindness. If eyewear can correct this problem, then it does qualify under IDEA.

Volkerpsychologie
For those phenomena that could not be carefully observed and measured in a laboratory, like religious beliefs, mythology, customs, and language, Wundt proposed this field of study. He believed that historical and comparative analysis was more appropriate in studying these higher-level mental functions.

Voluntarism
Considered the first school of thought in psychology; refers to Wundt's study of reaction times, perception, and attention, things he associated with a person's will and voluntary effort.

Widening gap
The gap between what a student with a disability knows and what their peers know, which widens as they advance in grade level.

Zeitgeist
Sometimes referred to as the "spirit of the times"; emphasizes the influences of developments in other sciences, political climate, technological advancements, and economic conditions on the development of psychology.

Zone of proximal development (ZPD)

According to Vygotsky, the learner's actual development involved the accumulated knowledge and potential for developing other cognitive abilities. The learner's potential development represented functions that had not materialized yet,
but were developing with environmental experiences. Thus, the ZPD was the difference between what the learner could do with assistance (from older peers or
adults) and what the learner could do alone.

Resources

Break the Cycle:
https://www.breakthecycle.org/

Coalition to Support Grieving Students:
https://grievingstudents.org/

The Cornell Research Program on Self-Injury and Recovery:
http://www.selfinjury.bctr.cornell.edu/about-self-injury.html

Dating Matters:
https://vetoviolence.cdc.gov/dating-matters

Dating Matters: Strategies to Promote Healthy Teen Relationships:
https://www.cdc.gov/ViolencePrevention/DatingMatters/index.html

Ending K-12 Sexual Harassment:
http://stopsexualassaultinschools.org/wp-content/uploads/2018/04/SSAIS
_FINAL.pdf

GLSEN Article:
https://www.glsen.org/article/glsen-releases-new-national-school-climate
-survey-report

GLSEN Study:
https://www.glsen.org/article/2017-national-school-climate-survey-1

Know Your Title IX:
https://www.knowyourix.org/

Life Signs Self-Injury Guidance and Network Support:
http://www.lifesigns.org.uk/how-to-react-when-your-friend-says-they-self
-injure/

Preventing, Assessing, and Intervening in Teenage Dating Abuse:
https://safesupportivelearning.ed.gov/get-smart-get-help-get-safe-teenage
-dating-abuse-training-specialized-instructional-support

S.A.F.E. Alternatives Resources for Schools:
http://www.selfinjury.com/schools/

The Safe Place to Learn:
https://safesupportivelearning.ed.gov/safe-place-to-learn-k12

Self-Injury Outreach and Support:
http://sioutreach.org/learn-self-injury/friends/#ffs-tabbed-110

Stop Sexual Assault in Schools:
http://stopsexualassaultinschools.org/metook12-resources/

That's Not Cool:
https://thatsnotcool.com/

Title IX:
https://www.titleix.com/k-12/

Title IX Blog:
http://title-ix.blogspot.com/

About the Authors and Contributors

Jennifer L. Martin, PhD, is an assistant professor in the Department of Teacher Education at the University of Illinois at Springfield. Prior to working in higher education, Dr. Martin worked in public education for 17 years, 15 of those as the department chair of English at an urban alternative high school for students labeled at risk for school failure in metropolitan Detroit. She is the editor of the two-volume series *Women as Leaders in Education: Succeeding Despite Inequity, Discrimination, and Other Challenges* (Praeger, 2011), which examines the intersections of race, class, gender, and sexuality for current and aspiring leaders from a variety of perspectives. Martin is also the editor of *Racial Battle Fatigue: Insights from the Front Lines of Social Justice Advocacy* (recipient of the 2016 AERA Division B's Outstanding Book Recognition Award; Praeger, 2015), which contains personal stories of the implications of doing social justice work in the field and in the university. Martin has numerous publications on bullying and harassment, educational equity, and issues of social justice, including *Teaching for Educational Equity: Case Studies for Professional Development and Principal Preparation, Volume 1* (2016) *and 2* (2017), and *Feminist Pedagogy, Practice, and Activism: Improving Lives for Girls and Women* (2017). Martin has been providing professional development workshops for teachers and administrators on culturally responsive teaching and leading in various school districts. Martin was invited by Kappa Delta Pi in 2015 to create a national curriculum on culturally responsive teaching and leading for the organization to be delivered in a one-day workshop. This curriculum has been delivered in many states throughout the nation. She is currently studying the development of culturally responsive leadership practices.

Sarah E. Torok-Gerard, PhD, is an associate professor in the Department of Psychology, Neuroscience, and Human Development at the University of Mount Union. Torok-Gerard earned her bachelor's in psychology from Mercyhurst College (2000) and then went on to earn her master's (2002) and PhD (2006) in educational psychology at the University at Albany, State University of New York. It was at SUNY Albany where she began her 16-year career as an educator, teaching courses in developmental and educational psychology. While teaching at Skidmore College, she completed her dissertation on the metacognitive and metalinguistic factors involved in reading acquisition and remediation. Her work earned her the Presidential Distinguished Doctoral Dissertation Award from the School of Education at the University at Albany in May 2006 and was subsequently published (2008). She also has published work involving the use of humor in classroom instruction (Torok, McMorris, Lin, 2004). A 12-year veteran at the University of Mount Union, Torok-Gerard has taught a vast array of courses outside of her trained area of expertise including sport psychology, the psychology of gender, and the psychology of prejudice. She has had a varied number of research interests throughout her career as well, including bullying intervention and prevention. This research led to her being awarded several grants, including a Great Cities, Great Service Mini-Grant (2009) and a Community Partner and Summer Program Grant (2012). These monies were allocated for service learning projects that partnered her Psychology of Gender students with area middle school students and the local YWCA. Torok-Gerard has also presented in a variety of different contexts, including the Eastern Psychological Association Conference (2004), an Early Childhood Oxford Roundtable, at Oxford University (2007), the Biennial Meeting of the Society for Research in Child Development (2007), and the North American Society for the Psychology of Sport and Physical Activity Annual Conference (2014). In 2015, she became certified through the American

Council on Exercise as a health coach after completing sabbatical research on the self-regulatory behaviors and motivational orientations of distance runners. In addition to her research and work in the classroom, Torok-Gerard has dedicated a considerable amount of her time to in administrative roles at the University of Mount Union, including serving as chair of her department for six years.

Brianna Boehlke is an undergraduate student at the University of Mount Union, where she is majoring in history with minors in adolescent to young adult education and gender studies. She is the former research assistant of Jennifer Martin. She is the vice president of philanthropy for Delta Sigma Tau and a member of the education honor society Kappa Delta Pi. She was honored with the Alliance YMCA's Volunteer of the Year award for 2017–2018, and she was the recipient of the Martin Luther King Jr. Award for her work in social justice in 2018. She has presented at international conferences including as the International Association of Research on Service Learning and Community Engagement and the Race and Pedagogy Institute.

Caitie Boucher is a graduate student at the University of Illinois Springfield studying to receive a master's degree in human development counseling, specializing in school counseling. She is a member of Psi Chi, the international psychology honor society, and Chi Sigma Iota, the international counseling honor society. Boucher plans to work with children and adolescents, helping them to understand and utilize their full potential while navigating academic and social/emotional developmental needs.

Courtney Cepec is an undergraduate student at the University of Mount Union majoring in English and minoring in writing and adolescent young adult education, and former research assistant of Jennifer Martin. She is president of her Kappa Delta Pi chapter, Omega Iota, a national education honor society on her campus. She has presented nationally three times at Kappa Delta Pi convocation in Indianapolis, Indiana, in November 2018, and internationally at the Race & Pedagogy Institute in Tacoma, Washington, in 2018. She plans a career in the field of education and hopes to work in an urban environment.

Taylor Cook received a master's degree in human development counseling from the University of Illinois Springfield, specializing in clinical mental health. She is a member of Psi Chi, the international psychology honor society; Kappa Delta Pi, the international honor society in education; and Chi Sigma Iota, the international counseling honor society. Cook discovered her passion for lifelong learning while working in a special education classroom during her undergraduate studies. She has since continued her work with children and adolescents in K–12 schools, in the university setting, and most recently at a behavioral health center. She is passionate about advocating for youth with behavioral and mental delays.

Halle O. Devoe is a graduate student at the University of Illinois Springfield pursuing a degree in school counseling, and plans on a career counseling in the high school setting and private practice. She is interested in spirituality and the concept being used to help students find their sense of self at a time in their lives when they are heavily influenced by others around them. She is passionate about helping kids prepare for life-long learning and psychological, spiritual, and emotional well-being.

Evan Hopkins graduated from the University of Illinois Springfield with a bachelor's degree in business administration with a minor in management information systems. He started substitute teaching while looking for new work, found a love for teaching, and is currently finishing his certification in elementary education. He has been a substitute teacher for two years, and plans to find work with students in the third to fifth grade range.

Grace A. Moll is a graduate student at the University of Illinois in Springfield working towards her degree in human development counseling with a school counseling concentration. Her long-term goal is to become a school counselor at the middle school level.

Dr. Kristine Turko earned MS and PhD degrees in psychology at Lehigh University, and a BS degree in psychology at Drexel University. She is currently completing the requirements to acquire her credential as a Board Certified Behavior Analyst (BCBA). Before becoming a faculty member at the University of Mount Union in 2006, she served as a visiting assistant professor at Lafayette College and an adjunct professor at Lehigh University. She also conducted research at the Moss Rehabilitation Research Institute and McNeil Consumer Products, both in Philadelphia, Pennsylvania. Turko's research interests include best practice for autism intervention in adult populations, and effective autism intervention training and education models for undergraduate students. Her work as the founder of the Spectrum Education Center supports her pedagogical interests related to improving the training of autism intervention professionals by facilitating relationships between clinical sites and academic institutions.

Index